Oracle Application Express 4 Recipes

Edmund Zehoo

Oracle Application Express 4 Recipes

ISBN-13 (pbk): 978-1-4302-3506-4

ISBN-13 (electronic): 978-1-4302-3507-1

President and Publisher: Paul Manning
Lead Editor: Jonathan Gennick
Technical Reviewer: Guillermo Alan Bort
Editorial Board: Steve Anglin, Mark Beckner, Ewan Buckingham, Gary Cornell, Jonathan Gennick, Jonathan Hassell, Michelle Lowman, James Markham, Matthew Moodie, Jeff Olson, Jeffrey Pepper, Frank Pohlmann, Douglas Pundick, Ben Renow-Clarke, Dominic Shakeshaft, Matt Wade, Tom Welsh
Coordinating Editor: Anita Castro
Copy Editor: Mary Behr
Compositor:Bytheway Publishing Services
Indexer: John Collin
Artist: April Milne
Cover Designer: Anna Ishchenko

Distributed to the book trade worldwide by Springer Science+Business Media, LLC., 233 Spring Street, 6th Floor, New York, NY 10013. Phone 1-800-SPRINGER, fax (201) 348-4505, e-mail orders-ny@springer-sbm.com, or visit www.springeronline.com.

For information on translations, please e-mail rights@apress.com, or visit www.apress.com.

Apress and friends of ED books may be purchased in bulk for academic, corporate, or promotional use. eBook versions and licenses are also available for most titles. For more information, reference our Special Bulk Sales–eBook Licensing web page at www.apress.com/bulk-sales.

The source code for this book is available to readers at www.apress.com. You will need to answer questions pertaining to this book in order to successfully download the code.

To my family,
for you are truly all I have.

Contents at a Glance

Contents

About the Author

Edmund Tan Zehoo is the Chief Technical Officer of an e-forms and workflows solution vendor based in Singapore. He took the role of lead architect in the design of several Rapid Application Development and workflow products, one of the most popular being the Rapidflows product. He has also spent the last eight years building performance-critical .NET solutions hosted on top of Oracle databases for large companies and governmental institutions in Singapore.

Edmund is a frequent speaker at various workflow conferences in Singapore and Malaysia, and he continually preaches about the synergistic power of using Oracle with the .NET framework. During his free time, he likes to explore the inner workings of the brain and mind, with the ultimate goal of writing intelligent software to emulate the behavior of the mind. He is also an avid believer in the Technological Singularity.

About the Technical Reviewer

Guillermo Alan Bort started working as First Line Support for Oracle customers before the support model switched to web-based Oracle Support. In the beginning, his area of interest was Linux System Administration, Oracle Database, and Oracle Applications; later, he focused on Oracle Database, working with high availability and disaster recovery scenarios in large scale environments. He supported several companies with outsourced database administration services and developed several APEX applications to control and share information across a multiregional team.

Acknowledgments

This book is the result of the combined efforts of a team of wonderful people with whom I've had the pleasure of working. I'll start with a special word of thanks to my editor Jonathan Gennick: thanks for giving this author halfway around the world a chance. Your encouraging remarks and insightful edits constantly remind me that authoring a book can indeed be so much fun.

My heartfelt gratitude also goes out to Anita Castro for her timekeeping and the always cheerful e-mails, Mary Behr for making me sound so much better in print, Dominic Shakeshaft and the Apress editorial board for giving me a shot at this book, and all the other Apress team members who've contributed to this book.

Last and definitely not least, I have a small but fiercely-loving family that I would like to individually thank: my mom and late dad for being the greatest parents one could ever hope for; my late godmother for instilling the bookworm in me; my brother and sister for their silly jokes; and the two people who've suffered the most during this project, my wife and daughter who've (yet again) had to put up without a husband and father for eight months—thank you for being the understanding family I knew you'd be.

CHAPTER 1

Introducing Oracle APEX

I still remember deploying my first Microsoft Access application 10 years ago for a head hunting agency. They had a user base of about 200 users (I can already hear some of you groan) and they needed a system to manage job applicants and the companies that want to hire them. And they tossed my meager development team of two an "uncompromisable" deadline of one month in which to conceptualize, develop, and test the system—and have it go live right after that.

Any self-respecting enterprise development team would have laughed off the ridiculous timeline, but for reasons unknown to ourselves (though I think the obscene amount of money offered for the job had something to do with our decision), we decided to have a go at it. We turned to the distant faraway lands of rapid application development (RAD). We found a match in Microsoft Access, and after confirming that the actual user concurrency rate would be low enough to squirm past Access's concurrency restrictions, we took the job.

Our two man team successfully developed and deployed the application within the one month timeframe, and the agency used it for at least five years before upgrading their systems. The point of the story is that were it not for the RAD tool, some projects would never see the light of day. Stories such as mine still echo in many corners of the Internet to this day.

RAD tools have come a long way since then. Now that most enterprise solutions are deployed entirely on the Web, it would only make sense for RAD tools to catch up, and they have. From simpler app creation tools such as the cloud-based Zoho App Creator and Google Apps to the more "serious" ones like APEX and Ruby on Rails, they've all made their debut on the Web; it is now easy as ever for anyone to set up their own sales force app or online bookstore app and have them all hosted on the Internet with a (metaphorical) click of a button.

RAD tools work exceptionally well in business scenarios; firstly because business apps are usually web-based, and secondly, because they consist mostly of CRUD (Create, Read, Update, and Delete) operations, the atomic operations at the heart of every database-centric application. For this same reason, APEX takes the cake; it integrates tightly with the Oracle database and handles CRUD very well through PL/SQL. APEX sits as a platform on top of the database, and in doing so, the applications you churn from APEX enjoy all the benefits available to the database (such as clustering support, for one).

In this chapter, you will learn about APEX through a few recipes that will help you get up and running with APEX in no time. These recipes will also provide a primer of sorts to familiarize you with basic APEX concepts. You will also learn how to use some of the team development tools available in APEX,

1-1. Deciding Whether to Use APEX

Problem

Your boss has just tasked you with a new project. You are not sure if APEX is the right tool for the project.

Solution

APEX offers shorter development times and ease of development, but there are scenarios where it's not the best tool for a project. It is important to have an idea of the full capabilities and limitations of a tool before you wield it. Consider using APEX for a project if:

- The application in mind is a web-based application consisting mostly of CRUD operations.

- Oracle is the only database your application needs to support, or there's minimal chance for a migration to a different database vendor.

- Your project has a short development timeline.

- Your development methodology requires rapid and successive iterations of prototyping or it features frequently evolving requirements.

- Your application needs to serve a high transaction volume.

- Your development team is well versed with PL/SQL and JavaScript.

Avoid using APEX if:

- Your application consists of modules that require a non-CRUD architecture, such as a message-driven or event-driven architecture.

- Your application needs to have a high degree of object reusability (across the logic and presentation tiers) and needs to strongly conform to traditional frameworks such as Object Oriented Programming (OOP) or Model View Controller (MVC).

- Your application consists of complex forms containing more than 100 database items (example: enterable fields) per page. (I would like to point out that hosting 100 fields or more in a single page is, from a user interface point of view, very bad design. However, your project requirements may demand you to do so anyway. If so, keep this limitation of APEX in mind.)

- Your application consists of reports that require more than 100 columns to be displayed in the same report.

- Your application consists of tables that require more than two columns as the primary key.

How It Works

As mentioned, APEX works very well for CRUD-based web-based business applications and sits as a platform on top of the Oracle database. APEX does this well because at its heart, it leverages the PL/SQL language to handle the business logic for the applications developed on top of it, and PL/SQL is the foundation for all database CRUD operations. A good benchmark is that if 75% of the application consists of CRUD alone, APEX would help to significantly reduce the time and effort needed to develop your application.

Also, APEX is a RAD tool, and many developers have given their testimonials on how RAD products have enabled them to deploy large scale systems in weeks instead of months (including myself in the opening section of this book). APEX also fits development teams that employ software development methodologies with a constantly evolving set of requirements, such as agile, or methodologies that frequently involve the need for successive iterations of prototyping. APEX is also well-suited for large-scale deployments. Consider these figures: Oracle hosts a free instance of APEX at http://apex.oracle.com, that receives an average of 1.4 to 1.5 million page views a week and hosts over 10,000 workspaces.

APEX applications practically live inside the Oracle database; its code modules consist mostly of PL/SQL, and any applications, forms, and reports exist as metadata in database tables. Because the business logic, UI, and data are all stored in the database, APEX has the benefit of eliminating the additional round trips required by other platforms that need to frequently communicate between the business and data tiers over the network. Thus, APEX applications easily outperform their traditional three-tier counterparts.

However, APEX is not database-independent, so there is a risk of a database vendor lockdown. Migrating an APEX application from an Oracle database to a Microsoft SQL Server-based one, for example, would most certainly mean rewriting the entire application from scratch. It is important to consider the range of databases that need to be supported by the application when considering whether to use APEX in your project.

There are also several technical limitations to note when using APEX, particularly in terms of the maximum number of database items that can be hosted on a single page. Table 1-1 lists a few of the current limitations for APEX, as stated on the Oracle website.

Table 1-1. APEX Component Limitations

Component	Description
Interactive reports	A single page supports one interactive report.
	Maximum of 100 columns per interactive report.
Classic reports	Maximum of 100 columns per classic report.
Forms	100 enterable items (input fields) per page.
	Maximum of 32767 bytes enterable for text area or rich text edit control.
	Maximum of two columns for primary keys.
Tabular forms	Maximum of one wizard-generated tabular forms per page.
	Maximum of 50 editable tabular form columns.
Item names	Maximum of 30 characters for item names referenced using bind variable syntax.
Validations	Maximum of 3,950 characters for text entered for validation.

Most of the business logic development for APEX is done using PL/SQL. Although PL/SQL does support function and code reusability to a degree, this does not extend outside of the business tier. For instance, in traditional development tools, you could create different buttons that all inherit from a single generic button class containing a common set of behavior. This level of OOP in the user interface is not supported in APEX.

Lastly, it's important to keep in mind that APEX is a platform with standard behavior and functionality. It doesn't offer the same freedom that a traditional development tool does, so if you need to achieve certain functionality that APEX does not provide out of the box, you will need to get your hands dirty with JavaScript, AJAX, and DHTML.

1-2. Identifying an APEX Deployment Model

Problem

You want to deploy APEX. You've heard there are a couple of different ways to do it, and you're not sure which deployment model would suit your needs.

Solution

The main decision fork when deploying APEX is deciding which HTTP server to use to serve your APEX applications. Oracle provides two types of HTTP servers:

- Oracle XML DB HTTP Server (embedded PL/SQL gateway)
- Oracle HTTP Server and mod_plsql

Choose the Oracle XML DB HTTP Server if:

- You want a simpler two-tier deployment (web browser and database server).
- Your priority is to simply get up and running in the shortest time possible with as little configuration as possible.
- You don't wish to install a separate server to host the HTTP server.
- You are deploying APEX on a personal PC as a standalone system.

Choose the Oracle HTTP Server and mod_plsql approach if:

- You want a full three-tier deployment (web browser, HTTP web server, and database server).
- You are deploying APEX in an enterprise environment and need access to an extensive set of web server configuration and log settings.
- You intend to expose the APEX application to the Internet. This is for security purposes and will be explained in detail in the "How It Works" section.
- You need Single Sign On (SSO) integration.
- You need mid-tier load balancing and failover features.

How It Works

The Oracle XML DB HTTP server contains the embedded PL/SQL gateway, which is installed together with a standard Oracle database installation. The embedded PL/SQL gateway runs in the Oracle XML DB HTTP server. This is illustrated in Figure 1-1.

Figure 1-1. Using Oracle XML DB HTTP as your web server

This deployment is a two-tier model and is easy to setup. The APEX engine and embedded PL/SQL gateway exist in the same database. Do note that a two-tier deployment may not be desirable in some cases, especially from the perspective of security. For example, if you are planning to expose your APEX applications to the Internet, this deployment model may not be desirable because the HTTP listener can't be separated from the database, so you would be exposing the database directly to the Internet as well.

Another disadvantage that arises from the tight coupling between the web server and the database is that in the event of database downtime, your web server will be down as well; this will prevent access to static data such as static web pages or images.

An embedded PL/SQL gateway also does not provide mid-tier load balancing or failover features. To scale your systems, you will need to depend on Oracle Real Application Clusters (RAC) technology at the database level. For these reasons, the embedded PL/SQL gateway is suited more for smaller deployments or standalone systems.

■ **Note** The Oracle XML DB HTTP Server with embedded PL/SQL gateway is not supported prior to Oracle Database Version 11*g*.

The Oracle HTTP Server and mod_plsql approach is essential for enterprise deployments due to the more extensive set of configuration and log settings available to the administrator as well as from a security standpoint. The Oracle HTTP Server runs on Apache and uses the mod_plsql plug-in to communicate with the APEX engine. The mod_plsql plug-in maps HTTP requests to stored procedures in the Oracle database over a Net8/SQL*Net connection. Figure 1-2 illustrates the Oracle HTTP server deployment in detail.

■ **Tip**   A Net8/SQL*Net connection is a transparent connection that transfers data between a client machine and the Oracle database. It allows services and applications to reside on different machines and communicate with each other as peer applications.

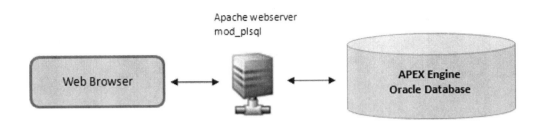

Figure 1-2. Using Oracle HTTP server as your web server

1-3. Installing Oracle APEX

Problem

You are tasked to install the latest version of Oracle APEX on top of an existing Oracle database installation (which happens to be running on a Windows-based server) and you have decided to use the embedded PL/SQL gateway as your web server.

■ **Note**   APEX installation is supported on a large number of platforms. The example and screenshots shown in this recipe will feature a Windows-based installation. The installation procedure for non-Windows based operating systems remain the same.

Solution

Execute the following steps to install APEX on your system:

1. Ensure that an existing Oracle database installation exists. If none is found, install an Oracle database (version 10.2.0.3 and above) first.

▓ **Note**   Some versions of the Oracle database include an earlier version of APEX built in. In any case, the following steps will still apply whether you are installing APEX from scratch or upgrading to a newer version of APEX

2. Download the software. The latest version of Oracle APEX (as of the date of writing this book) is version 4.0.2. You can download the latest version of APEX from the following URL:
    http://www.oracle.com/technetwork/developer-tools/apex/downloads/index.html

3. Unzip the contents of the downloaded APEX package into a folder named APEXFILES\APEX on your system (e.g.: C:\APEXFILES\APEX).

▓ **Note**   C:\APEXFILES\APEX will be your APEX home directory. It is important that your subfolder is named APEX.

4. Logon to SQL*Plus on your system as the SYSDBA.

5. You will need to create two tablespaces. Run the statements shown in Listing 1-1 in SQL*Plus.

Listing 1-1. Creating the APEX Tablespaces

```
CREATE TABLESPACE APEX datafile 'C:\oraclexe\oradata\XE\APEX.dbf'

SIZE 500M
EXTENT MANAGEMENT LOCAL
SEGMENT SPACE MANAGEMENT AUTO;

CREATE TABLESPACE APEX_FILES datafile 'C:\oraclexe\oradata\XE\APEX_FILES.dbf'
SIZE 100M
EXTENT MANAGEMENT LOCAL
SEGMENT SPACE MANAGEMENT AUTO;
```

■ **Note** Your Oracle home directory may be installed in a different path. Ensure that you change the path in the code above to reflect the correct location. In the example above, the Oracle database home path is `C:\oraclexe\oradata\XE`.

---

6. Now, set your working directory for SQL*Plus to `C:\APEXFILES\APEX`. The easiest way to do this (on Windows) is to first open a command prompt window, navigate to the folder, and then run the `sqlplus` command from that folder.

7. Login as SYSDBA again and type the following command:

```
@apxsqler
```

This command will roll back any subsequent SQL executed if an error occurs midway.

8. Next, run the APEX installation script by typing the following command. Execution may take a few minutes; you should see a lot of output stream past.

```
@apexins APEX APEX_FILES TEMP /i/
```

A snapshot of the output from running this statement is shown in Figure 1-3.

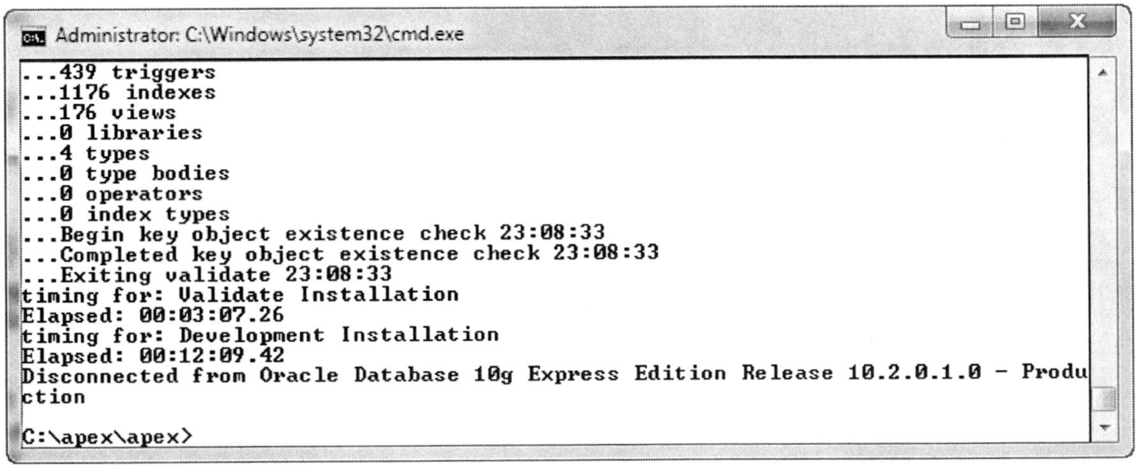

Figure 1-3. Apex installation output

9. To check if there are any errors during the installation, you can check the generated log files in the C:\APEXFILES\APEX folder. If there are any errors, undo the installation by logging on to SQL*Plus as SYSDBA and running the following command:

```
DROP USER FLOWS_030000 CASCADE
```

You will then need to resolve the errors in the log file before running the installation again.

■ **Tip**   The log file names carry the format Install<YYYY-MM-DD><HH24-MI-SS>.log

---

10. If there are no errors in the installation, logon to SQL*Plus again as SYSDBA and load the APEX images into the Oracle database by running the following statement:

```
@apxldimg.sql C:\APEXFILES
```

You should see the output shown in Figure 1-4.

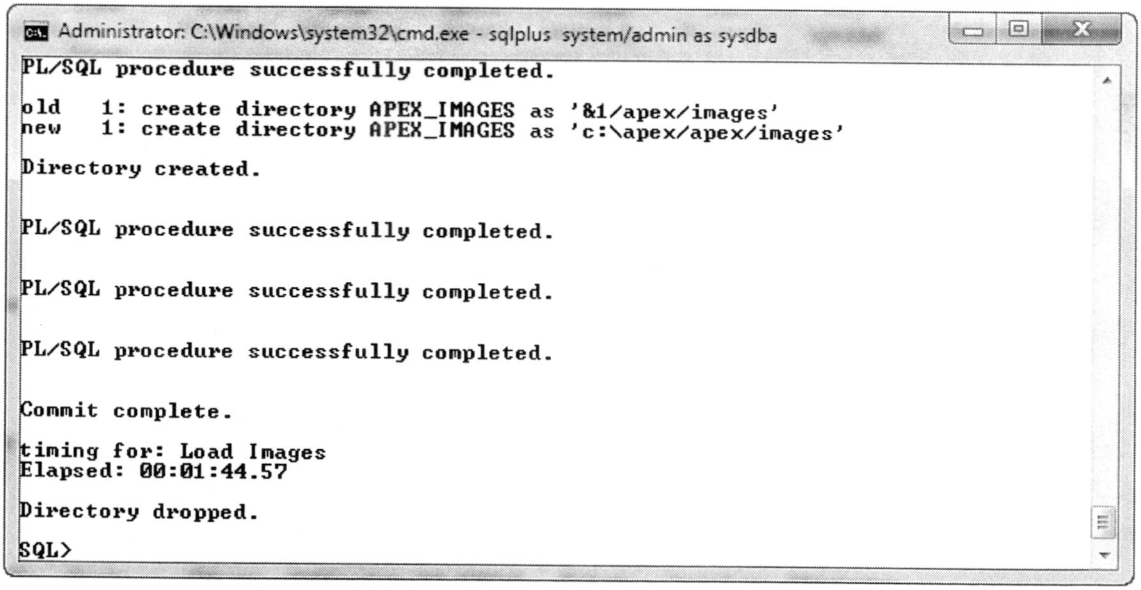

Figure 1-4. Apxldimg.sql output

■ **Note**   When running this step, ensure that the path provided points to the parent folder and not the folder where you unzipped your APEX installation files. The `apxldimg` script will append the `\APEX` suffix to your path.

---

11. Next, you need to force APEX to use the right paths for the APEX icon image and JavaScript files. Without doing this step, you might find that the login page for APEX loads up without any icons showing and with a bunch of JavaScript errors. Open the Windows command prompt and navigate to the `C:\APEXFILES\APEX\UTILITIES` directory. Run the `sqlplus` tool from this directory and logon as SYSDBA. Next, run the following statement:

```
@reset_image_prefix.sql
```

When prompted for the image prefix, simply press the Enter key to use the default (`/i/`). When this has completed successfully, you should see the output shown in Figure 1-5.

```
Administrator: C:\Windows\system32\cmd.exe                          □  ▢  ☒

...Update image prefix for all internal Application Express applications

PL/SQL procedure successfully completed.

...Purge all cached region and page entries

PL/SQL procedure successfully completed.

...Recompiling the Application Express schema

PL/SQL procedure successfully completed.

Image Prefix update complete
Disconnected from Oracle Database 10g Express Edition Release 10.2.0.1.0 - Produ
ction
```

Figure 1-5. Resetting the image prefix

12. Finally, set the password admin123 for the Administrator by running the following statement:

```
@apxxepwd.sql admin123
```

13. Now, try logging on to APEX using the following URL, substituting *yourserver* with your actual server name, IP address, or localhost (if you have installed APEX as a standalone system on your machine):

```
http://yourserver:8080/apex
```

You should see the login page shown in Figure 1-6.

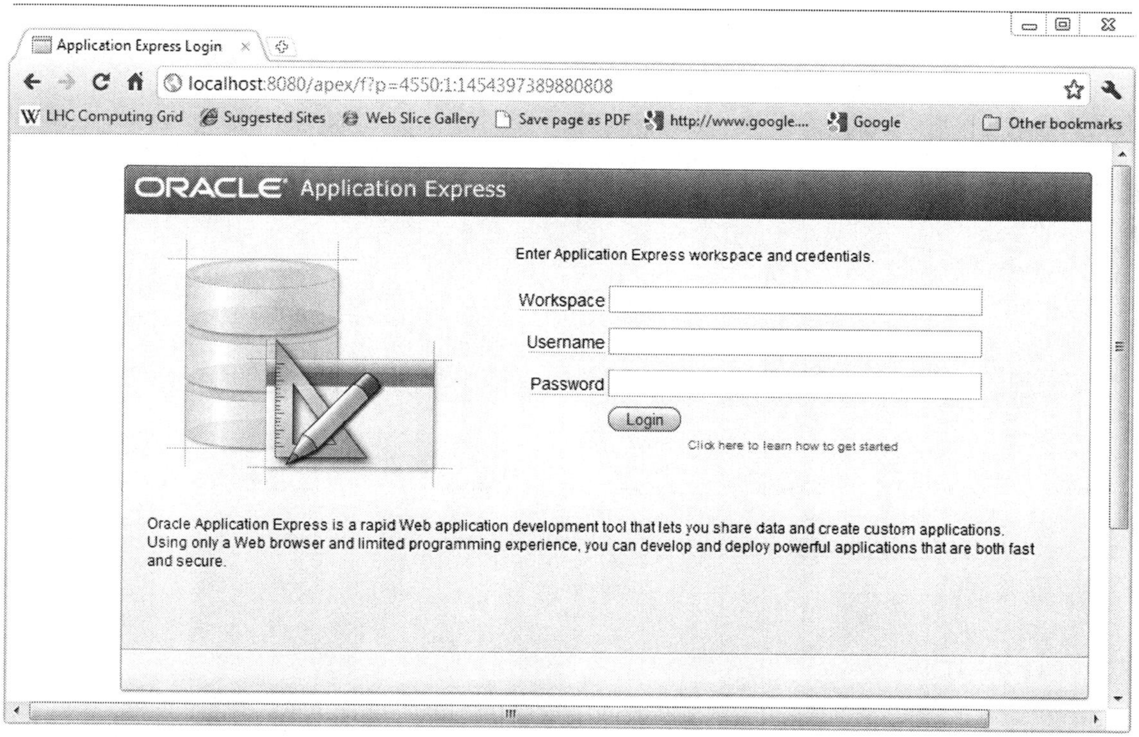

Figure 1-6. APEX login page

■ **Tip** If you are unable to see the login page in Figure 1-6, check if the port number specified in your URL is correct. Also check if you have unzipped the APEX files in the correct folders and referenced these folders correctly during the installation. If you are still unable to figure out what the problem is, it's always a good idea to peek in the generated APEX installation log files. More troubleshooting information is available at:

```
http://download.oracle.com/docs/cd/E17556_01/doc/install.40/e15513/trouble.htm#BABCHHAF
```

Set the workspace name to INTERNAL, the username to ADMIN, the password to admin123, and click the Login button. You should be able to see the page shown in Figure 1-7. This will indicate that your installation of APEX was successful.

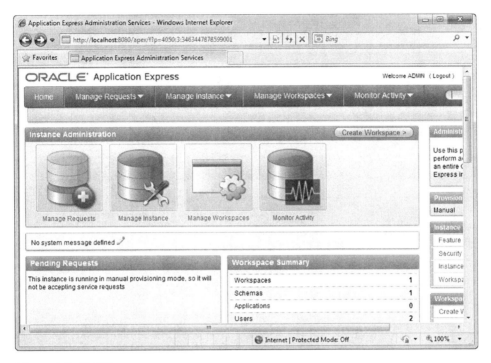

Figure 1-7. APEX home page

How It Works

The first thing you might have noticed when trying to install APEX is that there is no installer to speak of. If you look closer, you can see that the APEX installation files downloaded from the Oracle site are simply a bunch of PL/SQL script files.

The reason there is no installer is because Oracle APEX is basically a metadata repository. APEX applications, forms, and reports are nothing more than metadata and PL/SQL code stored in an Oracle database. An engine called the Application Express engine uses this metadata to render and process APEX web pages.

■ **Tip**   The fact that Oracle APEX, your applications, forms, and reports live entirely in the database makes backup a convenient process. Backing up an APEX application is no different from backing up any other Oracle database. Chapter 9 covers the backup process in detail.

To get an idea what APEX the product consists of, here are some figures from the Oracle website: APEX consists of approximately 425 tables and 230 PL/SQL packages containing 425,000+ lines of code.

1-4. Familiarizing Yourself with APEX-speak

Problem

You find yourself amidst seasoned APEX developers. Tongue-tied, you strain your mind to make sense of the jargon they're tossing across the table every minute or so. You don't speak APEX, and this is a serious problem.

Solution

Before embarking on APEX, you need to know the difference between workspaces, Websheets, and schemas. Table 1-2 explores in detail the various jargon used in APEX.

Table 1-2. APEX Jargon

Jargon	Description
Workspace	A workspace represents the working area for a team of developers. It allows different teams of developers to work in their own separate workspaces (in the same repository) and not have to interact with each other.
Application	An application is basically what it sounds like—the traditional notion of an "application." In Apex 4.0, you can build two different types of applications: a database application or a Websheet application.
Database application	A database application is a type of application built around an RDBMS. It typically consists of forms, views, and reports.
Websheet application	The Websheet is the latest addition to Apex 4.0. It is another type of application that lets you build and deploy web-based forms, business logic, and reports in a declarative manner.
Schema	Every APEX workspace is linked to one or more database schemas. A database schema stores the various database objects (such as tables) for each application.
Theme	A theme is collection of templates that define the look and feel (layout) of an APEX application.

Jargon	Description
Page	A page is the most basic unit of an APEX application and correlates to a web page. There are six different types of pages you can create: a blank page, report, form, tabular form, master detail, and "Report and Form."
Blank page	A blank page is an empty page that allows you to customize the contents on your own.
Report	There are two types of reports in APEX: classic reports and interactive reports
Classic report	A classic report is a static report that displays a list of records in a tabular format to the user.
Interactive report	An interactive report is a type of report that allows for user interaction—searching, filtering, sorting, column selection, highlighting, and so on—at view-time to retrieve the desired set of data in the report.
Form	A form allows for data entry. A form typically consists of a set of data controls and a Submit button.
Tabular form	A tabular form allows you to perform update, insert, and delete operations on multiple records at one time in a single screen. These records are displayed in a tabular format.
Master detail	The master detail page allows you to create forms with master-detail relationships from two tables.
Report and Form	A Report and Form page contains both a report and form in the same page. The most common usage of this type of page is when you need to key in search parameters in one page and have the search results show up in the same page. In this case, the search parameters can be entered through the form component, and the search results would show up in the report component of the page.

How It Works

APEX is a platform that can be used by several development teams simultaneously. Each workspace represents the working area for a team of developers. Inside each workspace, developers can create multiple applications. For instance, Team Alpha might be working on two applications (a sales force and a HRM application) while Team Beta might be working on an online bookstore application. This is summarized in Figure 1-8.

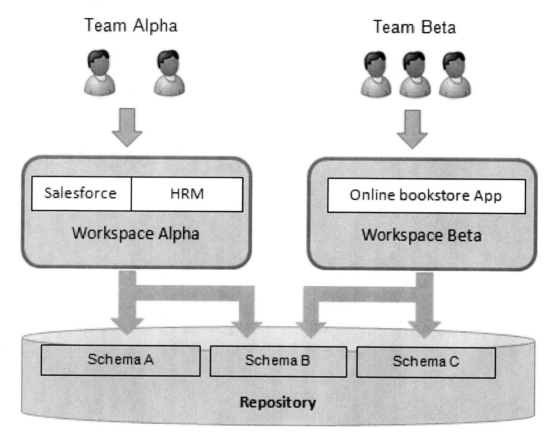

Figure 1-8. APEX workspaces

Within the context of an APEX workspace, there are a number of different objects and subobjects that can be created. Figure 1-9 illustrates the relationship between these different types of objects. If you get confused by the jargon again, refer to Table 1-2 for the definitions of these objects.

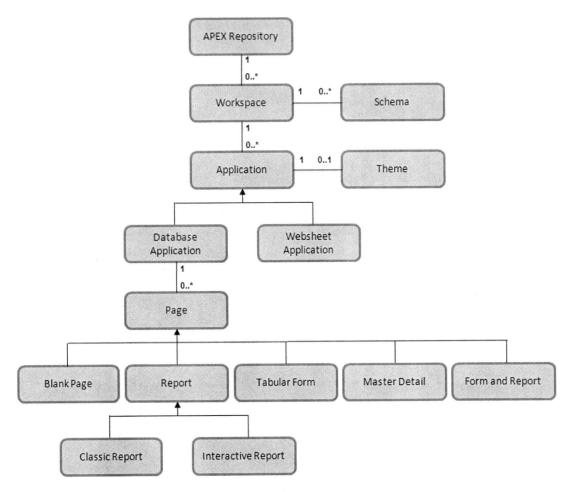

Figure 1-9. The relationship between various APEX objects

■ **Note** The atomic unit of a database application is a page. A database application essentially consists of a bunch of pages that can be a mix of data entry screens, reports, or tabular listings of data.

1-5. Setting up a Workspace for Team-based Development

Problem

You have just installed APEX. You now need to create a workspace so that development team Alpha (Sally and John) can develop their sales force application.

Solution

Here is how to set up for team-based development:

1. Log in to the APEX portal by typing `http://yourserver:8080/apex` in the address bar of your browser.

▒ **Note** Replace *yourserver* with your server name or IP address. If you have installed APEX locally, replace *yourserver* with localhost.

---

2. In the login window, specify Internal as the workspace, and login as the Administrator using the username and password you created earlier in Recipe 1-3.

3. After logging in successfully, click the Manage Workspaces menu item. Click on the Create Workspace link under the Workspace Actions section. Specify a workspace name, ID, and description in the ensuing page. You should now see the page shown in Figure 1-10.

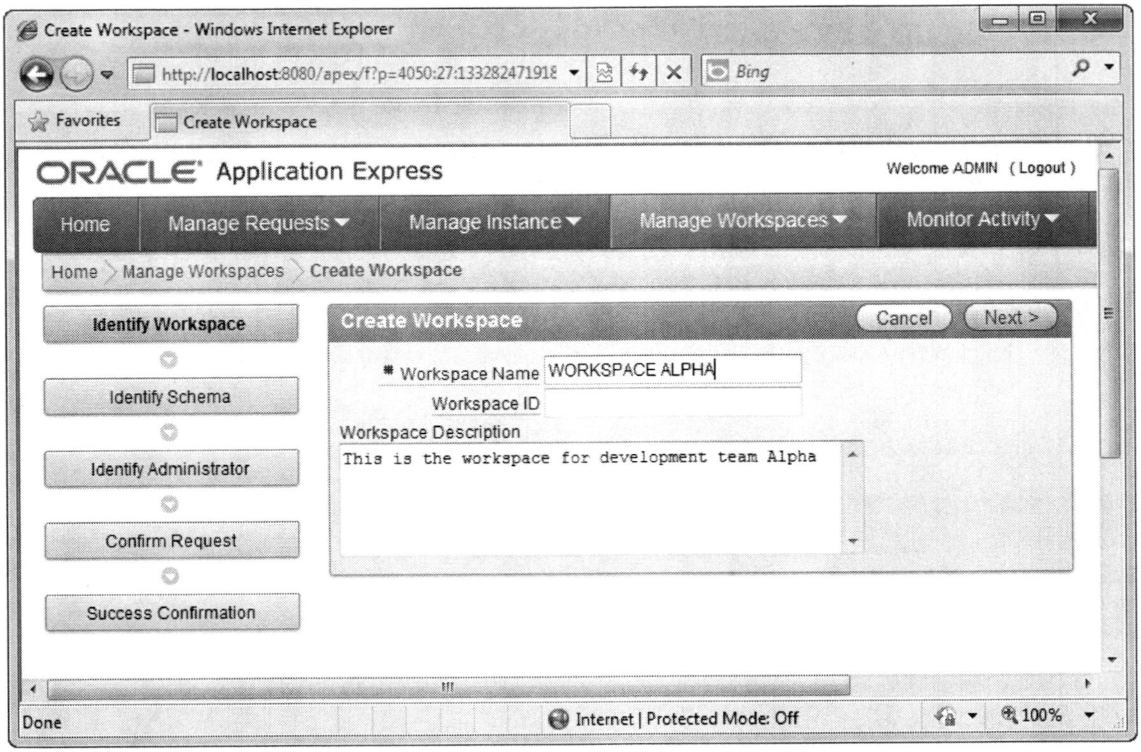

Figure 1-10. Creating a workspace

4. Click the Next button to continue. In this page, you can specify to use an existing database schema or to create a new one for the workspace. Figure 1-11 shows how you can create a new schema for the workspace.

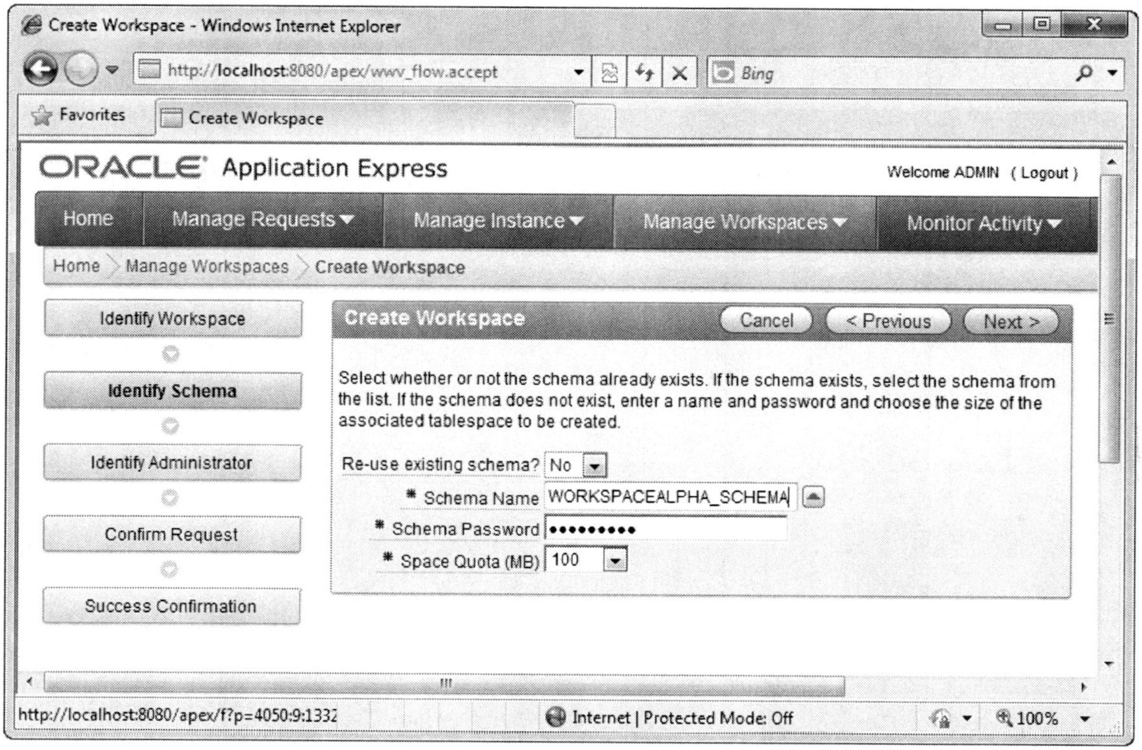

Figure 1-11. Creating a new schema for the workspace

5. Next, you'll be required to specify the Workspace Administrator user, password, and e-mail. See Figure 1-12.

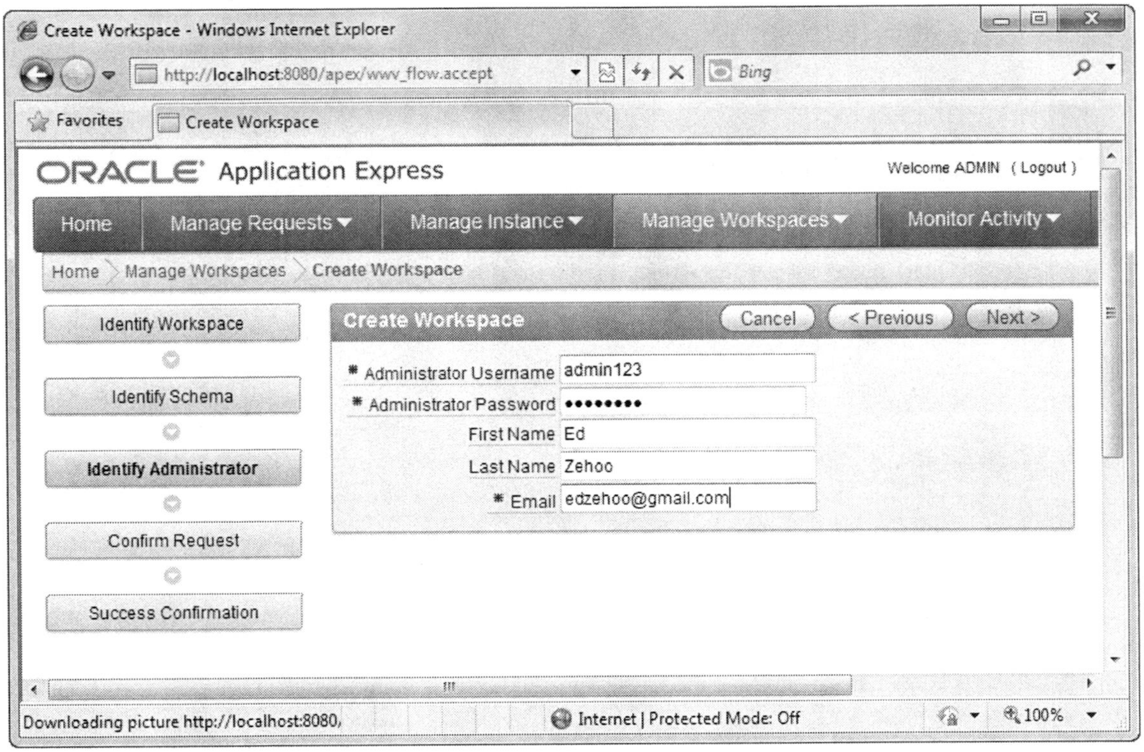

Figure 1-12. Specifying the Administrator details

6. Click the Next button to continue. Click through the remaining pages of the wizard to confirm workspace creation. You can browse your existing workspaces by navigating to the Manage Workspace ➤ Workspace Reports ➤ Existing Workspaces link. After you click the link, you should be able to see the Alpha workspace you have just created (highlighted in Figure 1-13).

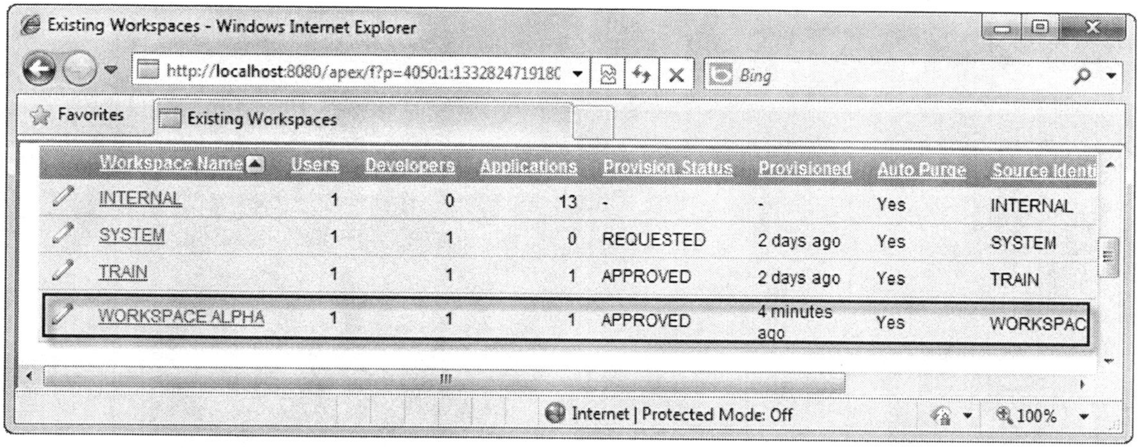

Figure 1-13. The team Alpha workspace

7. Now you will need to add the user accounts for the developers Sally and John to the workspace. Click on the Manage Workspaces menu, then click on the Manage Developers and Users link under the Workspace Actions section. In the ensuing page, click the yellow-colored Create User button, and fill in the details of the user in the next page. Be sure to select the WORKSPACE ALPHA workspace you created earlier as the workspace for this user account. Figure 1-14 illustrates this in detail. Click the Create button after you have filled in the form.

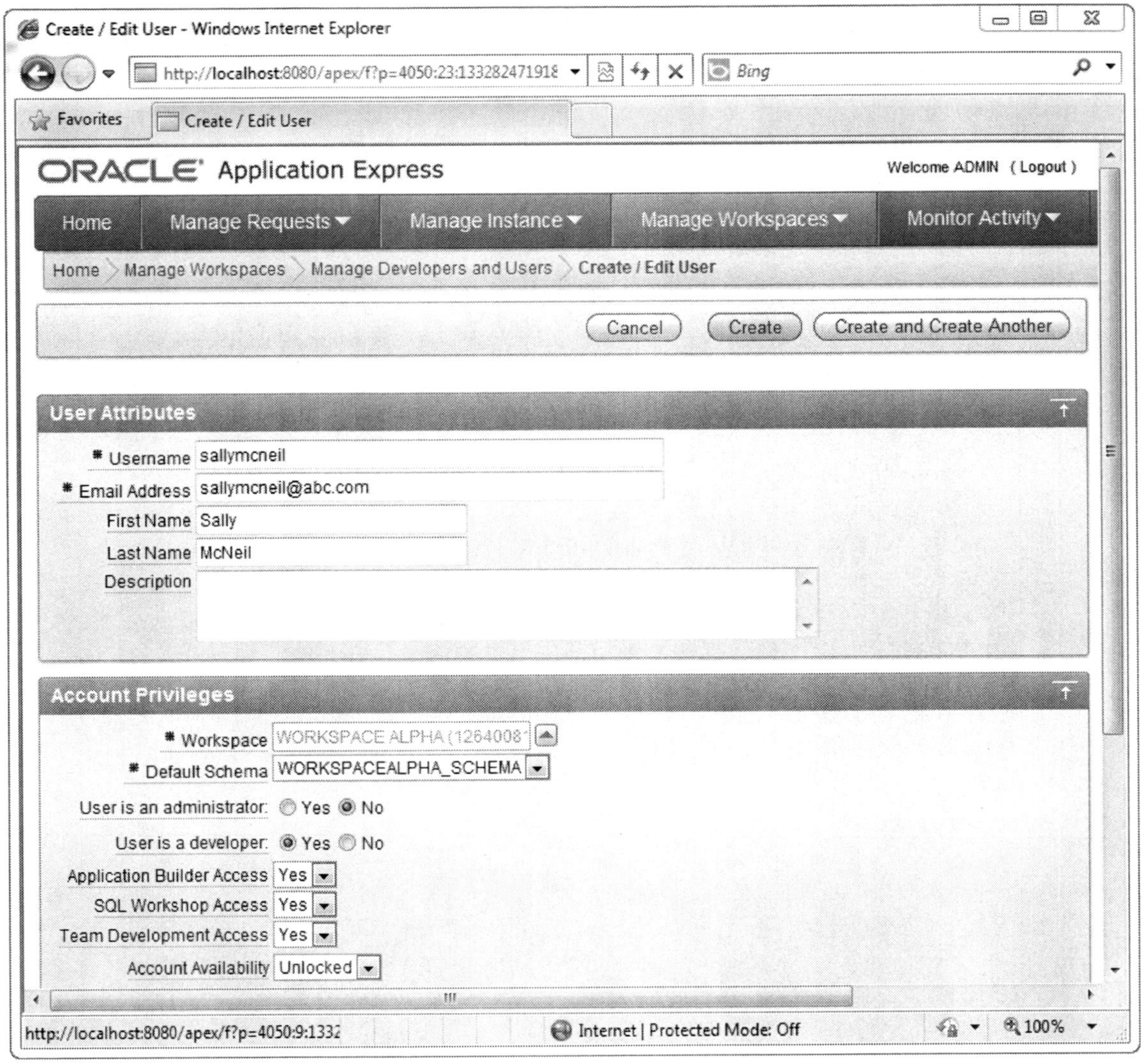

Figure 1-14. Creating a developer

8. Upon creating the user, you should be able to see the newly created account in the Manage Developers and Users page. It is now time to try logging on to your workspace as a developer. Click the Logout link in the top right corner of the page, and click the Login link to navigate to the Login page again. In the login page, specify WORKSPACE ALPHA as your workspace name, and specify the username and password for the developer account you created earlier (as shown in Figure 1-15).

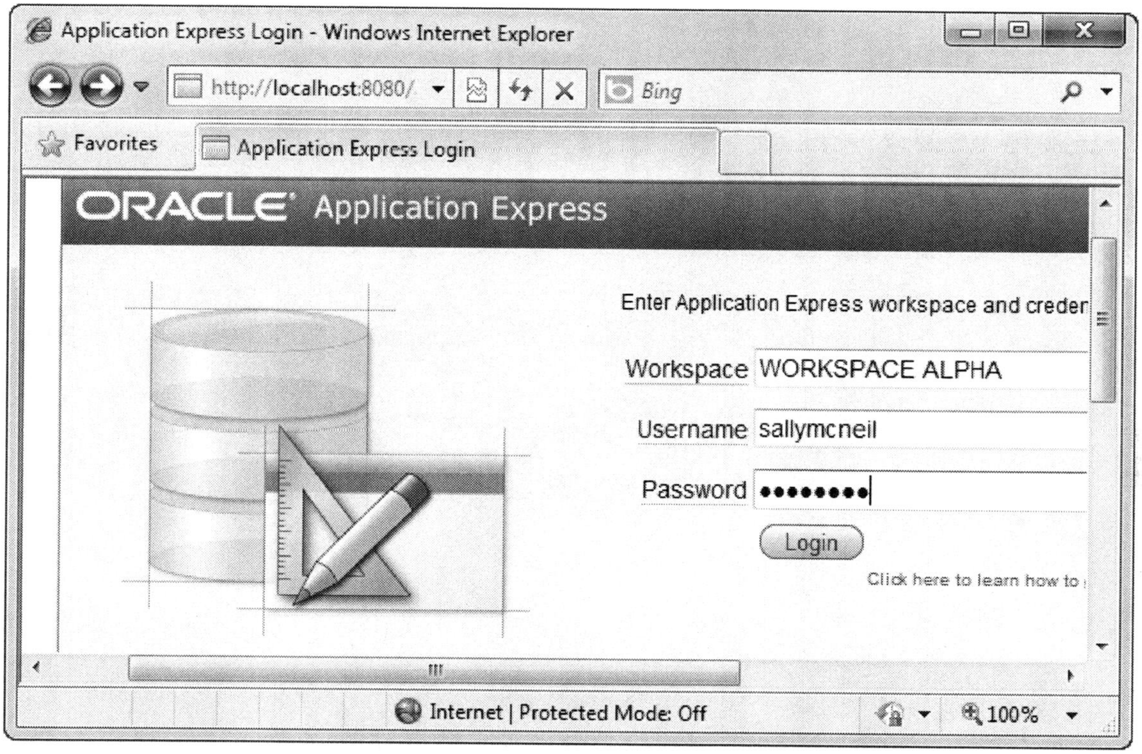

Figure 1-15. Logging on to your workspace

9. Click the Login button. If you were able to log on successfully, you should be able to see the workspace home page shown in Figure 1-16.

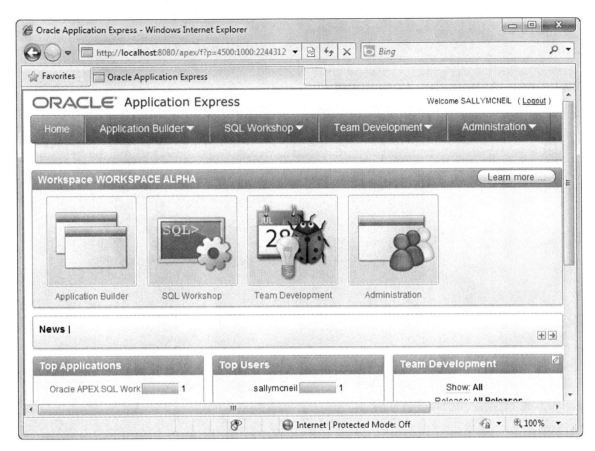

Figure 1-16. The workspace home page

How It Works

Workspaces, as introduced earlier in Recipe 1-4, represent the working area for a development team. For instance, in a typical APEX deployment, each department may be given their own workspace, which is self-administered and separate from other departments.

An APEX workspace can be configured to map to one or more database schemas. This allows any application, form, or report created in this APEX workspace to inherit all the permissions in the associated database schema. (Your application code would have access to all the database objects in that schema, as if it were logged on directly to that schema).

In a typical organization, an APEX Administrator would create workspaces as required for different development teams, then individually add the appropriate developer accounts for each workspace.

▓ **Caution** APEX workspaces are not to be confused with database workspaces. The latter is a shared virtual environment in which users can make version-controlled changes to data in a table. Database workspaces are a part of the Oracle Workspace Manager, a feature of the Oracle database.

1-6. Managing the Development Process

Problem

As project manager, you have established a set of features, milestones, and tasks for your development team. You need to leverage on the Software Configuration Management features of APEX to track the progress of your project.

Solution

To create and update a feature throughout your project, follow these steps:

1. Login to a workspace in your APEX portal.

2. Click on Team Development ➤ Features ➤ Create Feature.

3. Fill in the details of the feature you wish to develop in the software (as shown in Figure 1-17).

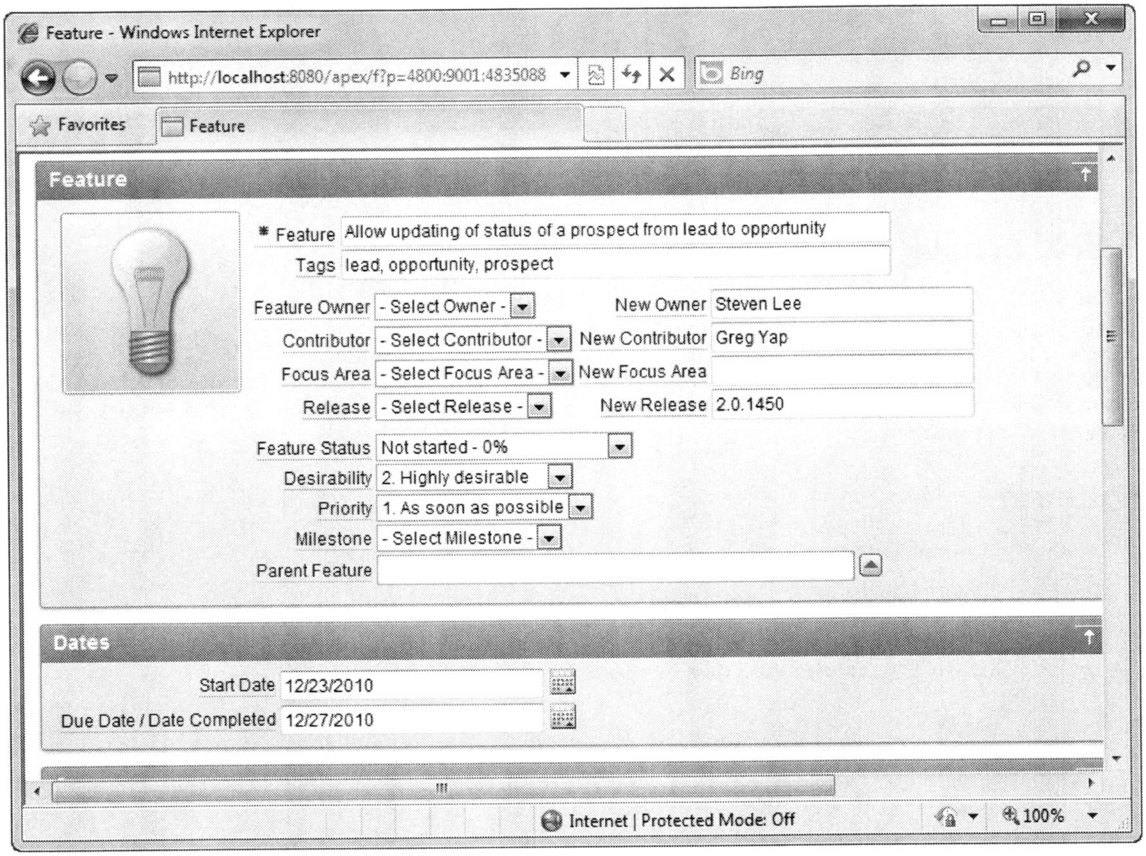

Figure 1-17. Creating a feature

4. Click the Create Feature button.

5. You have created a feature, which is now viewable by all developers in the workspace.

6. If a developer has completed this feature, and he now wishes to change the status of the feature, he will first need to navigate to `Team Development ➤ Features ➤ Features tab`.

7. You should be able to see a list of all your features in this page. You can search for your feature through this page as well. Once you have located the feature you created earlier, click on the Edit icon next to your feature (see Figure 1-18).

Figure 1-18. Browsing the list of features

8. In the next page, change the Status field of the feature to Complete - 100% and click the Apply Changes button.

9. If you navigate to the Team Development ➤ Features ➤ Dashboard tab, you can see a dashboard containing a summary of your list of features (as shown in Figure 1-19).

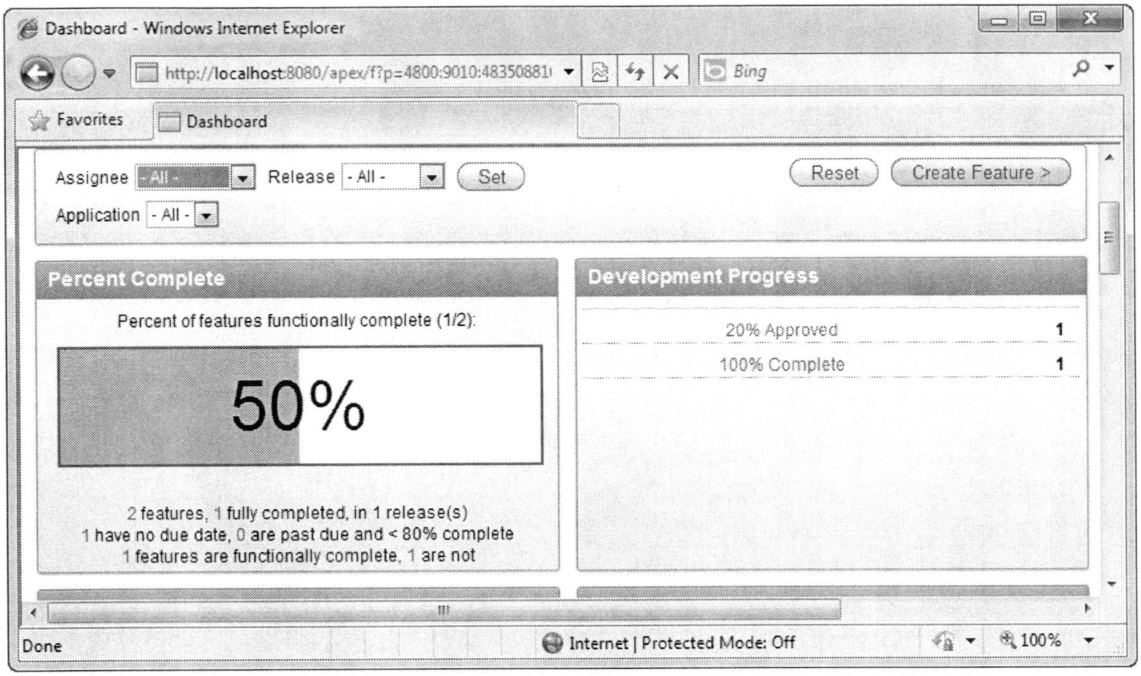

Figure 1-19.The Features dashboard

10. The Calendar tab shows your feature development deadlines in a visualize calendar format, the History tab shows you the latest updates made to the list of features, and the Focus Areas and Owners tab shows the distribution of features among the various persons involved in a doughnut chart.

■ **Tip**   The steps involved in creating milestones, tasks, and reporting bugs are very similar to those for creating a feature. To access each item, click on the corresponding icon in the Team Development menu.

How It Works

The new Team Development module provided in version 4.0 of APEX provides a way for stakeholders (your end users) to log in and track the status of feature requests and to even insert their feedback as they use the application you've developed!

APEX Team Development is also a great boon for development teams that use a SCRUM-based methodology like agile in their projects. One of the basic tenets of agile is that features can be added in any order at any time, and more importantly, a working product can be released at any iteration.

Using Team Development, you can quickly create a new release; group a bunch of features, milestones, and tasks under that release; and track its progress through the various dashboards in the portal. When the release is made available to the end users, they log on to the portal to test your application and provide feedback (through the integrated Team Development Feedback feature). This allows the project manager to incorporate these feedback and establish a new release plus a new set of features, milestones, and tasks.

This iterative process can occur many times to produce incremental releases of an application every week or so and suits very well the rapidly evolving nature of requirements prevalent in the agile development approach.

CHAPTER 2

Application Data Entry

Most business database-centric applications generally function in the same manner. An application is built around a table, say a Customer table. An end user needs to add new data to this table (in this case, a new customer record). He or she also needs to modify existing data and delete customer records from this table. Data records in this table usually take the appearance of a grid, accompanied by the New, Edit, and Delete buttons that allow the end user to modify the grid's contents. The New and Edit buttons typically take the user to a separate detail page—a form—that displays the set of fields in a more streamlined manner for data entry.

As you move towards increasingly complex examples like sales order forms or expense claim request forms, you can dress up your application with increasingly sophisticated bells and whistles—data validation, calculated fields, complex form behavior, access rights, web service calls and so on. At its heart, though, a business application still consists of basic CRUD (Creating, Reading, Updating, and Deleting) operations.

This recurring pattern is the underlying foundation that makes the entire concept of Oracle APEX work. It takes care of the tedious work of setting up basic data entry screens and binding it to the database table. After that, you are given the freedom to add the bells and whistles you want to each page to make them behave the way you want them to.

This chapter provides you with several recipes to help you create the CRUD foundation for your application. It will guide you through creating two different application types—the standard database application and the Websheet application (a new feature in APEX 4.0). You will learn how to generate the data entry forms for both and then modify them slightly to use a richer set of UI controls. I will also explore how you can speed up data entry by using a special type of form called the tabular form.

2-1. Creating a Database Application

Problem

You need to create a database application that contains a data entry form to manage a master list of customers and their details.

Solution

It's best to approach this problem in two parts. First, create the customer table. Then create the application, including a data entry form.

Creating the Customers Table

Here's how to create the customers table:

1. Login to an existing APEX workspace as a developer.

■ **Note** You can refer to Recipe 1-5 for more information on how to create a workspace.

---

2. You will now need to create the Customers table. Click on the SQL Workshop ➤ Object Browser menu item. In the ensuing window, click the Create button in the top right corner, and choose the Table menu item.

3. You will be presented with a window that allows you to define your database table. Specify a name for the table and define a few fields for the table. You may create a mix of NVARCHAR2, NUMBER, and DATE fields. This is shown in Figure 2-1.

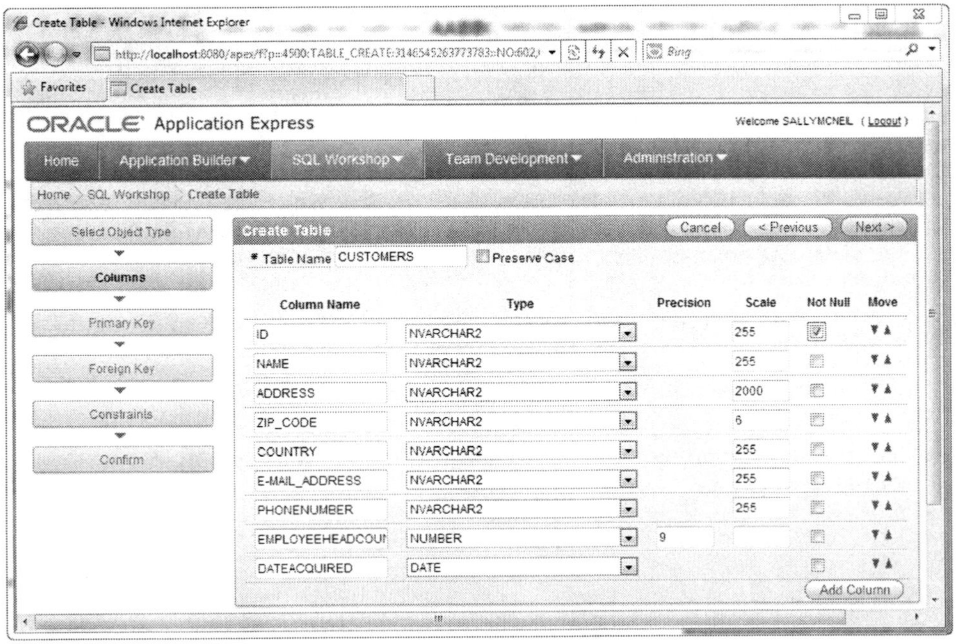

Figure 2-1. Creating the Customers table

4. Click the Next button to continue. You can define a primary key in this screen, if needed. Set the primary key to the ID field of your table, as shown in Figure 2-2.

■ **Tip** Several APEX functions, like editing a record from a report page, require a primary key to be defined on the table or view upon which the report is based. You can read up more about report pages in Recipe 2-2.

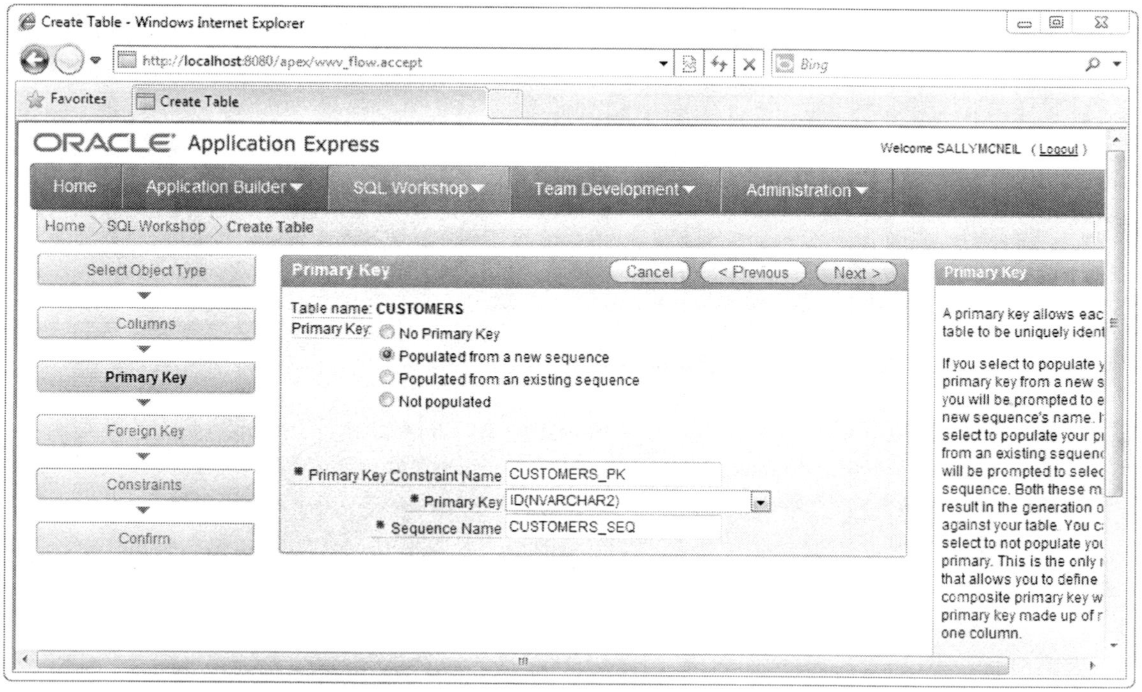

Figure 2-2. Defining the primary key

5. Click the Next button. The next page allows you to define a foreign key (if available). Since there isn't one at the moment, skip this page and click the Next button again. In the next page, you can define constraints on your table. You may, for example not want to have duplicate records (two records of a particular company with the same name). Choose to create a unique constraint on the Name field, as shown in Figure 2-3.

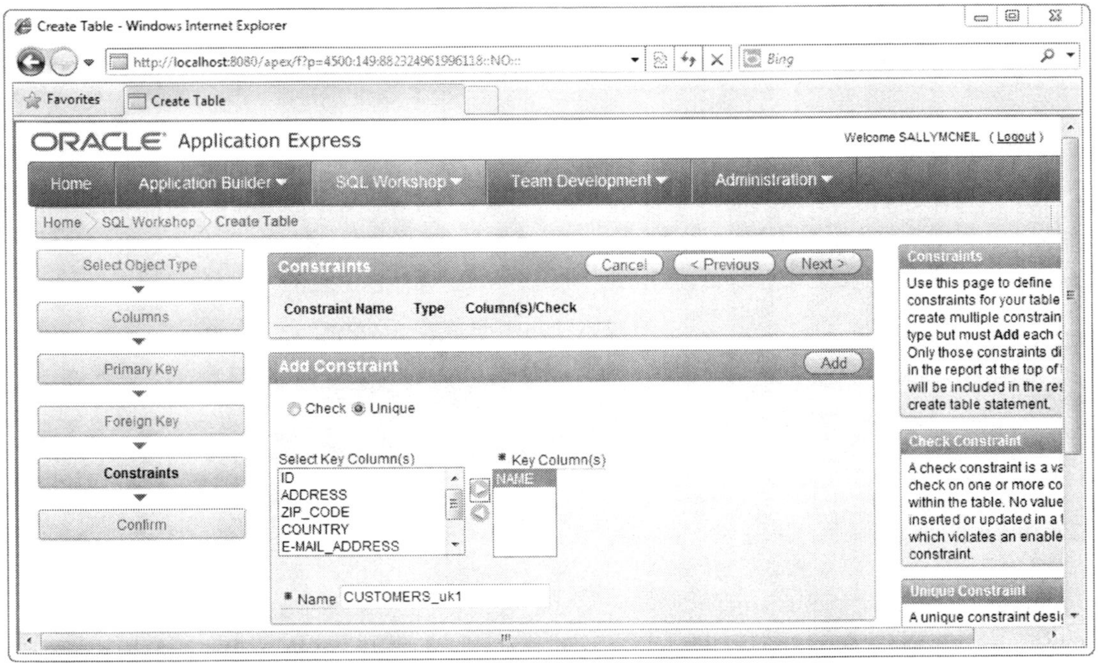

Figure 2-3. Defining constraints on the Customers table

6. Click the Next button. You can see a summary of the table that will be created. Click the Create button to confirm the request, after which your table will be generated. If you browse your list of tables, you should see the Customers table appear in that list (shown in Figure 2-4).

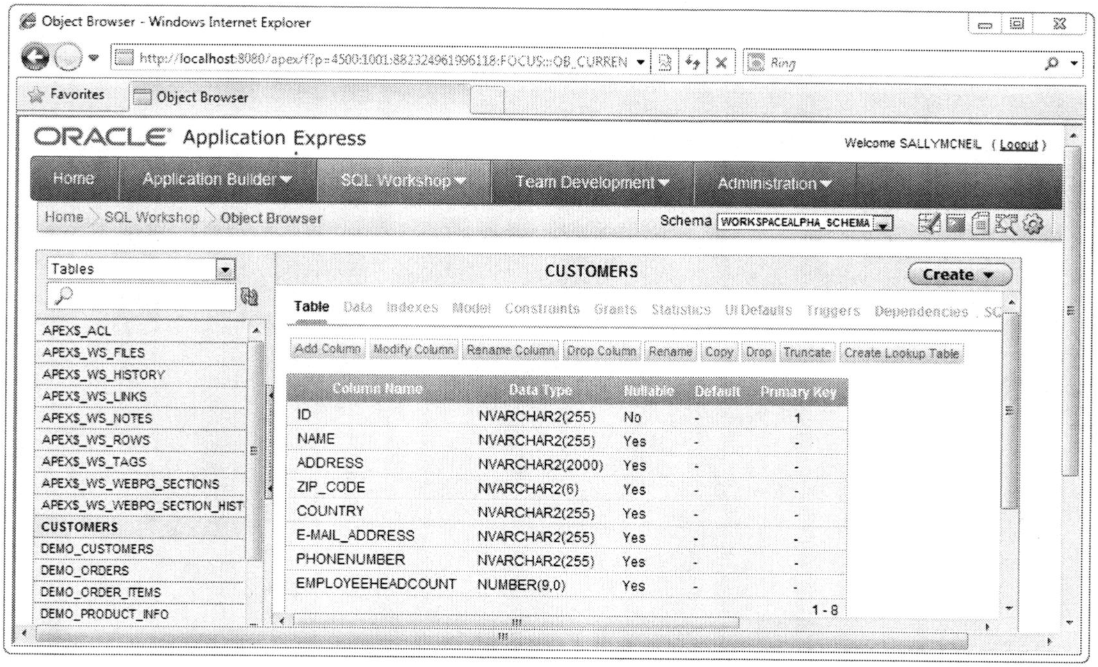

Figure 2-4. The Customers table in the Object browser

Creating the Database Application and Data Entry Form

Now it's time to create the database application.

1. To create a new database application, click the Application Builder ➤ Database applications menu item in the workspace home.

2. The application builder wizard will be displayed (as shown in Figure 2-5). Choose the Database application type.

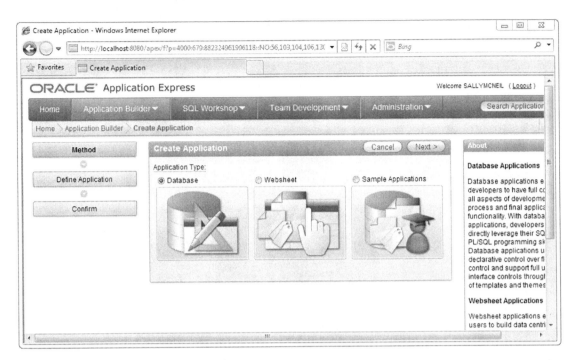

Figure 2-5. Application Builder wizard

3.   Next, you will need to specify a name for your application. Use Sales Force as the application name. Choose to create the application from scratch. Click on the Next button.

4.   You will now see a section of the wizard called Pages. Here you can define the list of pages contained in your application. Create a blank page; this will be the home page of your application. Choose the blank page type and specify My Home as your page name (see Figure 2-6). When you are done, click the Add Page button.

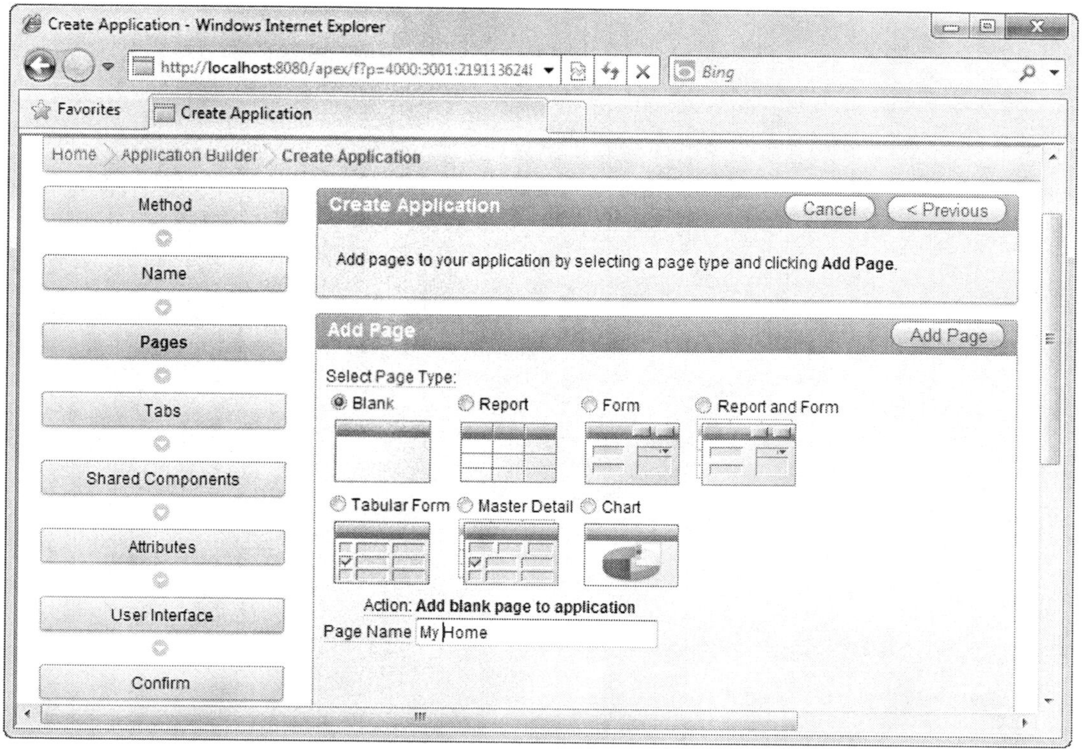

Figure 2-6. Creating a blank page as the home page

5. In this same area, you will be able to create the data entry page. Choose the Form page type. In the Subordinate to Page field, select the My Home page. In the table name field, choose an existing table from the database; in your case, the Customers table you created earlier. After you are done, click the Add Page button. This step is shown in detail in Figure 2-7.

■ **Tip** The Subordinate to Page field gives APEX some information on how your pages are structured. This, in turn, defines the default navigation scheme generated by APEX later. For instance, setting the Customers form as the subordinate to the My Home page will cause APEX to automatically generate a link to the Customers form in the home page.

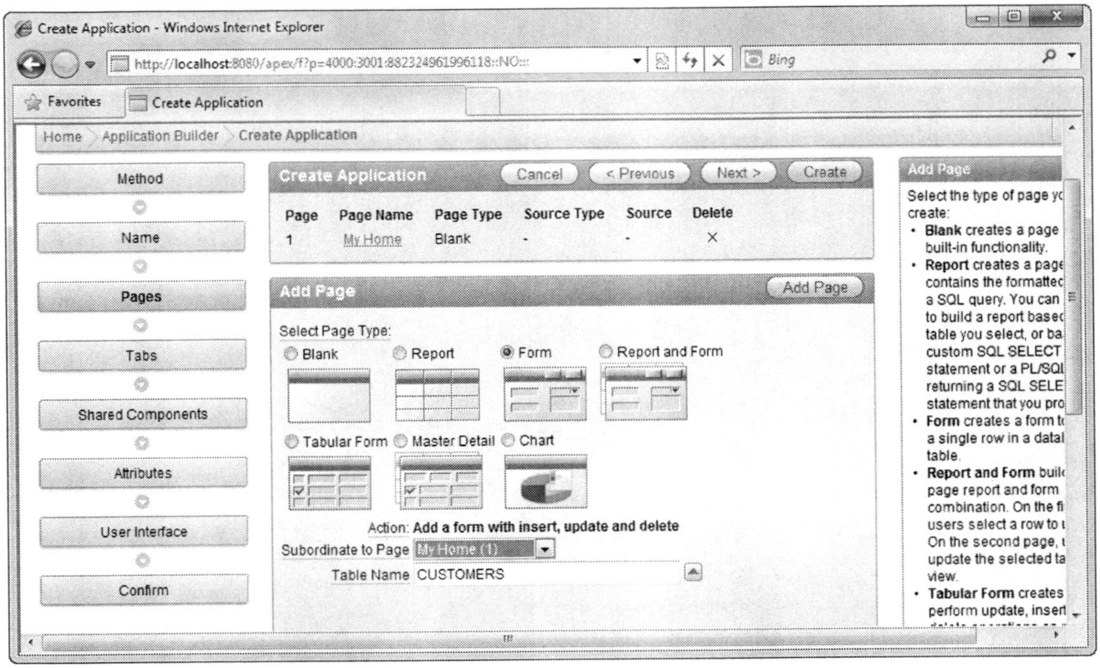

Figure 2-7. *Creating the Customers data entry page*

6. When you are done, click the Next button. In the next page, you can define tabs for your application. Use the default settings and proceed to the next page. You may also skip the Shared Components, Attributes, and UI wizard pages for now. Click the Create button to create the application. You will be required to reconfirm your settings one more time.

7. After your application is successfully created, you will see the screenshot shown in Figure 2-8. (Note that a Login page is automatically generated in your application). Click the Run Application icon to try out your application!

Figure 2-8. The SalesForceApp application was created successfully!

8. You will first see the Login page. Log in with the same credentials as the developer account you used earlier to log in to your workspace. After you've logged in to your application, you should see the home page shown in Figure 2-9. Note that a link to the Customers page has been automatically generated on the home page.

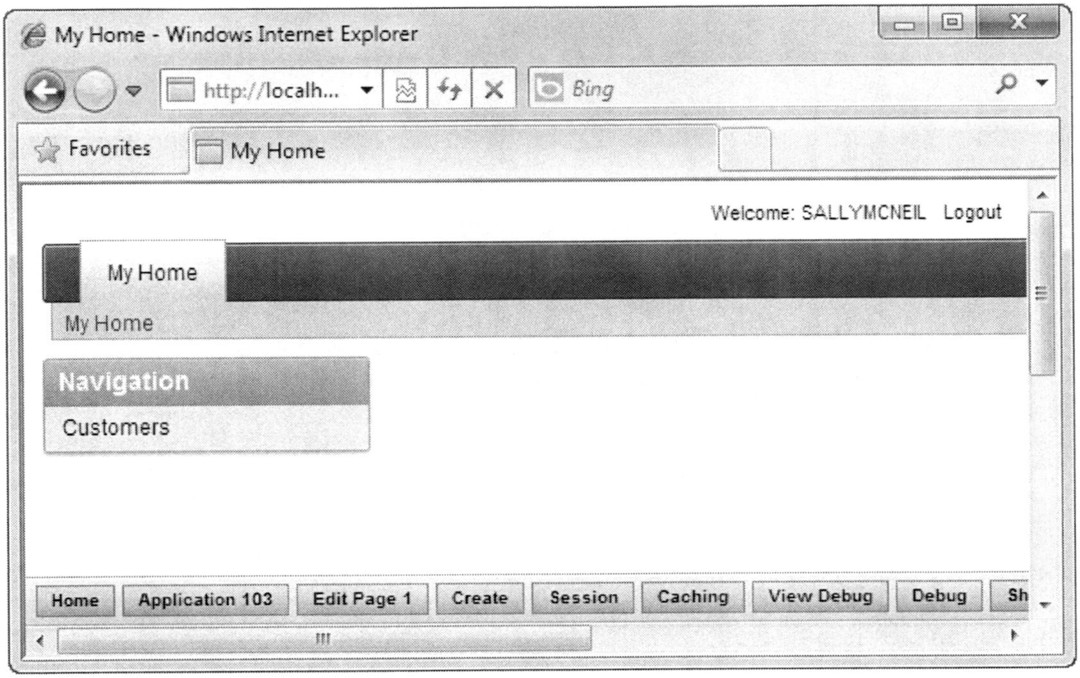

Figure 2-9. The home page of your application

9. Click the Customers link to open the Customers data entry form. You can see your form here (with the full list of fields from the Customers table). Enter some information in this form and click the Create button when you are done. This is shown in Figure 2-10.

■ **Note** The generated controls on the form depend on the field type declared in the database table. For instance, a date field in the database would generate a date picker control on the form.

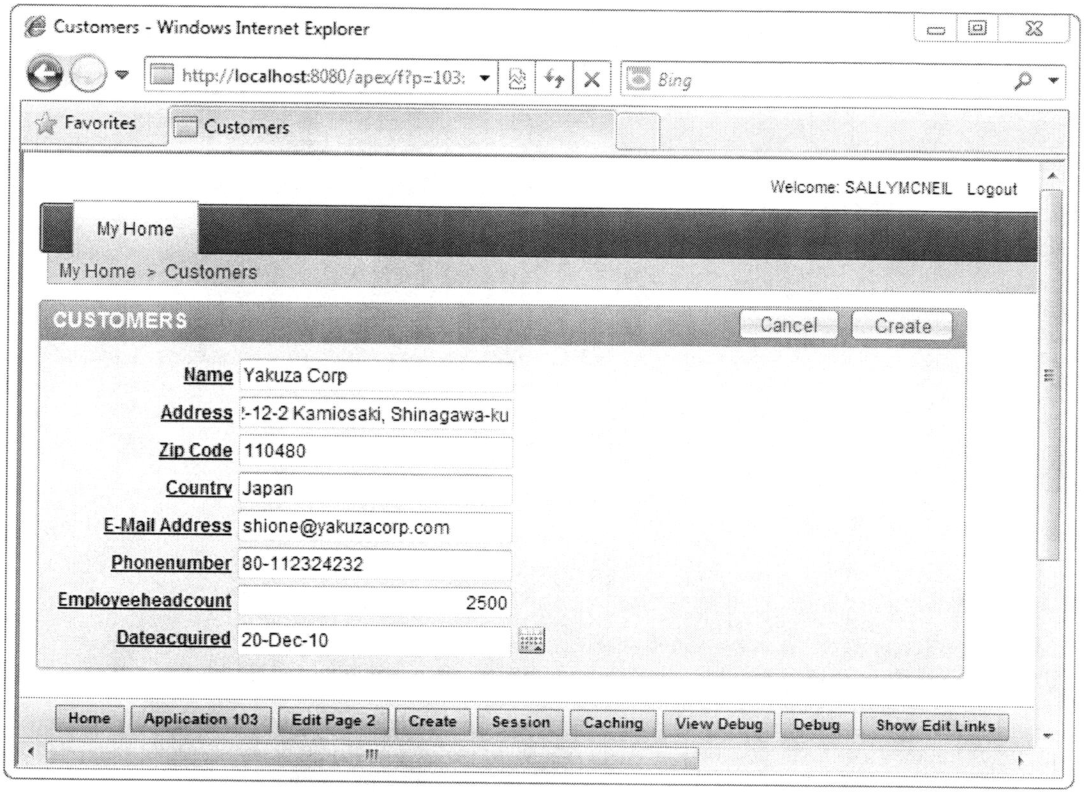

Figure 2-10. The Customers data entry page

10. When you have created the record, log out from the application and click the
Home button in the bottom bar to return to the workspace. Navigate to the
object browser in the SQL Workshop, and take a peek at the data in this table.
You should be able to see the newly created record in your database table (see
Figure 2-11).

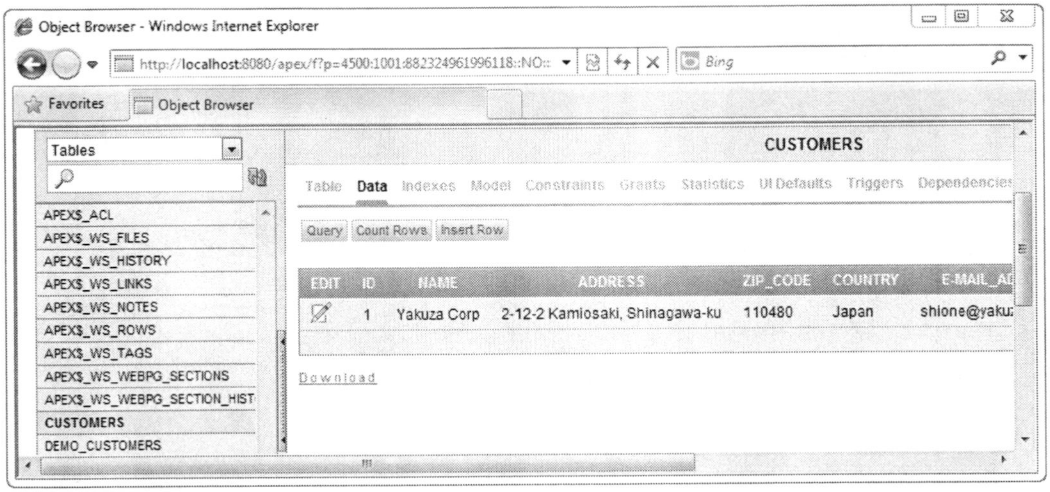

Figure 2-11. The newly created customer record

How It Works

The Database Application type is the most common application type in APEX. It allows you to set up pages (specifically forms and reports) that allow you to quickly generate the CRUD user interfaces around an existing database table.

A typical APEX application starts off with the developer (or database designer) defining the full set of database tables needed for the application. This can be done using the Object Browser tool or by running PL/SQL script in the SQL Workshop section of APEX. It is also possible to create the database objects—tables, indexes, constraints, sequences, etc.—using an external tool, a set of DDL in a script, or importing the schema from another database.

Once the tables are all generated, the APEX developer generates the desired forms and reports from the schema of these database tables. Once the forms are in place, the developer refines these generated pages by adding validation routines, JavaScript functionality, complex form behavior, access rights settings, and so on.

2-2. Creating a Report to Manage Your Data

Problem

Your users want to create two pages: a data entry form and another page to retrieve the data they have just entered. The application also needs to display previously entered data to the users row by row in a grid (listing) format and provide a way for them to edit and delete their data.

Solution

Execute the following steps to create a report to show existing records:

1. Open the Sales Force application in the workspace (connected as a developer).

2. Click the Create Page button in the top right corner. In the ensuing window, choose the Form page type. In the next page (Figure 2-12), choose the Form on a Table with Report page type. Click the Next button to continue.

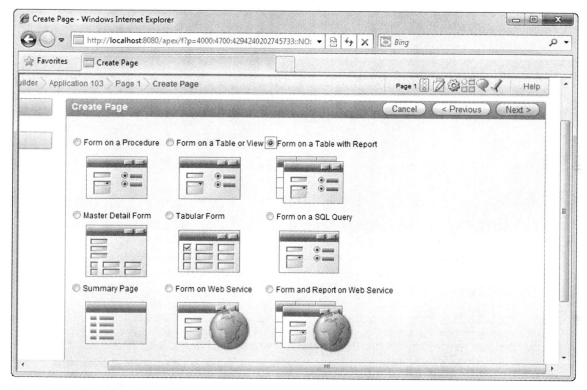

Figure 2-12. Choosing the page type

3. In the next page, use the default settings. Click the Next button to proceed to the table/view selection page. Choose the Customers table and click the Next button. Use the default settings for the next two pages of the wizard. You will eventually see the page in Figure 2-13 that allows you to define the columns available in the report. Highlight (select) all columns and click the Next button.

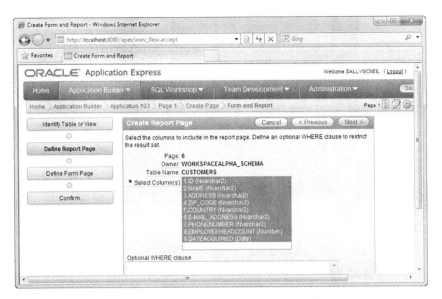

Figure 2-13. Specifying the list of columns to include in the report

4.　Use the default settings for the next four pages of the wizard. After that you will see a page that allows you to select the columns available in the form. Select all the columns.

■ **Tip**　At this point, you may run into the **Column Names must be valid Oracle Identifiers** error. This may happen if you include certain fields from the Oracle database that are reserved keywords or contain invalid characters. The Oracle database exercises a higher level of freedom with regards to field names compared to APEX. You can view Oracle's rules for naming database objects at the following link: `http://download.oracle.com/docs/cd/E11882_01/server.112/e17118/sql_elements008.htm#SQLRF51129`.

5.　In the next page, you can decide if you want to let your users insert, update, or delete records from the Customers table through the report. Leave all the options as Yes (see Figure 2-14).

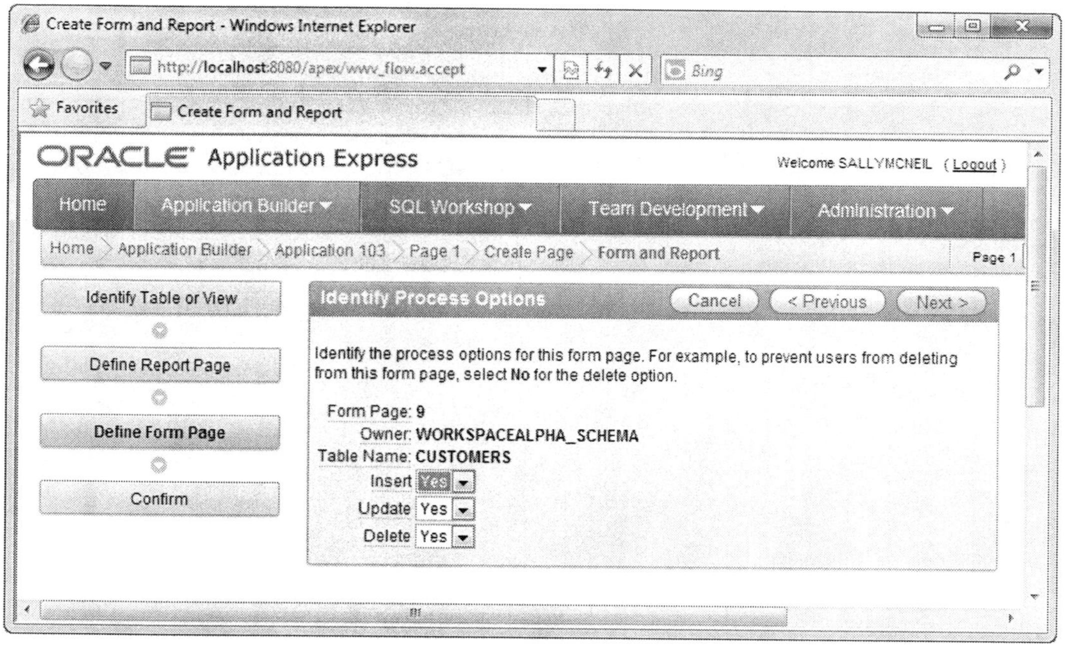

Figure 2-14. Process options on the form

6. Click the Next button and click Finish to finalize your configuration and to create the form and report. After that, return to your application home. You should be able to see two new pages in your application: Report on CUSTOMERS and Form on CUSTOMERS. You can see these in Figure 2-15.

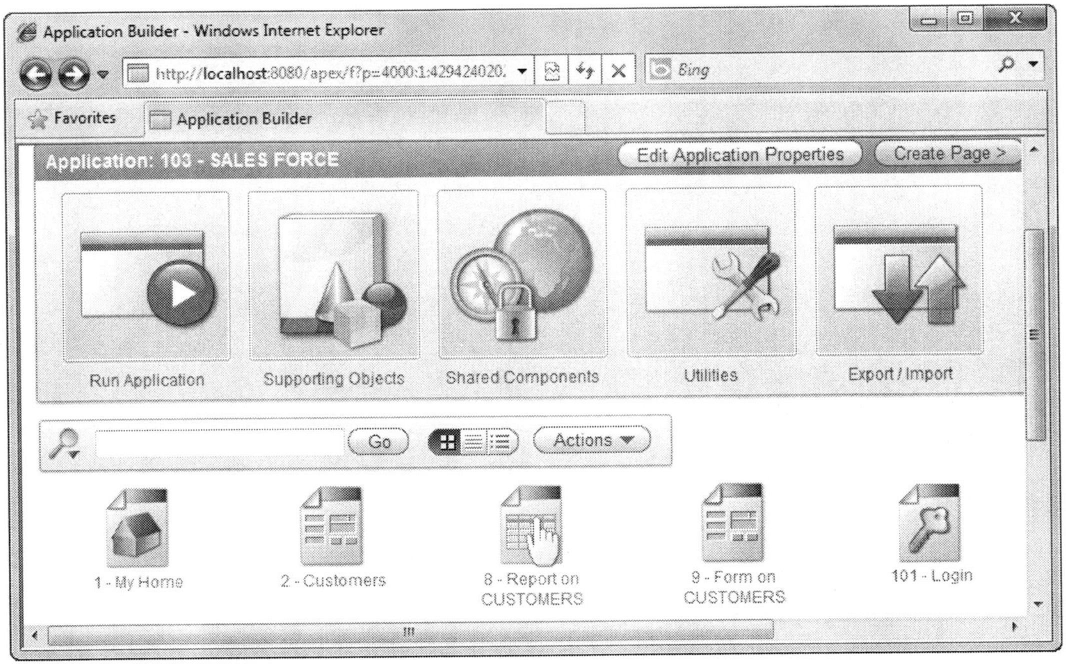

Figure 2-15. The newly created report and form

7. Now you need to create a link to the report and form in your home page. Navigate to the application home, and click the 1-My Home page. This should display the configuration area for the page. Under the Page Rendering section, navigate to Regions ➤ Body (3), right click on the Navigation item and choose the Edit List menu item. This should display the page shown in Figure 2-16.

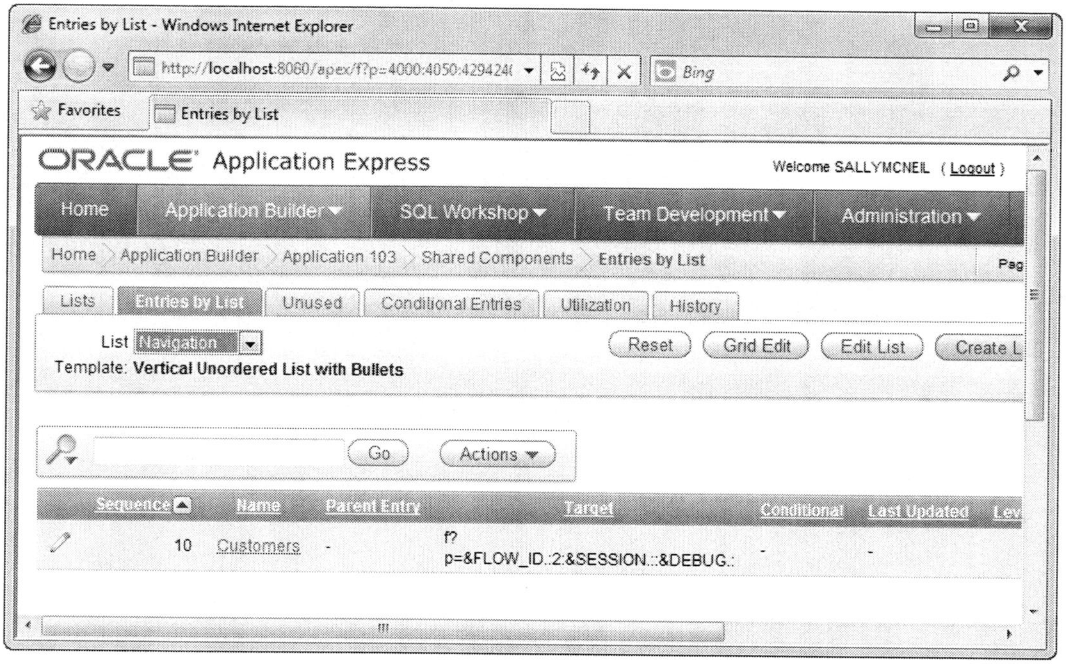

Figure 2-16. The Entries by List page

8. Click the Create List button in the top right corner. This will display a new page allowing you to configure the settings for the navigation list. Specify My List of Customers as the List Entry Label (this is the caption that is displayed on the link), and choose the Report on CUSTOMERS page for the page field. When you are done, click the Create button. You should now see your newly created link in the Entries by List page.

9. Now, navigate to your application and run the application. You should now see the new My List of Customers link in your application home page area, as shown in Figure 2-17.

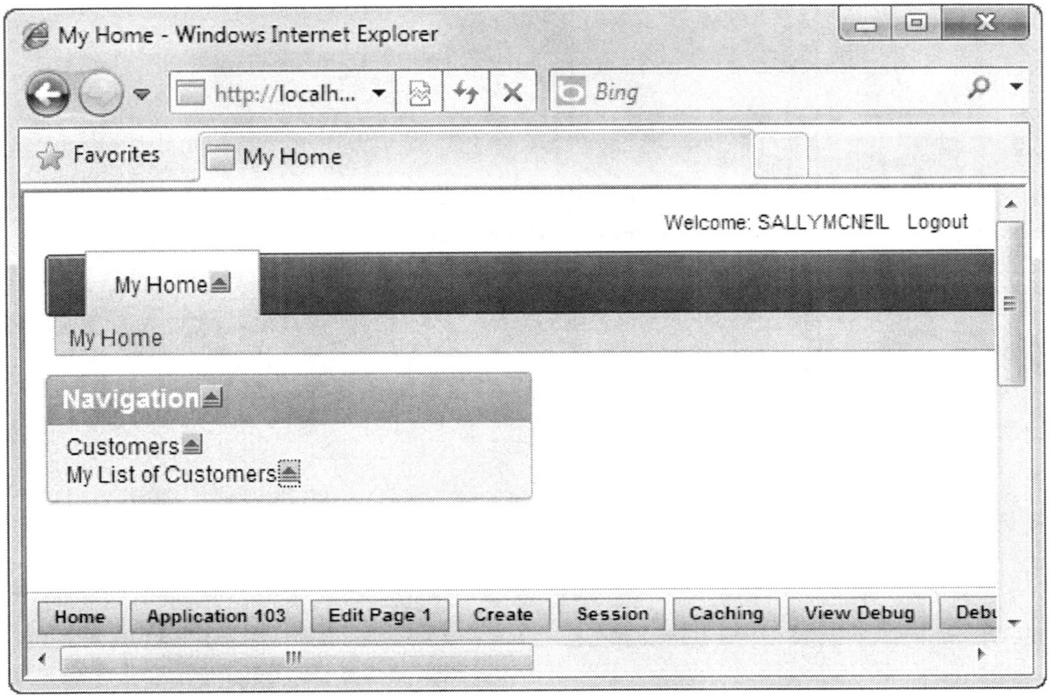

Figure 2-17. The application home page area

10. Click the My List of Customers link. You should be able to see the records from the Customers table show in the table. Click the Create button to add a new record to the list. You will see the associated form show (as shown in Figure 2-18). Fill out this form and click the Create button.

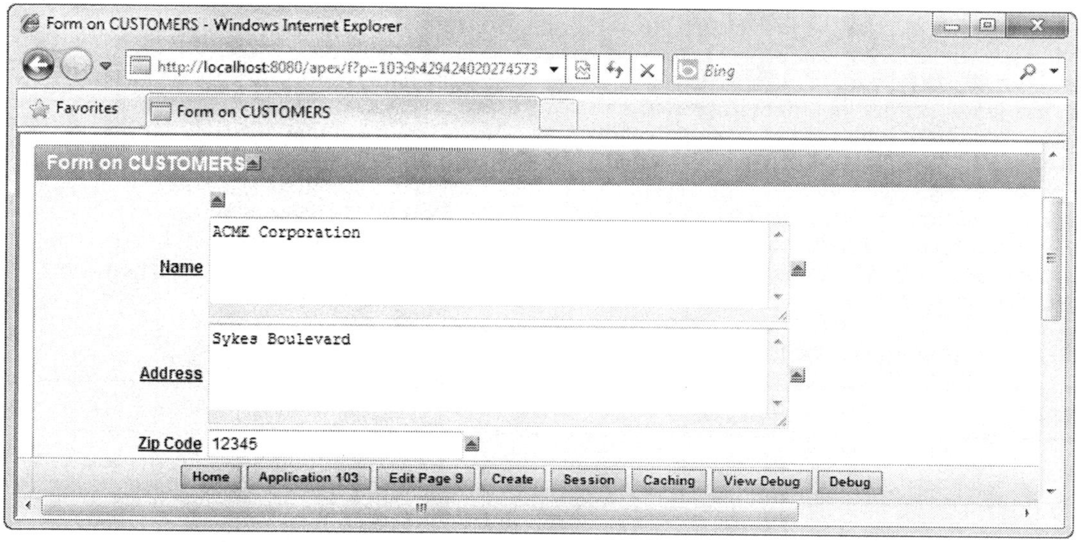

Figure 2-18. The customer details form

11. Once you have added the new record, you will be able to see it in the list (as shown in Figure 2-19). You can also edit an existing record by clicking the little paper and pen icon to the left of the table.

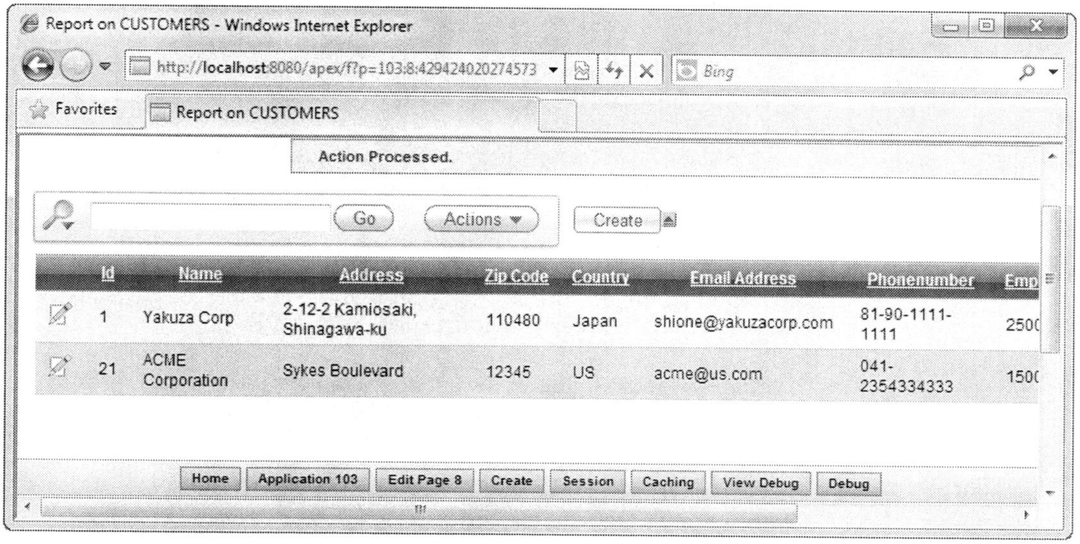

Figure 2-19. The newly created record

How It Works

A report is an object type in APEX that refers to a listing of multiple data records displayed in a tabular format. The word "report" is a bit of a misnomer since its usage in APEX covers much more than just generating traditional data reports. A report in APEX (specifically an interactive report) is commonly used to present a list of records to the user so that he/she can modify or delete them from the underlying table. In this manner, the function of the report can be considered similar to that of a view.

Reports can also be used in detail forms with master-child relationships where the report takes the appearance of a table inside the master form. Multiple child records can then be entered into this table.

Reports come with a lot of built-in functionality; Table 2-1 lists some of the default functionality provided with reports.

Table 2-1. *Functionality Built Into Reports*

Functionality	Description
Filter	Perhaps the most powerful feature of reports, filters allow the end user (in real time) to define a set of filters that can instantly apply to the full set of rows displayed in the report. Filters modify the query to the database in real time; this means that the dataset sent to APEX for processing is just the information displayed to the user.
Paging	Records in reports are automatically paged by APEX. The end user can dynamically change the page size (number of rows displayed in a single page).
Sorting	The end user can easily sort via each column in the report in real time.
Grouping	The end user can dynamically group records by a certain field or combination of fields.
Highlighting	The end user can choose to dynamically highlight rows based on certain criteria (for example, highlight in red all invoice records with amount larger than $10,000).
Create Computed Columns	The end user can dynamically create additional columns that are computed from data in existing columns. The end user can define very complex formulas to perform this computation.
Chart	The end user can dynamically create a chart view of the existing data in the report. With a few clicks, the end user could create a complex pie chart, for example, to visualize the data in the report.
Aggregate	The end user can use aggregate functions (for example, summation) that calculate an aggregate value of all data in a column of the report and displays it at the bottom of the column. This can be combined with grouping.

2-3. Changing Field Item Types in a Form

Problem

You need to change the item type of several fields on the form from a text area to a single-line text box.

Solution

To change the field type of a text area to a single-line text box, follow these steps:

1. Navigate to the application home and click the Form on CUSTOMERS form. This will display the page configuration area. In the Page Rendering section, expand the Regions ➤ Body (3) ➤ Form on Customers ➤ Items node and double-click the field you would like to modify (see Figure 2-20).

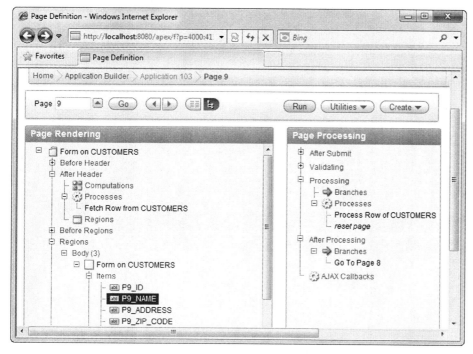

Figure 2-20. *The field setting on the form*

2. In the Edit Page Item page, change the field type of the field from Textarea to a Text Field (as shown in Figure 2-21).

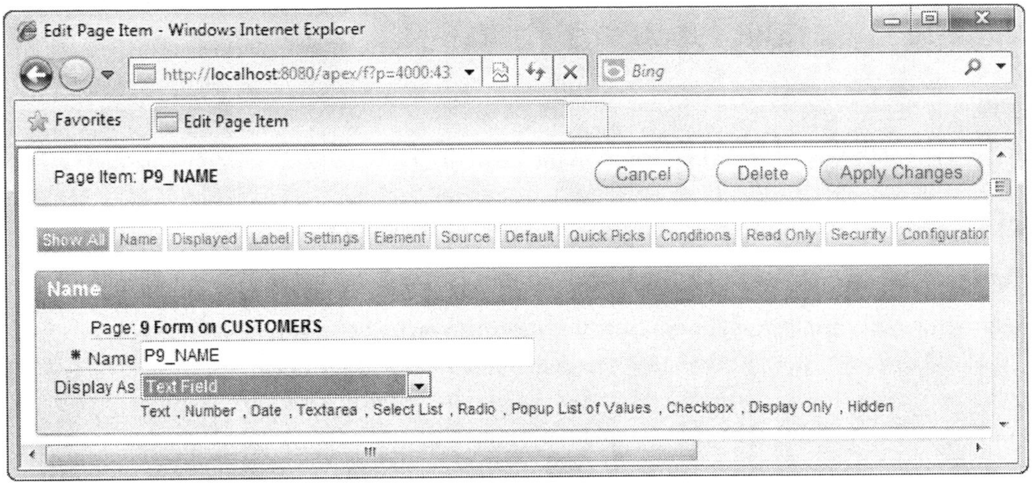

Figure 2-21. The field settings page

3. Click the Apply Changes button. Run the application and open the My List of
    Customers page. Choose to create a new record. In the form page, you should
    be able to observe that the field type of your field has changed accordingly
    (shown in Figure 2-22).

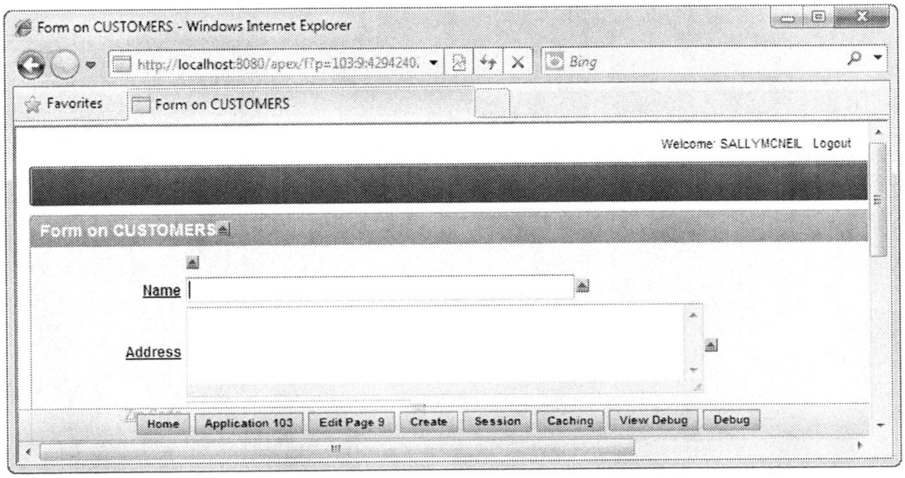

Figure 2-22. The reflected changes in the Form on CUSTOMERS form

How It Works

The Page Rendering section provides an overview of the back-end wiring of each page. It lists every field used on the form and provides tools to manipulate every aspect of the fields from visual layout to validation behavior.

2-4. Selecting from a List of Values in a Form

Problem

You need to create a List of Values (LOV) as a drop-down list for the Country field in the Customers form. This LOV must be dynamic and should be managed in a separate table.

Solution

Here's how to create a form field allowing users to select from a LOV:

1. Using the Object Browser tool in the SQL Workshop, create a new table named Countries with two columns: CountryName and Remarks. Insert some sample data into the tables; for example, create records for Japan, US, and Singapore in the CountryName field.

■ **Tip**   Recipe 2-1 describes how to use the Object Browser tool to create tables.

---

2. Navigate to the application home and click the Form on CUSTOMERS form. This will display the page configuration area. In the Page Rendering section, expand the Regions ➤ Body (3) ➤ Form on Customers ➤ Items node and double-click the Country field.

3. In the ensuing page, change the Display As field type to a Select List. This indicates a drop-down list. When you do this, you will also notice that a new tab named List of Values will appear at the top. Click on this tab.

4. In the ensuing page, click the Create Dynamic List of Values link. This will launch a pop-up window that allows you to configure the dynamic list. In the pop-up window, use the default table/view owner, and click the Next button.

5. In the next page of the wizard, choose the Countries table. Set CountryName as both the Display column and Return Value. Click the Next and Finish buttons consecutively to complete the configuration. You will see the generated SQL in the List of Values `definition` area (shown in Figure 2-23).

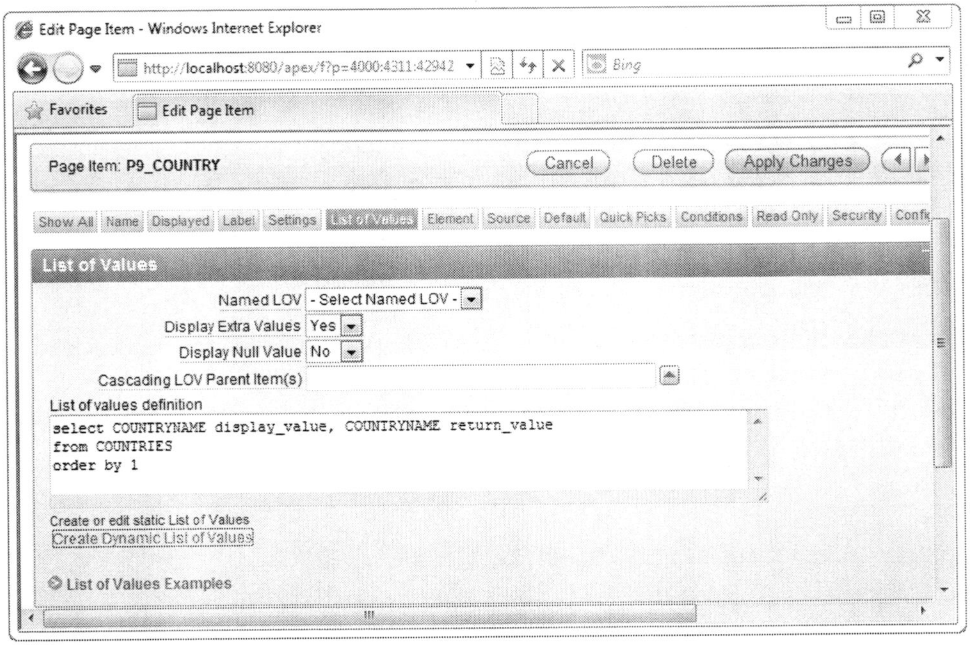

Figure 2-23. *The generated SQL in the LOV definition area*

6. Click the Displayed tab, and set the Height to 1. This will convert the select list from a list box to a drop-down list.

7. Click the Apply Changes button. Run the application, click the My List of Customers link, and choose to create a new record. You will notice that the field for Country has changed to a drop-down list containing the values stored in your Countries table (shown in Figure 2-24).

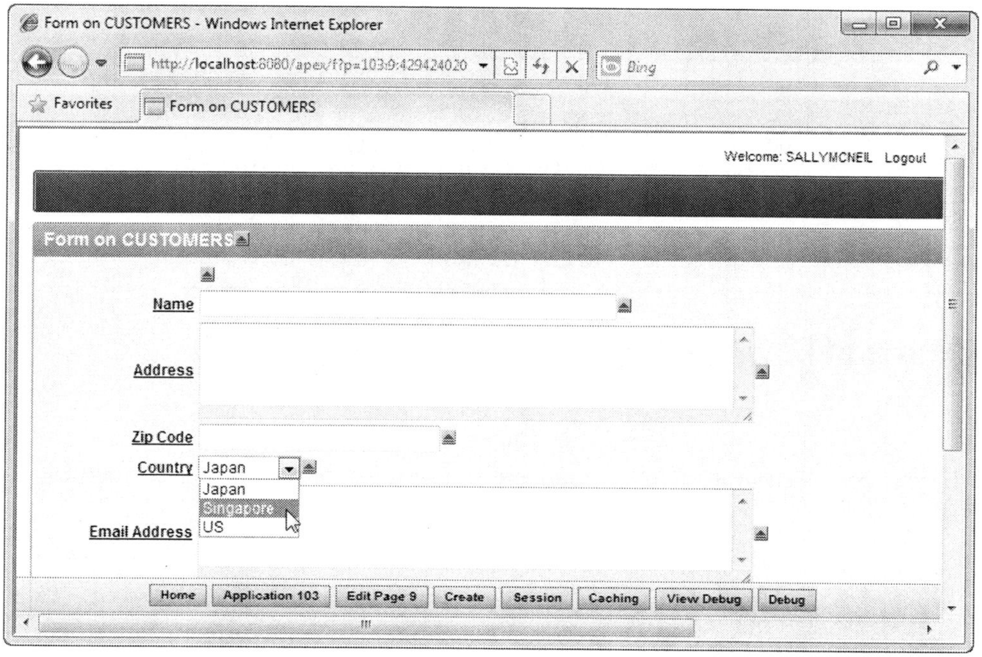

Figure 2-24. The Country drop-down list

How It Works

Oracle APEX provides five different types of controls that allow the user to pick from a list of values. They are described in Table 2-2.

Table 2-2. Item Types Providing LOV Functionality

Item Type	Description
Checkbox	You can create multiple checkboxes (a checklist) that users can tick on the form. The LOV area allows you to define the caption and value of each checkbox.
Radio Group	The Radio Group type allows you to pick a single value from a list of values using radio buttons. The LOV area allows you to define the caption and value of each radio button.
Popup LOV	The Popup LOV is a selection control where you can select a value from a list in a pop-up window.

Item Type	Description
Select List	A select list can take the appearance of a list box (if the Height property is set to a value larger than 1) or a drop-down list (if the Height property is set to 1). The LOV contained in a Select List are defined in the LOV area.
Shuttle	A shuttle basically comprises two list boxes that allow you to shuttle (or add) items from one box to the other.

2-5. Uploading and Downloading Files in a Form

Problem

You need to let the user upload an attachment—a company profile (in any file format)—along with each customer record.

Solution

Here's how to create a file upload field in your form:

1. Using the Object Browser tool in the SQL Workshop, add a new BLOB column to the Customers table, and name the column CompanyProfile.

2. Navigate to the application home and click the Form on CUSTOMERS form. This will display the page configuration area. In the Page Rendering section, expand the Regions ➤ Body (3) ➤ Form on Customers node and right-click the Items node. Choose the Create Page Item menu item.

3. In the ensuing page, select the File Browse field type and click Next. In the next page, change the Item Name to P9_COMPANYPROFILE. Use the default settings for the rest of the pages in the wizard. After you have created the page item, double-click on the item in the Page Rendering section.

4. In the item configuration page, click the Source tab, and change the Source type to Database Column. Set the Source value or expression field to the name of your BLOB database field, COMPANYPROFILE. Click the Apply Changes button to save your changes.

5. Now, run the application, click the My List of Customers link, and choose to create a new record. You will notice the new company profile field in the form. Click the Browse button and select any text-based file in the file picker dialog (as shown in Figure 2-25). Click the Create button in the top right corner to save the record. The contents of the file will be written into the BLOB column.

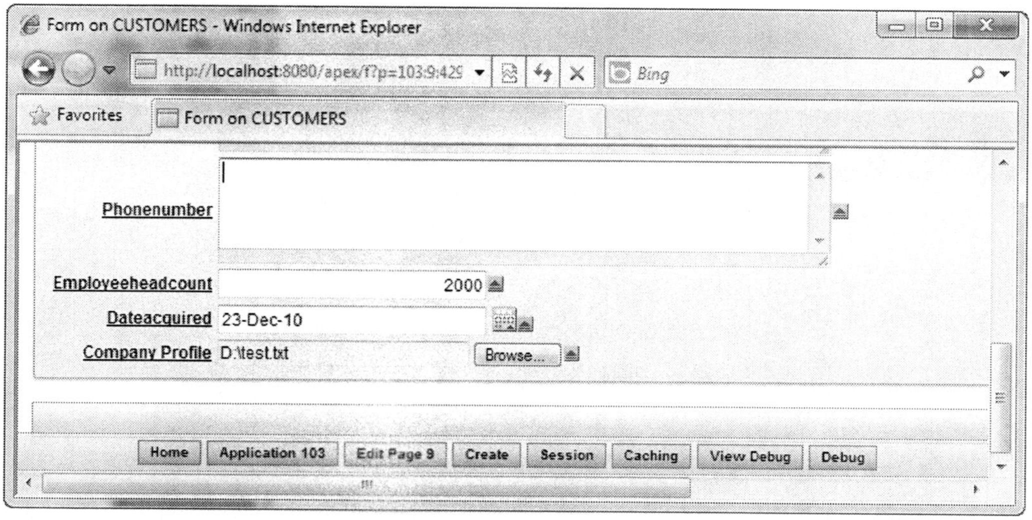

Figure 2-25. The Company Profile file upload field in action

6. Now try to edit the record you have just created. In the form window, you will be able to see a little Download link next to the file upload control. Click the Download link to download the contents of the file (as shown in Figure 2-26).

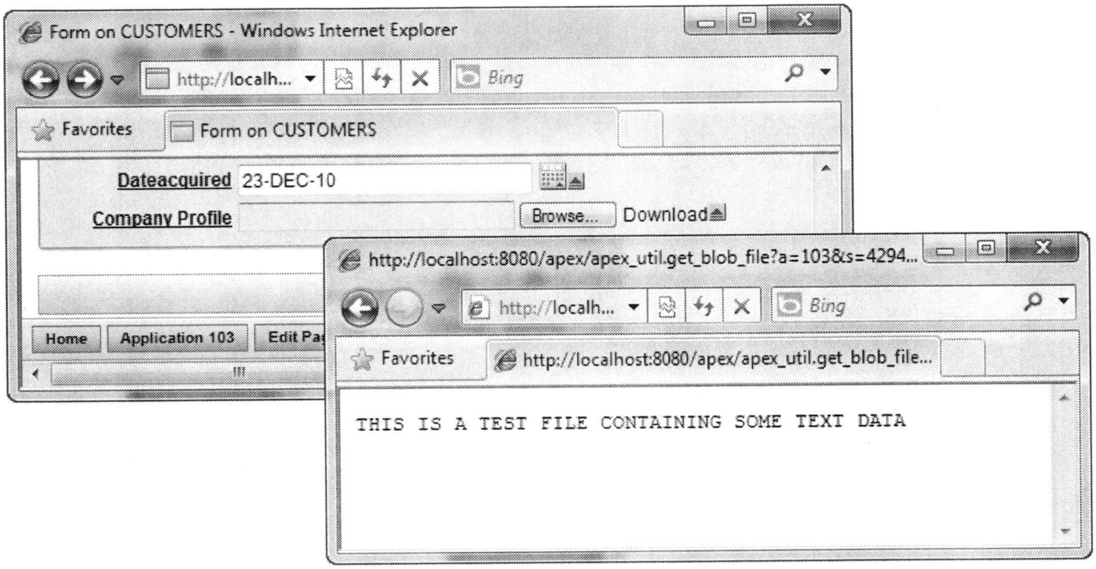

Figure 2-26. Downloading data from a BLOB field

How It Works

When you use the BLOB field to store your file attachments, the content of your file attachments are stored in the BLOB field after an upload is made via an APEX form. Likewise, when a download is initiated, the contents of the BLOB field are downloaded to the client browser.

2-6. Using Tabular Forms to Speed Up Data Entry

Problem

You have lots of data to key into your application. You need a better and faster way to edit and insert data records.

Solution

Execute the following steps to create a tabular data-entry form:

1. Navigate to the application home. Create a new page, and choose the tabular form as the type of the page. Click the Next button.

2. In the next section of the wizard, you are allowed to choose the type of operations allowed on the tabular form. Leave it as the default (Update, Insert, and Delete) and proceed to the next page.

3. Choose the Customers table from the list. In the next page, select all columns to include in the tabular form. This is shown in Figure 2-27.

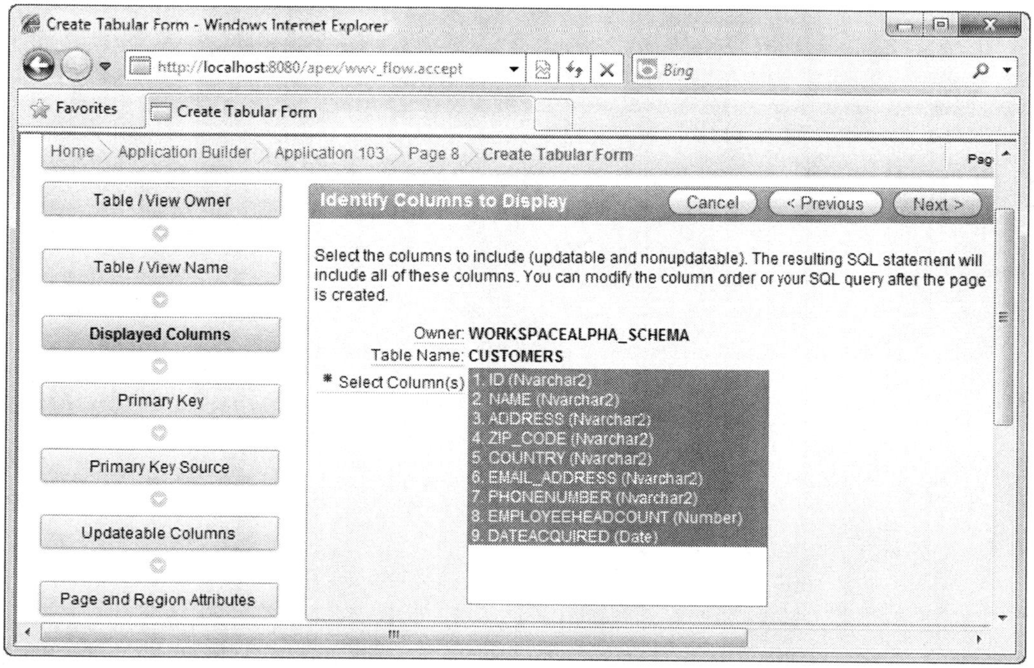

Figure 2-27. Selecting the list of columns to include in a tabular form

4. Use the default settings on all the subsequent pages. At the end of the wizard, click the Run Page icon to run your tabular form.

5. You should be able to see the tabular form, as shown in Figure 2-28. You will be able to modify your data by changing values directly in the cells of the table. You will also be able to delete and add rows from this table using the buttons provided at the top and bottom of the table. Once you are done modifying your data, click the Submit button to save your changes.

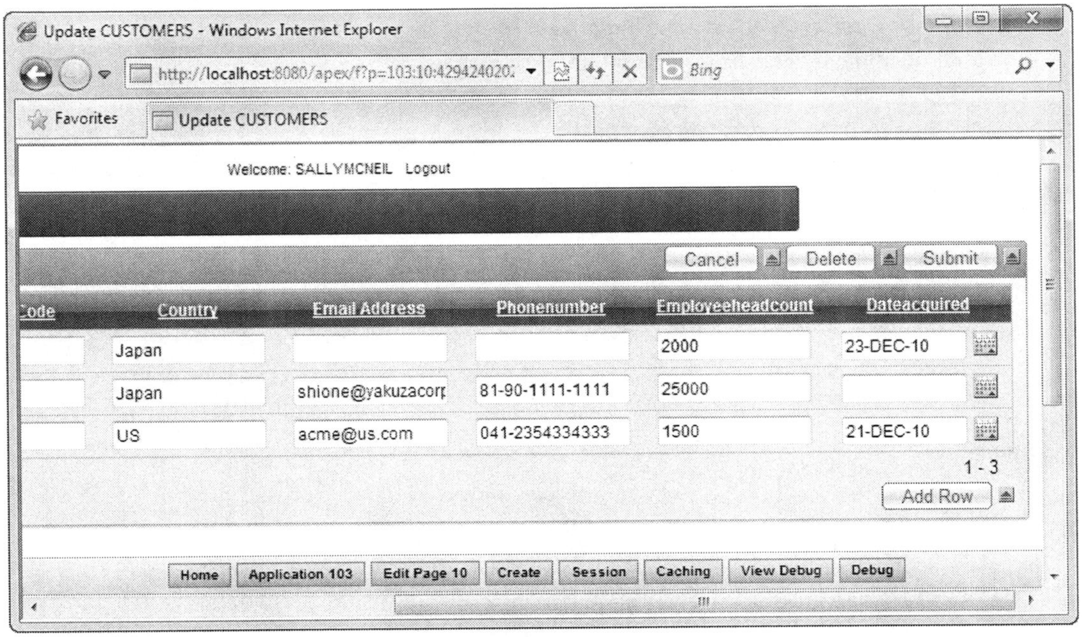

Figure 2-28. The tabular form in action

■ **Tip** You might also want to include a link from your application home page directly to this tabular form. Steps 7 to 9 in Recipe 2-2 explain how to do this in detail.

How It Works

Tabular forms help you to quickly set up grids that allow you to do inline editing of tabular data. The objective of the tabular form is to allow the end user to modify multiple records and to submit all the changes at once. This reduces network traffic when many users need to update multiple data records frequently.

The tabular forms feature provides rich UI controls for each column during inline editing. For example, a Country column could present a dropdown containing a list of countries to pick from when editing the tabular form.

2-7. Creating a Websheet Application

Problem

You have a Microsoft Excel spreadsheet containing a huge list of data—a list of all your customers. You need to get this entire list onto the Web so that users can modify it via a web interface, and you need to do this in the shortest possible time.

Solution

Here's how to create a Websheet application using data from a Microsoft Excel spreadsheet:

1. Click on the Application Builder main menu item, and click the Create button. Choose to create a Websheet application.

2. Change the name of the application to CustomersWebSheet.

3. Click the Create button to create the Websheet. You should see your Websheet application in the workspace home (see Figure 2-29).

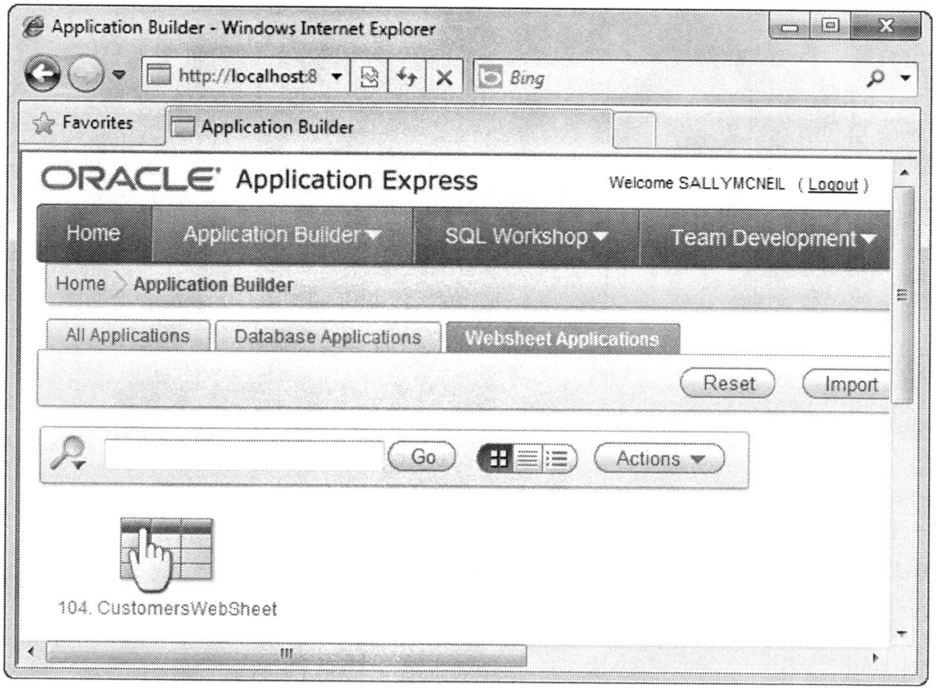

Figure 2-29. The newly created CustomersWebSheet application

4. Click on your Websheet application and click the Run button.

5. Login to the Websheet application using your developer credentials

6. In the application, click the Data main menu item and select the Create submenu item.

7. In the wizard, choose to create a data grid, and click the Next button.

8. In the next page, choose to create the data grid via Copy and Paste (as shown in Figure 2-30).

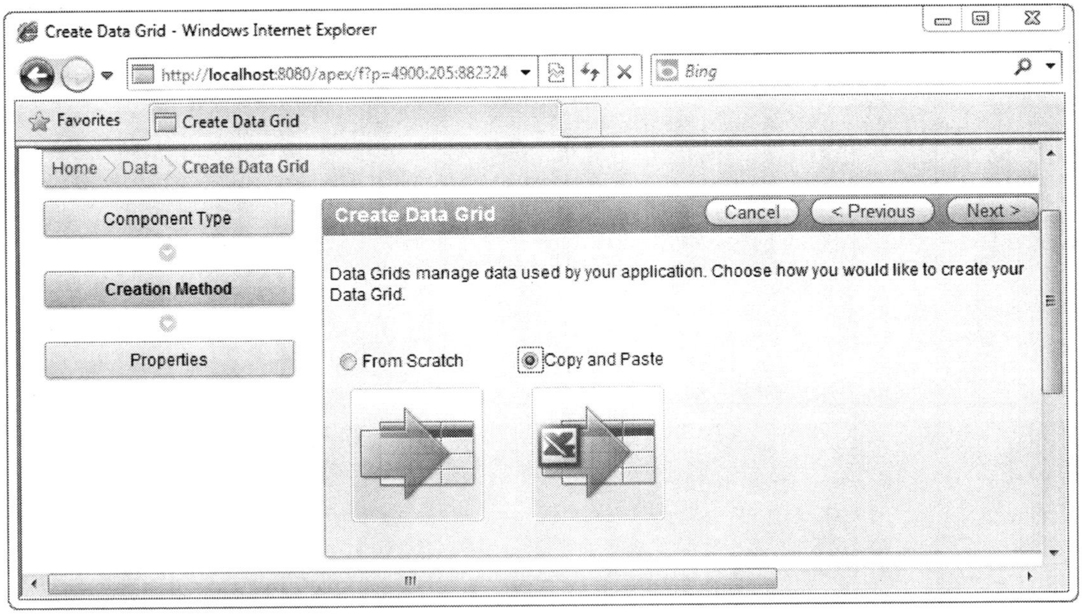

Figure 2-30. Create data grid via cut and paste

9. In the next page, specify Customers as the name of your data grid. You will now need to copy all the data from your Excel spreadsheet (as shown in Figure 2-31) and paste it into the large text area in this page (shown in Figure 2-32).

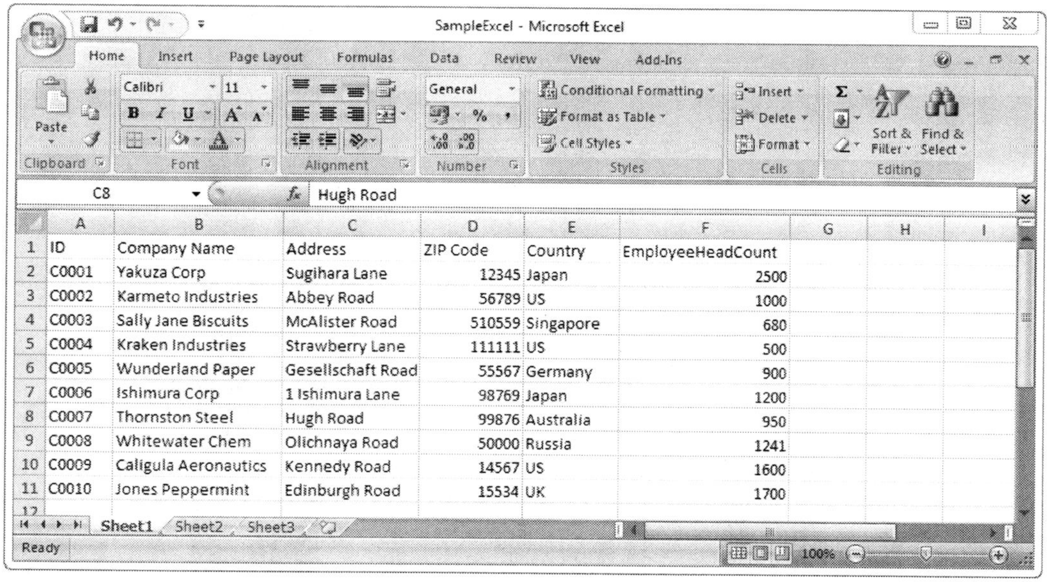

Figure 2-31. Copy the contents from your Microsoft Excel file...

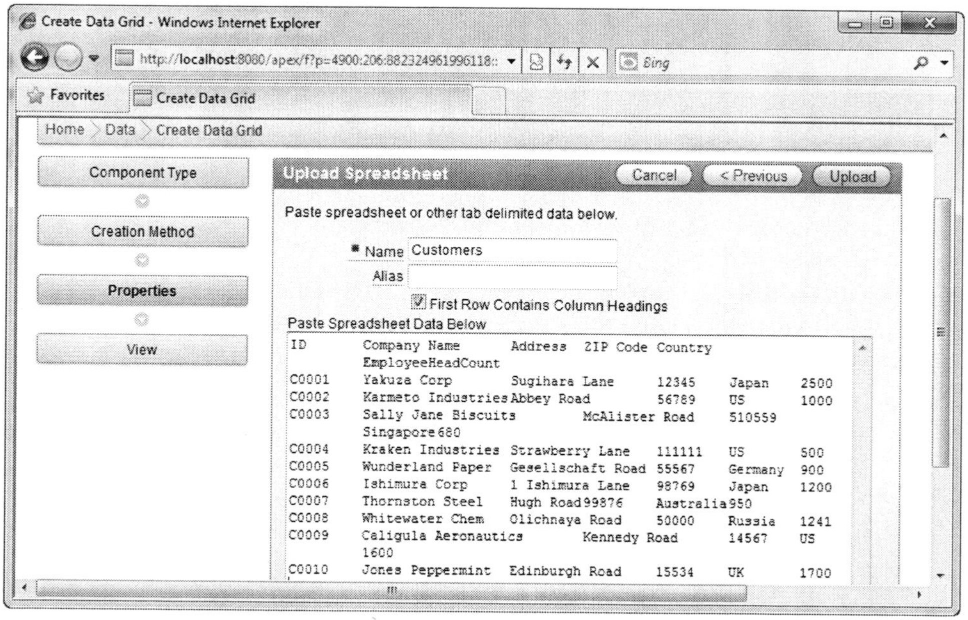

Figure 2-32. ...and paste them in the large text area here...

63

10. Next, click the Upload button. You will find your spreadsheet data magically arranged neatly in a data grid (see Figure 2-33)!

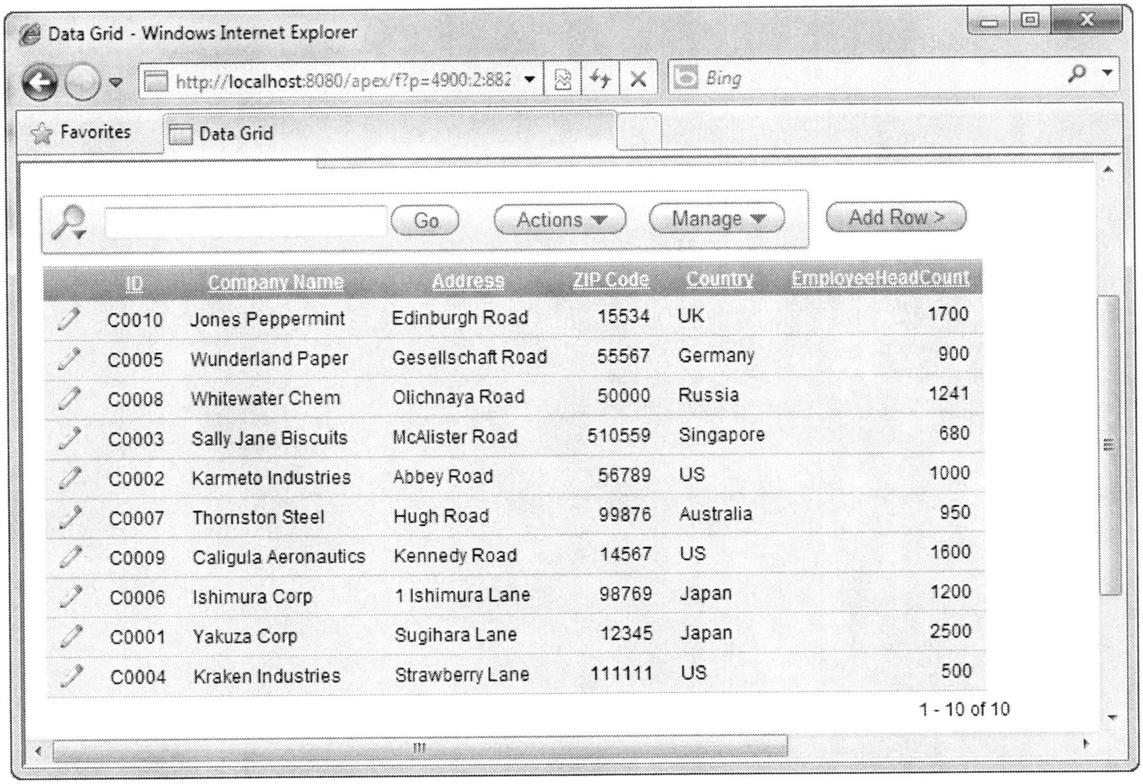

Figure 2-33. ...and here's your spreadsheet data neatly arranged in a data grid!

11. You can now edit the Websheet directly by clicking on any cell in the table (as shown in Figure 2-34). Use the Edit icon at the left side of each row (which opens up a form generated from your Excel sheet columns) to add new rows to the table and so on.

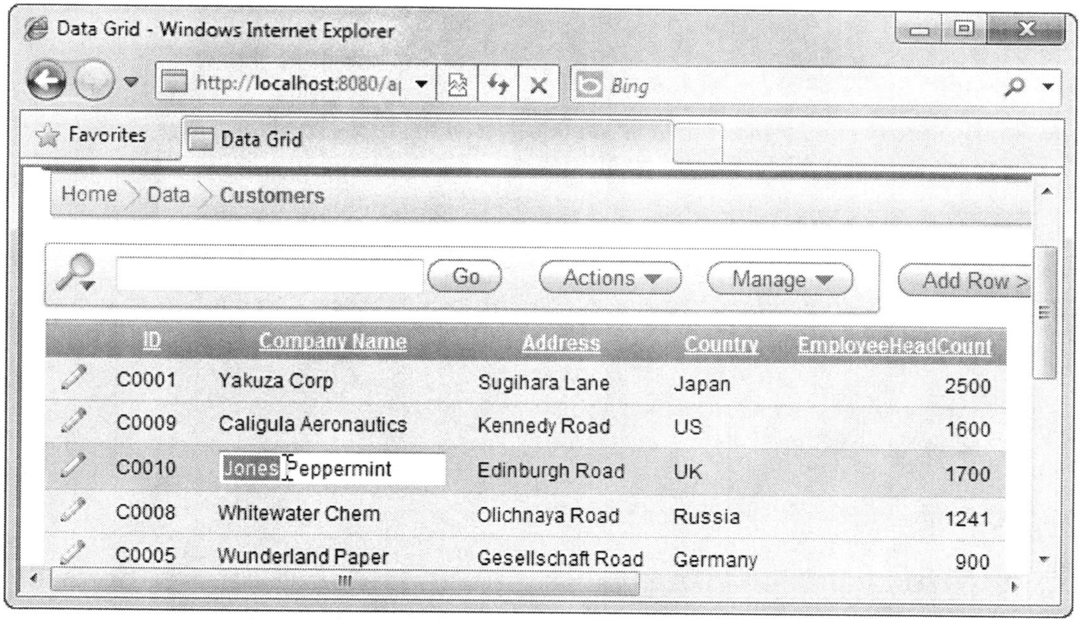

Figure 2-34. Editing data in a Websheet

How It Works

Worksheets provide a convenient way of converting an entire spreadsheet into an editable grid that provides all the standard functionality a report provides—including validation, paging, sorting, highlighting, and so on.

Note that worksheet applications work slightly differently under the hood. A worksheet data grid does not map directly to a database table as a form does. Worksheet data is stored in the internal APEX$_WS_ROWS table.

■ **Tip**   You can inspect the contents of the APEX$_WS_ROWS table using the Object Browser tool in the SQL Workshop.

2-8. Changing the Item Type of a Websheet Column

Problem

You need to create a Websheet that uses different controls for different columns. For example, your users want to use a drop-down list (containing the list of different countries) for the Country column.

Solution

Here's how to create a drop-down list for a column in the Websheet:

1. Navigate to the CustomersWebSheet application and run it. Log in to the application using your developer credentials.

2. Open the Customers data grid.

3. Click on the Manage drop-down button, and click the Columns ➤ Column Properties menu item.

4. You will see the Column Properties page. Select the Country column from the Column Name field.

5. Under the Display As field, choose Select List.

6. Under the List of Values section in Figure 2-35, select the New List of Values based on Current Values item. This will retrieve the whole list of unique values from the Country column in the spreadsheet data you pasted earlier.

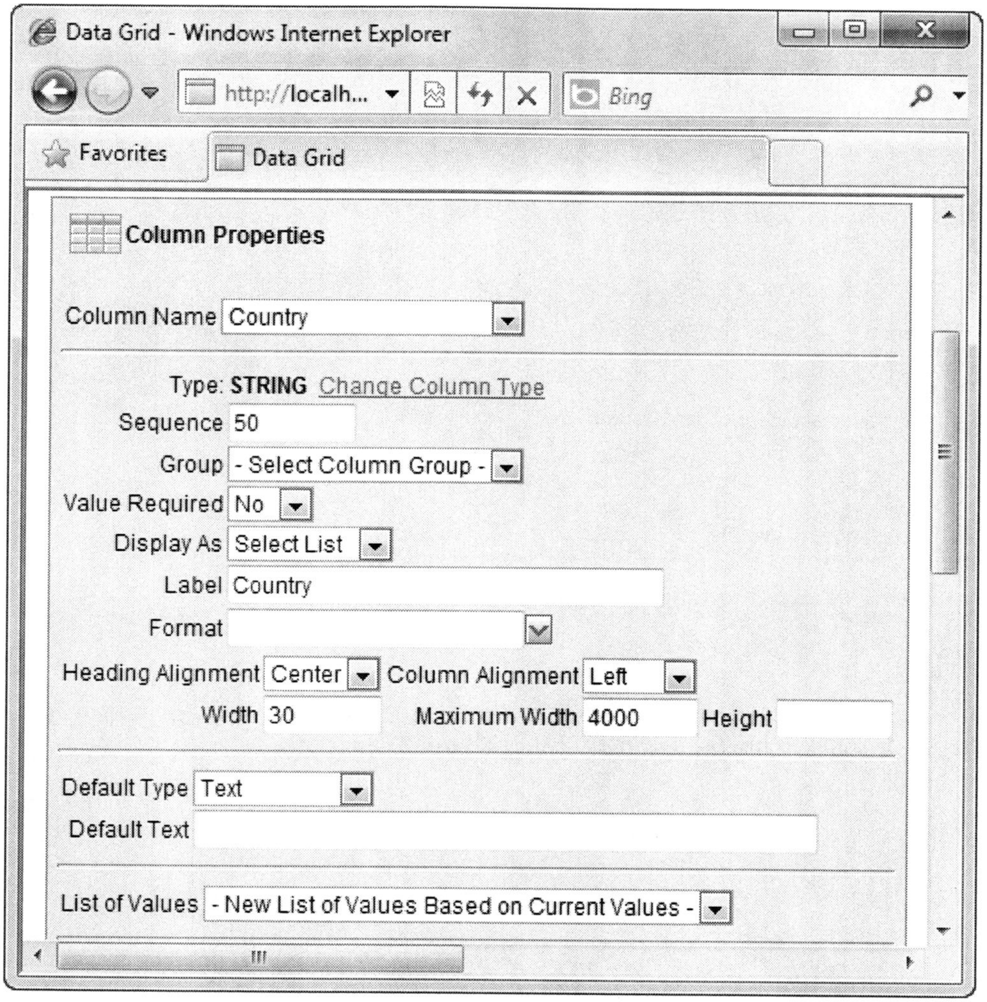

Figure 2-35. Modifying Country column properties

7. Click the Add Row button when you are done. When you click on any cell in the Country column on the data grid, you will now notice a drop-down list containing the list of countries instead of the usual text box (see Figure 2-36).

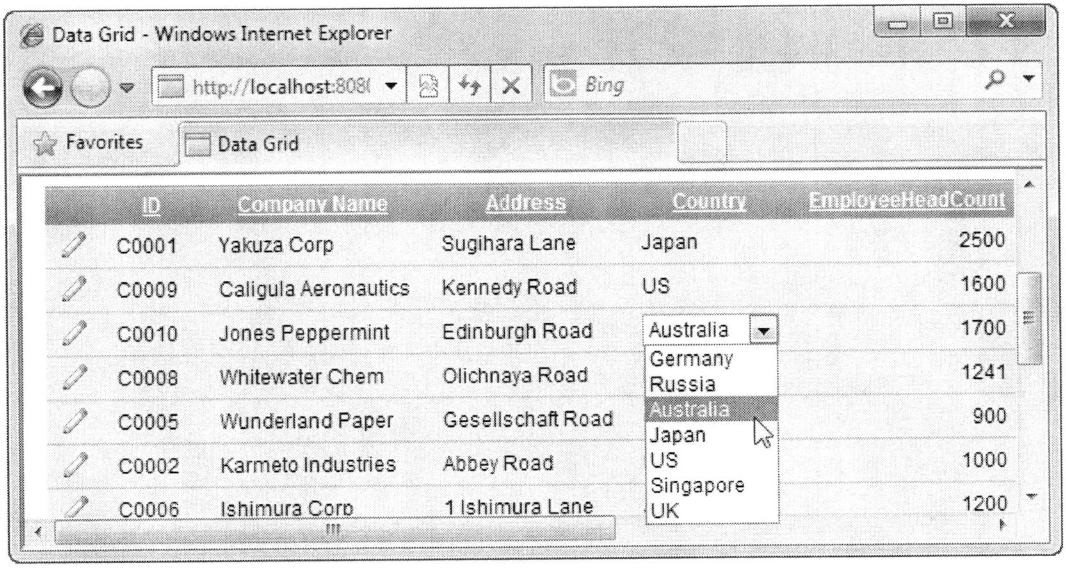

Figure 2-36. Drop-down list inside a Websheet data grid

How It Works

Just like reports, you can easily change the item type of each column in the Websheet. The list of item types available to the Websheet is limited, however, to the following item types:

- Date picker
- Read only
- Select list
- Text
- Text area

▨ **Note** For select lists in Websheets, you can only define a static list of items (separated by comma) in the LOV. The select lists in Websheets do not support dynamic lists like forms do.

2-9. Modifying Values in a Websheet in Bulk

Problem

You have a thousand-row list of data in your Websheet. You need to change the word "Road" in all addresses to "Street."

Solution

Here's how to change data en masse in a Websheet:

1. Navigate to the CustomersWebSheet application and run it. Log in to the application using your developer credentials.
2. Open the Customers Data grid.
3. Click on the Manage drop-down button, and click the Rows ➤ Replace menu item.
4. In the ensuing page, enter Road in the Find What field and Street in the Replace With field (as shown in Figure 2-37). Click the Apply button when you are done.

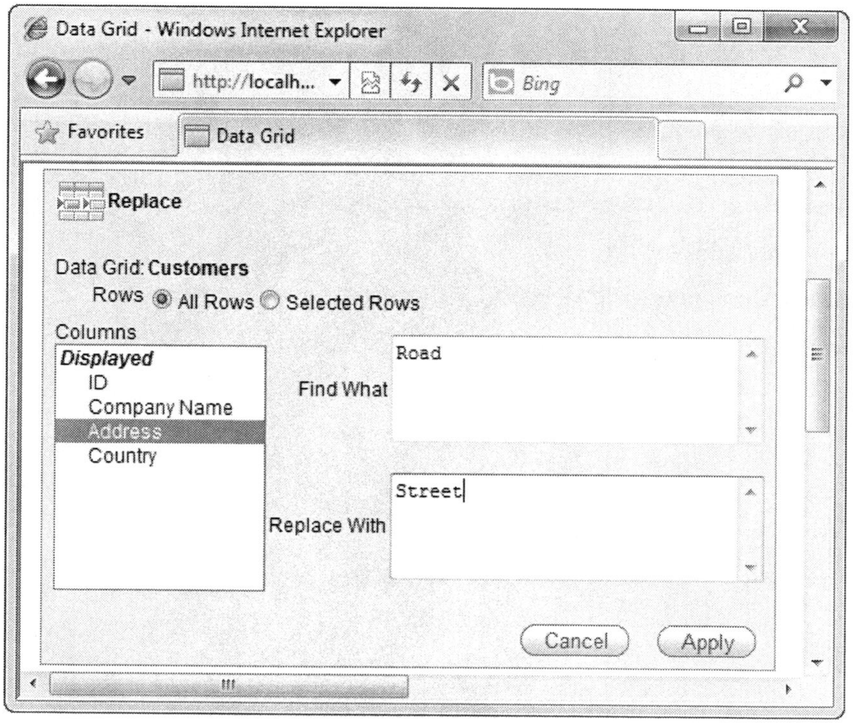

Figure 2-37. Replacing "Road" with "Street"

5. You will find all phrases of "Road" replaced with "Street" in your Websheet (as shown in Figure 2-38).

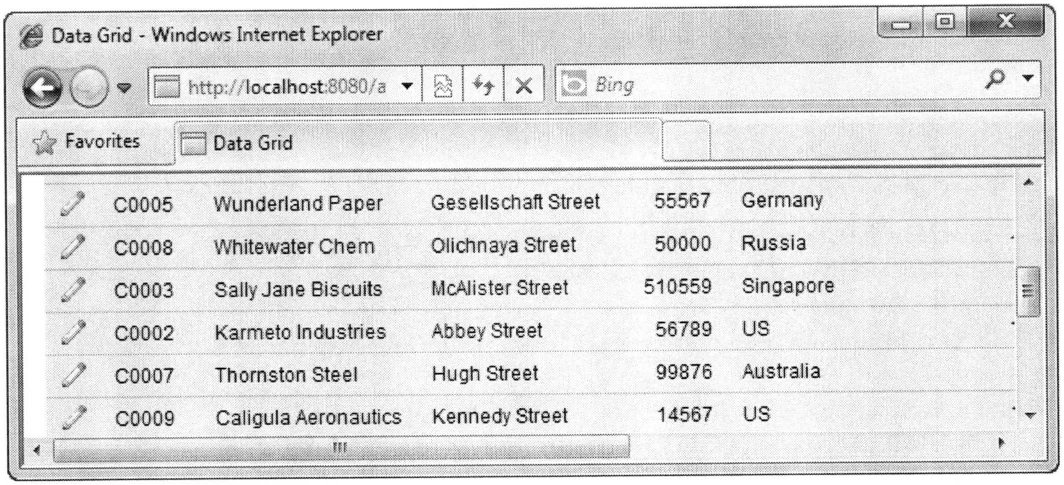

Figure 2-38. Phrase replacement in a Websheet

How It Works

Websheets provide a few tools to help you modify data en masse in a data grid. The following bulk edit actions are supported:

- Replace a value in a certain column with another value for all rows.

- Set a column to a certain value for all rows.

- Fill columns containing null values with data from the previous row.

CHAPTER 3

Wiring up Application Logic

If you are an ASP.NET developer, you're probably familiar with the codebehind model introduced by Microsoft to separate the presentation from the logic layer. In a codebehind page, execution of code is event-based. You specify blocks of code to execute when a page loads or when a button is clicked.

The APEX logic layer works in a similar fashion. Perhaps the best way to summarize how it works is this: Page execution is segmented into different chronological events—points at which application logic can be inserted. For instance, the back end execution of a typical APEX page is segmented into two major events, Page Rendering and Page Processing, both of which consist of smaller events that can trigger application logic.

An APEX developer can insert application logic using mostly PL/SQL statements and JavaScript, both of which can also be generated using the wizards provided by APEX. (In fact, if you don't count PL/SQL as "code," it's possible to create an entire bookstore or salesforce application from scratch without writing a single line of code!)

APEX is different from traditional development tools in that it is geared at churning out business applications in the shortest amount of time possible. In meeting that goal, APEX enforces a strict framework that expects business applications to be developed in a certain way. For instance, every form is expected to display information, provide client-side validation and server-side validation, and perform back-end processing at specific points in its lifetime. Applications developed on APEX are limited in nature to this type of flow, and trying to write logic to do something outside this norm may not be as easy as it would be using a traditional development tool. This means that you can't use APEX to create games (not great ones, at least), but you can certainly use it to create business applications—especially database-centric ones—very quickly.

In this chapter, I explore the APEX logic layer in detail and show you how to perform common tasks in APEX.

3-1. Adding Server-side Validation to Your Form

Problem

You are creating a form to handle patient discharges from a hospital. When nurses fill in the form, they are required to enter the Social Security number of the patient. Before the record can be created, the form data must be validated at the back end—the patient's Social Security number must be checked against a payment history table. If the payment record exists (if the patient has paid for his or her treatment), the discharge is allowed. If not, the discharge form must display an error message.

Solution

Before you can test the solution in this recipe, you will need to set up some sample database and form objects. After that, you will explore how you can add server-side validation to these forms. Let's start by creating the sample objects.

Setting up the Sample Objects

To create the sample objects, please follow these steps:

1. Create the PaymentHistory table shown in Listing 3-1 using the SQL Workshop or PL/SQL.

Listing 3-1. The PaymentHistory Table

```
CREATE table "PAYMENTHISTORY" (
    "SOCIALSECURITYNO" NVARCHAR2(9),
    "AMOUNTPAID"       NUMBER(6,2)
)
```

2. Create the patient discharge table shown in Listing 3-2 (with the DISCHARGEID field set as the primary key), then create a database application and set up a data entry form on top of this table.

Listing 3-2. The PatientDischarge Table

```
CREATE table "PATIENTDISCHARGE" (
    "DISCHARGEID"             NVARCHAR2(10),
    "PATIENTNAME"             NVARCHAR2(255),
    "PATIENTSOCIALSECURITYNO" NVARCHAR2(9),
    "DATEOFDISCHARGE"         DATE,
    "DISCHARGEREMARKS"        NVARCHAR2(2000),
    constraint  "PATIENTDISCHARGE_PK" primary key ("DISCHARGEID")
)
/

CREATE sequence "PATIENTDISCHARGE_SEQ"
/

CREATE trigger "BI_PATIENTDISCHARGE"
  before insert on "PATIENTDISCHARGE"
  for each row
begin
  if :NEW."DISCHARGEID" is null then
    select "PATIENTDISCHARGE_SEQ".nextval into :NEW."DISCHARGEID" from dual;
  end if;
end;
/
```

░ **Tip**   Refer to Recipe 2-1 for more information on how to set up a data entry form.

---

3. Add a sample record to the PaymentHistory table with the Social Security
    number 123456789. This can be done by executing the SQL in Listing 3-3.

Listing 3-3. Creating the Sample Record in the PaymentHistory Table

```
INSERT INTO PAYMENTHISTORY(SOCIALSECURITYNO,AMOUNTPAID) VALUES('123456789',500)
```

Adding Server-side Validation

To add server-side validation to your form, follow these steps:

1. Navigate to the Page Processing section of the Page Definition area in the
    patient discharge form.

2. Under the Validating node, right click the Validations node and click the
    Create button (as shown in Figure 3-1).

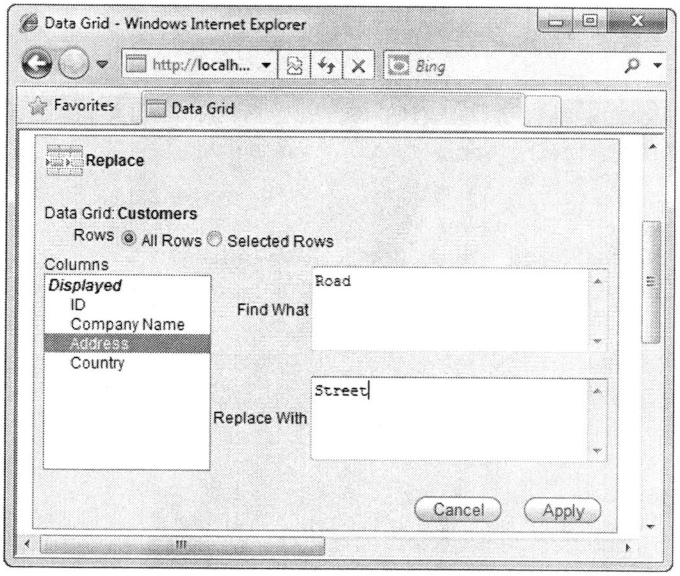

Figure 3-1. Launching the Create Validation wizard

3. You should now see the Create Validation wizard. In the first page of the wizard, choose the Item Level Validation item (see Figure 3-2).

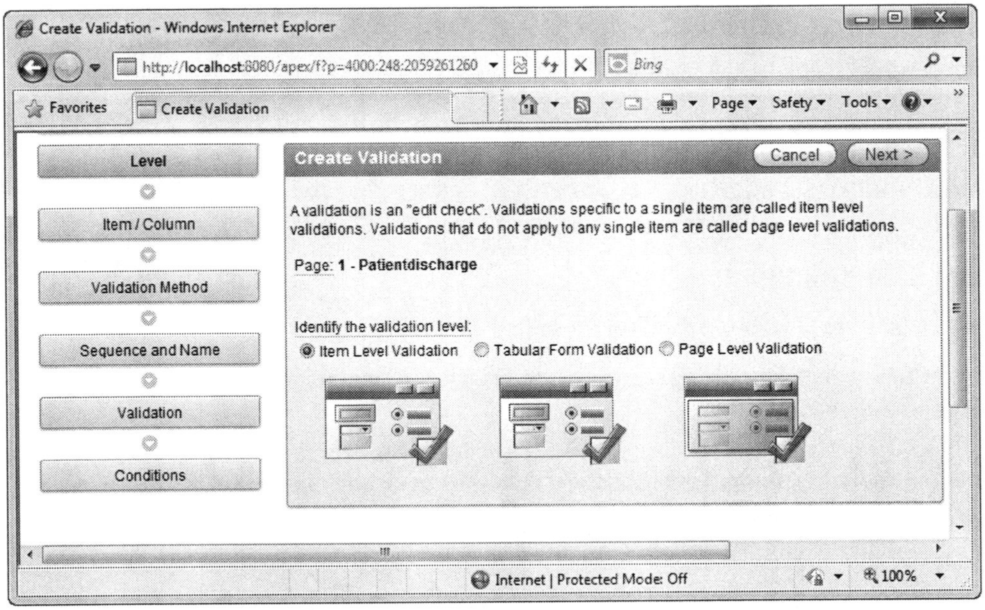

Figure 3-2. Selecting the type of validation

4. In the next page of the wizard, select the PATIENTDISCHARGE: 1. P1_PATIENTSOCIALSECURITYNO (Patientsocialsecurityno) item as the item to be validated.

5. In the next page, choose the PL/SQL validation method, and next the Function Returning Boolean PL/SQL validation type.

6. Use the default values in the next (Sequence and Name) step. Proceed to the next (Validation) step and enter the PL/SQL validation code shown in Listing 3-4.

Listing 3-4. PL/SQL Validation Code

```
DECLARE
      CT INTEGER;
BEGIN
      SELECT COUNT(*) INTO CT FROM PAYMENTHISTORY WHERE
      SOCIALSECURITYNO = :P1_PATIENTSOCIALSECURITYNO;
```

```
        IF CT>0 THEN
            return true;
        ELSE
            return false;
        END IF;
END;
```

7. In the same step, specify an error message to display when the validation fails, as shown in Figure 3-3.

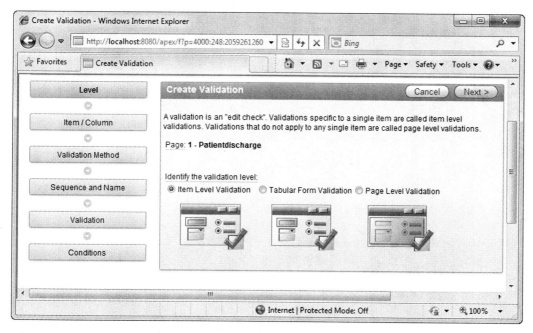

Figure 3-3. Specifying validation behavior

8. Proceed to the next step. Select the CREATE option for the When Button Pressed field, as shown in Figure 3-4.

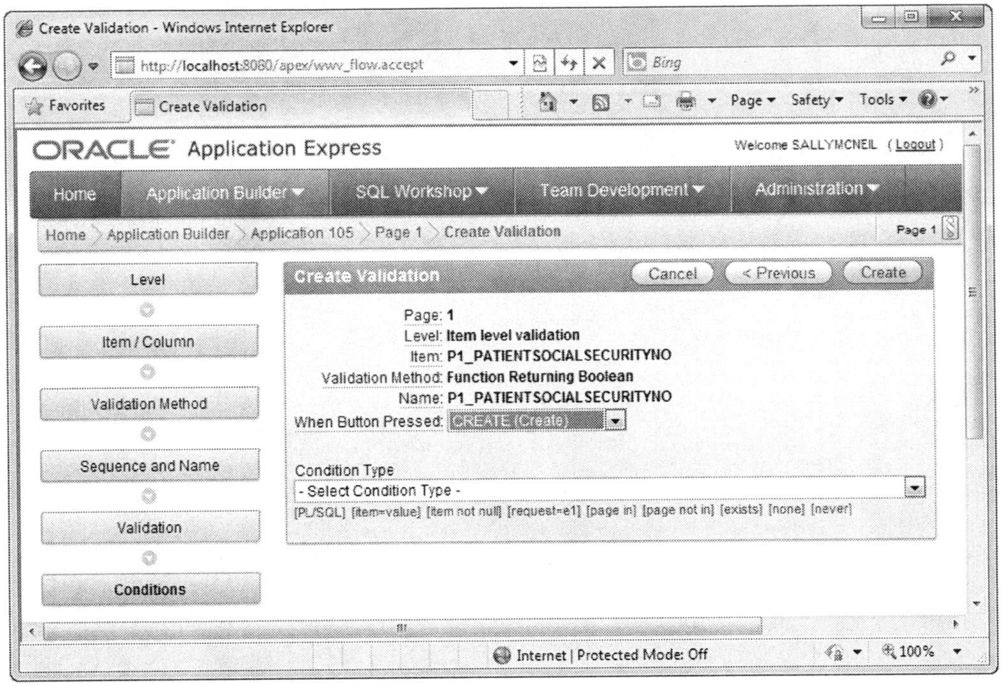

Figure 3-4. Specifying validation behavior

9. Click the Create button to create the validation rule.

10. Now run the form. You will be able to see the Patient Discharge form show. Key in any value other than 123456789 in the PatientSocialSecurityNumber field. Click the Create button. You should see your validation error message displayed at the top of the page (as shown in Figure 3-5). If you key in the value 123456789 (which exists in the PaymentHistory table), the error will not show.

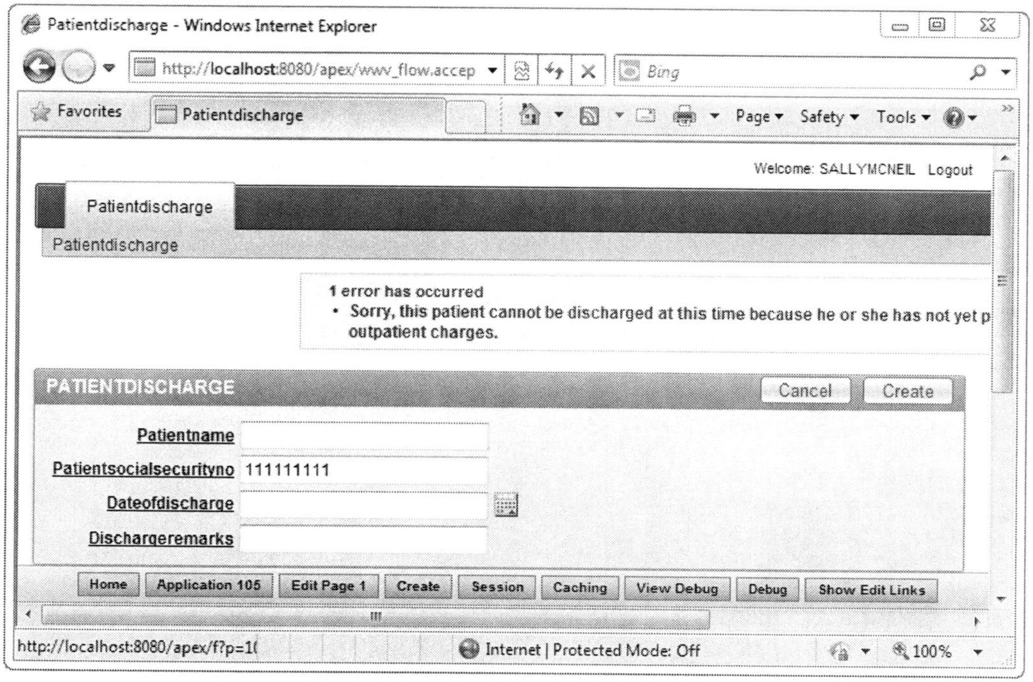

Figure 3-5. *Validation in action*

How It Works

First, a little about server-side validation. Server-side validation, as opposed to client-side validation requires a round trip to the server. There are basically three types of server-side validation in APEX.

Item Level Validation: Use this when your validation involves only one page item at a time.

Tabular Form Validation: Use this to validate tabular forms (more on this in Recipe 3-2).

Page Level Validation: Use this when your validation involves multiple page items in the form (for example, ensuring that the start date is earlier than the end date).

The Condition Type field allows you to specify the conditions under which the validation will be applied. For example, you might not need to check for payment if the person being discharged happens to be a VIP patient at that hospital. You might include a checkbox in the Patient Discharge form that indicates that the patient is a VIP member if checked. The condition configuration allows you to then create a rule that can check for this flag, and if ticked, to skip the validation.

3-2. Adding Server-side Validation to Your Tabular Form

Problem

You have a tabular Employee form, and you need to perform server-side validation. You need to ensure that the Social Security number is not left empty when submitting the form.

Solution

To add server-side validation to your tabular form, follow these steps:

1. Create the table shown in Listing 3-5.

Listing 3-5. *The Sample Employee Table*

```
CREATE table "EMPLOYEE" (
    "EMPLOYEENAME"      NVARCHAR2(255),
    "EMPLOYEETYPE"      NVARCHAR2(10),
    "SOCIALSECURITYNO"  NVARCHAR2(10),
    "EMPLOYEEID"        NVARCHAR2(10),
    constraint   "EMPLOYEE_PK" primary key ("EMPLOYEEID")
)
/

CREATE sequence "EMPLOYEE_SEQ"
/

CREATE trigger "BI_EMPLOYEE"
  before insert on "EMPLOYEE"
  for each row
begin
  if :NEW."EMPLOYEEID" is null then
    select "EMPLOYEE_SEQ".nextval into :NEW."EMPLOYEEID" from dual;
  end if;
end;
```

2. Create a database application/tabular form on top of the EMPLOYEE table.

▨ **Tip**   Recipe 2-6 shows you how to create a tabular form.

---

3. Navigate to the Page Rendering section of the Page Definition area of your tabular form.

4. Expand the following node: Employee ➤ Regions ➤ Body (3) ➤ EMPLOYEE ➤ Report Columns, right click on the SOCIALSECURITYNO field, and click on the Create Validation submenu item, as shown in Figure 3-6.

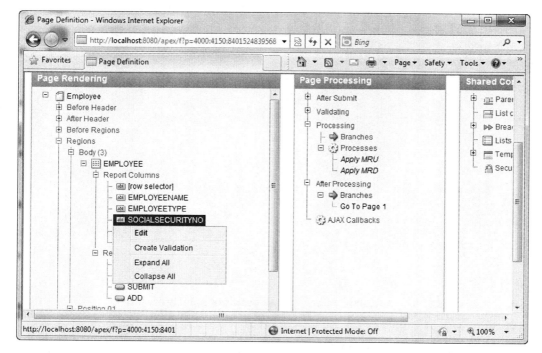

Figure 3-6. Adding validation to the SOCIALSECURITYNO field

5. On the next page, choose the Column Not Null validation type (you are checking to ensure SocialSecurityNo field is not left empty). Use the default settings on the next page.

6. On the page after that, you will be allowed to specify the error message shown if the validation fails. Enter the following error message: "Please specify the employee's Social Security number."

7. In the next page, choose ADD (Add Row) for the When Button Pressed field. Save the changes and run your tabular form. Leave the Social Security number field empty and try to submit the tabular form. You should see the screen shown in Figure 3-7.

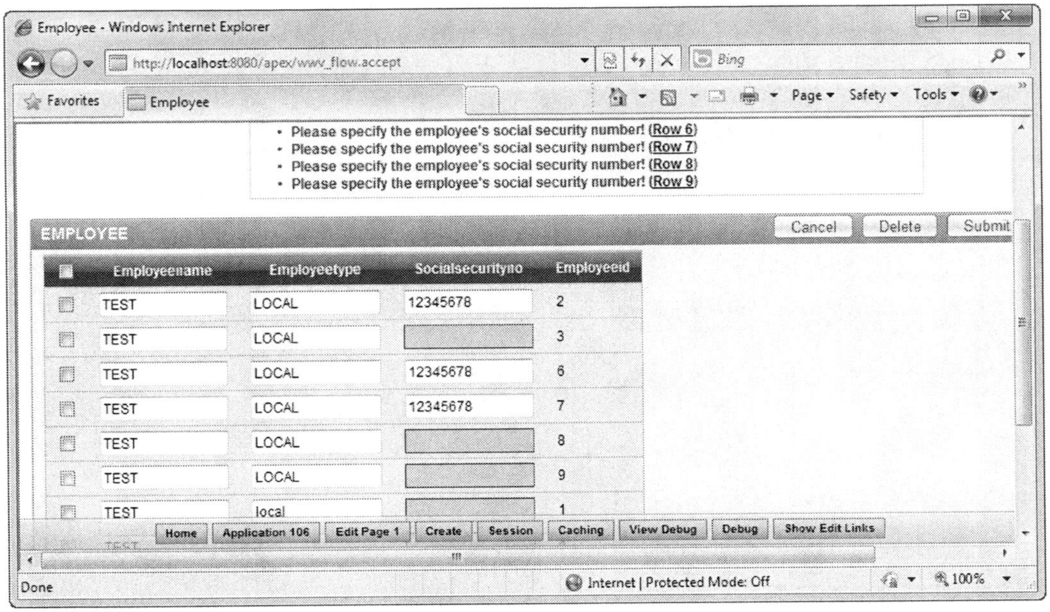

Figure 3-7. Tabular Form validation in action

How It Works

You can insert simple validation in any of the following four events of the tabular form:

- When the user clicks the ADD (Add row) button.
- When the user clicks the CANCEL button.
- When the user clicks the DELETE button.
- When the user clicks the SUBMIT button.

▓ **Note** Not all of the standard form's validation options are available to a tabular form. For instance, the tabular form does not support the complex type of PL/SQL validation you saw in Recipe 3-1.

3-3. Adding Client-side JavaScript Validation to Your Form

Problem

Upon moving the focus away from a numerical field on a standard form, you need to instantly check if the value entered is within a certain range and display an error message if it isn't. You want to do this using JavaScript so that you can eliminate a round trip to the server.

Solution

To add client-side validation to your form, follow these steps:

1. Create the table shown in Listing 3-6 and create a database application/data entry form based on the table.

Listing 3-6. The Sample Salaries Table

```
CREATE table "SALARIES" (
    "PAYROLLID"     NVARCHAR2(255),
    "EMPLOYEENAME"  NVARCHAR2(255),
    "SALARY"        NUMBER(6,2),
    constraint  "SALARIES_PK" primary key ("PAYROLLID")
)
/

CREATE sequence "SALARIES_SEQ"
/

CREATE trigger "BI_SALARIES"
  before insert on "SALARIES"
  for each row
begin
  if :NEW."PAYROLLID" is null then
    select "SALARIES_SEQ".nextval into :NEW."PAYROLLID" from dual;
  end if;
end;
/
```

2. Navigate to the Page Rendering section of the Page Definition area of your form.

3. Right click on the root node (your data entry form) and choose the Edit submenu item.

4. In the next page, navigate to the HTML Header and Body Attribute tab. In the HTML Header field, enter the JavaScript code shown in Listing 3-7. You should see the screen shown in Figure 3-8. Click the Apply Changes button

Listing 3-7. Validation JavaScript

```
<script type="text/javascript">
  function validSalary(object){
    if(parseInt(object.value)>5000)
    alert('Salary must be a figure below $5000');
  }
</script>
```

Figure 3-8. Specifying the validSalary JavaScript function

5.   After doing this, navigate to the Page Definition area of your form again. Right click on the P1_SALARY form item under Salaries ➤ Regions ➤ Body (3) ➤ Salaries ➤ Items menu in the Page Rendering section. Click the Edit item in the pop-up menu.

6.   Navigate to the Element tab, and type the code shown in Listing 3-8 in the HTML Form Element Attributes field (as shown in Figure 3-9).

Listing 3-8. Adding a JavaScript Event Handler to the Salary Field

```
onblur="validSalary(this);"
```

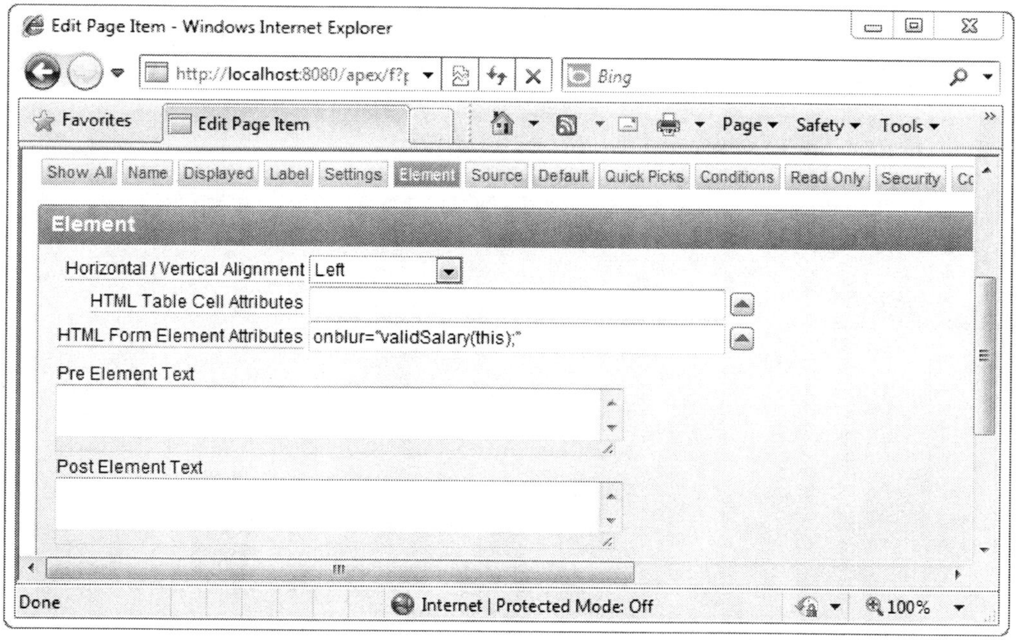

Figure 3-9. Adding validation to the SOCIALSECURITYNO field

7. Apply your changes. Now run the form. If you enter a value larger than 5000 in
    the Salary field and navigate away from the field, it will show a JavaScript pop-
    up error message like the one shown in Figure 3-10.

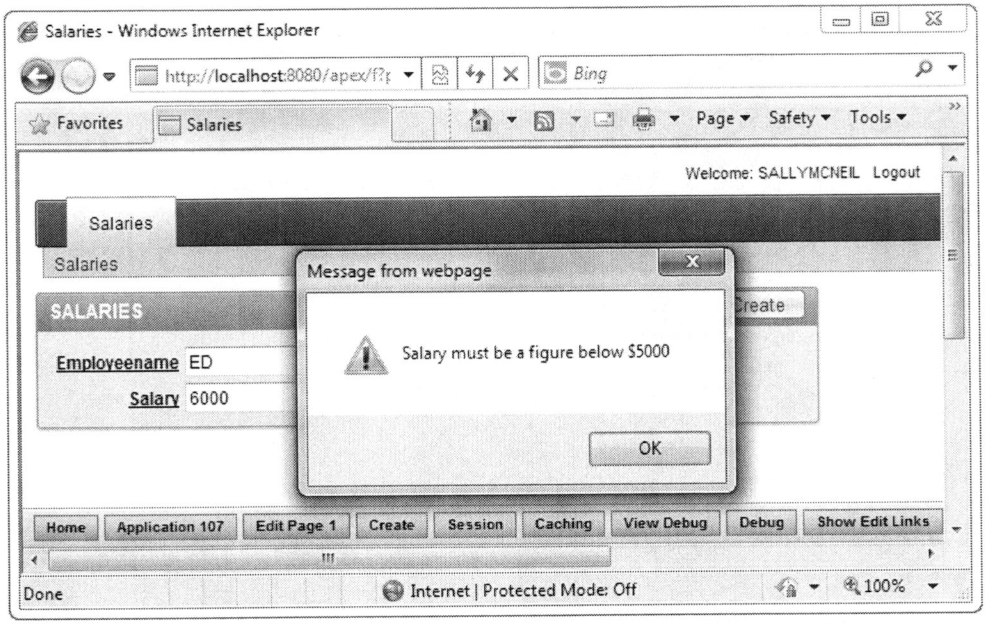

Figure 3-10. Client-side validation in action

How It Works

Client-side validation in APEX is implemented entirely in JavaScript, and is useful because it does not incur an additional round trip to the server. You typically use client-side validation when you need to:

- Check for missing values.

- Check if a numerical or date value falls within a certain range.

- Check if the length of a particular value exceeds a maximum number of characters.

The HTML Header and Body Attribute section of the form allows you to insert blocks of JavaScript that are included together when a particular page is rendered. You can use this section to insert a list of JavaScript functions that can be selectively called from any item in the form.

The HTML Form Element attribute field, as you saw earlier, allows you to specify JavaScript event handlers for each page item on the form. You can make calls to JavaScript functions defined in the HTML Header and Body Attribute section from this area.

3-4. Changing the List of Items in a Drop-down List Dynamically

Problem

You have a drop-down list. When you change the values in this drop-down list, you want the values in another drop-down list to also change. In other words, you want to create a cascading drop-down list.

For example, you have an equipment request form. When you submit a request, you can zoom in on a specific equipment using the category and subcategory drop-down list. When you change the equipment category, the subcategory list refreshes to show only the equipment relevant to that category.

Solution

To test the solution in this recipe, you will first need to set up some sample database and form objects. After that, you will create a cascading relationship between the two drop-down lists. Let's start with the sample objects.

Setting up the Sample Objects

To setup the sample objects used in this recipe, follow these steps:

1. Create the tables shown in Listing 3-9.

Listing 3-9. Sample Equipment Request Tables

```
CREATE table "EQUIPMENTREQUEST" (
    "REQUESTID"    NVARCHAR2(10),
    "CATEGORY"     NVARCHAR2(255),
    "SUBCATEGORY" NVARCHAR2(255),
    constraint    "EQUIPMENTREQUEST_PK" primary key ("REQUESTID")
)
/

CREATE sequence "EQUIPMENTREQUEST_SEQ"
/

CREATE trigger "BI_EQUIPMENTREQUEST"
  before insert on "EQUIPMENTREQUEST"
  for each row
begin
  if :NEW."REQUESTID" is null then
    select "EQUIPMENTREQUEST_SEQ".nextval into :NEW."REQUESTID" from dual;
  end if;
end;
/

CREATE table "CATEGORY" (
    "CATEGORYNAME" NVARCHAR2(255),
    "CATEGORYID"   NUMBER(6,2),
```

```
        constraint  "CATEGORY_PK" primary key ("CATEGORYID")
)
/

CREATE sequence "CATEGORY_SEQ"
/

CREATE trigger "BI_CATEGORY"
  before insert on "CATEGORY"
  for each row
begin
  if :NEW."CATEGORYID" is null then
    select "CATEGORY_SEQ".nextval into :NEW."CATEGORYID" from dual;
  end if;
end;
/

CREATE table "SUBCATEGORY" (
    "SUBCATEGORYNAME"   NVARCHAR2(255),
    "PARENTCATEGORYID"  NUMBER(6,2),
    "SUBCATEGORYID"     NUMBER(6,2),
    constraint  "SUBCATEGORY_PK" primary key ("SUBCATEGORYID")
)
/

CREATE sequence "SUBCATEGORY_SEQ"
/

CREATE trigger "BI_SUBCATEGORY"
  before insert on "SUBCATEGORY"
  for each row
begin
  if :NEW."SUBCATEGORYID" is null then
    select "SUBCATEGORY_SEQ".nextval into :NEW."SUBCATEGORYID" from dual;
  end if;
end;
/
```

2. Now create the sample data shown in Listing 3-10. The MODEM and
    NETWORK CARD subcategory items belong to the parent HARDWARE
    category, whereas the LOTUS NOTES and SHAREPOINT subcategory items
    belong to the parent SOFTWARE category. The foreign key in this case is the
    PARENTCATEGORYID column.

Listing 3-10. Creating Sample Data

```
INSERT INTO CATEGORY(CATEGORYID,CATEGORYNAME) VALUES(1,'SOFTWARE')
/
INSERT INTO CATEGORY(CATEGORYID,CATEGORYNAME) VALUES(2,'HARDWARE')
/
```

```
INSERT INTO SUBCATEGORY(SUBCATEGORYNAME,PARENTCATEGORYID,SUBCATEGORYID) VALUES('LOTUS
NOTES',1,1)
/
INSERT INTO SUBCATEGORY(SUBCATEGORYNAME,PARENTCATEGORYID,SUBCATEGORYID)
VALUES('SHAREPOINT',1,2)
/
INSERT INTO SUBCATEGORY(SUBCATEGORYNAME,PARENTCATEGORYID,SUBCATEGORYID) VALUES('NETWORK
CARD',2,3)
/
INSERT INTO SUBCATEGORY(SUBCATEGORYNAME,PARENTCATEGORYID,SUBCATEGORYID) VALUES('MODEM',2,4)
/
```

3. Now create a database application/standard entry form on top of the
    EquipmentRequest table. Go to the Page Definition > Page Rendering view of
    the form, and change (edit) the CATEGORY field to a Select List. Choose to
    create a dynamic LOV for the field, setting CATEGORY, CATEGORYNAME, and
    CATEGORYID as the table name, display column, and return value,
    respectively.

▓ **Tip**   Refer to Recipe 2-4 to find out how to create a dynamic drop-down list.

---

4. Repeat the same for the SUBCATEGORY field, using SUBCATEGORY,
    SUBCATEGORYNAME, and SUBCATEGORYID instead as the table name,
    display column, and return value, respectively.

5. Edit the CATEGORY field again, and under the Default tab, enter 1 as the
    Default value. This will set the default selected value in the category drop down
    to SOFTWARE.

6. Test your form. You should be able to see two drop-down lists containing the
    data you entered earlier, but with no cascading relationship between them at
    the moment, as shown in Figure 3-11.

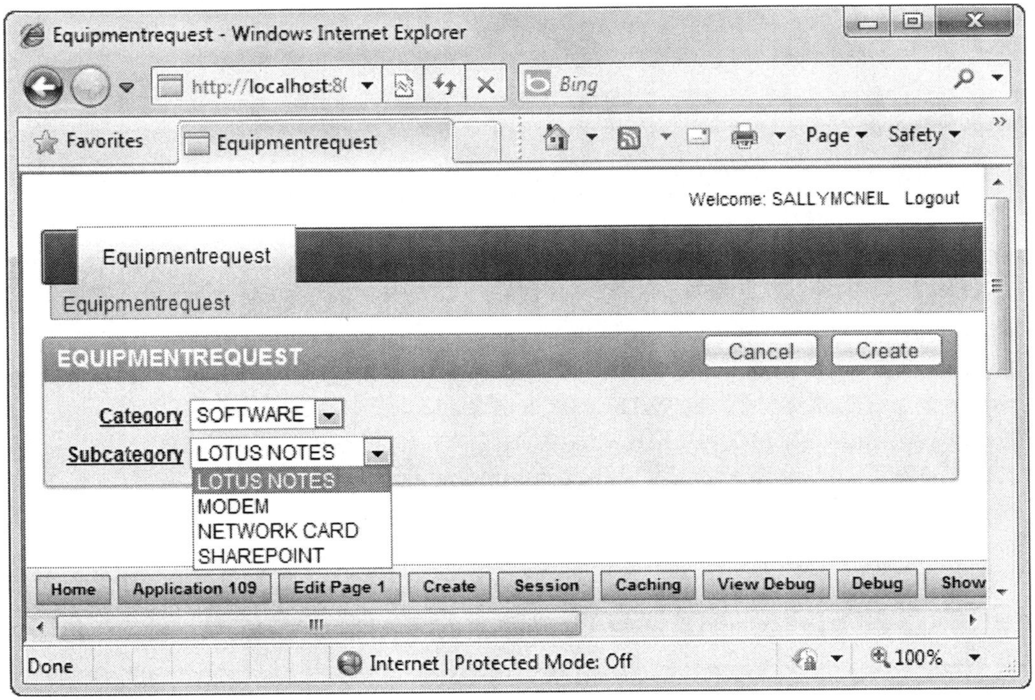

Figure 3-11. *Drop-down lists without cascading relationship*

Creating the Cascading Relationship

To create a cascading relationship between the two drop-down lists, follow these steps:

1. In the Page Definition > Page Rendering view, edit the SUBCATEGORY field. Navigate to the List Of Values tab. Set the Cascading LOV Parent Item(s) field to P1_CATEGORY.

2. In the List of Values definition area, add the filter WHERE PARENTCATEGORYID=:P1_CATEGORY to the SQL. You should now have the screen shown in Figure 3-12.

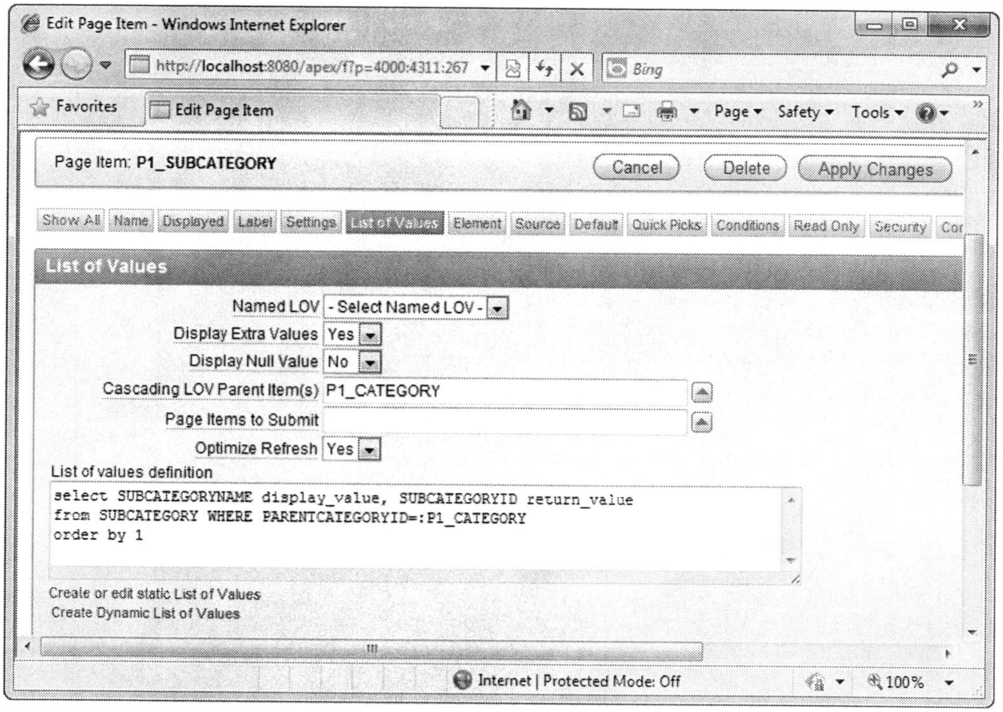

Figure 3-12. Creating the cascading relationship

3. Apply your changes and run the form again. Note that when you change the selected category, the subcategory drop-down list will only show the items relevant to that category (see Figure 3-13).

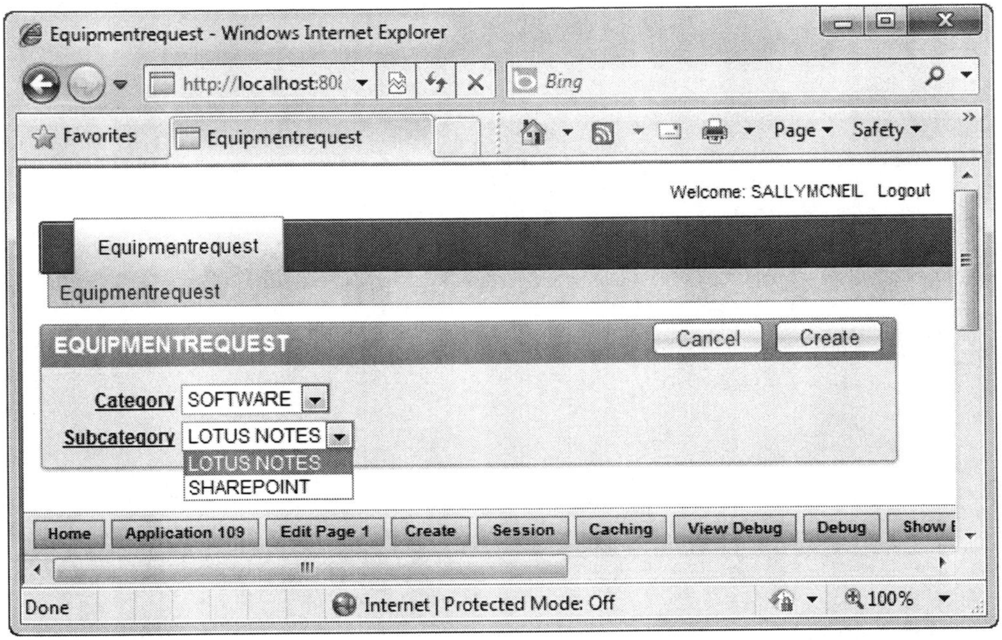

Figure 3-13. The cascading relationship in action

How It Works

You can easily specify the List of Values (LOV) returned in a dynamic drop-down list using PL/SQL in the List of Values tab of the Select List page item.

You might also have noticed that you can reference form fields directly in your PL/SQL code using the :ItemName syntax (a colon, followed by the name of the page item). This allows you to create dynamic PL/SQL code that uses data keyed in from the form on the fly for further processing.

3-5. Disabling or Hiding a Section of a Form Dynamically

Problem

You have a list of fields on a standard form you wish to hide (set invisible) depending on what was specified in another field. Taking the sample employee table in Recipe 3-2 as context, you might choose to hide the employee's Social Security number if the employee type was keyed in as LOCAL.

Solution

To create a dynamic action to hide a section of a form, follow the following steps:

1. Create a database application/standard entry form from the EMPLOYEE table from Recipe 3-2.

2. Create a standard entry form from the EMPLOYEE table.

3. Navigate to the Page Definition area of the form. Right click on the
    P1_EMPLOYEETYPE field and choose the Create Dynamic Action menu item.

4. In the first page of the wizard, choose the Standard dynamic action type. Next,
    assign a name to your dynamic action.

5. In the next page of the wizard, specify LOCAL in the Value field (as shown in
    Figure 3-14).

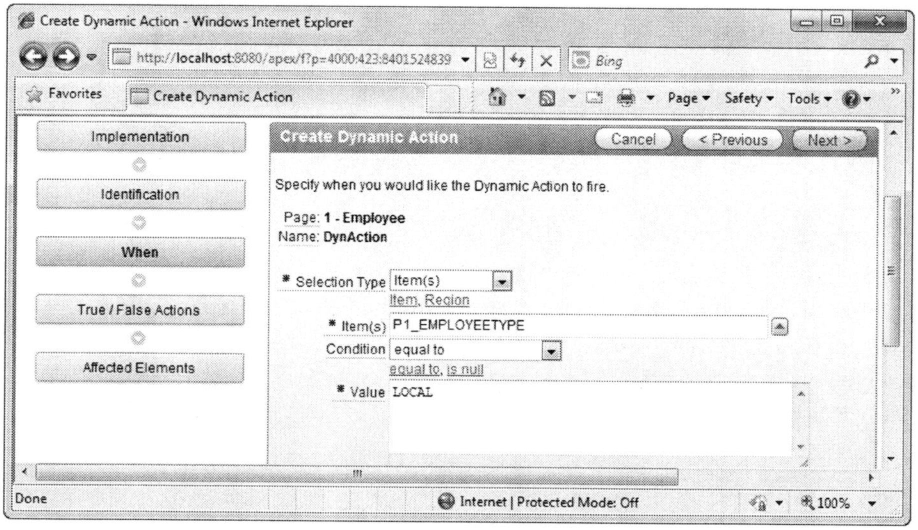

Figure 3-14. Configuring the dynamic action

6. In the next page of the wizard, specify the Hide option. Ensure that the Create
    Opposite Action checkbox is ticked.

7. Next, you will be requested to select the fields you want to hide. Select item(s)
    from the Selection Type field, and add P1_SOCIALSECURITYNO to the box on
    the right (as shown in Figure 3-15).

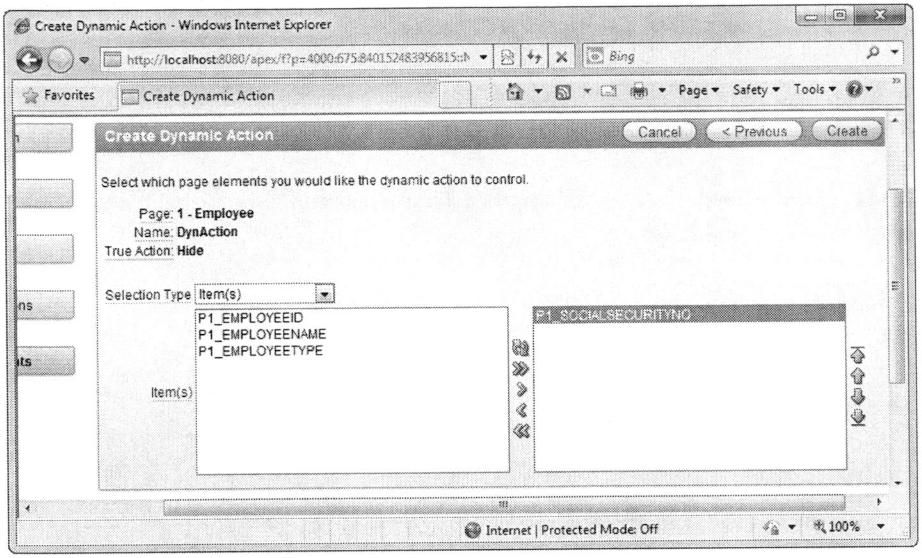

Figure 3-15. Specifying the target of the dynamic action

8. Click the Create button. Now, run your form. Type LOCAL into the Employee Type field. Once you have done that, navigate away from the field. The Social Security Number field immediately disappears from view (as shown in Figure 3-16). If you type anything other than LOCAL in the employee type field, the behavior will not apply.

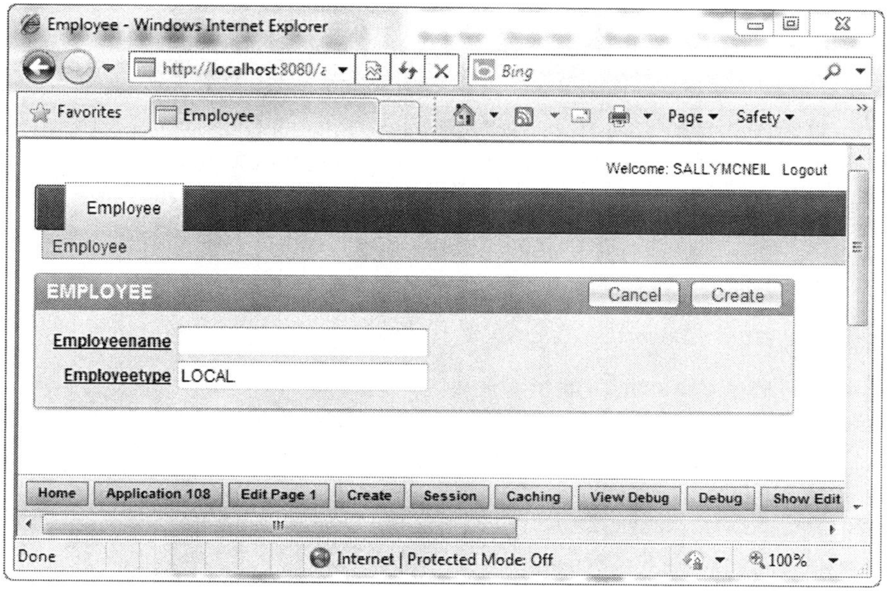

Figure 3-16. Dynamic action running in your form

How It Works

A dynamic action is client-side behavior applied on a particular page item, typically implemented using a combination of JavaScript and AJAX. APEX provides wizards, such as the one you saw earlier in this recipe to auto-generate client-side behavior. Dynamic actions are great if you want to:

- Dynamically hide or show certain sections of your form when something happens on your form (eg: a particular piece of data was entered or a field was double-clicked).

- Enable or disable certain fields on your form when something happens on your form.

■ **Note** Previously, APEX developers had to manually write JavaScript/AJAX code to create dynamic behavior. In Apex 4.0, the wizards allows you to easily generate dynamic client-side behavior—shielding the developer from the intricacies of JavaScript programming.

3-6. Storing Computed Values

Problem

You need to run certain values keyed in through the form through some computation before storing the final value in the database. Using the sample `Salaries` table in Recipe 3-3 as an example, you might want run some computations on the salary before saving the amount in the database.

Solution

To create a computed field in your form, follow these steps:

1. Navigate to the Page Definition area of the Salaries form. Right-click on the Computations node in the `After Submit` root node under the Page Processing section.

2. In the first page of the wizard, choose the Item on This Page location type. In the next page, select P1_SALARY for the Compute Item field and PL/SQL Function Body for the type field.

3. In the next page, you will be able to specify the computation to apply. For instance, you may use the following PL/SQL to specify that all salary entered should be stored with a 20% extra increment in the database:

```
return (:P1_SALARY * 20)/100 + :P1_SALARY
```

4. Save your changes and run the form. Try keying in a value of 500 in the salary field (as shown in Figure 3-17) and creating the record.

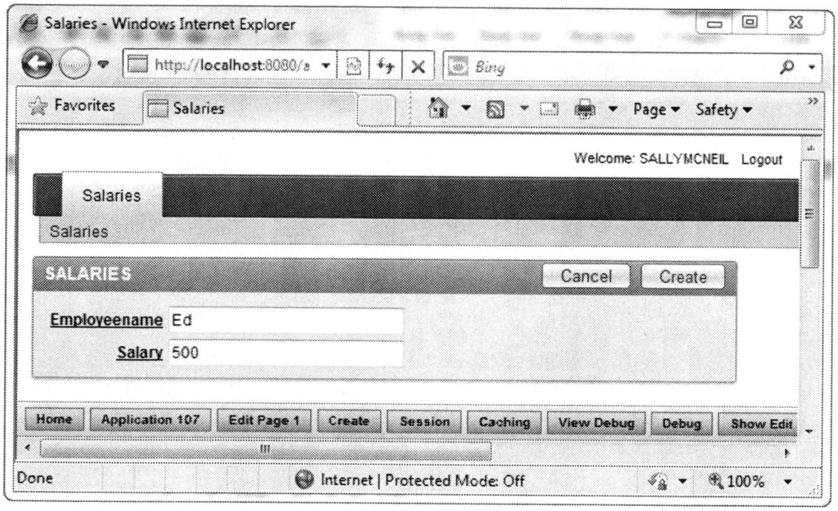

Figure 3-17. Running the Salaries form

5. Now, inspect your database using the Object Browser. You can see that the computation has been applied on your data (as shown in Figure 3-18).

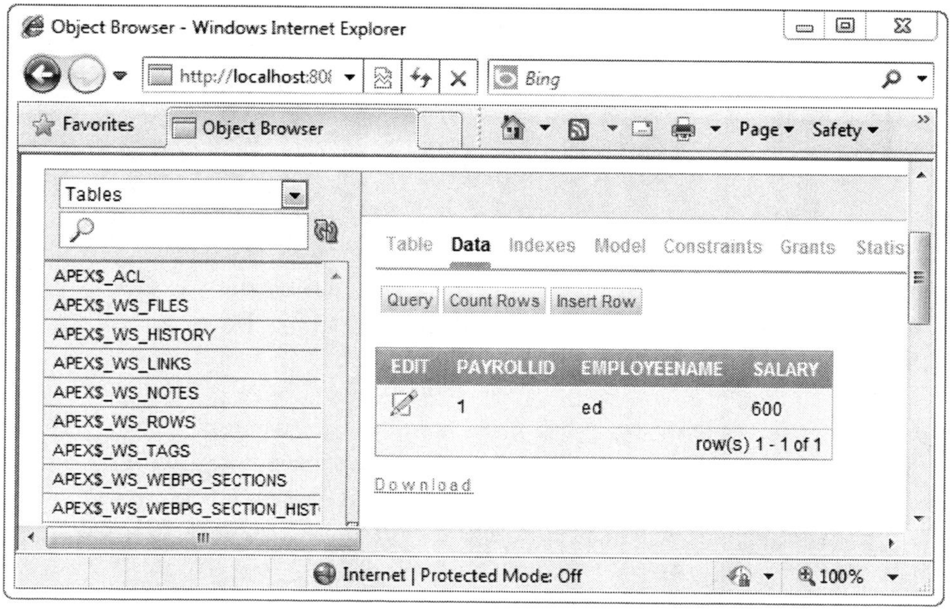

Figure 3-18. The computed value stored in the database

How It Works

APEX computations allow you to apply computational algorithms at different events in your form. It can be used to either display a computed value (for example, a monetary amount after a currency conversion) to the end user (through a read-only text page item field) or to save the computed value in the database.

3-7. Interacting with a Web Service

Problem

When you click a button in your form, you need to connect to a web service, pass it a parameter, and have the web service return a value that you can then display on your form. For example, you may want to display the latest currency conversion rate (retrieved from a web service) for two different currencies specified through your form.

Solution

To test the solution in this recipe, you will first need to set up a sample form. After that, you need to add a reference to the web service to your application. Finally, you will need to make use of that reference in your form. Let's start by creating the sample form.

Creating the Sample Form

To create the sample form used in this recipe, follow these steps:

1. The first thing you need to do is to create a sample form to key in the currency codes (and to also display, in the same form, the currency rate retrieved via the web service).

2. Create a new application and add a blank page to the application. In the Page Definition > Page Rendering area, create a new page item (a TEXT field) named P1_FROMCODE. Use default settings for this page item. After that, create another text field page item named P1_TOCODE with similar settings. Next, create a NUMBER field page item named P1_RETURNEDRATE.

3. Next, create a button in the form. Right click on the Items node and choose Create Button. Specify P1_GETCURRENCYRATE as the name of the button, set the Label field as Get Currency Rate, and change the button style to a HTML Button (as shown in Figure 3-19). Finally, click Create Button.

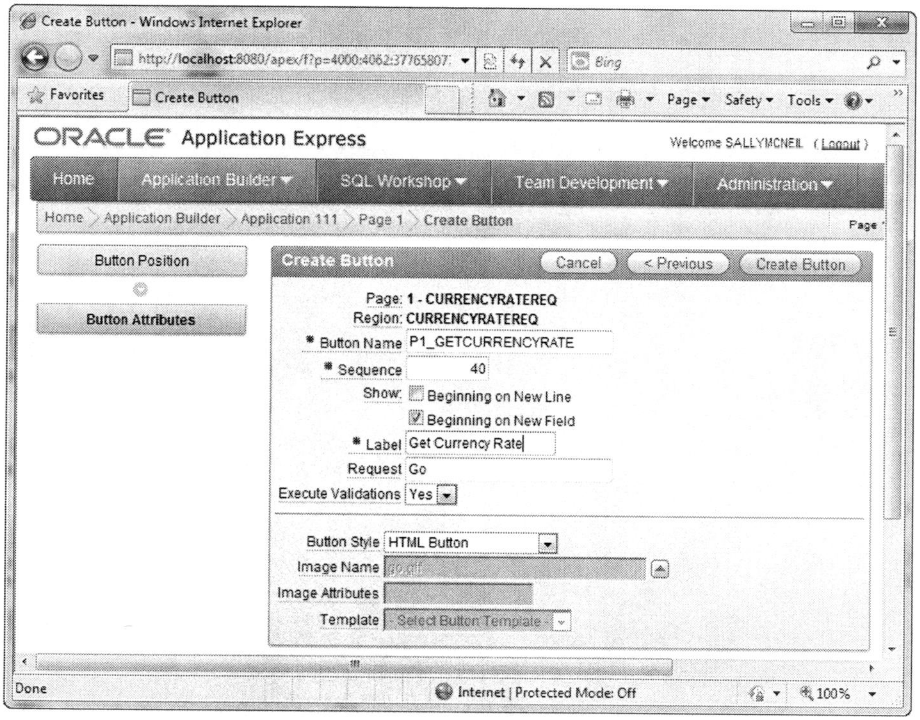

Figure 3-19. Configuring the Get Currency Rate button

4. You should now have the screen shown in Figure 3-20.

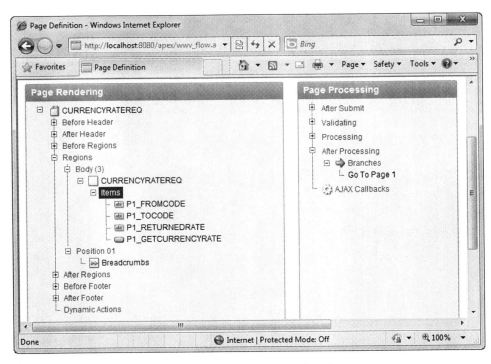

Figure 3-20. The list of page items in the CurrencyRateReq form

Adding the Web Service Reference

To add a web service reference to your application, follow these steps:

1. You now need to add the reference to the web service. Navigate to your application home, and click the Shared Components icon. In the Logic section, click Web Service References. Click on the Create button to add a new web service reference.

2. In the first page of the wizard, choose the Based on WSDL option. Click No when asked if you would like to search a UDDI registry to find the WSDL. In the next page of the wizard, specify `www.webservicex.net/CurrencyConvertor.asmx?wsdl` in the WSDL Location field (as shown in Figure 3-21).

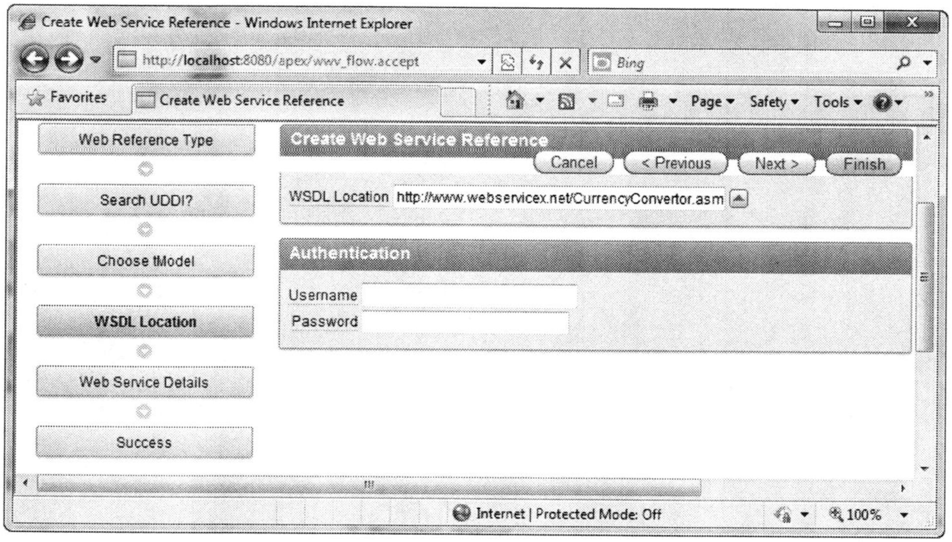

Figure 3-21. *The web service URL*

3. Click the Finish button. The web service should be created successfully.

Calling the Web Service from Your Form

To make use of the web service reference in your form, follow these steps:

1. In the Page Definition ➤ Page Processing area, right click on Processes under After Submit and click the Create button.

2. Choose the Web Services process type. In the next page, specify a name for the process. In the following page, choose the CurrencyConverter web service in the Web Service Reference field. Another Operation field will appear instantly. Choose the ConversionRate operation. This will, in turn, show a list of input parameters and output parameters for the webservice method.

3. For the From Currency parameter in the Webservice Input Parameters section, use the little arrow button on the right of the text field to choose the P1_FROMCODE field from a pop-up list. Choose P1_TOCODE for the To Currency field. Make sure the Source for both parameters is set to Item.

4. For the Webservice Output Parameters section, choose to store the results in Items. Specify P1_RETURNEDRATE in the Value field of the ConversionRateResult parameter. When you are done with the configuration, you should have something that looks like the screenshot in Figure 3-22.

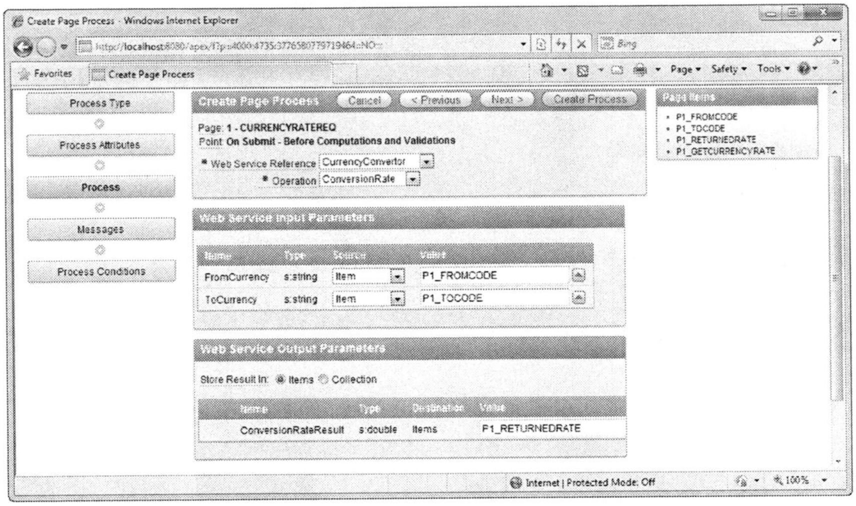

Figure 3-22. *Specifying web service details*

5. In the next page of the wizard, you can specify a success and error message to display when the web service call succeeds or fails, respectively. Proceed to the next step of the wizard where you can choose to have the web service called when the Get Currency Rate button on your form is clicked. Choose P1_GETCURRENCYRATE in the When Button Pressed field (as shown in Figure 3-23).

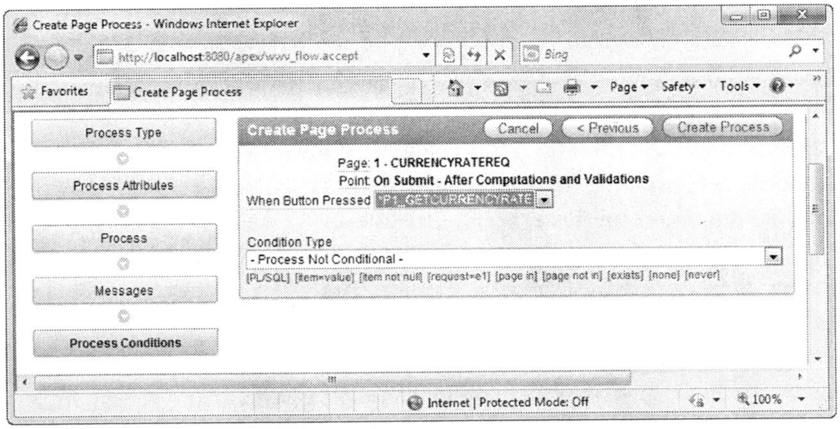

Figure 3-23. *Hooking up the web service execution to the Get Currency Rate button*

6. Finally, click the Create Process button to complete the wizard. Now run your form. Specify the three-letter currency code in the FromCode and ToCode fields, and click the Get Currency Rate button. You should be able to see the currency rate returned in the ReturnedRate field (as shown in Figure 3-24).

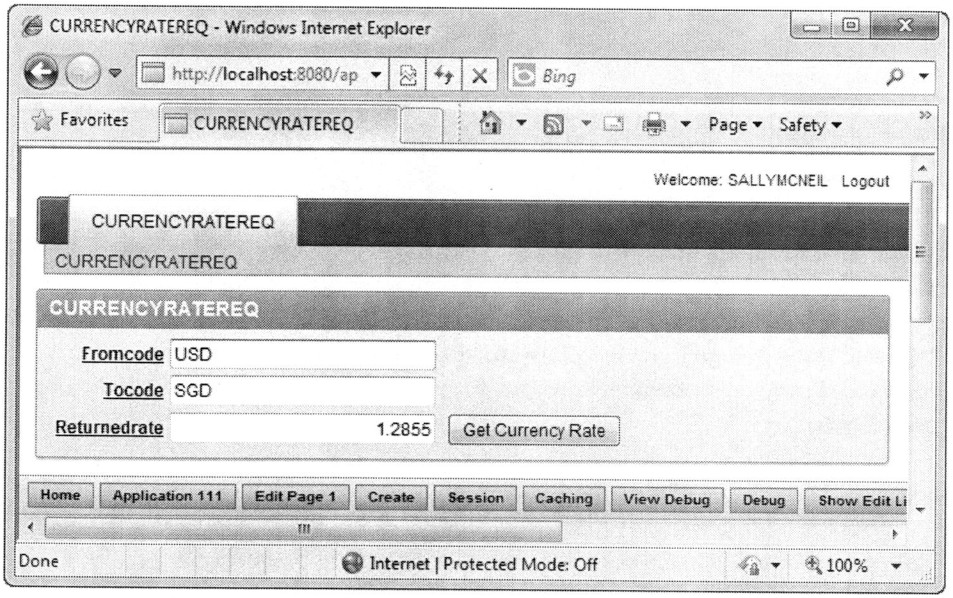

Figure 3-24. The web service call in action

■ **Note** As the web service used in this example is hosted online, you will need to ensure that the server hosting your APEX instance has a live connection to the Internet for this sample to work.

How It Works

The Web Service References section provides a global shared area that allows you to define web service data sources. Centralizing your web service references in one location instead of hard-coding them all over your application can make your application easier to maintain when the URL or address of the web service changes.

Web services can be called at any point in the execution of your form—when your form loads up, when a button is clicked, or when a particular condition is met. APEX also supports two different types of web-services: RESTful web services and WSDL-based web services.

3-8. Running a PL/SQL Process when Saving the Page

Problem

Upon submitting a form, you want to save some of the data entered through the form in a separate table. For example, you have a Patient Discharge form. When you create a record in this form, you need to create a corresponding entry in the Payment History form.

Solution

To run a PL/SQL process when saving the page, follow these steps:

1. Create the sample tables in Recipe 3-1.

2. Create a new database application/standard data entry form over the PATIENTDISCHARGE table.

3. In the Page Definition ➤ Page Processing area of the Patient Discharge form, right click on the Processes node under the Processing node, and choose the Create menu item.

4. In the first step of the wizard, choose the PL/SQL item.

5. Specify the name of the process in the next page of the wizard, and select On Submit - After Computations and Validations for the Point field.

6. In the next page, specify the PL/SQL shown in Listing 3-11. You should now have the screen shown in Figure 3-25.

Listing 3-11. Inserting Data into Another Table

```
INSERT INTO PAYMENTHISTORY(SOCIALSECURITYNO,AMOUNTPAID) VALUES (:P1_PATIENTSOCIALSECURITYNO,0)
```

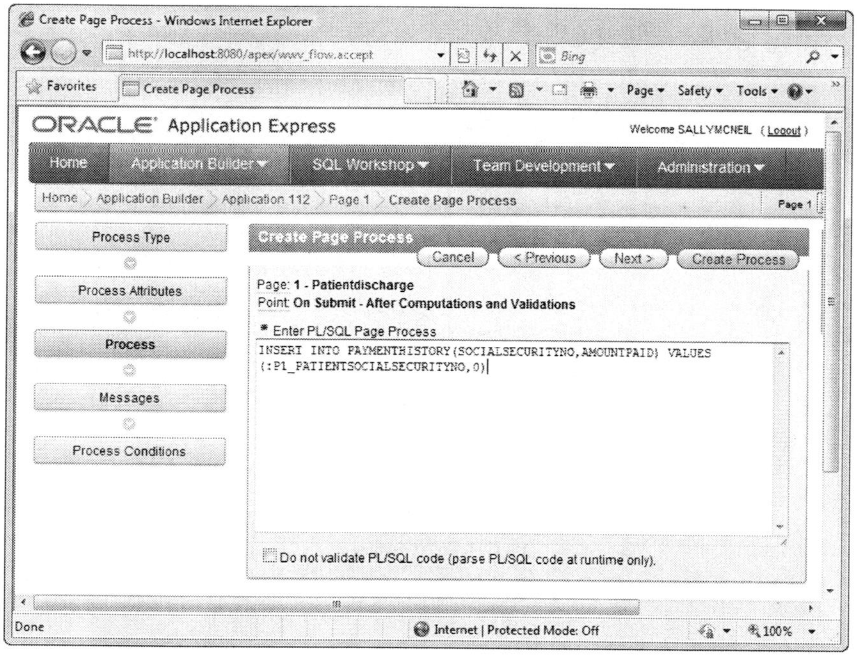

Figure 3-25. Specifying the process details

7. Save your changes and run the form now. Key in 99999999 in the Social Security Number field and create the record. Using the Object Browser, open the PAYMENTHISTORY table. You should be able to see a new record automatically created in this table with the Social Security number 99999999.

How It Works

A process is a server-side task that executes when a certain event occurs in your form. There are a number of different process types that can be generated via the wizard (for example, running a PL/SQL script, sending an e-mail, or calling a web service). You can even create processes to dynamically modify session states in your application. Through the wizard, processes can also be tied to button items on your form such that when a button is clicked on the form, the process would immediately execute.

■ **Tip** Processes can also be initiated from client-side JavaScript events. By inspecting postback parameters, different server-side processes can be made to execute.

3-9. Sending an E-mail from the Form

Problem

You need to send an e-mail when you click a button on the form. You also want to use data entered through the form as various parameters in the e-mail.

Solution

To test the solution in this recipe, you will first need to create the sample database and form objects. Then you will need to invoke the Send Email process from your form. Let's start by creating the sample objects used in this recipe.

Creating the Sample Object

To create the sample objects used in this recipe, follow these steps:

1. Create the table shown in Listing 3-12, and create a new database application/data entry form over the table.

Listing 3-12. The PatientDB Table

```
CREATE table "PATIENTDB" (
    "PATIENTNAME"       NVARCHAR2(255),
    "PATIENTEMAIL"      NVARCHAR2(255),
    "PATIENTDIAGNOSIS"  NVARCHAR2(2000),
    "PATIENTID"         NVARCHAR2(10),
    constraint  "PATIENTDB_PK" primary key ("PATIENTID")
)
/

CREATE sequence "PATIENTDB_SEQ"
/

CREATE trigger "BI_PATIENTDB"
  before insert on "PATIENTDB"
  for each row
begin
  if :NEW."PATIENTID" is null then
    select "PATIENTDB_SEQ".nextval into :NEW."PATIENTID" from dual;
  end if;
end;
/
```

Sending the E-mail

To invoke the Send E-mail process from your form, follow these steps:

1. In the Page Definition ➤ Page Rendering section of the PatientDB form, add a new button item named Send E-mail. Change the button type to a HTML button, and set the label of the button to Send Email.

2. In the Page Definition ➤ Page Processing section of the PatientDB form, right click on Processes under the Processing node, and choose to create a new process.

3. In the first page of the wizard, choose the Send E-mail process. Next, specify a name for the process. In the next page, specify the contents and recipient of the e-mail. You can use the substitution syntax (for example, &P1_PATIENTNAME) to insert data from your form into the e-mail. The figure shown in Figure 3-26 shows the configuration for a typical e-mail that uses the patient's e-mail address and name entered through the form.

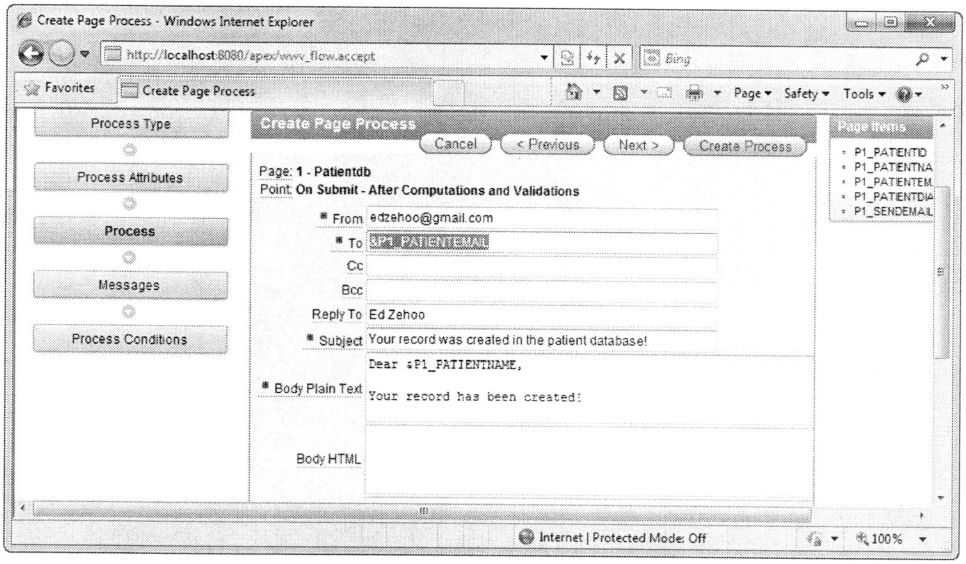

Figure 3-26. Specifying the details of the e-mail

4. In the next page, specify the success or failure message to display. In the following page of the wizard, specify the P1_SENDEMAIL field in the When Button Pressed field.

5. Save the changes and run the form. Specify a functioning e-mail address in the Patient e-mail field. Click the Send Email button. An e-mail should be sent to the address you've specified.

How It Works

Sending an e-mail is also a server-side process. Outbound e-mails are not sent out immediately (unless you specified to do so in the Process configuration wizard), but are queued until a DBMS_JOB job dequeues it and sends it out.

CHAPTER 4

Customizing Look and Feel

Customizing application look and feel is one of the most important aspects of solution delivery. It is the process that defines how your application is presented to the end user. APEX is extremely flexible in this area, letting you customize not just the color schemes, headers and footers of a page, but even the attributes for the controls it uses on your form.

Half of the time, users like yourself don't just create standalone web applications for an intranet environment. I know many developers that use APEX because they needed an easier way to integrate forms into their public-facing web site. Think about the "Apply for a job" section of a public web site, for instance. When visitors click on the link, they shouldn't feel like they're being redirected to an entirely new portal. The "Apply for a job" form should look and feel no different from any other page on the site. To achieve that purpose, the developer needs to make the form's color scheme, header, and footer conform to the rest of the web site.

APEX provides the facilities for you to change every aspect of the user interface in your applications. You will take a look at the basics of doing so in this chapter.

4-1. Adding an Image Header to Your Form

Problem

You need to add an image in the header area of your form.

Solution

To add an image to the header area of your form, follow these steps:

1. Click on an existing application in the Application Builder.

2. Click the Shared Components icon. In the ensuing page, click the Images link under the Files section, as shown in Figure 4-1.

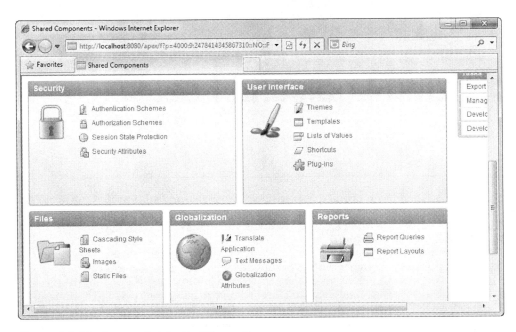

Figure 4-1. *The Images link in the Files section*

3. In the ensuing page, click the yellow Create button in the top right corner. Choose your application from the list, and browse for a banner image (GIF, JPG or PNG file) to upload. When you're done, click the Upload button.

4. You should now see your image in the application, as shown in Figure 4-2.

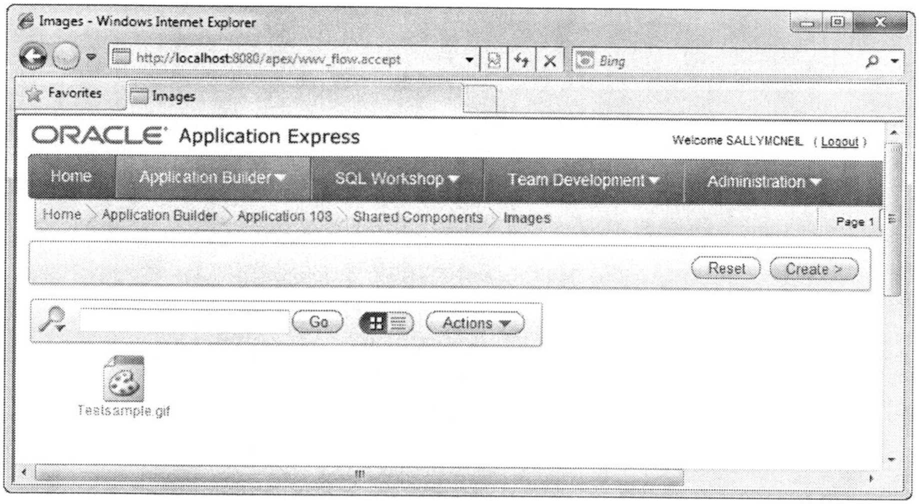

Figure 4-2. The Testsample.gif image

5. Now, navigate to an existing form in the application and click on it to view its Page Definition.

6. In the Shared Components area of the form, expand the Templates node, followed by the Region node, right-click on the Form Region node, and choose the Edit menu item (as shown in Figure 4-3).

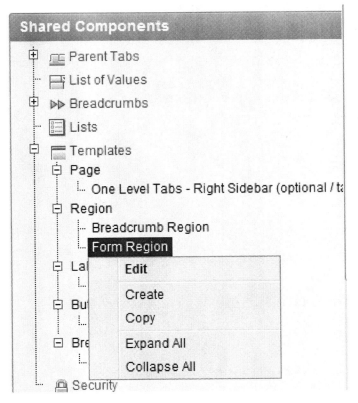

Figure 4-3. *Navigating to the Form Region template definition page*

7. In the ensuing page, click the Definition tab. Add the following HTML tag above the DIV tag in the template box:

```
<img border="0" src="#APP_IMAGES#Testsample.gif">
```

8. You should now have the screen shown in Figure 4-4.

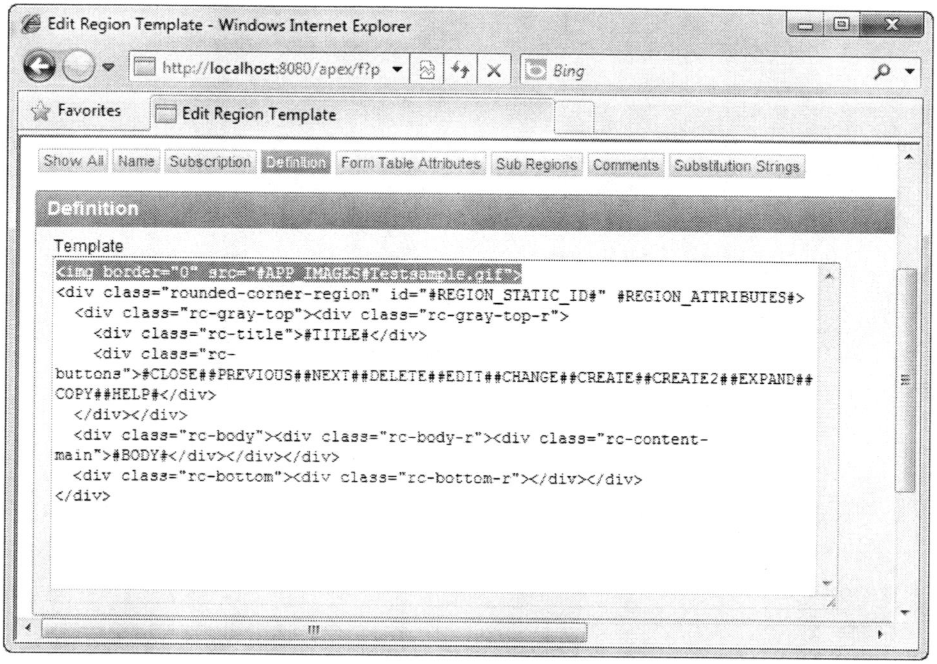

Figure 4-4. Including the Testsample.gif image in the template

9. Save your changes and run the form. You should now see your image at the top of the form, as shown in Figure 4-5.

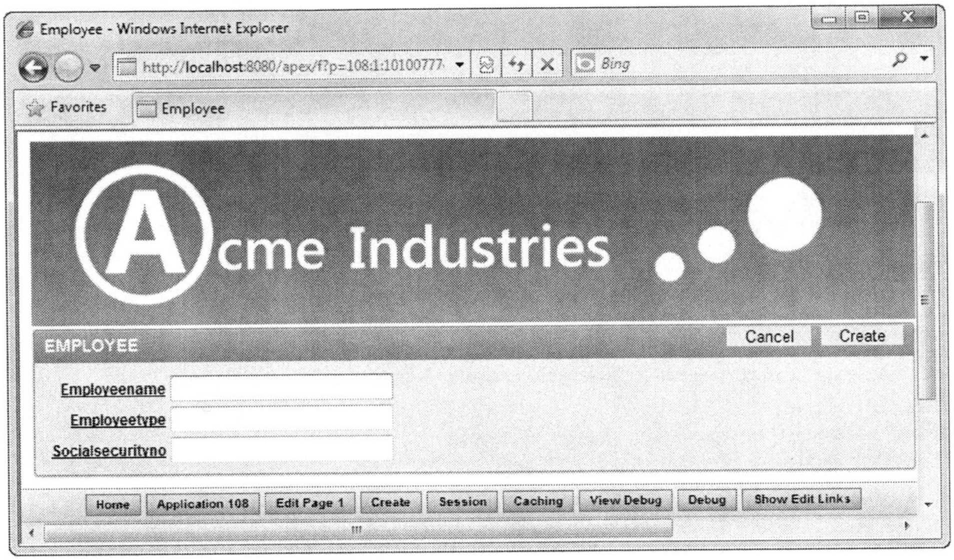

Figure 4-5. The new image header in your form

■ **Caution** Image names are case-sensitive! If you don't use the correct case, your image may not show up at all.

How It Works

Before proceeding, you should be aware of various terminology used in APEX when you embark on modifying the look and feel of an application. Table 4-1 describes some of this terminology.

Table 4-1. Some APEX Terminology

Term	Description

Template	A template is an HTML string that represents a User Interface element in an APEX application. For example, the standard template for a button looks something like this:
	
	`<button value="#LABEL#" onclick="#LINK#" class="button-gray" type="button">`
	
	`  <span>#LABEL#</span>`
	
	`</button>`

Term	Description
	The flexibility with templates is that developers can actually modify these templates, creating a standard template that is used throughout the entire application or workspace. For instance, simply by modifying an existing button template to include a width tag `<button width="300px"` all buttons in the entire application would instantly have a width of 300 pixels wide. In fact, developers can even change the HTML entirely, replacing <button> tags with <img> tags to create image buttons.
Theme	Every type of control and user interface element in APEX is represented by a template. A complete collection of these templates is known as a theme. In other words, a theme is a collection of templates. Themes make it easy for your developers to skin your applications and switch from one theme to another with a few clicks of the mouse.

Substitution String	In the button template example, you might have noticed special tags like #LABEL# (phrases enclosed between two hash symbols (#)). These are called substitution strings and provide an easy way for developers to insert dynamic fields in a template.
	
	For instance, #LABEL# actually represents the text that will be displayed on top of the button. They are substituted with actual values (in this case, the button text) when your form is rendered by APEX. Try to think of it as mail merge.
	
	In this fashion, you could reposition and move these substitution strings around to achieve interesting effects. For instance, you could write an onclick JavaScript handler to prompt a confirmation box that displays the text of the button as part of its message using the #LABEL# substitution string.
	
	`<button value="#LABEL#" onclick="if (confirm('Are you sure you wish to click the #LABEL# button'))`
	`#LINK#" ...`

Now that you know these terms, let's look at how user-uploaded images are used in APEX. APEX treats images as resources that can be reused many times within an application or within a workspace. The first step before you can use any images in your application is to import it. The Shared Components area of your application, as its name indicates, is a global area where pages can reference to retrieve an image resource.

When an image has been uploaded into this global area, you can easily refer to it from any part of your page template. However, you can't just refer to it using its file name; you must also specify the path to the file name. The path is not specified as a URL, but as a substitution string; APEX replaces it with the actual URL later on. If you uploaded your image to an application, you should use the #APP_IMAGES# substitution string, as you've seen earlier in this recipe. To use it, simply append the name of the file right after the substitution string (without any slash in between), like so:

```
#APP_IMAGES#myfile.jpg
```

You can also use #WORKSPACE_IMAGES# if you have uploaded your image to a workspace instead (so that other applications in the workspace can make use of the image).

4-2. Adding Custom CSS Styles to Your Page

Problem

You need a quick way to declare several stylesheet classes and have them apply on some elements in your form.

Solution

To add a custom CSS style to your page, follow these steps:

1. Click on an existing application in the Application Builder.

2. Navigate to an existing form in the application and click on it to view its Page Definition.

3. In the Page Rendering area of the form, right click on the form root node and choose the Edit menu item.

4. In the ensuing window, click the HTML Header and Body Attribute tab, and paste the style sheet class shown in Listing 4-1. (You should now have the same screen as shown in Figure 4-6).

Listing 4-1. A Sample Style Class

```
<style>
.specialstyle
    {
    font-family : Verdana;
    font-size : 12pt;
    color : #FF0000;
    font-weight : bold;
    text-align :left ;
    vertical-align : middle;
```

```
}
</style>
```

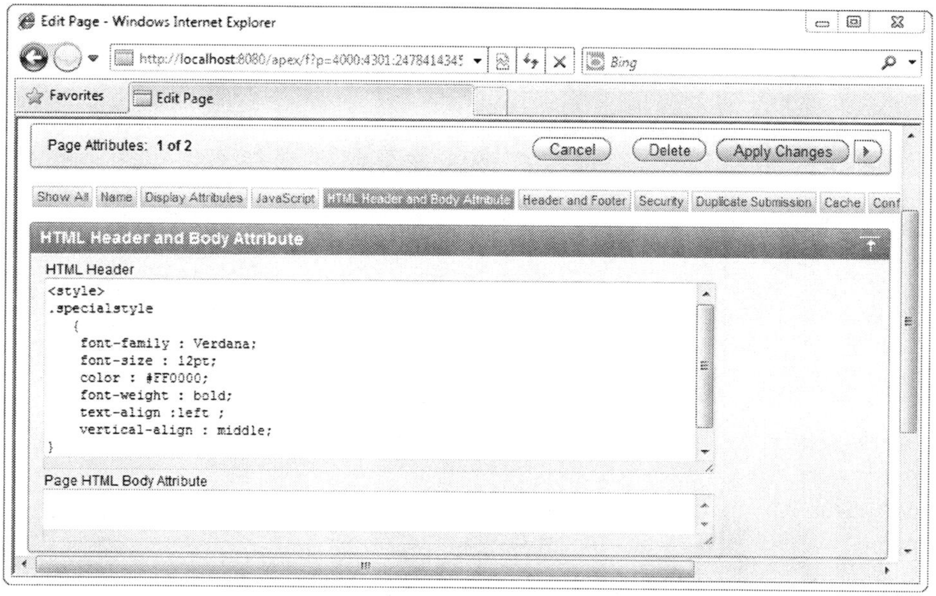

Figure 4-6. Declaring a custom style in the HTML header

5. Click the Apply changes button to save the form. Navigate back to the Page Definition area of the form.

6. In the Shared Components section, expand the Templates node, and further expand the Button node. Right click on the deepest Button node, and choose the Edit menu item.

7. In the ensuing window, click the `Definition` tab, and change the class of the button to "specialstyle," as shown in Figure 4-7.

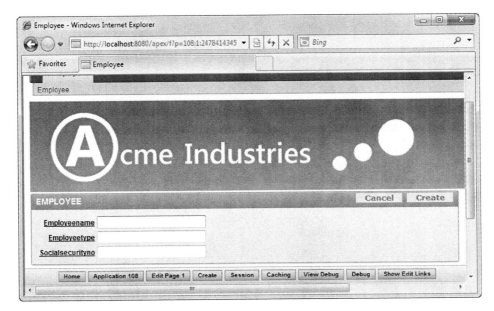

Figure 4-7. Referencing the specialstyle style

       8.   Save your changes, and run the form. You should now see your form with the buttons in red, as declared in the stylesheet class (see Figure 4-8).

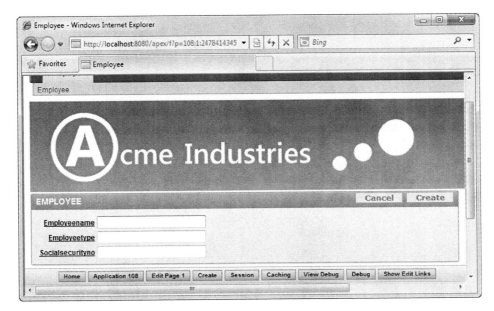

Figure 4-8. The specialstyle style applied on your form

How It Works

If you need to declare some stylesheet classes quickly and use them in your forms (without the need to reuse these classes in other forms), a good place to declare them is under the HTML Header and Body Attribute section, as you've seen earlier in this recipe. Whatever you've entered in this section is rendered as-is at the top of the web page generated by APEX.

Once declared, you can reference any of those styles directly via the name of the style class.

■ **Caution** By placing your stylesheet class in the HTML Header and Body Attribute section, you make it available to the form alone and not to other forms in your application. To create a set of styles that can be used globally throughout your application or workspace, please consider using custom CSS files instead (covered in Recipe 4-3).

4-3. Using a Custom CSS File

Problem

You have a large number of stylesheet classes stored in a .css file, and you need to reference this css file in your application so that you can apply custom styles to some elements on your form.

Solution

To use a custom CSS file, follow these steps:

1. Create a new CSS file (using Notepad or any other editor tool) with the text shown in Listing 4-2.

Listing 4-2. A Sample CSS File

```
.buttonstyle_incss
{
font-family : Verdana;
color : #FFFFFF;
font-weight : bold;
text-align :left ;
vertical-align : middle;
width:150px;
height:25px;
background-color:#000000;
}
```

2. Click on an existing application in the Application Builder.

3. Click the Shared Components icon. In the ensuing page, click the Cascading Style Sheets link under the Files section.

117

4. Click the Create button to add a new style sheet to your application. In the ensuing page, browse for your .CSS file and click the yellow Upload button in the top right corner.

5. You should now see your CSS file, as shown in Figure 4-9.

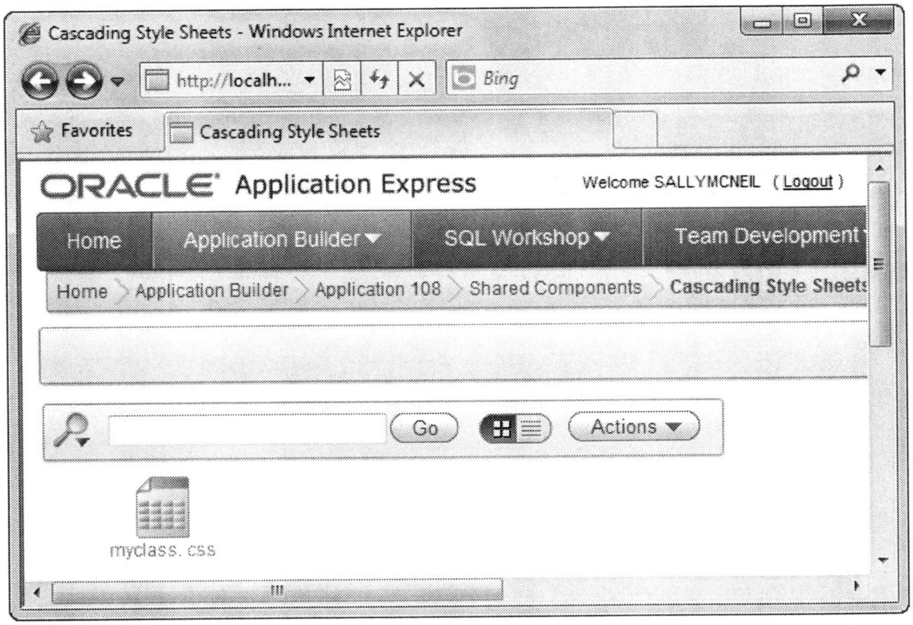

Figure 4-9. The newly uploaded myclass.css file

6. Navigate to the Page Definition area of your form. Right click on the root form node and choose the Edit menu item.

7. In the ensuing page, click the HTML Header and Body Attribute tab. In the HTML Header textbox, type the following code, substituting myclass.css with the name of your uploaded css class. Take care to note that the class name is case sensitive.

```
<link href="#WORKSPACE_IMAGES#myclass.css" rel="stylesheet" type="text/css" />
```

8. You should now have the screen shown in Figure 4-10.

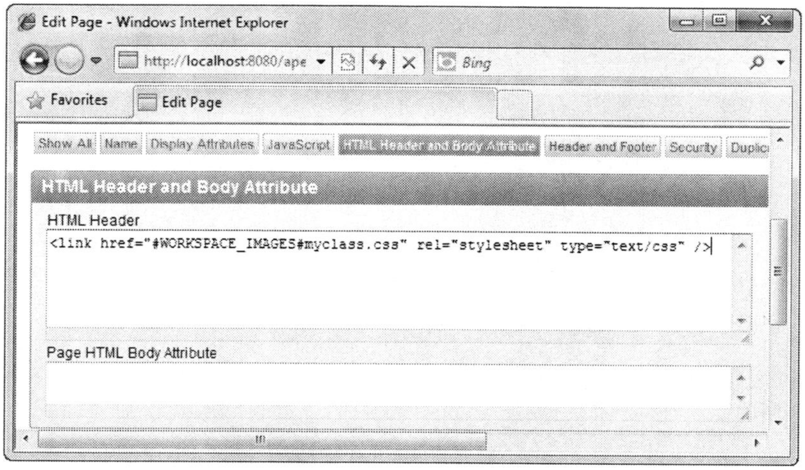

Figure 4-10. Referencing the myclass.css file

9. Save your changes and return to the Page Definition area of your form. In the Shared Components section, expand Templates ➤ Button, right-click on the deepest Button node, and choose the Edit menu item.

10. Click the Definition tab in the ensuing page, and set the Class property of the button to the name of your class in the CSS stylesheet: buttonstyle_incss. You should have the screen shown in Figure 4-11.

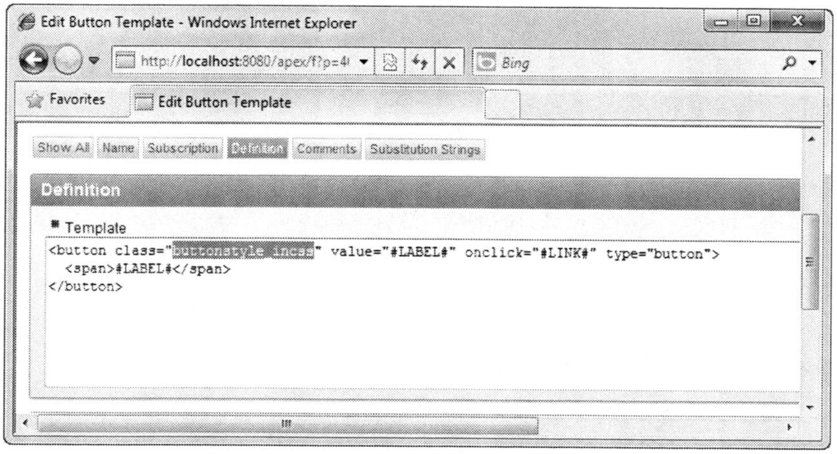

Figure 4-11. Referencing the buttonstyle_incss style in your CSS file

11. Save your changes and run the form. The buttons on your form have taken on the white-font-on-black-background style defined in your attached CSS file, as shown in Figure 4-12.

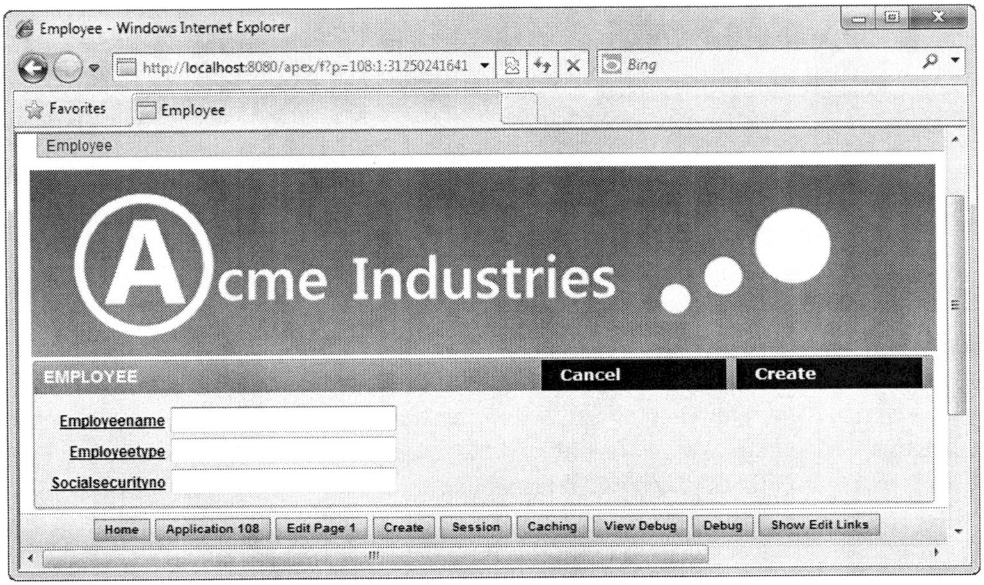

Figure 4-12. The CSS file applied on your form

How It Works

CSS files are also treated as resources in APEX. You can upload a CSS file globally and reuse it in any application in a workspace. Just like standard web application development, you have to declare the CSS file before you can use any of the styles inside. You can do so by including the standard HTML declaration for CSS files in the HTML Header and Body Attributes section of the form, like so:

```
<link href="#WORKSPACE_IMAGES#myclass.css" rel="stylesheet" type="text/css" />
```

> **Note** The href property of the HTML declaration needs an actual path to the CSS file, so you need to include the #WORKSPACE_IMAGES# substitution string to tell APEX where to look for it.

4-4. Creating a New Theme in Your Application

Problem

You like your new white-font-on-black-background button, so much so that you want this button to be the de facto standard for all your other applications. You wish to create a special theme that includes this button as a default, so that the theme can be easily reused by developers for other applications.

Solution

To use a new theme, you must first create the theme, and then switch the application theme to your new theme.

Creating a New Theme

To create a new theme, follow these steps:

1. Click on an existing application in the Application Builder.

2. Click on the Shared Components icon, and click on the Themes link inside the User Interface section (as shown in Figure 4-13).

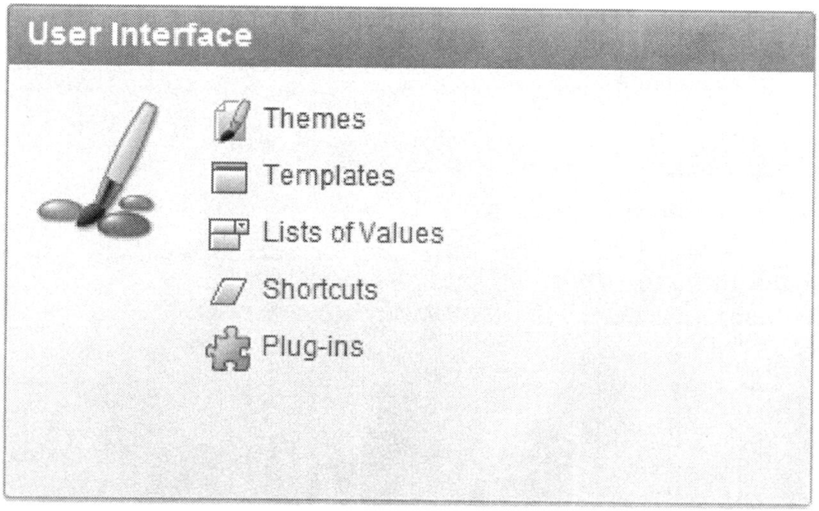

Figure 4-13. The Themes link in the User Interface area

3. In the ensuing window, click the Create button to start the Theme Creation wizard.

4. In the first step of the wizard, choose to create the theme from the repository.

5. Next, choose a theme from the list of themes (choose any theme you wish). Finally, click the Create button to create the theme.

6. You should now see your newly created theme in the Themes area, as shown in Figure 4-14. I chose the Theme 8 (Orange) theme.

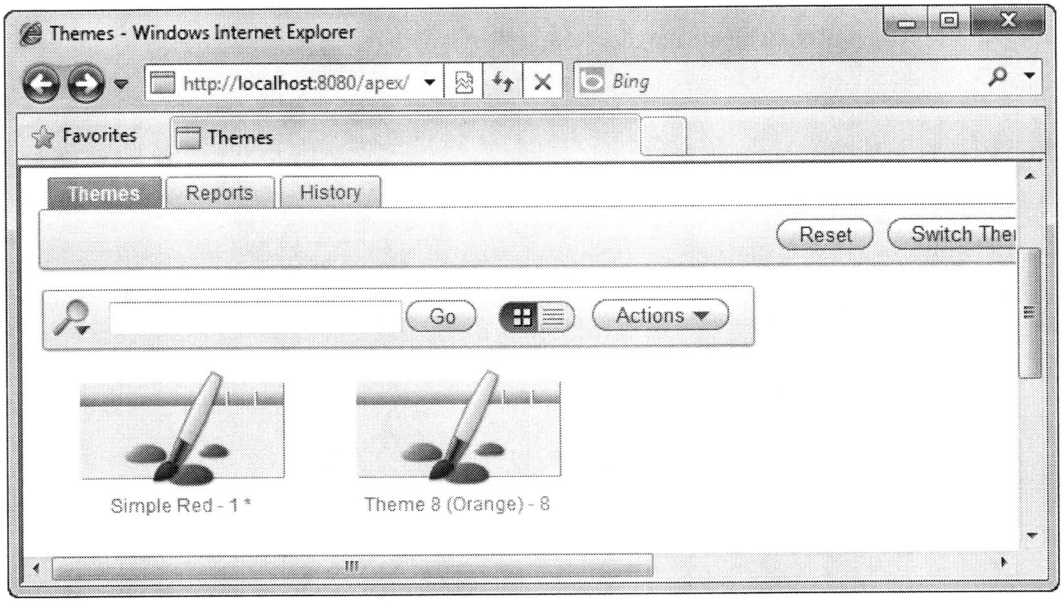

Figure 4-14. The newly created theme (Theme 8 (Orange) - 8)

7. Now that you have a theme, you need to modify it to include your custom button template. Click on the theme. You should now see a screen that looks like Figure 4-15.

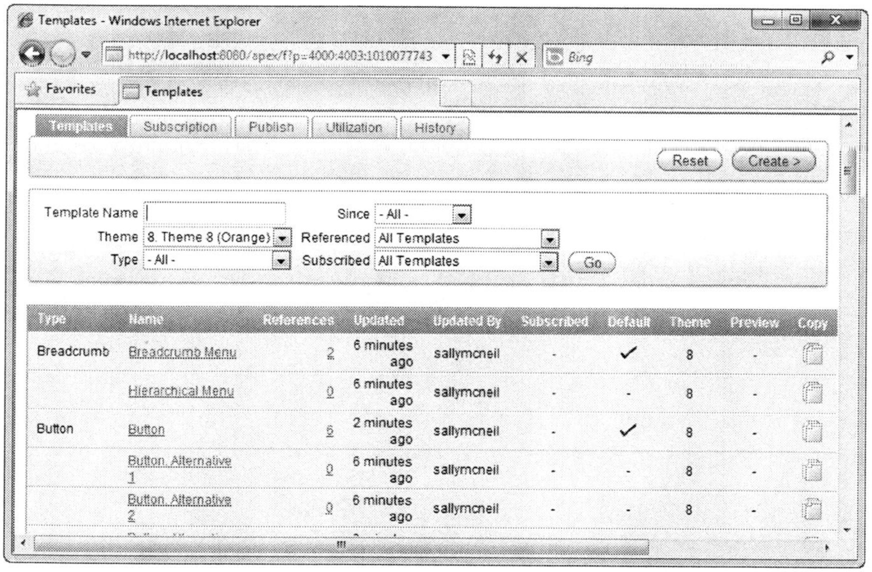

Figure 4-15. The contents of a theme

8. In this screen, click the Button link in the Button Type section. In the ensuing page, copy the button template from Recipe 4-3, and paste it in the Template field under the Definition area. You should now have the screen shown in Figure 4-16. Save your changes.

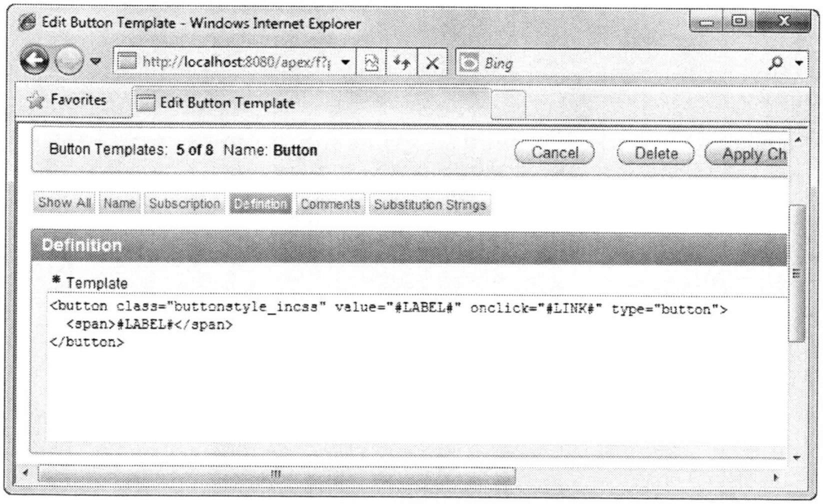

Figure 4-16. Modifying the button template in the theme

Switching the Application Theme

To switch your application theme to the newly created theme, follow these steps:

1. Return to the Shared Components section of your application. Under the same User Interface area, click the Themes link again.

2. Click the Switch Theme button. You should now see the screen shown in Figure 4-17. Choose to switch to your newly created theme.

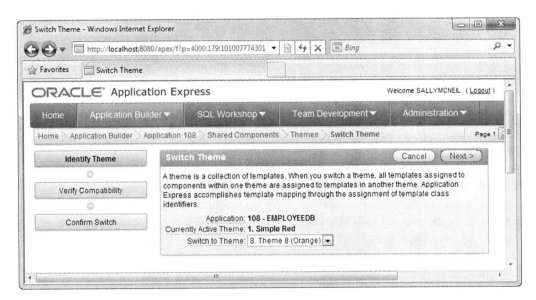

Figure 4-17. Switching the active theme of an application

3. Navigate to the next step of the wizard and confirm the theme switch. After you have successfully switched the theme, a message stating so will be displayed. Now, run your application one more time. You should see the new theme applied, together with your custom white-font-on-black-background button template (as shown in Figure 4-18).

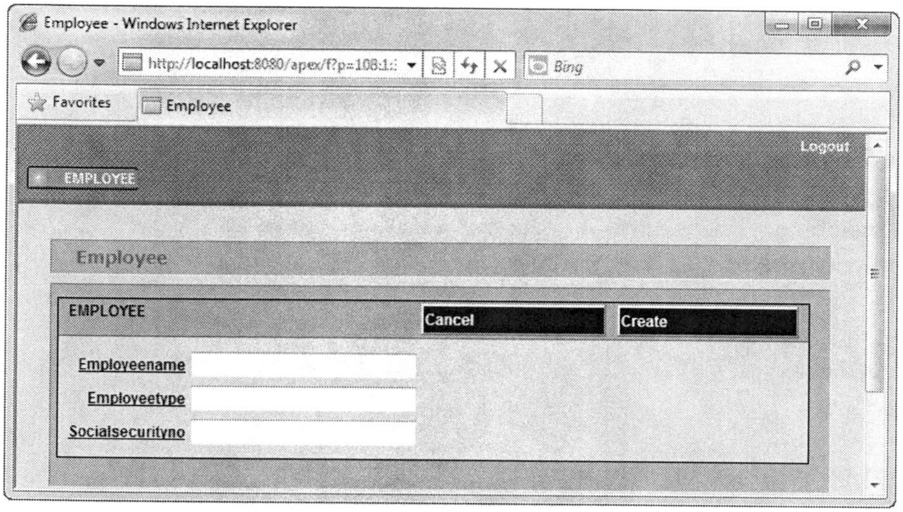

Figure 4-18. The new theme applied on your form

How It Works

As mentioned in Recipe 4-1, themes are collections of templates, and they are a good way to manage your user interfaces. A theme includes a template for every single type of user interface element in APEX. Themes allow you to easily skin your application and to switch between them.

You can also easily create new variations of a theme by making a duplicate copy of it in APEX and individually modifying the templates contained inside.

▓ **Note** There are web sites that sell or provide APEX themes. ApexSkins is one such site; go to
www.apexskins.com.

4-5. Modifying Form Control Templates

Problem

Your application runs well. One day, someone in the office deletes some important data by mistake. High-level politics kick in, and your not-so-IT-savvy bosses decide it's a great idea to have all buttons in your form prompt for an additional pop-up confirmation before doing anything. Given that some of your existing forms have numerous buttons, and it wouldn't be very fun changing your forms one button at a time, you look for a faster alternative.

Solution

Modify the form control template in order to change the behavior for all buttons at once. Here are the steps to follow:

1. Open the existing form in your application.

2. In the Page Definition area of the form, expand the Templates node in the Shared Components section. Look for the Button node, and expand that as well.

3. Right-click on the deepest Button node, and choose to Edit the item (as shown in Figure 4-19).

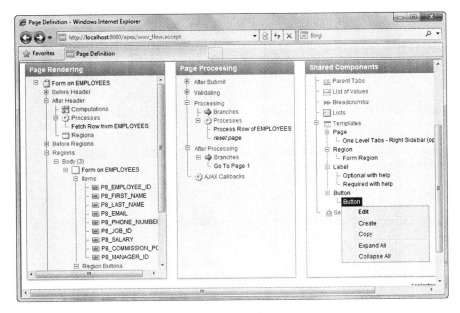

Figure 4-19. *The new theme applied on your form*

4. In the ensuing popup window, look for the Definition panel. In the Template field, modify the APEX button template to include a confirmation pop-up JavaScript in the onclick event of the button (as highlighted in bold in Listing 4-3).

Listing 4-3. *Modifying the Default Button Template*

```
<button value="#LABEL#" onclick="if (confirm('Are you sure?')) {#LINK#};" class="button-gray"
type="button">
```

```
<span>#LABEL#</span>
</button>
```

5. You should now have the screen shown in Figure 4-20.

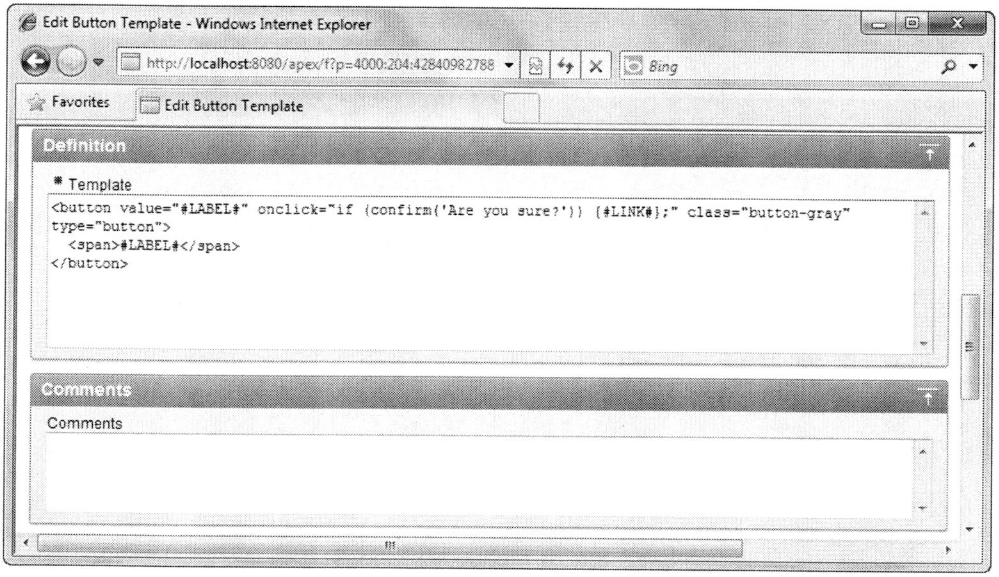

Figure 4-20. *The new button template*

6. Save your changes and run the form. Click on any button in your form. You should now see a JavaScript confirmation pop-up window appear, allowing you to cancel or confirm your action, as shown in Figure 4-21.

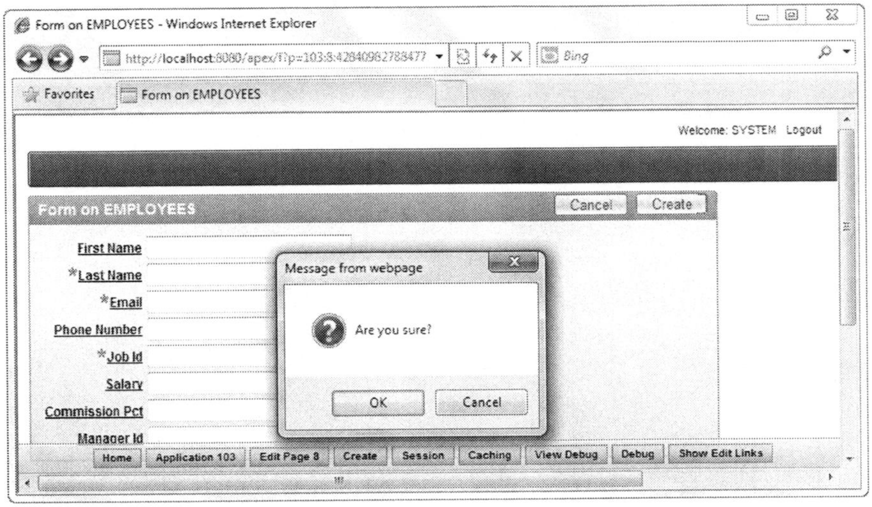

Figure 4-21. The new button in action

How It Works

To APEX, a button may not necessarily be a button, and a textbox not necessarily a textbox. Zen-speak aside, how APEX represents each form control is entirely customizable by the developer. For instance, APEX ships with the following default template for a button:

```
<button value="#LABEL#" onclick="#LINK#;" class="button-gray" type="button">

   <span>#LABEL#</span>
</button>
```

But the fact that APEX exposes this template to you and lets you modify it means that you can, for instance, replace the previous HTML with something else entirely. Once you do that, every time an APEX application needs to render a button, it would render your HTML.

This flexibility means that you can, for instance, to change all buttons in your form to image buttons simply by changing the button template. Or, in the case of this recipe, add additional functionality not present in the default control.

4-6. Creating Reusable Code Snippets

Problem

You have been tasked by your bosses to create an area in *all* your application forms to display the current system date in this fashion: "The date today is XXXXXXXX." You know you can write a simple one-line PL/SQL to generate this label inside every form, but knowing your bosses better, you know they're going to change their finicky minds the next day on how the date is presented. With this in mind, you need a way to centralize the point of change in your application, so that when you change the text in one location, it will automatically take effect in all your application forms.

Solution

Create a shortcut and reference that shortcut from each of your pages.

To create a shortcut, follow these steps:

1. Open an existing application.

2. Click the Shared Components icon.

3. In the User Interface section, click the Shortcuts link shown in Figure 4-22.

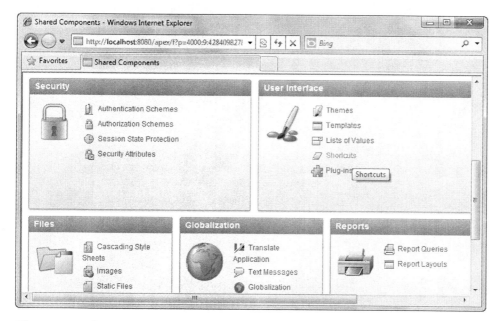

Figure 4-22. The Shortcuts link

4. In the next window, click the Create button, and choose to create the shortcut from scratch.

5. Click the Next button. Specify MY_DATE_CAPTION as the name of the shortcut, change the Source Type to PL/SQL Function Body, and type the following text into the Shortcut field:

```
return 'The date today is ' || to_char(sysdate,'DD/MM/YYYY HH24:MI:SS');
```

6. You should now see the screen shown in Figure 4-23.

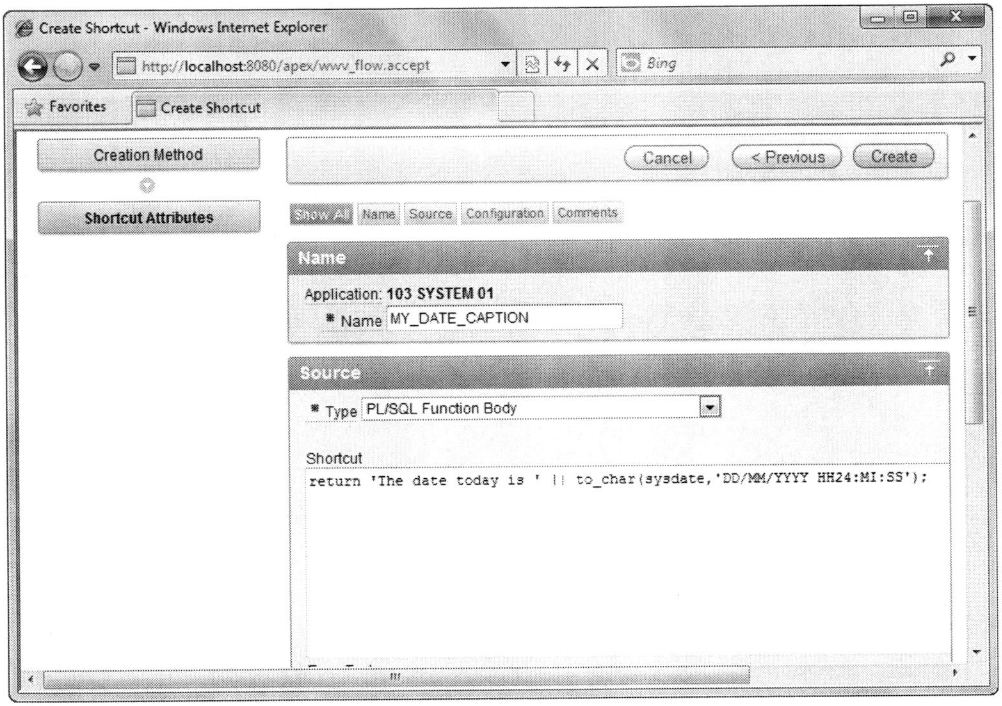

Figure 4-23. Specifying the source for the shortcut

7. Click the Create button to create the shortcut. You should now see the newly created shortcut shown in Figure 4-24.

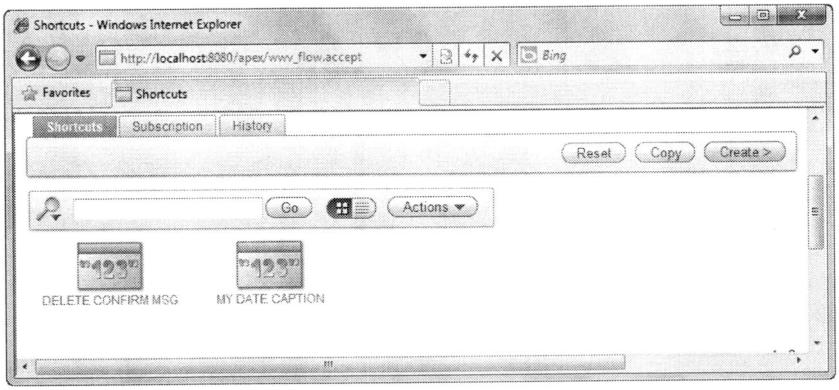

Figure 4-24. The newly created shortcut

To reference the shortcut from your form, follow these steps:

1. Open an existing form.

2. In the Page Definition area of the form, create a new region (Right-click on the Form ➤ Regions ➤ Body node in the Page Rendering section and click the Create menu item).

3. Choose the HTML region type in the wizard.

4. In the next page of the wizard, choose HTML Text (with shortcuts), as shown in Figure 4-25.

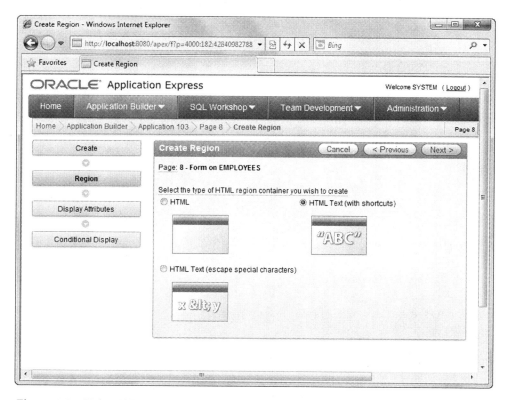

Figure 4-25. Using HTML Text (with shortcuts) in a region

5. In the next step, specify a title for the region.

6. The next step will allow you to specify the HTML Text Region source. Type in the name of the shortcut you created earlier, encased between the double quotes (as shown in Figure 4-26).

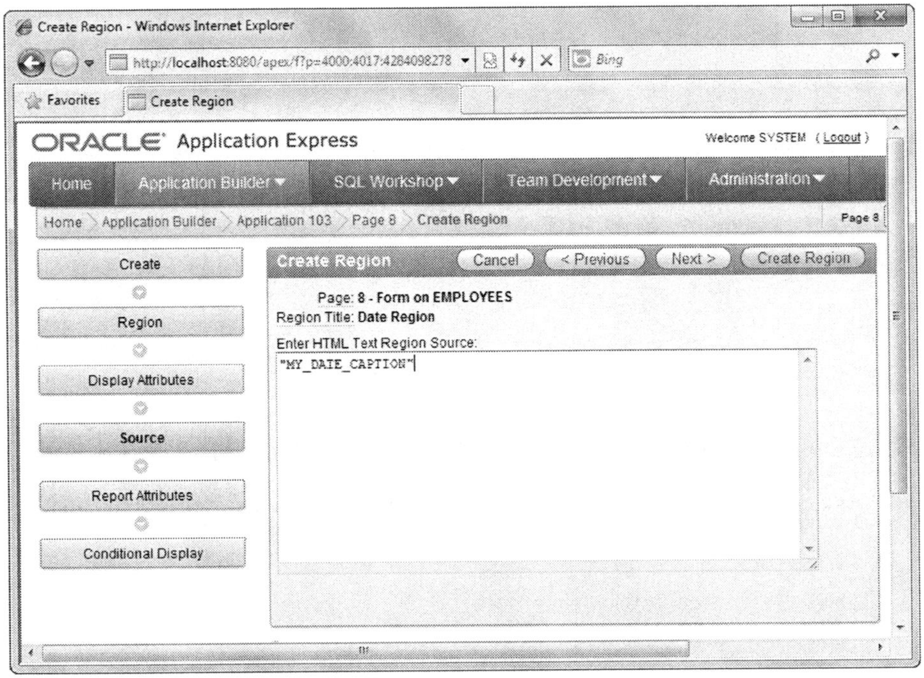

Figure 4-26. Referencing the shortcut from the region

7. Now click the Create Region button.

8. You should now see the date value appear in the region of your form, as shown in Figure 4-27.

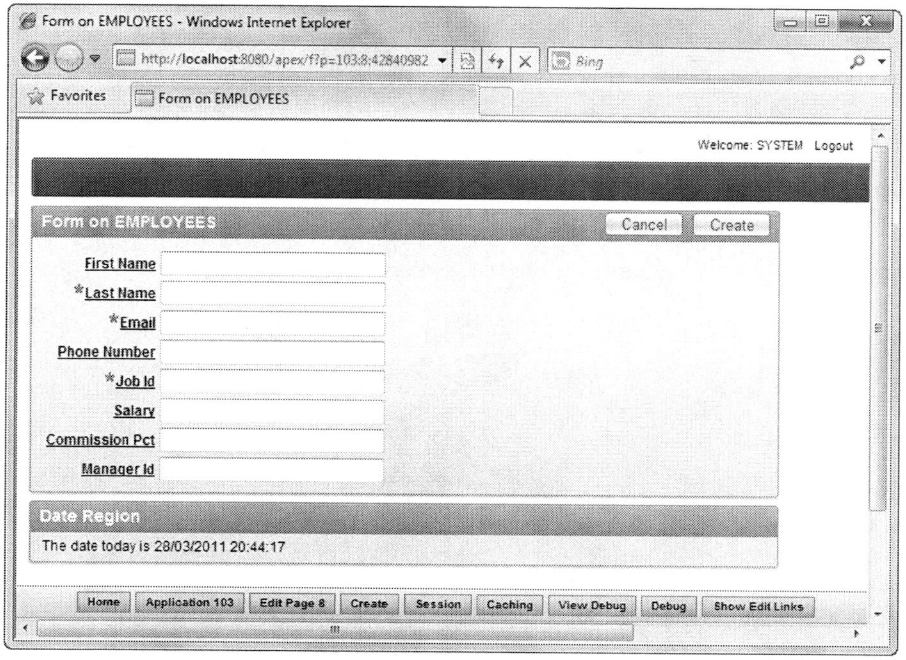

Figure 4-27. The shortcut in action

How It Works

Instead of hardcoding information directly inside a form, you can choose to have them externally represented as a dynamic variable, referenced from your application whenever required. In APEX, such a variable is called a shortcut.

There are many benefits to using shortcuts. For instance, if your boss decides that the text should be changed from "The date today is" to "Current date is", you can just change it in the shortcut, and every part of your application that uses the shortcut will display the correct text

4-7. Extending the UI via Plug-ins

Problem

You need to create a form control that isn't available in the existing APEX control toolbox. You plan to also share this control with your colleagues, so you need to make this control reusable.

Solution

You decide to use APEX plug-ins to implement the control. In this recipe, you will create a specialized hyperlink control (that will bring the user to the Google web site) as an example.

Creating the Plug-in

To create the plug-in, follow these steps:

1. Open an existing application.

2. Click on the Shared Components icon.

3. Click the Plug-ins link in the User Interface section, as shown in Figure 4-28.

Figure 4-28. The Plug-ins link

4. In the plug-in configuration page, specify GOOGLELINKIE as the name of the plug-in and mygooglelinkie as the internal name of the plug-in. Ensure that the Type field is set to Item.

5. In the Source area, type the text shown in Listing 4-4.

Listing 4-4. The Render Function

```
function RENDER_LINKIE (

p_item                  in apex_plugin.t_page_item
, p_plugin              in apex_plugin.t_plugin
, p_value               in varchar2
```

```
, p_is_readonly          in boolean
, p_is_printer_friendly in boolean )
return apex_plugin.t_page_item_render_result
is
    retval apex_plugin.t_page_item_render_result;
begin
    htp.p('<a href="http://www.google.com">Jump to Google</a>');
    return retval;
end;
```

6. Ensure that you set the Render Function Name (under the Callbacks section) to the name of your PL/SQL function (RENDER_LINKIE). You should now have the screenshot shown in Figure 4-29.

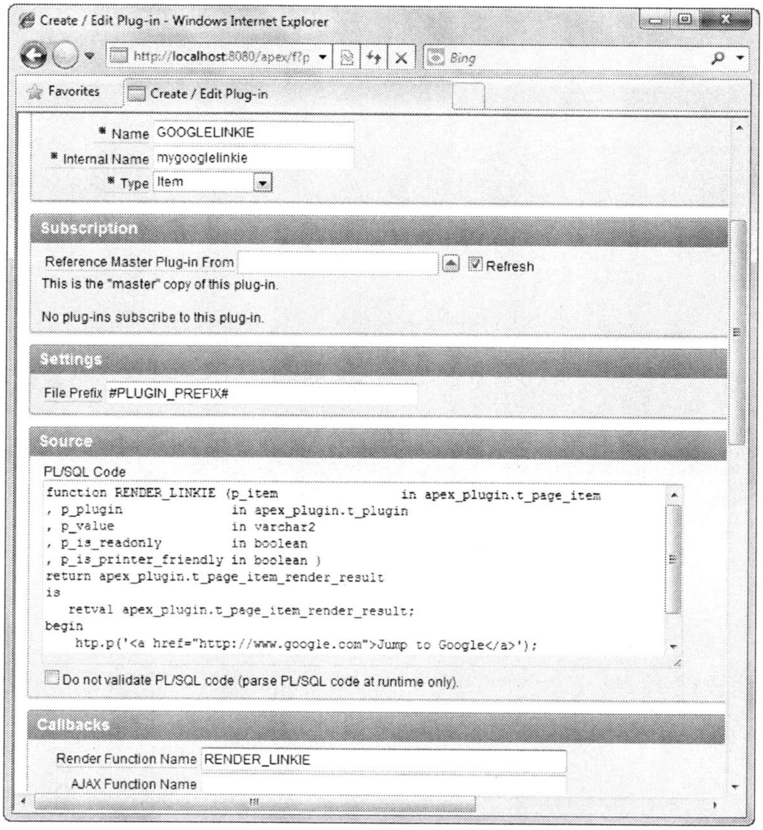

Figure 4-29. Specifying the details of the plug-in

7. Click the Create button to create the plug-in.

Using the Plug-in

To use the plug-in in your application, follow these steps:

1. Open an existing form.

2. In the Page Rendering area of the form, create a new Page Item.

3. Choose Plug-ins from the list of item types available in the first step of the wizard, as shown in Figure 4-30.

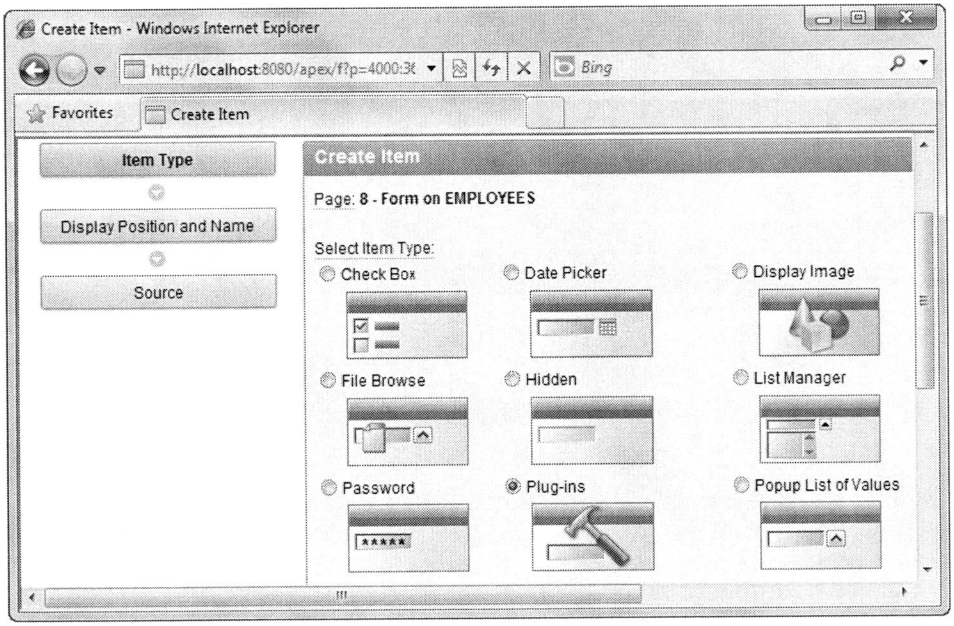

Figure 4-30. The Plug-ins item type

4. Choose the GOOGLELINKIE plug-in in the next step of the wizard, as shown in Figure 4-31.

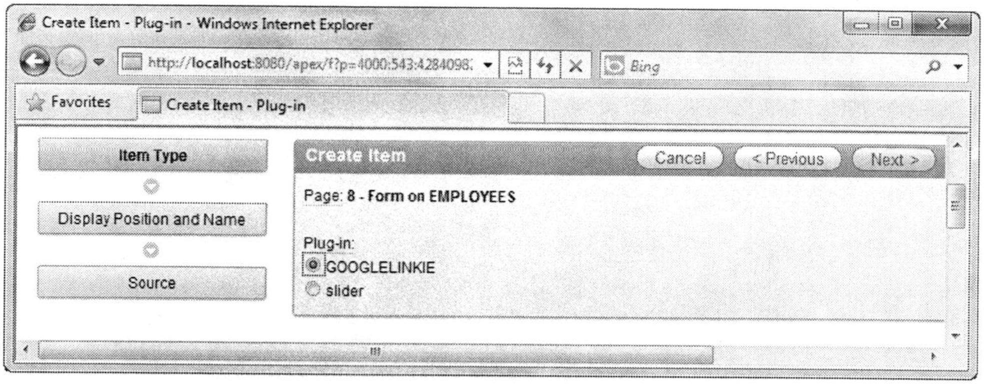

Figure 4-31. Choosing the GOOGLELINKIE plug-in

5. Complete the rest of the wizard using the default settings to create the page item.

6. Now run your application. You can see your control show up in the form ("Jump to Google") shown in Figure 4-32. Clicking on it will bring you to the Google web page.

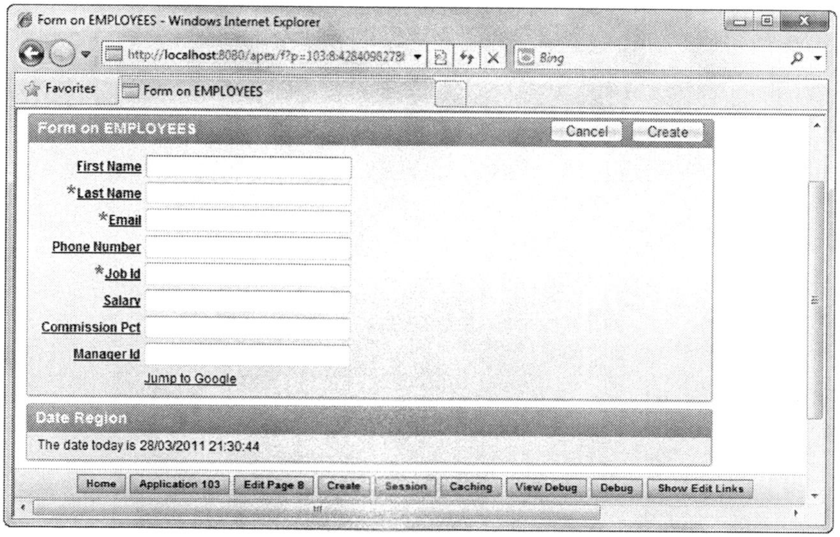

Figure 4-32. The Google Linkie plug-in in action

How It Works

Plug-ins are a way to extend the existing control toolset in APEX. The anatomy of a plug-in is quite straightforward. You supply a PL/SQL function for the plug-in, and that function is used to render the HTML (and accompanying JavaScript) for the control.

If you take a closer look at the PL/SQL function you specified earlier, you can see a statement that looks like the following:

```
htp.p('<a href="http://www.google.com">Jump to Google</a>');
```

Note that htp is a package that allows you to write HTML output from your plug-in. Using this function, you can render any HTML or JavaScript necessary to achieve the functionality you wish in your plug-in.

Using the plug-in framework in APEX, you can build an extensive set of functionality-rich and reusable plug-ins that you can share among your colleagues (or even sell online!).

CHAPTER 5

Visualizing Your Data

One of the key areas in which APEX really shines is its ability to create many different views to visualize the data in your database. If you have at least one numerical field in your table, you can massage your data to create vivid pie, doughnut, bar or candlestick charts that are either static or animated. If you have at least one date or time field in your table, you can magically populate your records on a calendar using that field. If you have a bunch of sales data, you can display it on top of each country on a beautiful high resolution map.

The rich platform that is APEX allows you to create (in a matter of minutes) hundreds of new ways to look at your data—something you wouldn't usually be able to pull off on your own in traditional programming. (Try writing your own animated chart engine or map renderer!)

The neat thing is that views in APEX are also considered pages, so they conform to the rest of the APEX architecture, which means you can apply templates, themes, processes, behavior, and so on to these pages. This chapter focuses on how to set up and use some of the basic views in APEX. By the end of the chapter, you will have an idea of the different type of views available in APEX.

5-1. Creating a Classic Report

Problem

You have two tables: an employee table and an employee leave table. You need to extract information from both tables and present it in a static report. In other words, you need to create a tabular read-only report combining data from multiple tables in the database.

Solution

This solution consists of two steps. You must first create the sample objects (that will be used for the other recipes in this chapter). After that you will create the report itself.

Step 1: Creating the Sample Objects

The sample objects you will create are the employee and employee leave tables. Execute the code shown in Listing 5-1 using the SQL Workshop.

Listing 5-1. Creating the Sample Objects

```
CREATE table "EMPLOYEES" (
    "EMPID"          NVARCHAR2(10),
    "EMPNAME"        NVARCHAR2(255),
    "EMPTITLE"       NVARCHAR2(255),
    "EMPDEPARTMENT" NVARCHAR2(255),
    constraint  "EMPLOYEES_PK" primary key ("EMPID")
)
/

CREATE TABLE  "EMPLEAVE"
(   "EMPID" NVARCHAR2(50),
    "LEAVEDATE" DATE,
    "LEAVETYPE" NVARCHAR2(255),
    "LEAVEREASON" NVARCHAR2(255),
    "LEAVEID" NVARCHAR2(50),
    CONSTRAINT "EMPLEAVE_PK" PRIMARY KEY ("LEAVEID") ENABLE
)
/

INSERT INTO EMPLOYEES(EMPID,EMPNAME,EMPTITLE,EMPDEPARTMENT) VALUES('E1','Janet
Harris','CFO','Finance')
/
INSERT INTO EMPLOYEES(EMPID,EMPNAME,EMPTITLE,EMPDEPARTMENT) VALUES('E2','Greg Yap','Senior
Developer','IT')
/
INSERT INTO EMPLEAVE(EMPID,LEAVEDATE,LEAVETYPE,LEAVEREASON,LEAVEID)
VALUES('E1',TO_DATE('20090329', 'YYYYMMDD'),'Sick Leave','Flu','L1')
/
INSERT INTO EMPLEAVE(EMPID,LEAVEDATE,LEAVETYPE,LEAVEREASON,LEAVEID)
VALUES('E1',TO_DATE('20100517', 'YYYYMMDD'),'Maternity Leave','Maternity','L2')
/
INSERT INTO EMPLEAVE(EMPID,LEAVEDATE,LEAVETYPE,LEAVEREASON,LEAVEID)
VALUES('E2',TO_DATE('20090314', 'YYYYMMDD'),'Emergency leave','To visit a dying friend','L3')
/
```

Step 2: Creating the Report

To create the classic report, follow these instructions:

1. Create a new application, and choose to create a new page in this application.

2. Choose the Report page type.

3. In the next step of the wizard, choose the Classic Report type, as shown in
   Figure 5-1.

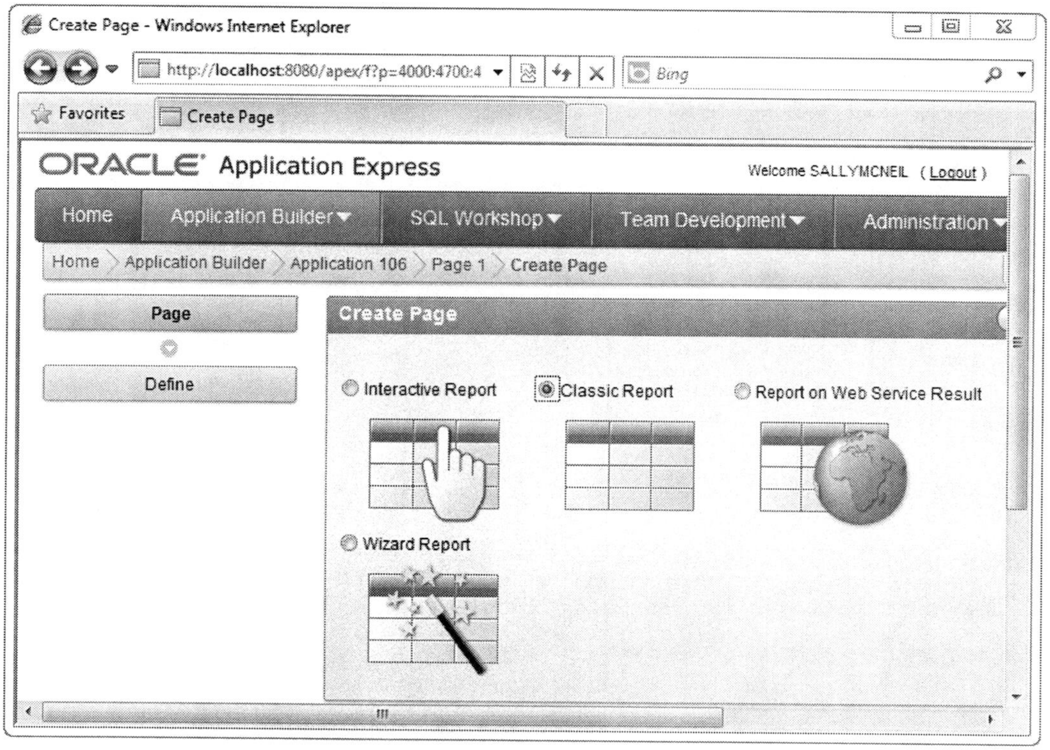

Figure 5-1. The Classic Report

4. Next, specify a name for your report. After you've done that, skip past the next step. You will now be allowed to enter the SQL statement for the report. Specify the SQL statement shown in Listing 5-2.

Listing 5-2. Specifying the SQL for the Classic Report

```
SELECT * FROM EMPLOYEES LEFT JOIN EMPLEAVE ON EMPLOYEES.EMPID=EMPLEAVE.EMPID
```

You should now see the screenshot shown in Figure 5-2.

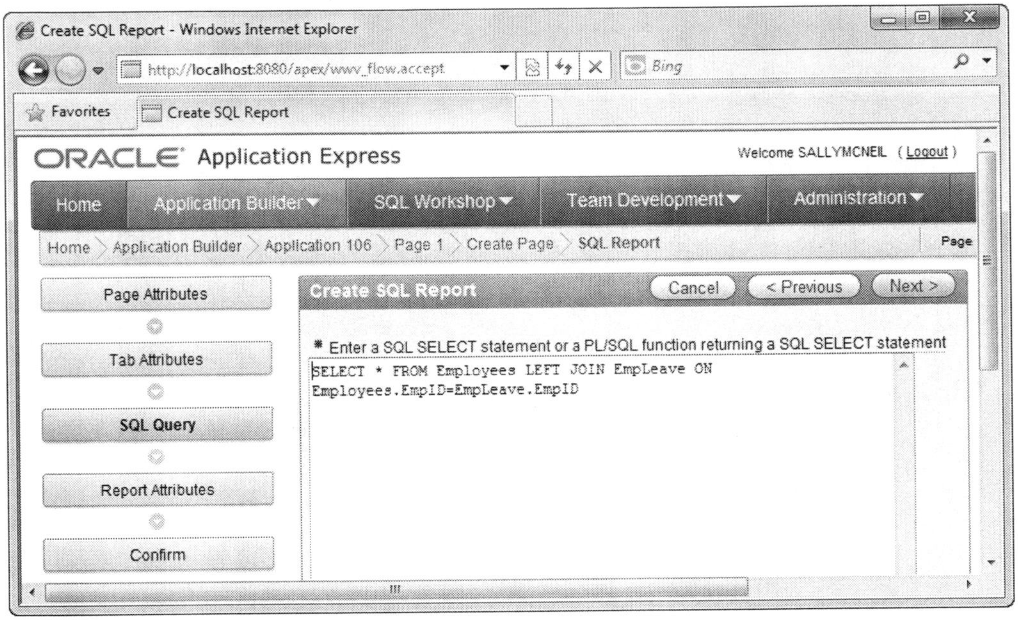

Figure 5-2. *Specifying the SQL for the classic report*

5.   Click through the rest of the wizard until the end.

6.   Run the report. You should see the list of combined data as displayed in Figure
5-3.

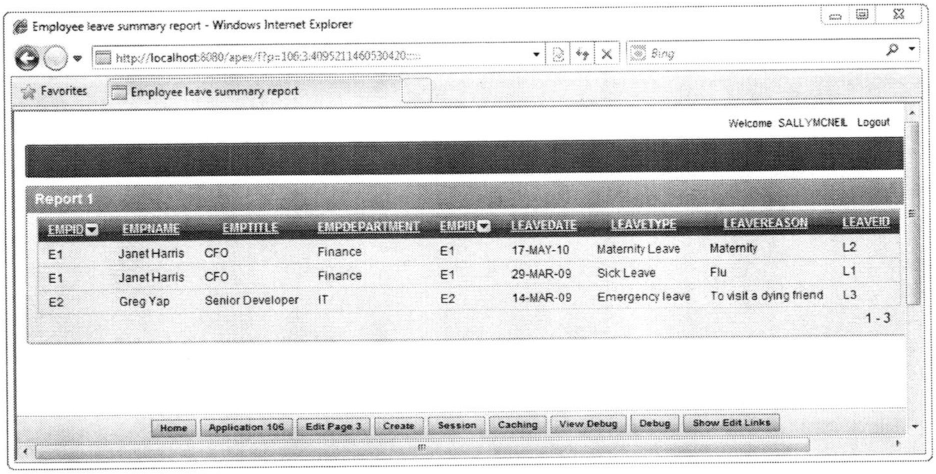

Figure 5-3. *The classic report in action*

How It Works

You first encountered reports in Chapter 2. There are basically two types of reports: Interactive Reports and Classic Reports. Classic Reports are static—they simply display information—while Interactive Reports allow you to interact with the information. Both reports can combine results from more than one table, as shown in this recipe.

5-2. Creating Parameterized Reports

Problem

Your management wants to be able to dynamically filter the information shown in their reports. Using the sample data from Recipe 5-1, your management wants to be able to narrow down to the list of leave records for a specific employee.

▒ **Note** If you haven't already done so, please execute Listing 5-1 to create the sample data used for this recipe.

Solution

To create a parameterized report, follow these instructions:

1. Open an application and choose to create a new page.

2. Choose the Report page type in the first step of the wizard, as shown in Figure 5-4.

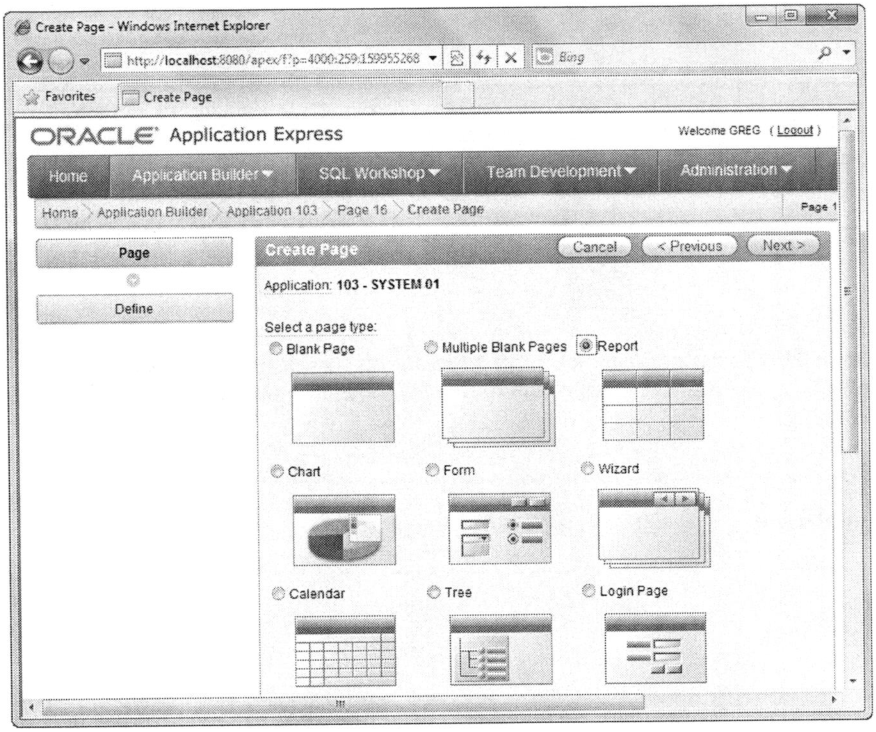

Figure 5-4. The report page type

3. In the next step, choose the Interactive Report type.

4. Skip through all the steps in the wizard until you reach the step that allows you to specify the SQL statement for the report. When you reach this step, specify the SQL shown in Listing 5-3.

Listing 5-3. Specifying the SQL for the Interactive Report

```
SELECT e1.EmpName, e1.EmpTitle, e1.EmpDepartment, e2.LeaveDate, e2.LeaveType, e2.LeaveReason,
e2.LeaveID FROM Employees e1 LEFT JOIN EmpLeave e2 ON e1.EmpID=e2.EmpID
```

5. In the same step, select Unique Column for the Uniquely Identify Rows by field, and LeaveID for the Unique Column field. You should now have the screen shown in Figure 5-5. Click Next to continue.

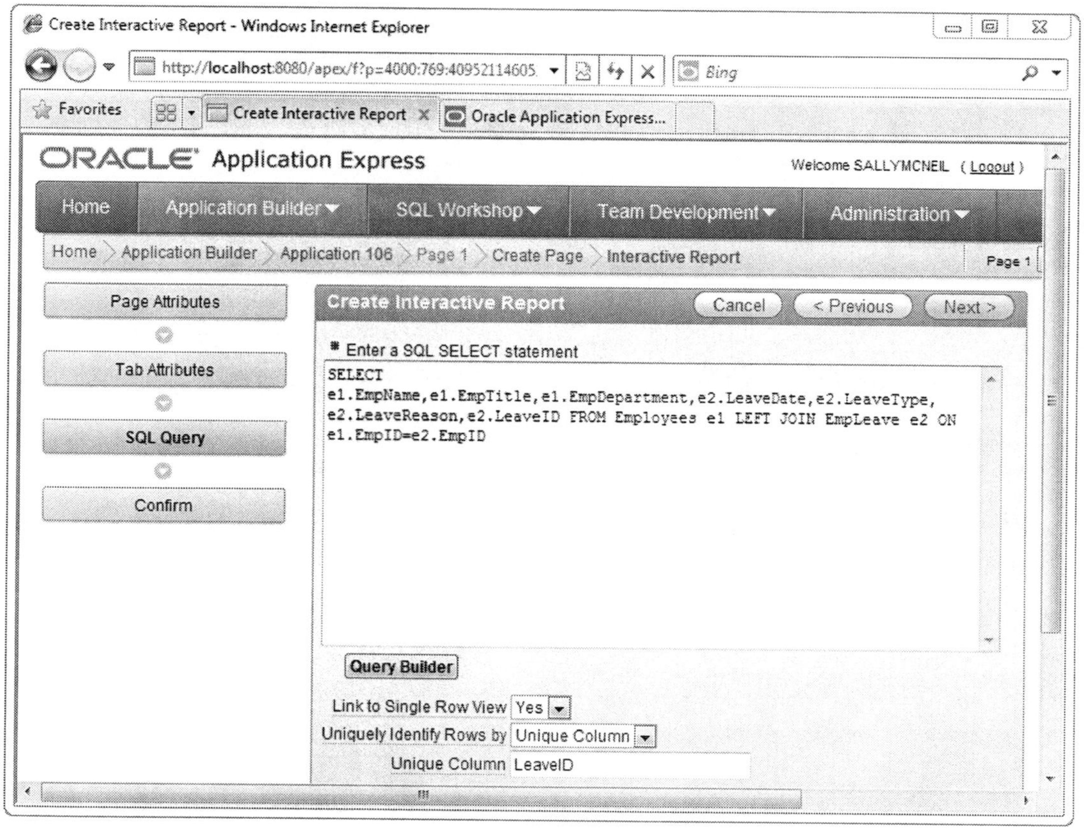

Figure 5-5. Specifying the SQL for the Interactive Report

6. Skip to the last step to complete the wizard. Now run your report. You should see the list of data you saw in Recipe 5-1, with the addition of a new search bar at the top of the list.

7. Click the magnifying glass icon in the search bar and choose the Empname entry, as shown in Figure 5-6.

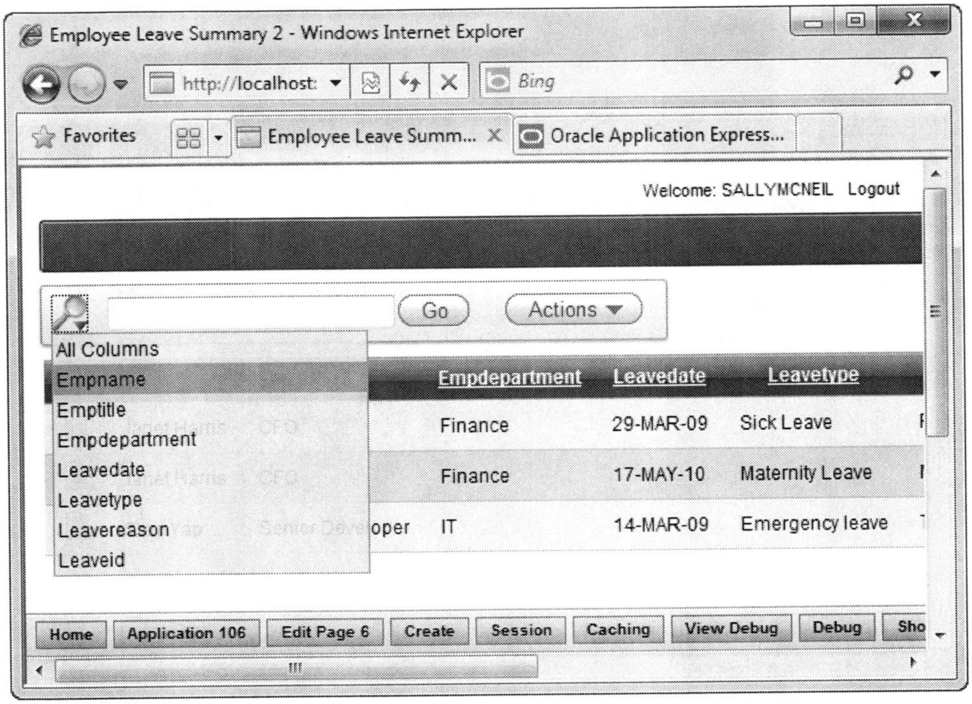

Figure 5-6. Searching by employee name

8. Once you have done that, the search bar now allows you to search by employee name. Key in Janet, and click Enter to begin the search. The list of results shown in the report is now filtered to show only those entries that match your search criteria (see Figure 5-7).

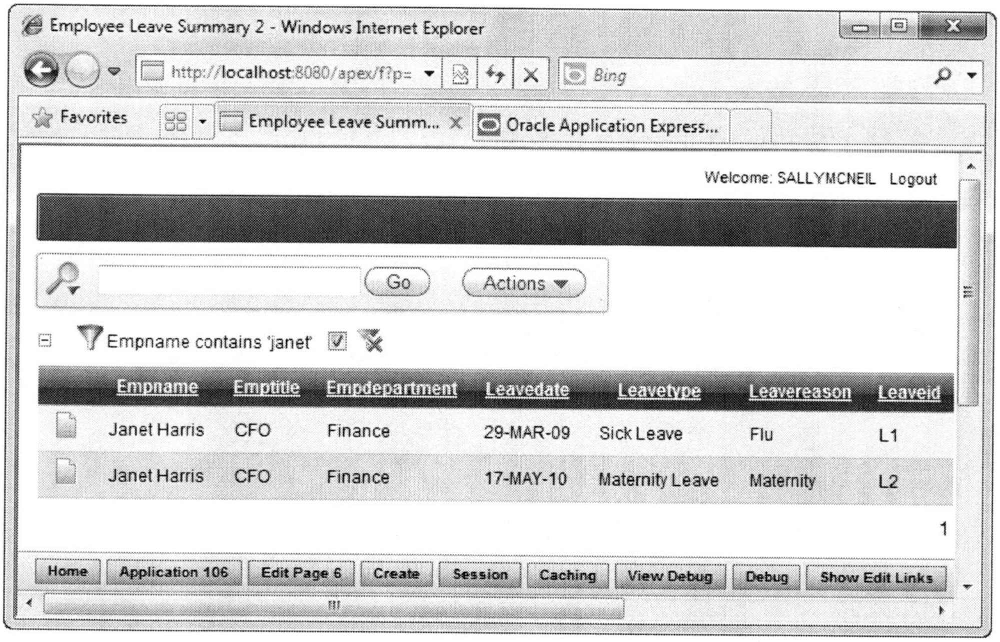

Figure 5-7. *The filtered list of results*

How It Works

Interactive Reports come with a built-in search bar that allows end users to quickly and dynamically apply filters on the list of results shown in the report. In this recipe, you can see how you were able to switch the mode of the search bar to make the report search using a particular field, in this case the Employee name field.

5-3. Visualizing Data in Graphical Charts

Problem

You wish to present data in the form of a chart so that you can analyze the data at a glance. For example, you wish to analyze the frequency of leave taken for each employee—and you want to visualize this information in the form of a 3D pie chart.

▓ **Note** If you haven't already done so, please execute Listing 5-1 to create the sample data used for this recipe.

Solution

To create a page to view your data in a 3D pie chart, follow these instructions:

1. Open an application and choose to create a new page.

2. Choose the Chart page type in the first page of the wizard, as shown in Figure 5-8.

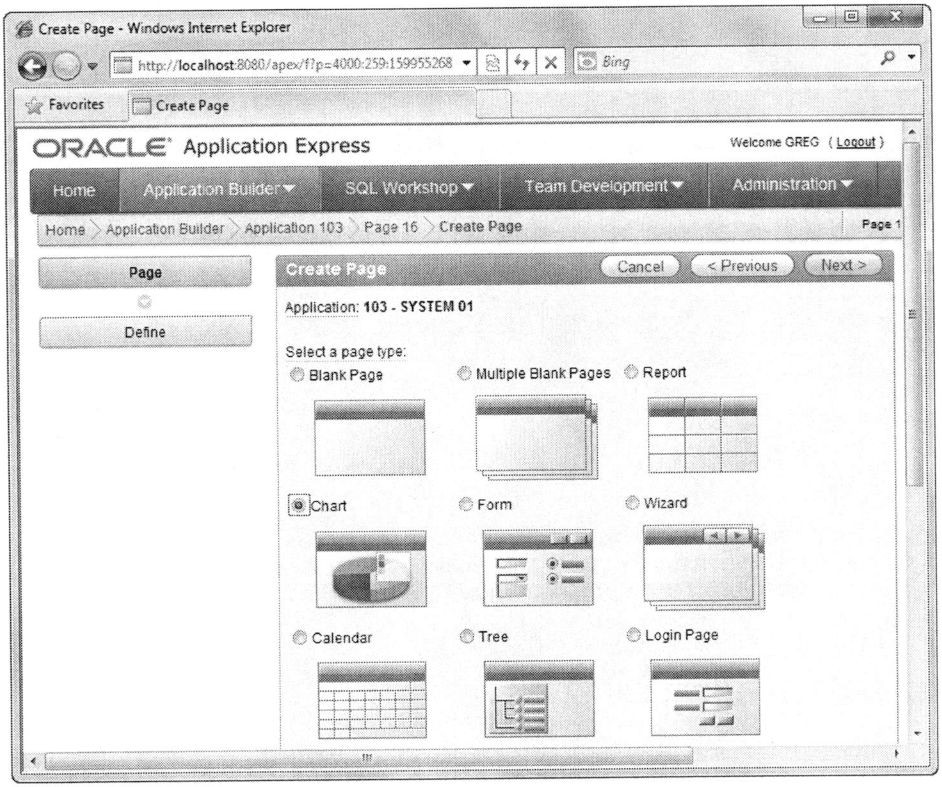

Figure 5-8. The chart page type

3. In the next step, choose Flash Chart.

4. In the following step, you need to specify the type of chart you wish to use. Choose the Pie & Doughnut chart type.

5. In the next step, you are yet again presented with a choice of charts, as shown in Figure 5-9. Choose the 3D pie chart.

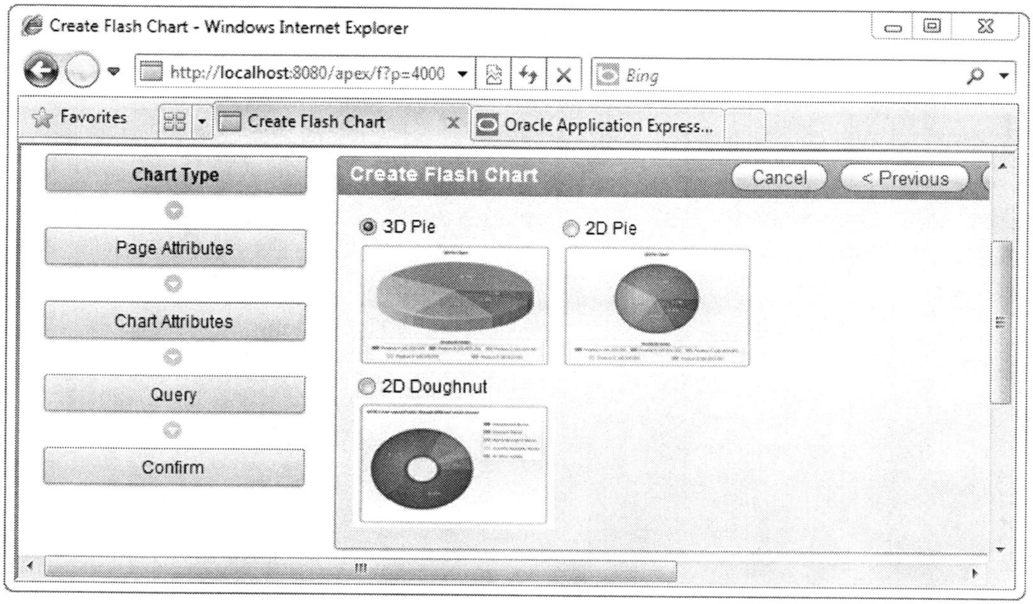

Figure 5-9. Choosing the 3D pie chart

6. Specify Employee Leave Frequency as the name of your page in the next step of the wizard.

7. Click through the next step. You will now be requested to specify the chart title and animation style. Specify Employee Leave Frequency as the Chart Title and Side From Left for the Chart Animation field, as shown in Figure 5-10.

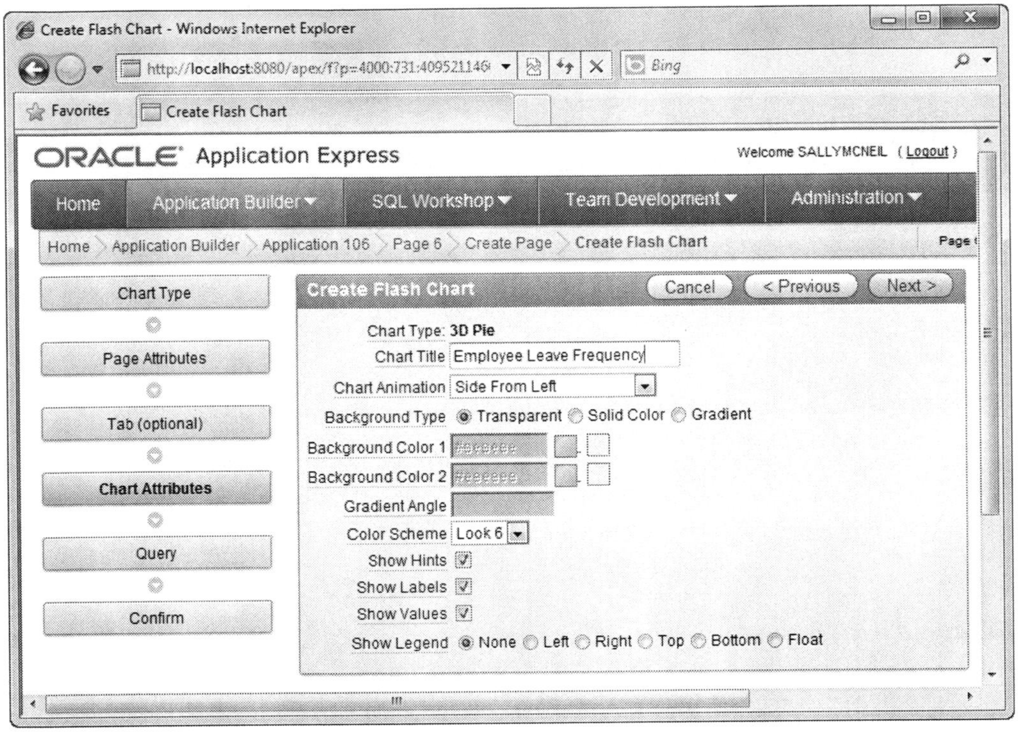

Figure 5-10. Specifying the chart settings

8. In the next step, you will specify the SQL statement that returns a dataset used to render the chart; use the code in Listing 5-4.

Listing 5-4. Specifying the SQL for the Chart

```
SELECT '',EmpName,count(*) FROM Employees INNER JOIN EmpLeave ON
    Employees.EmpID=EmpLeave.EmpID GROUP BY EmpName
```

9. You should see the screen shown in Figure 5-11.

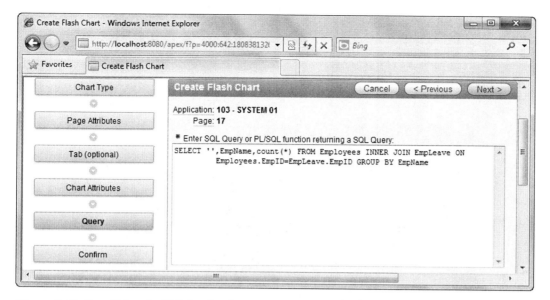

Figure 5-11. Specifying the SQL for the chart

10. Complete the wizard and run the chart page. You should see a nice animated pie chart showing the frequency of leave taken for each employee (see Figure 5-12).

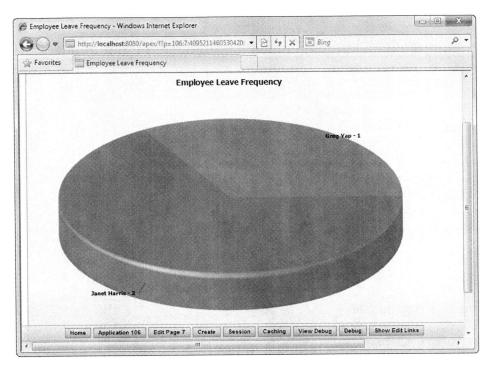

Figure 5-12. The animated chart

How It Works

The concept behind most views in APEX is similar: the heart of a view consists of the SQL statement that you feed it. APEX simply takes the dataset resulting from the SQL query (the dataset is expected to be in a certain format) and displays it appropriately.

Chart views are no different conceptually from any other view. For pie charts specifically, APEX always expects the second field in the SQL query to be the label that is displayed on the chart for the series. The third field is the numerical value for that series.

▓ **Note** The format of the SQL query differs for different types of charts. You can always refer to the sample SQL scripts provided in the same SQL definition page in the wizard. (APEX is nice enough to provide hints in their wizards.)

5-4. Visualizing Data in a Multi-Series Chart

Problem

Your boss has tasked you to retrieve two series of data (global and local sales) and have the amounts displayed in a single chart. You instantly recognize that your boss wants to look at a multi-series chart but you're unsure how to proceed.

Solution

To create a multi-series chart, you will first need to create the sample table and data used for this recipe. To do so, follow these instructions:

1. Run the following SQL to create the COMPANYSALES table and the corresponding data:

```
CREATE TABLE  "COMPANYSALES"
    (    "ID" NVARCHAR2(50),
         "GLOBALREVENUE" NUMBER(9,2),
         "LOCALREVENUE" NUMBER(9,2),
         "PRODUCT" NVARCHAR2(255),
          CONSTRAINT "COMPANYSALES_PK" PRIMARY KEY ("ID") ENABLE
    )
/

INSERT INTO "COMPANYSALES" ("ID","GLOBALREVENUE","LOCALREVENUE","PRODUCT")
VALUES(1,1000,2000,'CAR ENGINES')
/
INSERT INTO "COMPANYSALES" ("ID","GLOBALREVENUE","LOCALREVENUE","PRODUCT")
VALUES(2,1500,1900,'SAILBOATS')
/
INSERT INTO "COMPANYSALES" ("ID","GLOBALREVENUE","LOCALREVENUE","PRODUCT")
VALUES(3,200,4000,'BIKES')
/
```

To setup the multi-series chart, follow these instructions:

1. Open an existing application and choose to create a new page.

2. Choose the Chart page type.

3. In the next page of the wizard, choose the Flash chart type.

4. In the next page, choose the Column chart type, as shown in Figure 5-13.

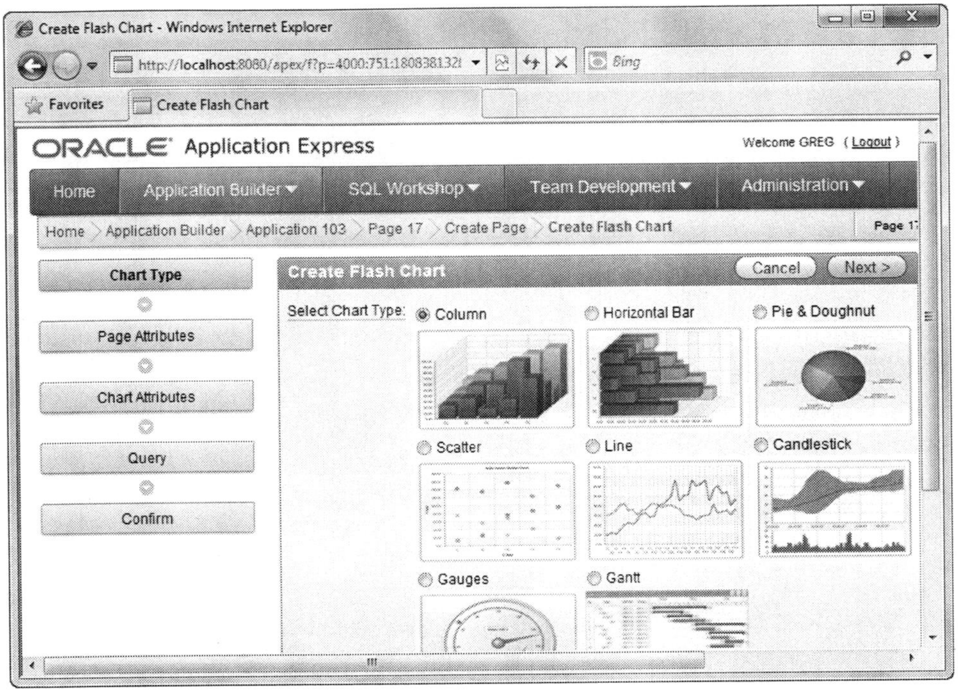

Figure 5-13. *The column flash chart type*

5. In the next page, choose the 3D Stacked Column chart type, as shown in Figure 5-14.

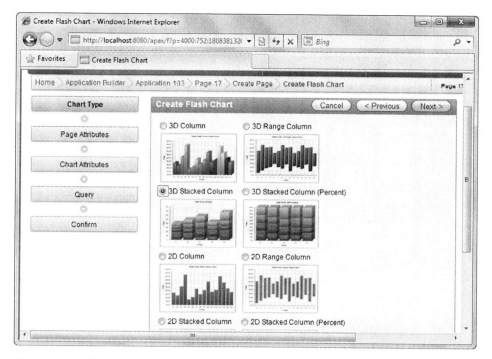

Figure 5-14. *The 3D Stacked Column chart type*

6. Skip the next two steps of the wizard. In the Chart Attributes step, specify the title for the chart as Global & Local Sales Summary, as shown in Figure 5-15.

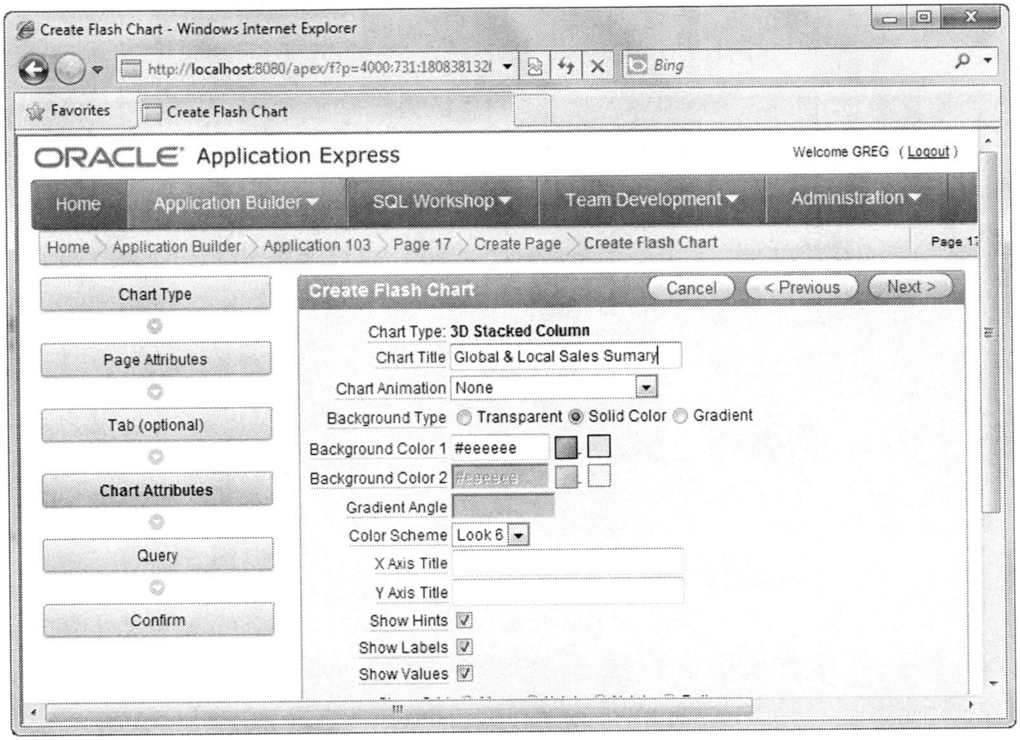

Figure 5-15. *Specifying the chart title*

7. In the next step, specify the following SQL datasource query for the chart:

```
SELECT NULL , PRODUCT, LOCALREVENUE, GLOBALREVENUE FROM COMPANYSALES
```

8. You should now see the screenshot shown in Figure 5-16.

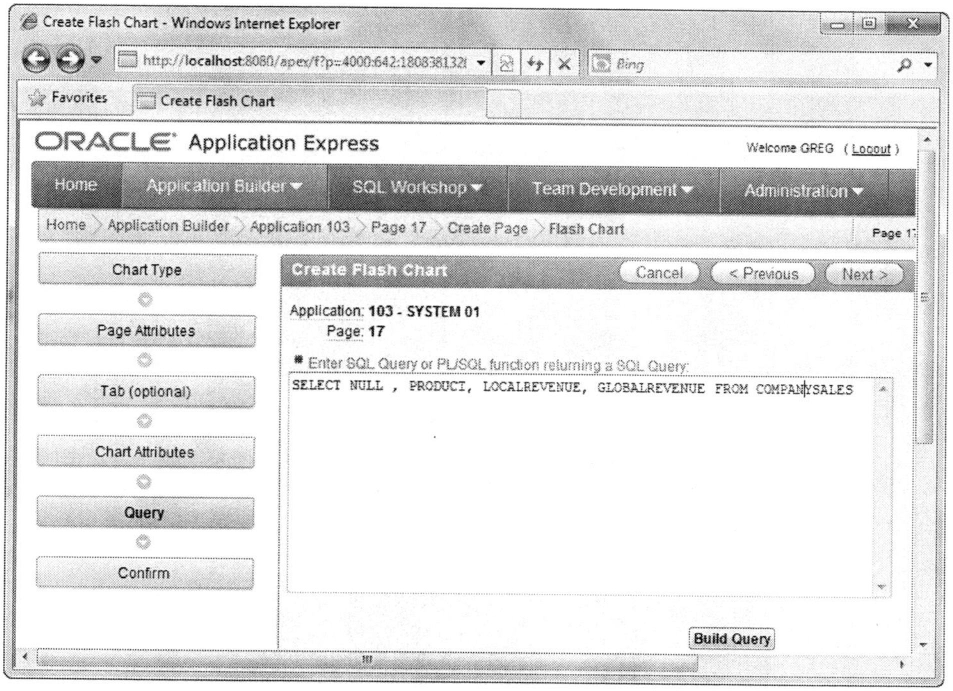

Figure 5-16. Specifying the SQL data source for the chart

9. Complete the wizard and run the form. You should see the multi-series chart shown in Figure 5-17.

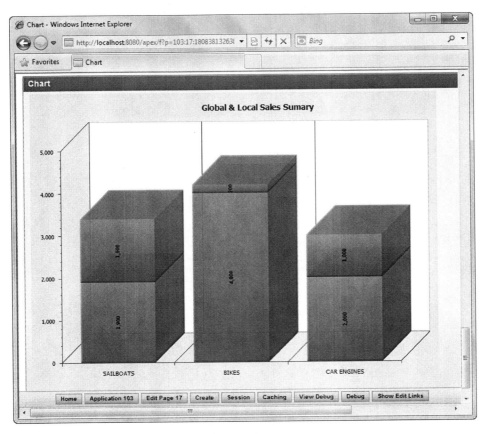

Figure 5-17. The multi-series bar chart in action

How It Works

APEX supports multi-series charts and they are easy to configure. Let's examine the SQL you used for the chart.

```
SELECT NULL , PRODUCT, LOCALREVENUE, GLOBALREVENUE FROM COMPANYSALES
```

The first SQL field denotes a link (this allows you to specify a hyperlink URL to apply on each bar in the chart such that when you click on it, you can either drill-down further into yet another chart or be redirected to an entirely different page.

The second SQL field allows you to specify the label for the chart. As you can see in Figure 5-15, the label captions are displayed at the bottom of each bar.

The third, fourth, and nth fields in the SQL statement denote the values to use for each series of data. In this recipe, for instance, the LOCALREVENUE and GLOBALREVENUE fields form the first and second series of data for the chart.

5-5. Visualizing Data on a Calendar

Problem

You want to see data plotted on a calendar. The report you've created to display the employee leave records is great, but you need to visualize it in a more intuitive manner. You wish to have the records displayed in a calendar based on the leave date of each individual record.

▨ **Note** If you haven't already done so, please execute Listing 5-1 to create the sample data used for this recipe.

Solution

Here are the steps to follow to create a page to view your data on a calendar:

1. To run the sample in this recipe, you need to first add a new record to the EmpLeave table. Run the query shown in Listing 5-5 via SQL workshop. Take note to change the date of the LEAVEDATE in this query to reflect the current month and year.

Listing 5-5. Inserting an Additional Sample Record

```
INSERT INTO EMPLEAVE(EMPID,LEAVEDATE,LEAVETYPE,LEAVEREASON,LEAVEID)
VALUES('E1',TO_DATE('20110110', 'YYYYMMDD'),'Maternity Leave','Maternity','L4')
```

2. Open an application and choose to create a new page.

3. Choose the Calendar page type in the first page of the wizard, as shown in Figure 5-18.

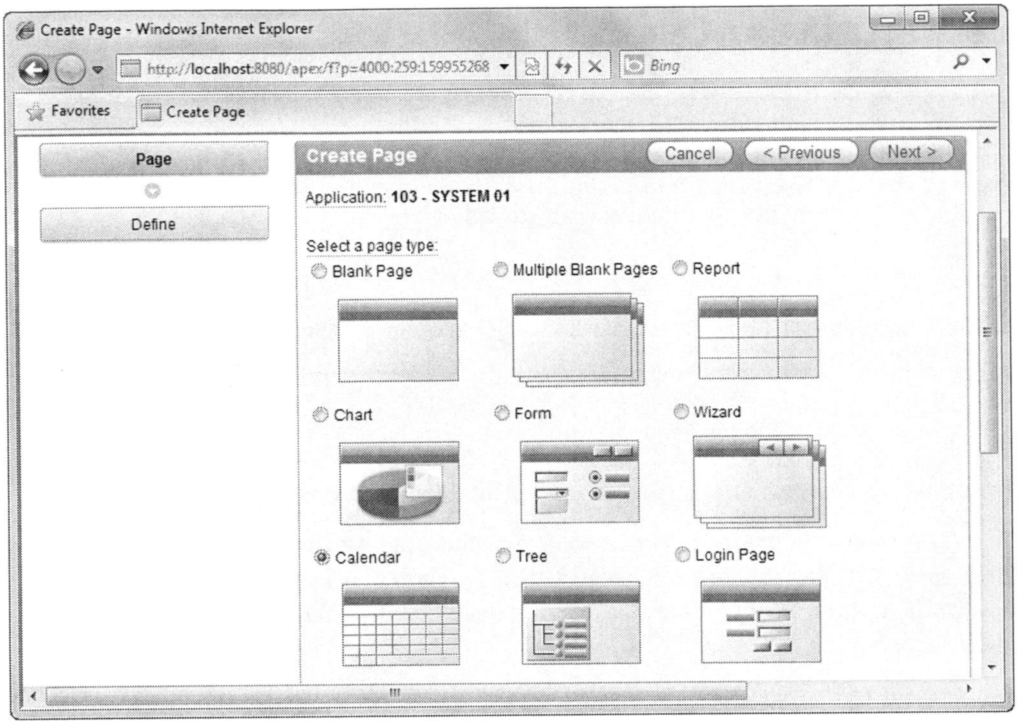

Figure 5-18. The Calendar page type

4. In the next step, choose SQL calendar.

5. Specify Employee Leave calendar as the name of your page.

6. Click through the next step. You will now see an area where you can define the SQL for the calendar; specify the SQL shown in Listing 5-6.

Listing 5-6. Specifying the SQL for the Calendar

```
SELECT EmpName, Leavedate FROM Employees,EmpLeave WHERE Employees.EmpID=EmpLeave.EmpID
```

7.You should now see the screen shown in Figure 5-19.

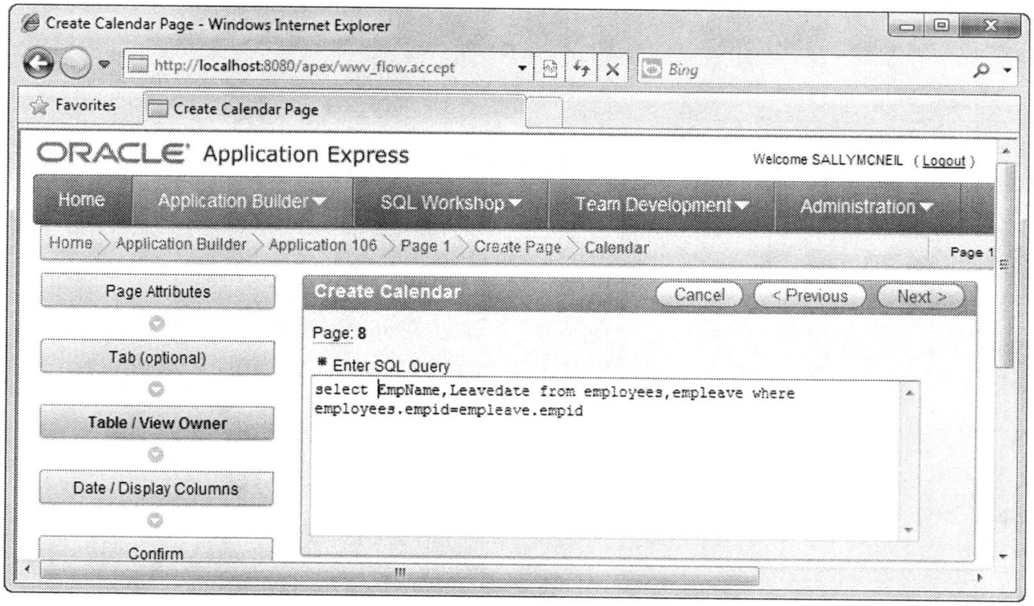

Figure 5-19. Specifying the SQL for the calendar

8. In the next step, you will be asked to specify the database field to use for the date column and the display column. Select LEAVEDATE for the date column and EMPNAME for the display column.

9. Navigate to the end of the wizard and run your calendar page. You should see the record you've just created show up in the calendar, as shown in Figure 5-20.

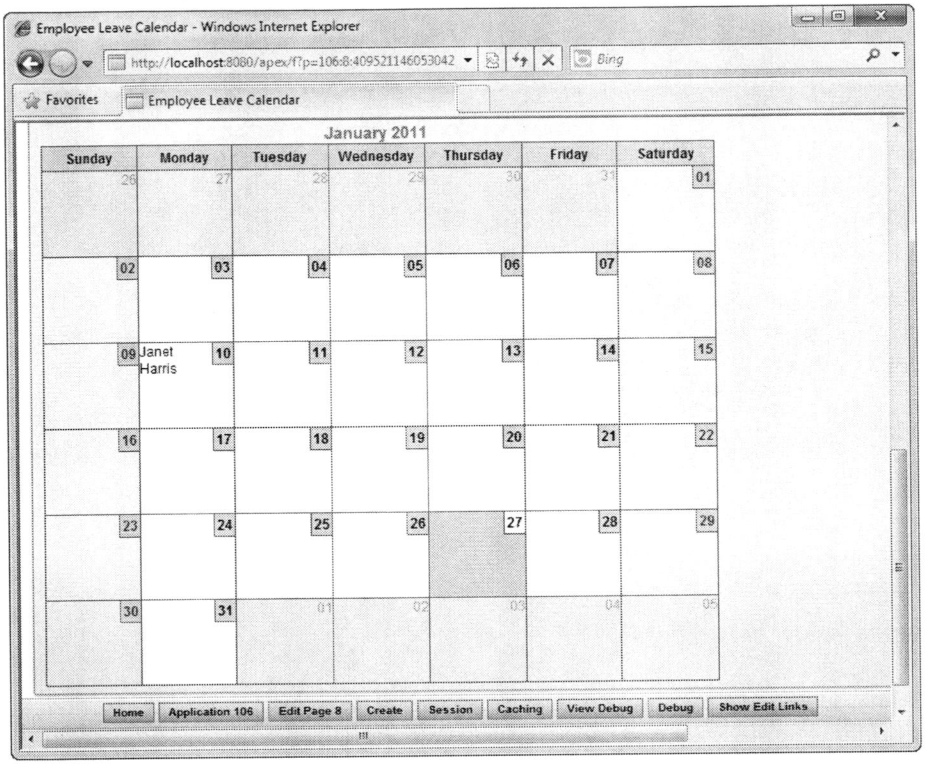

Figure 5-20. *The calendar in action*

How It Works

Calendar views are also similar to chart views in the sense that the SQL you specify has to adhere to a specific format. In the calendar view case, the first field in the SQL query refers to the label that will be displayed on the calendar while the second field in the query refers to the date field that is used to populate your records on the calendar.

5-6. Visualizing Data on a Map

Problem

You have a database table containing the total sales data for a number of countries in Europe. Your boss wants you to have that data populated on top of a map of Europe. You have less than a day to get it done and you are not sure how to proceed.

Solution

To create a visual map on your page, you must first set up the sales data sample table used in this recipe. To do so, follow these instructions:

1. Create the sample sales table by running the SQL shown in Listing 5-7.

Listing 5-7. Ccreating the Sample SalesData Table

```
CREATE TABLE  "SALESDATA"
   (    "SALES" NUMBER(9,2),
        "ID" NVARCHAR2(50),
        "COUNTRY" NVARCHAR2(255),
         CONSTRAINT "SALESDATA_PK" PRIMARY KEY ("ID") ENABLE
   )

INSERT INTO SALESDATA(SALES,ID,COUNTRY) VALUES(5000,1,'UNITED KINGDOM')

INSERT INTO SALESDATA(SALES,ID,COUNTRY) VALUES(6000,2,'IRELAND')

INSERT INTO SALESDATA(SALES,ID,COUNTRY) VALUES(6780,3,'FRANCE')
```

To create a map to display the data from the SalesData table, follow these instructions:

1. Open an existing application and choose to create a new page. Choose the Map page type in the first page of the wizard, as shown in Figure 5-21.

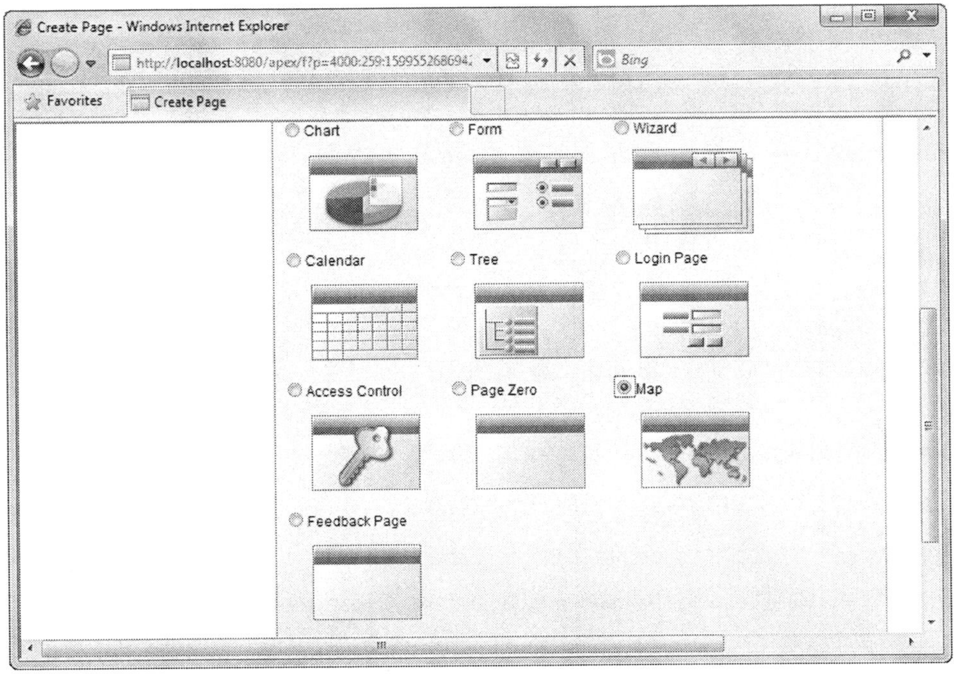

Figure 5-21. The Map page type

2. In the next page of the wizard, choose the World and Continent Maps item shown in Figure 5-22. We choose this map instead of the European maps collection because we want a map that displays all the European countries in a single view. The European maps collection displays single European countries.

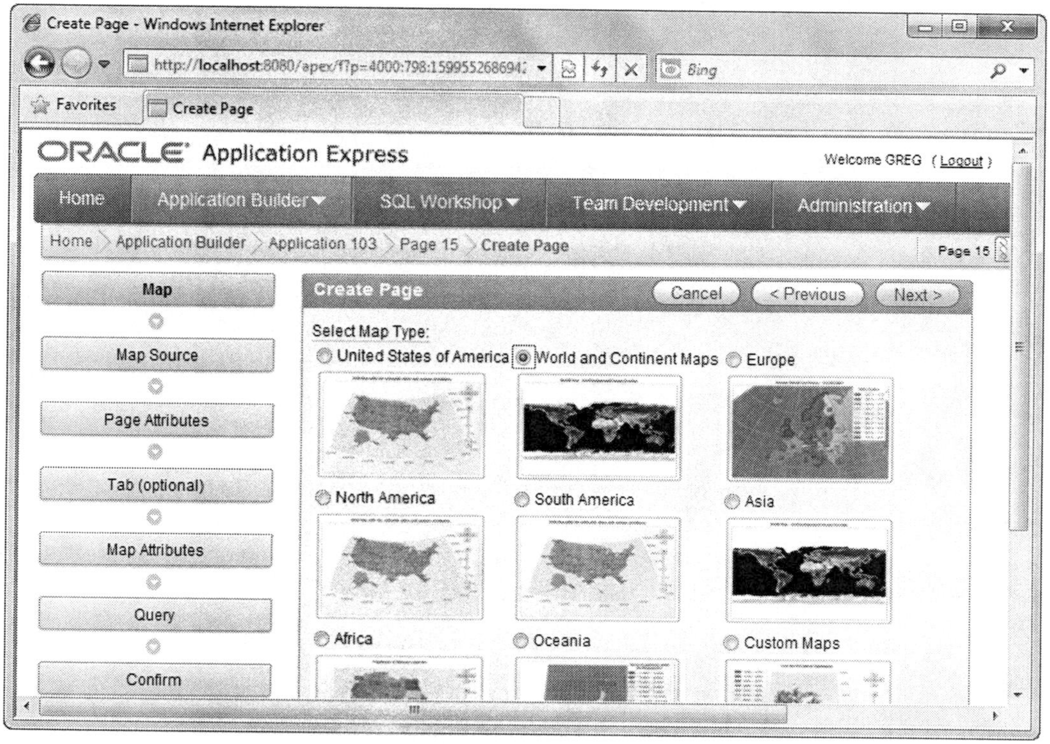

Figure 5-22. The World and Continent Maps package

3. In the next page, choose the Europe (without Russia) map shown in Figure 5-23. Of course, you may choose the Europe map if you have data that includes sales statistics for Russia.

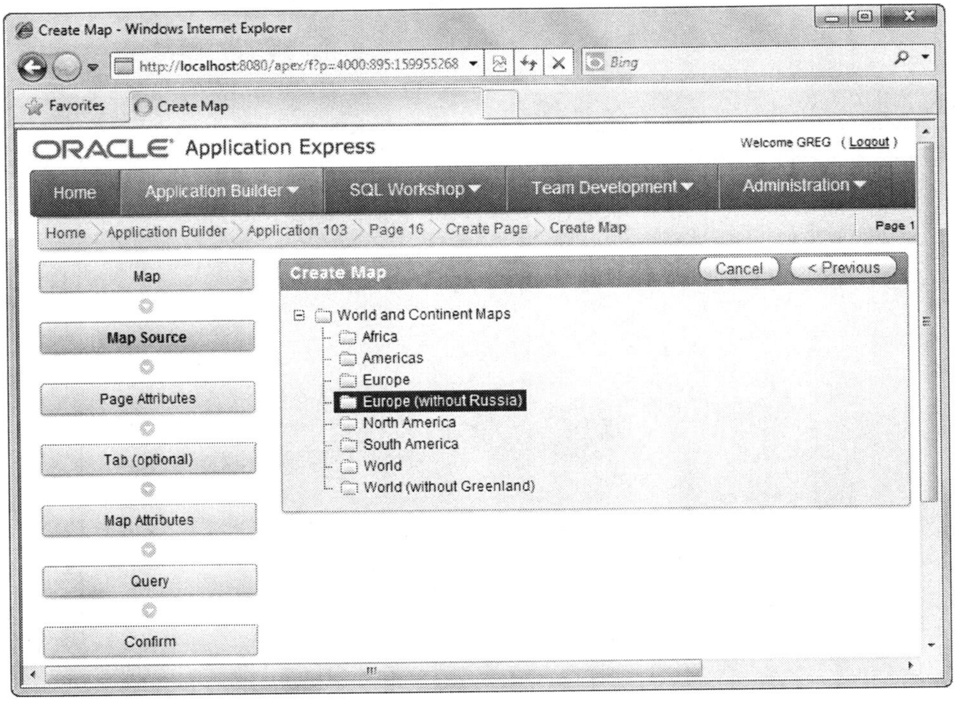

Figure 5-23. The Europe (without Russia) map

4. Skip past the next two pages of the wizard.

5. At the Map Attributes step of the wizard, specify a map title (such as ACME EUROPEAN SALES).

6. In the next page of the wizard, specify the following SQL query:

```
SELECT NULL LINK, COUNTRY, SUM(SALES) FROM SALESDATA GROUP BY COUNTRY
```

7. You should now see the screen shown in Figure 5-24.

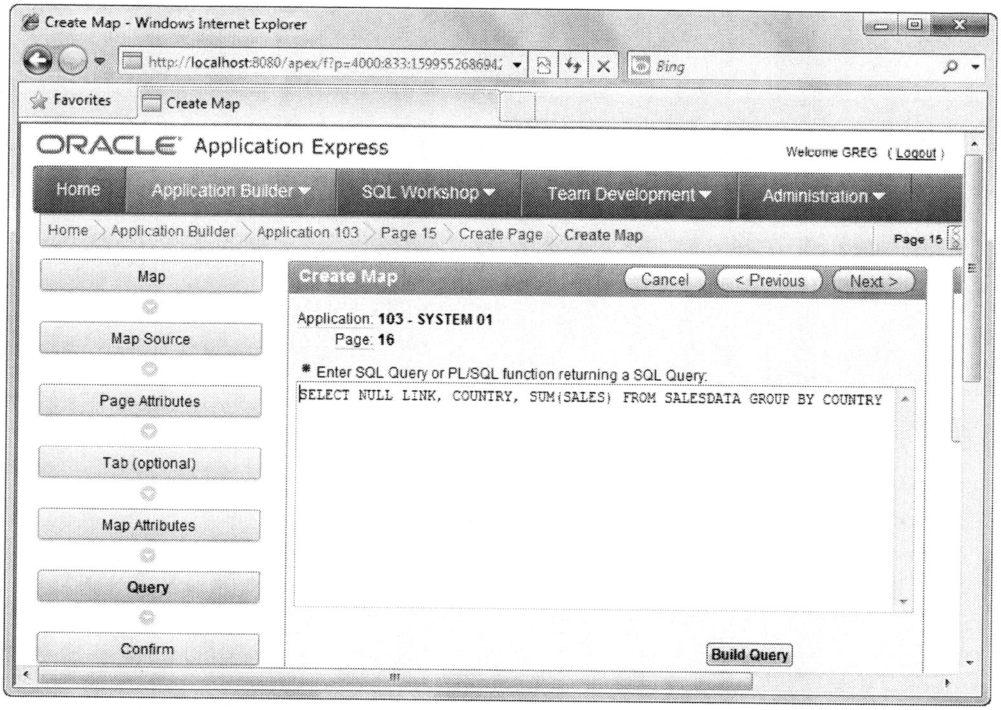

CHAPTER 5 VISUALIZING YOUR DATA

Figure 5-24. Specifying the datasource for the map

8. Skip the next step of the wizard and click the Finish button to create the map.

9. Run the page. You should see the map with your sales data displayed on each corresponding country, as shown in Figure 5-25.

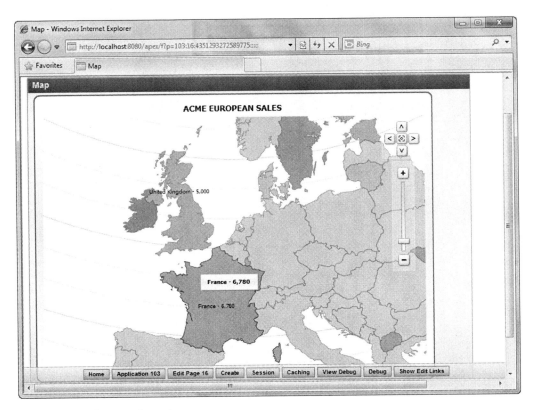

Figure 5-25. The map in action

10. If you mouseover each country, you can see a little tool tip displaying the total sales amount for that country. You can also zoom in/zoom out and pan the map using the navigation tools at the right.

How It Works

You can represent data on visual maps packaged with the APEX software. APEX provides a rich set of maps of different parts of the world, and it allows you to overlay statistical data on top of these maps.

You might have noticed that APEX matched your data to the visual maps using the name of the country you've provided. Is it possible, then, to get the full list of country names, state names, or province names that are intrinsically recognized by APEX? APEX uses the third-party AnyMap component to render its maps (and as a sideline note, the AnyCharts component to render its Flash charts). The country names mentioned earlier are actually defined by the AnyMap product. If you navigate to the AnyMap online documentation at http://anychart.com/products/anychart/docs/users-guide/index.html?maps-overview.html and go to Maps ➤ Maps Reference ➤ World ➤ World and Continent Maps ➤ Europe without Russia, you will see the full list of country names for this region (also shown in Figure 5-26).

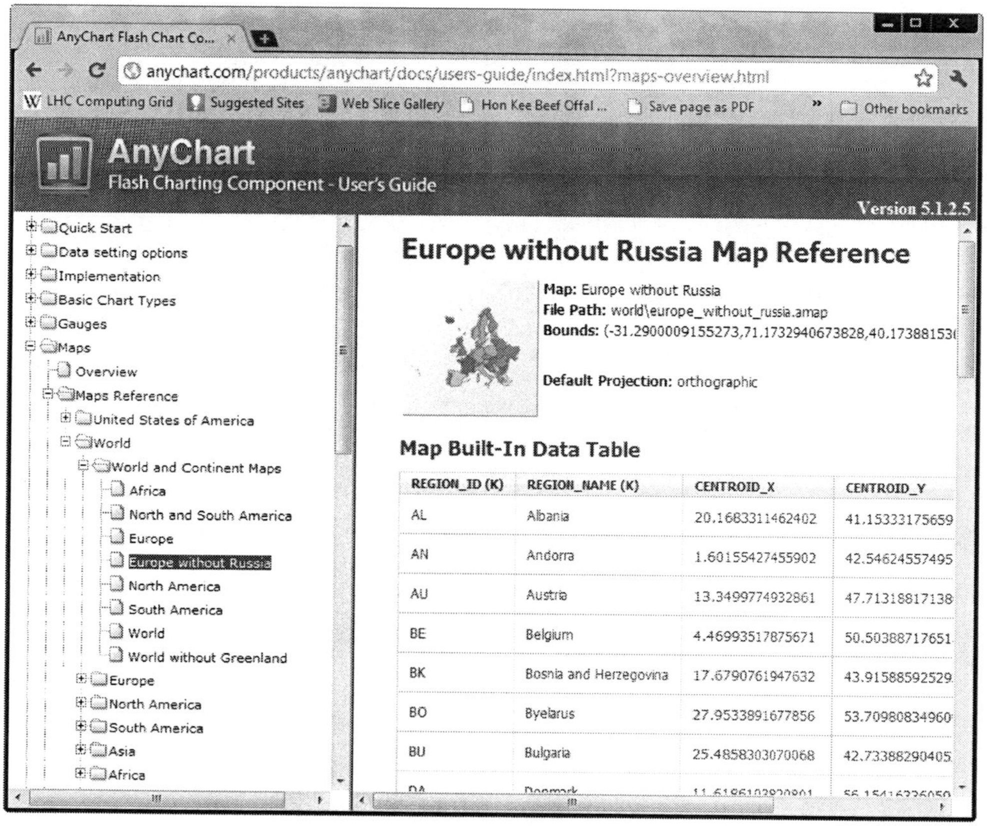

Figure 5-26. AnyMap documentation

> **Note** This type of mapping technology is different compared to, say, Google maps in the sense that these are not navigation maps, nor do they allow positioning of objects on the maps using GPS coordinates. These maps are used more to highlight or complement statistical data (for instance, showing the population of each country, total sales for each province in a country, and so on).

5-7. Putting it all Together into a Dashboard Page

Problem

You need dashboard functionality. You need to display a graphical chart and report for simultaneous viewing on the same page. For example, you'd like to create a dashboard showing employee leave frequency along with a list of all employees, and you want the employee leave frequency displayed as a pie chart.

Solution

To create a dashboard that combines a pie chart and a report, please follow these instructions:

1. Open an application and create a new page.

2. Choose to create a Blank page.

3. When requested, specify HR Dashboard as the name of the page.

4. Click through till the end of the wizard. After the page is created, choose to Edit the page.

5. In the Page Rendering section of the page, right-click on the Regions node and click the Create item in the pop-up menu shown in Figure 5-27.

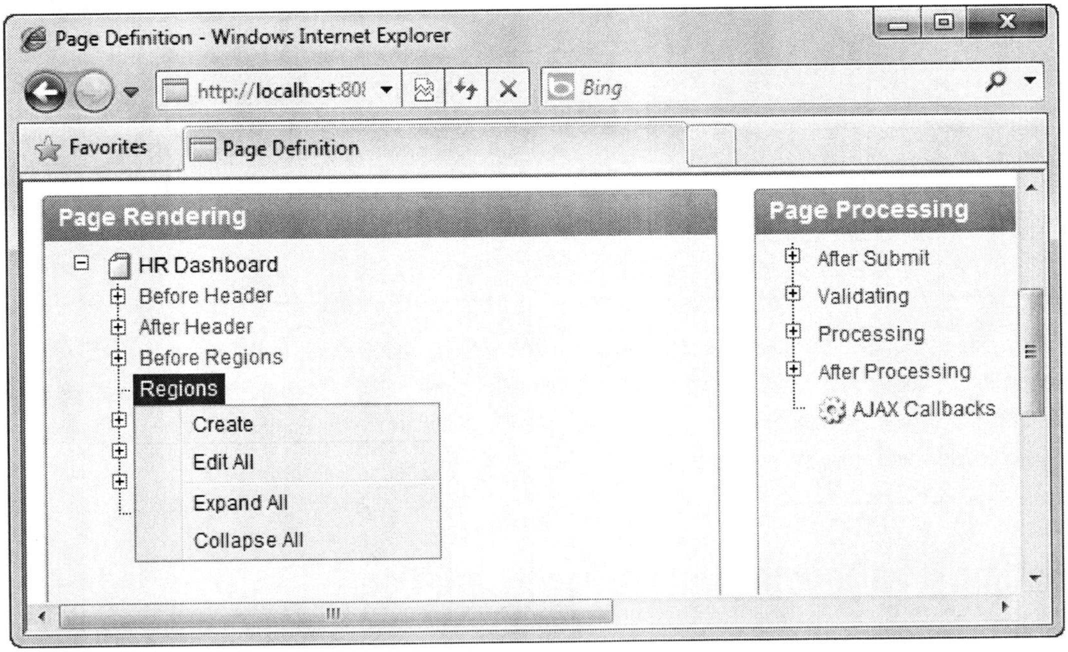

Figure 5-27. Creating a new region

6. In the first step of the wizard that pops up, choose the Chart item. Choose Flash Chart in the next step, then Pie & Doughnut in the next, and finally 3D Pie. Specify Employee Leave Frequency as the title of the region. In the next step of the wizard, specify the same title for the Chart and choose Side from Left for the animation style.

7. When you get to the SQL Statement area, specify the SQL shown in Listing 5-8.

Listing 5-8. Specifying the SQL for the Chart Region

```
SELECT '',EmpName,count(*) FROM Employees INNER JOIN EmpLeave ON
Employees.EmpID=EmpLeave.EmpID GROUP BY EmpName
```

8. Complete the wizard to create the region. You should see your newly created region, as shown in Figure 5-28.

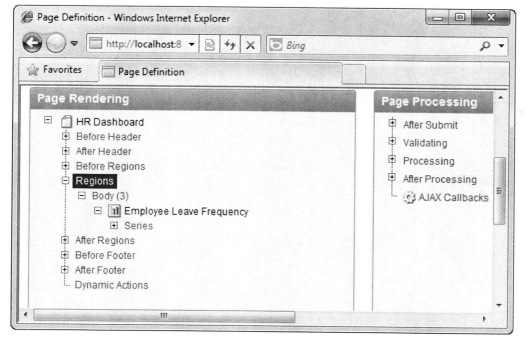

Figure 5-28. The newly created region

9. Now you need to create another region. Right click on the Regions node and choose Create again.

10. This time, choose Report as the region type. Choose the SQL Report type in the next step, and specify the region title as Employee Listing in the following step.

11. When you get to the SQL area, specify the SQL shown in Listing 5-9.

Listing 5-9. *Specifying the SQL for the Report Region*

```
SELECT EMPID, EMPNAME, EMPTITLE, EMPDEPARTMENT FROM Employees
```

12. Complete the wizard to create the region. Now run the page. You should see your pie chart and employee list all in the same page, as shown in Figure 5-29.

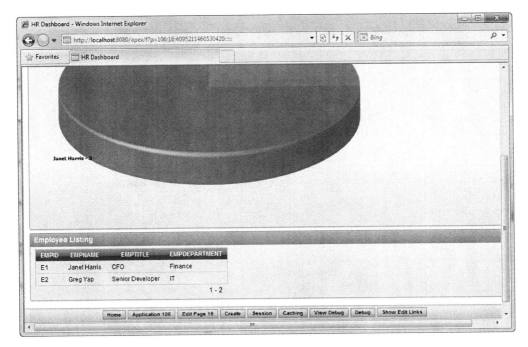

Figure 5-29. *The dashboard in action*

How It Works

Regions are APEX's way of organizing visual information within a single page. Using regions, you can even mix data entry forms and charts together in the same page. Regions are highly flexible; they can also be positioned anywhere you wish. In this way, you can create dashboards that convey a mix of information from different sources in different ways.

CHAPTER 6

Globalizing the Application

I am sure there has been at least one occasion when you've taken a flight to a foreign country, proudly presented your painstakingly crafted application consisting of hundreds of web pages and a beautiful UI, only to be asked if everything could be in Thai. No? You've been lucky!

Contrary to popular opinion, more than 60% of the world does not speak English. Moreover, each country has different locality specifications: Americans use the USD currency, the English use the pound or Euro, and quite interestingly, the French use the comma symbol instead of the dot in their numerals.

In today's environment where the Internet and the rise of cloud computing has truly brought the world closer together, it is inevitable that your application will be used by people from different parts of the world. It is thus important to consider more than just your own country or locality when developing applications, and especially when developing applications to be deployed on the Internet. Globalization, via Oracle's language and locale features, is the answer.

Globalization support consists of the following areas:

- Entering of double-byte characters such as those used in Japanese or Chinese.

- Translation of an application user interface into various languages.

- Display and data entry formats for currencies, time zones, and date/time values.

Recipes in this chapter explore these three areas of concern and the various facilities APEX provides to address them.

6-1. Setting up for Double-Byte Character Input

Problem

You have created forms that accept input in double-byte character sets such as those used in Chinese and other languages. Not only must your fields accept such characters, but you must enable users to key in such characters using an English-language keyboard.

Solution

To set up a Windows 7-based operating system to support data entry in Chinese, follow these steps:

■ **Note** This example illustrates how to set up the Chinese Input Method Editor (IME) on Windows 7. For other operating systems, please check your operating system manual.

---

1. Click the Windows Start button and navigate to the Control Panel.

2. Double-click the Region and Language icon in the control panel to launch it, as shown in Figure 6-1.

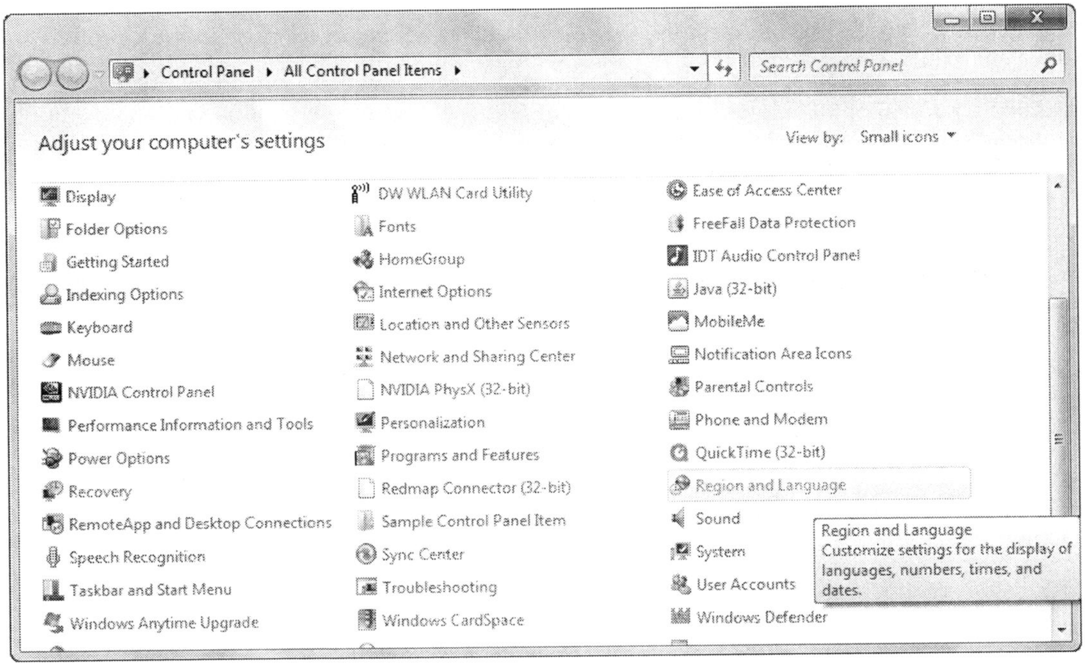

Figure 6-1. The Region and Language settings

3. In the ensuing pop-up window, click the Keyboards and Languages tab and click the Change Keyboards button. Another pop-up window, shown in Figure 6-2, will appear.

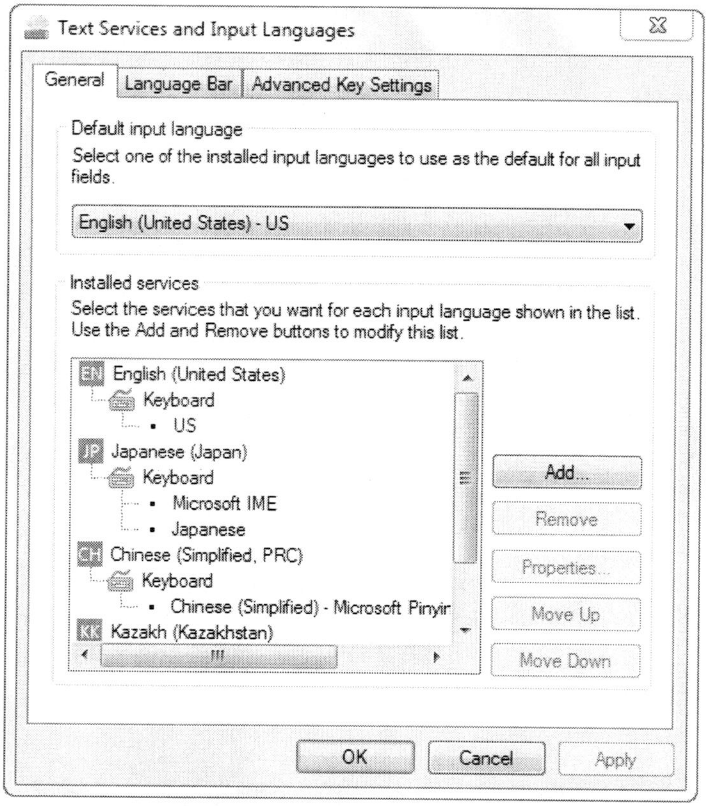

Figure 6-2. The list of IMEs installed on your system

4. Click the Add button, and look for the Chinese (Simplified, PRC) node. Expand this node and under the Keyboard node, pick the Chinese (Simplified) - Microsoft Pinyin ABC Input Style entry, as shown in Figure 6-3.

Add Input Language

Select the language to add using the checkboxes below.

- ⊞ Bengali (India)
- ⊞ Bosnian (Cyrillic, Bosnia and Herzegovina)
- ⊞ Bosnian (Latin, Bosnia and Herzegovina)
- ⊞ Breton (France)
- ⊞ Bulgarian (Bulgaria)
- ⊞ Catalan (Catalan)
- ⊟ Chinese (Simplified, PRC)
  - ⊟ Keyboard
    - ☑ Chinese (Simplified) - Microsoft Pinyin AB
    - ☐ Chinese (Simplified) - Microsoft Pinyin Ne
    - ☐ Chinese (Simplified) - US Keyboard
    - ☐ Chinese Simplified QuanPin (version 6.0)
    - ☐ Chinese Simplified ShuangPin (version 6.0)
    - ☐ Chinese Simplified ZhengMa (version 6.0)
    - ☐ Show More...
- ⊞ Chinese (Simplified, Singapore)
- ⊞ Chinese (Traditional, Hong Kong S.A.R.)
- ⊞ Chinese (Traditional, Macao S.A.R.)

OK

Cancel

Preview...

Figure 6-3. Installing a Chinese IME

5. Click the OK button to add the keyboard. Apply the new settings and close all windows. Your operating system should have the Chinese IME installed now.

6. Open a text editor tool, such as Notepad, and make sure the window has received input focus.

7. In the bottom right corner of your Windows desktop, the current default language should be EN (English), as shown in Figure 6-4.

Figure 6-4. The language toolbar

8. Click on the EN symbol and change your keyboard to CH (Chinese), as shown in Figure 6-5.

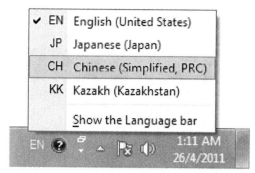

Figure 6-5. Changing the default language to Chinese

9. The language bar should change into a slightly longer one (with more icons), as shown in Figure 6-6. Make sure to change the second symbol to • (as highlighted in the red box in Figure 6-6).

Figure 6-6. Enabling Pinyin input

10. Type the following text on your keyboard: nihao shijie. This roughly translates to "Hello World" in Chinese.

11. When you hit the space character, your English text is instantly translated into Chinese. You should see the screen shown in Figure 6-7.

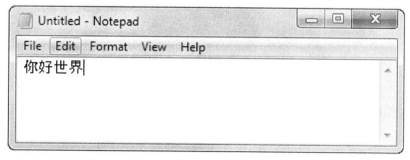

Figure 6-7. Hello World in Chinese

How It Works

Many books start off assuming that the reader knows how to enter double-byte characters. I assume that most of my readers are American and thus might not have ever experienced keying in data in a double-byte language like Chinese, Japanese, or Korean.

This recipe serves as a quick guide to setting up an Input Method Editor (IME) on a Windows-based operating system and using it to input double-byte characters. The Pinyin IME you've seen in this recipe is one of many ways for users to key in Chinese characters, in this case by typing their phonetically equivalent via Roman letters.

6-2. Supporting Double-Byte Data Entry

Problem

One of the forms you create in APEX requires the user to key in data in a double-byte language such as Japanese.

Solution

This solution consists of two steps. First, you must create the sample objects (these will also be used for the other recipes in this chapter). Then you'll create the application on top of those example objects.

Step 1: Creating the Sample Objects

The sample object you will create is the customers table. Create it by executing Listing 6-1 via the SQL Workshop. Note that the table columns are defined as NVARCHAR2, which is Oracle's national language version of VARCHAR2.

Listing 6-1. Creating the Sample Objects

```
CREATE table "MYCUSTOMERS" (
    "CUSTNAME"    NVARCHAR2(255),
    "CUSTREMARKS" NVARCHAR2(2000),
    "CUSTID"      NVARCHAR2(50),
    constraint  "MYCUSTOMERS_PK" primary key ("CUSTID")
)
/
```

Step 2: Creating and Running the Application

Now, create and run the application to key in some Japanese text. Here are the steps to follow:

1. Create a new application. In this application, create a new form and interactive report on top of the MyCustomers table.

2. Run the form. Using a Japanese Input Method Editor (IME), key in some Japanese text, as shown in Figure 6-8. Save the data by clicking the Create button.

■ **Tip** For further information on how to create a form on a table with report, please see Recipes 2-1 and 2-2.

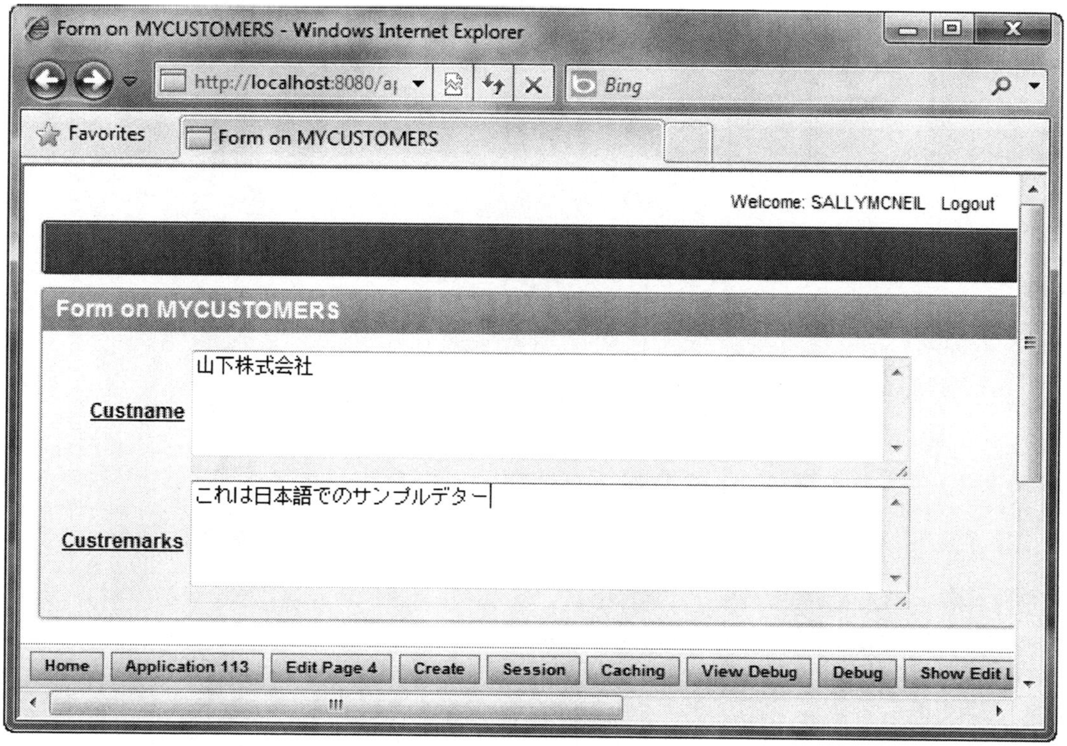

Figure 6-8. Keying in Japanese characters

3. Run the report. You should see the Japanese text you just entered, as shown in Figure 6-9.

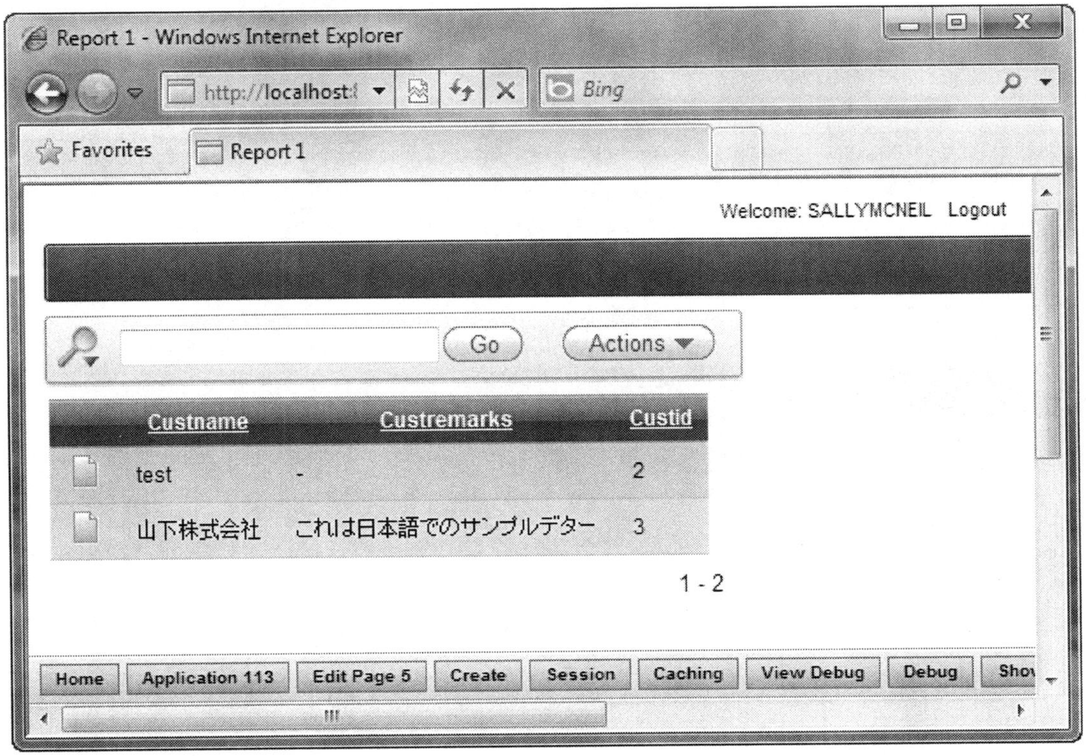

Figure 6-9. Viewing the Japanese characters in the database

How It Works

East-Asian languages use the double-byte format. To support double-byte data, the fields in the database table must be defined using the N-prefixed data types. For instance, you must use NVARCHAR2 instead of VARCHAR2, and NCHAR instead of CHAR.

For other languages such as Spanish, German, or Italian (which are single-byte character languages), you will not need to use the N-prefixed data types. This will help save space in your database because, as you can probably guess, N-prefixed data types take up double the amount of space in the database.

6-3. Translating Your User Interface Into Another Language

Problem

Depending on the browser language preference setting, you need your application to display the user interface (all labels, messages, names, and field captions) in the corresponding preferred language of the application user.

Solution

To translate your application UI to another language, follow these steps:

- Set globalization attributes.
- Map to a translated application.
- Seed translatable text to the translation repository.
- Export the XLIFF file.
- Translate the XLIFF file.
- Import the XLIFF file.
- Publish the translated application.
- Test your translated application.

Step 1: Set Globalization Attributes

Execute the following steps to set the globalization attributes for an application. These steps use the application from Recipe 6-1 as the basis for an example.

1. Open the application you created in Recipe 6-1, and click the Shared Components icon.
2. At the bottom of the page, under the Globalization section, click the Globalization Attributes link (as shown in Figure 6-10).

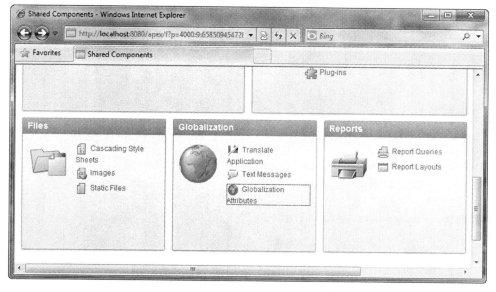

Figure 6-10. Globalization Attributes settings

3. Set the Application Primary Language to English and the Application Language Derived From field to Browser (use browser language preference), as shown in Figure 6-11.

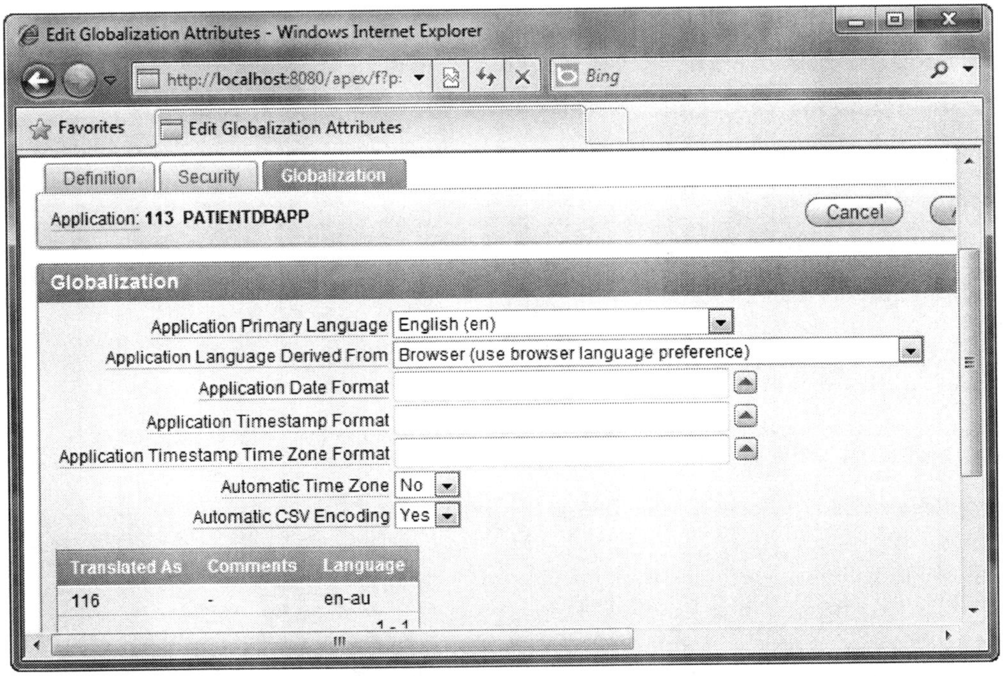

Figure 6-11. Setting the primary language of the application

4. Click the Apply changes button when you're done.

Mapping to a Translated Application

To map your primary language application to the translated application, follow these steps:

1. Return to the Shared Components page. This time, click the Translate Application link (also in the Globalization section).

2. You will now see a page that looks like Figure 6-12.

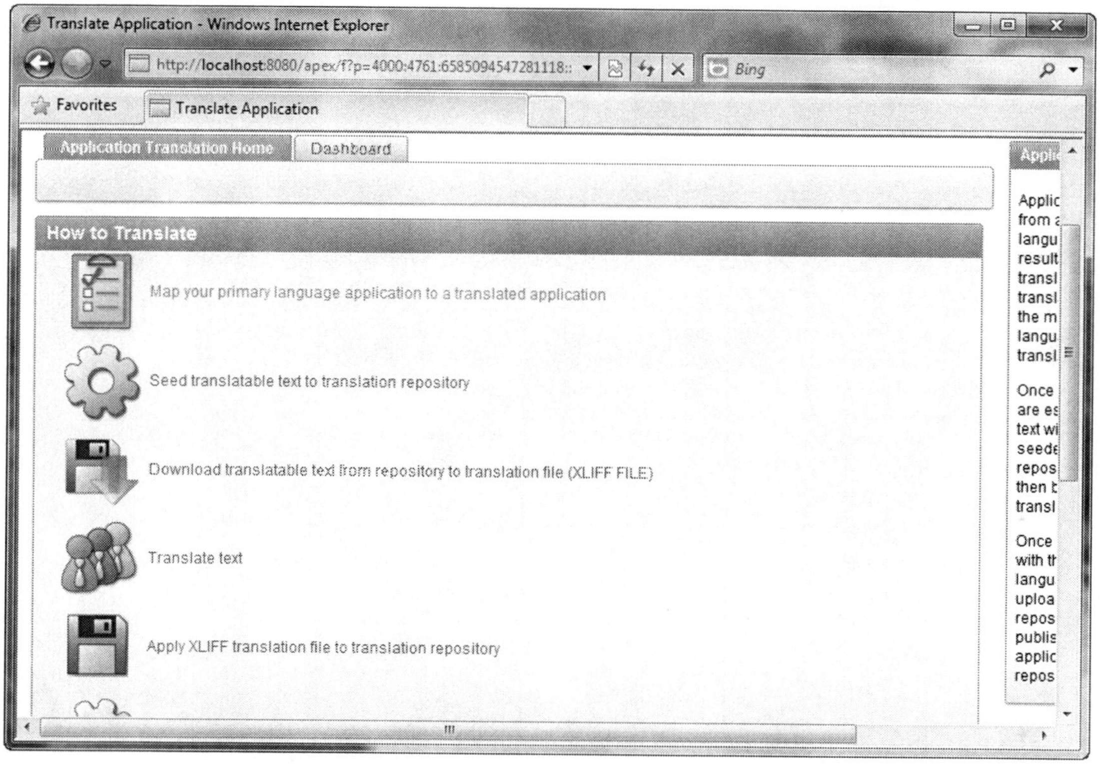

Figure 6-12. The various steps in translating an application

3. Click the first link, "Map your primary language application to a translated application."

4. Create a new mapping by clicking the Create button. In the ensuing pop-up wizard, key in any unique integer value for the Translation Application field.

5. For the language code, set the language to Icelandic (is), and the image directory to is. You may specify some comments if you wish, but this is optional. You should see something similar to Figure 6-13.

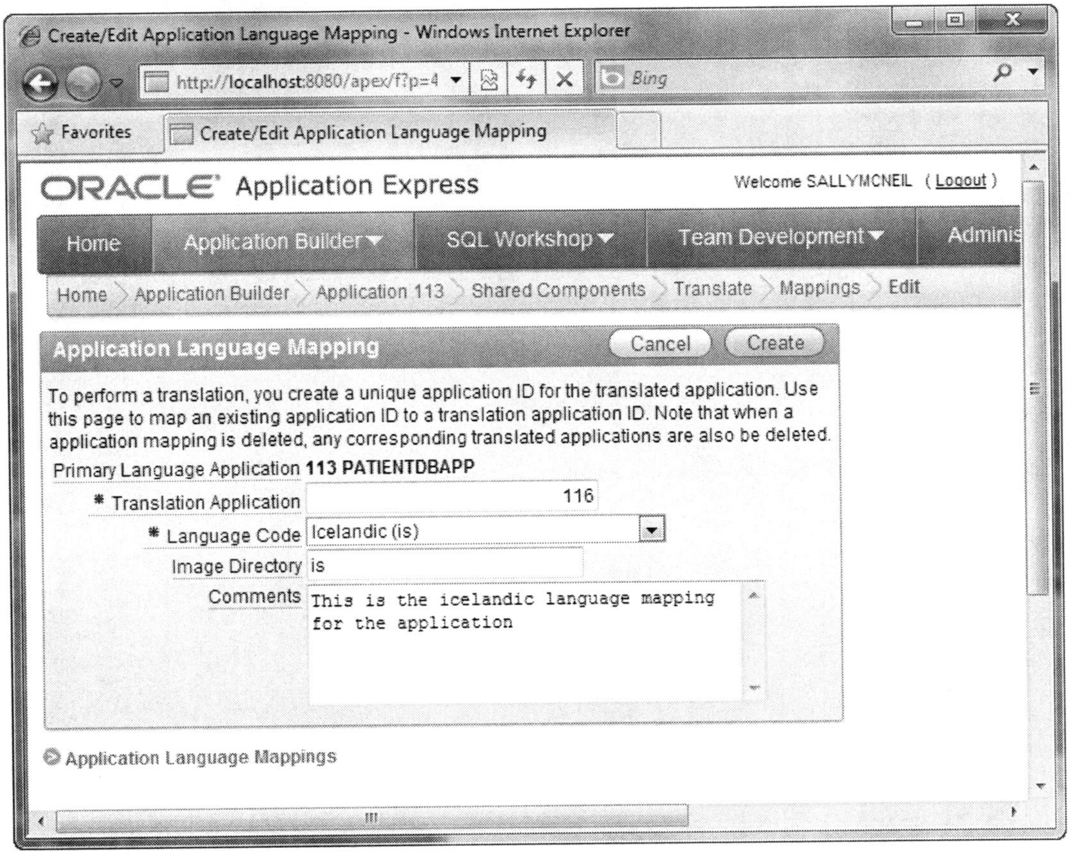

Figure 6-13. Defining the application language mapping

6. Click the Create button. You will see the created mapping record in the following page (as shown in Figure 6-14).

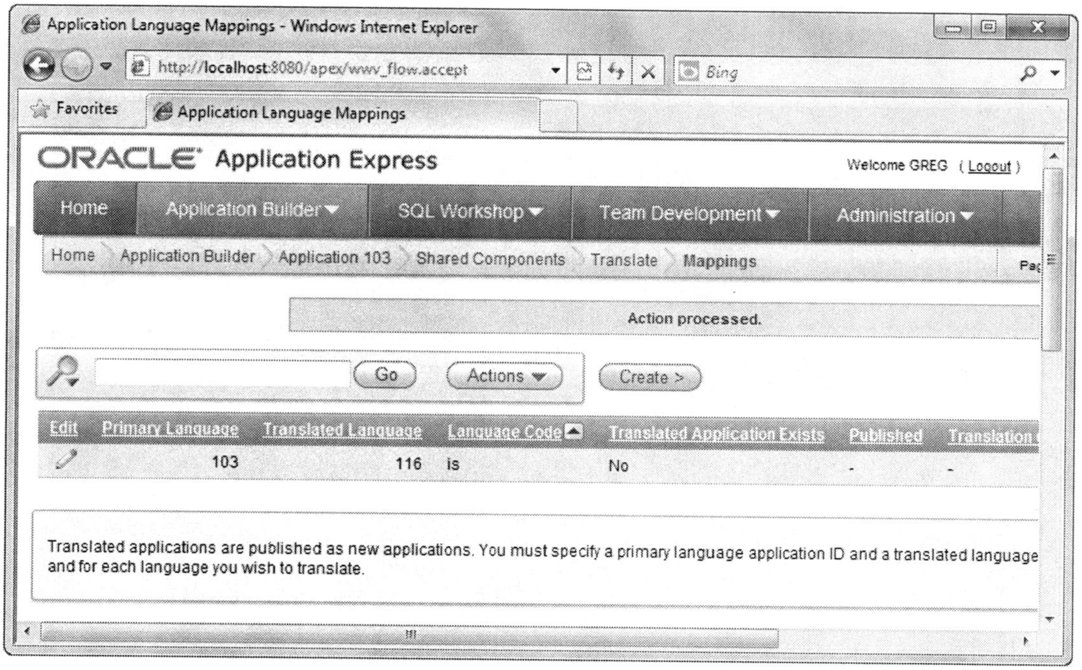

Figure 6-14. The created mapping record

Step 2: Seed Translatable Text to the Translation Repository

To map your primary language application to the translated application, follow these steps:

1. Return to the main Translate page. Click the second link shown in Figure 6-15, "Seeding translatable text to the translation repository."

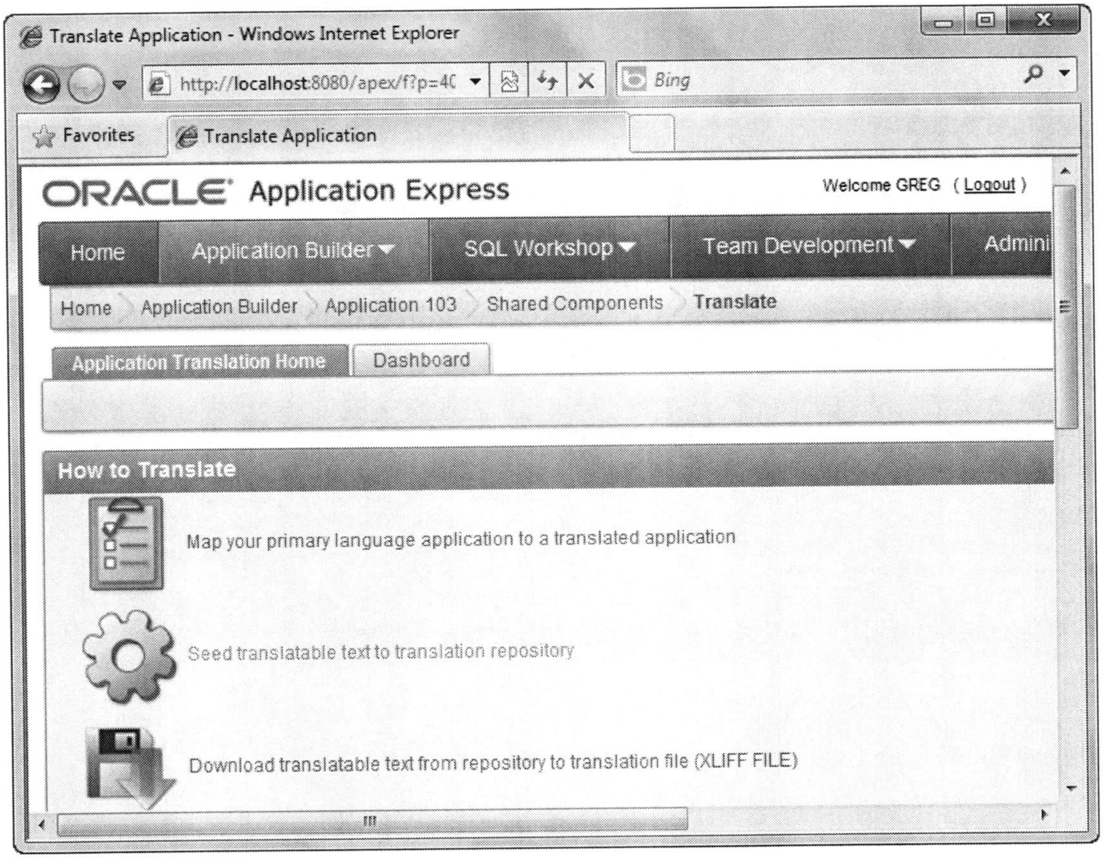

Figure 6-15. Seeding translatable text to translation repository

2. In the wizard, choose the "(Your primary language Application ID) >>116 (is)" entry from the drop-down list for the Language Mapping field, and click Next to continue. The value of 116 refers to the "to-be-translated" application ID.

3. Click the Seed Translatable Text button to complete the wizard.

4. You should see a brief summary of the seeding process, as shown in Figure 6-16.

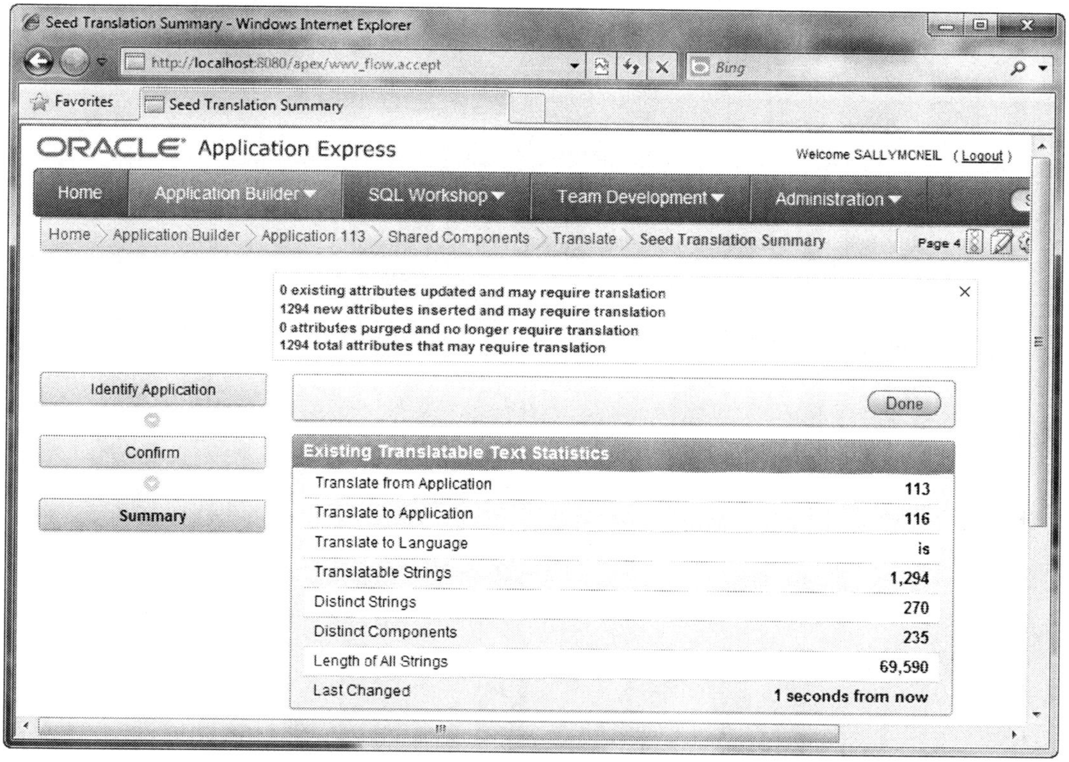

Figure 6-16. *Seeding statistics*

Step 3: Export the XLIFF File

To export the text resources used in your application to an XLIFF file, follow these steps:

1. Return to the main Translate page. Click the third link shown in Figure 6-17, "Download translatable text from repository to translation file (XLIFF FILE)."

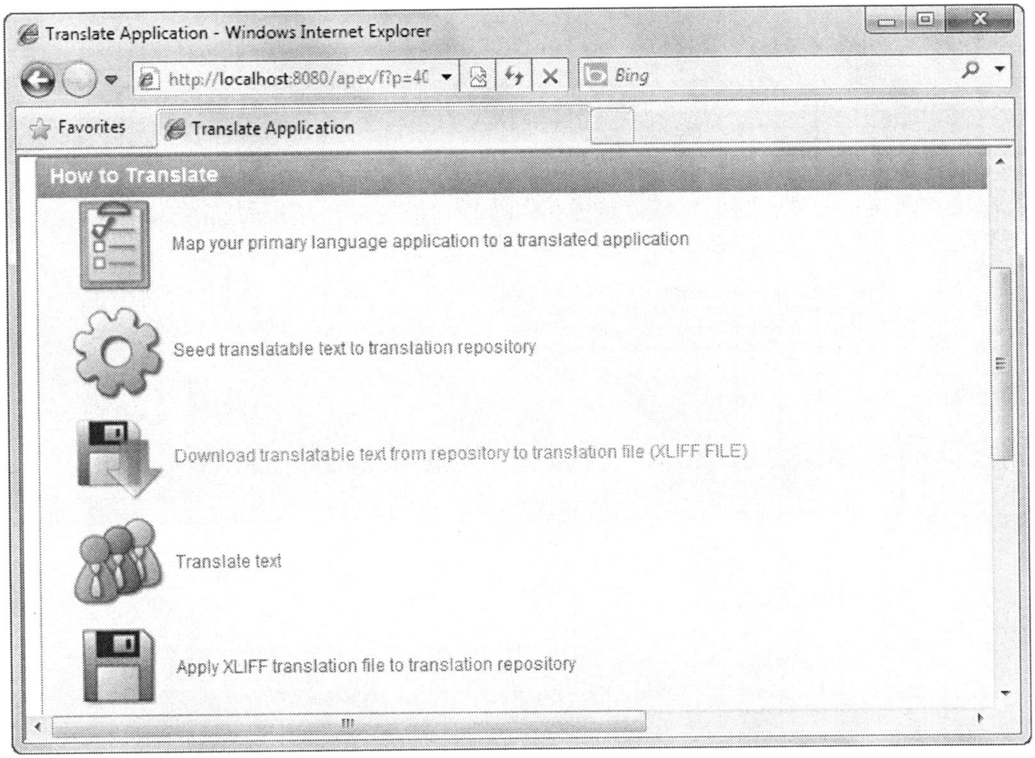

Figure 6-17. Exporting to an XLIFF file

2. In the ensuing configuration page, you need to download the XLIFF file for the complete application. Set the Application Translation field to the "(Your primary language Application ID) >>116 (is)" entry.

3. Ensure that the Include XLIFF Target Elements checkbox is selected.

4. Choose to export all translatable elements, as shown in Figure 6-18.

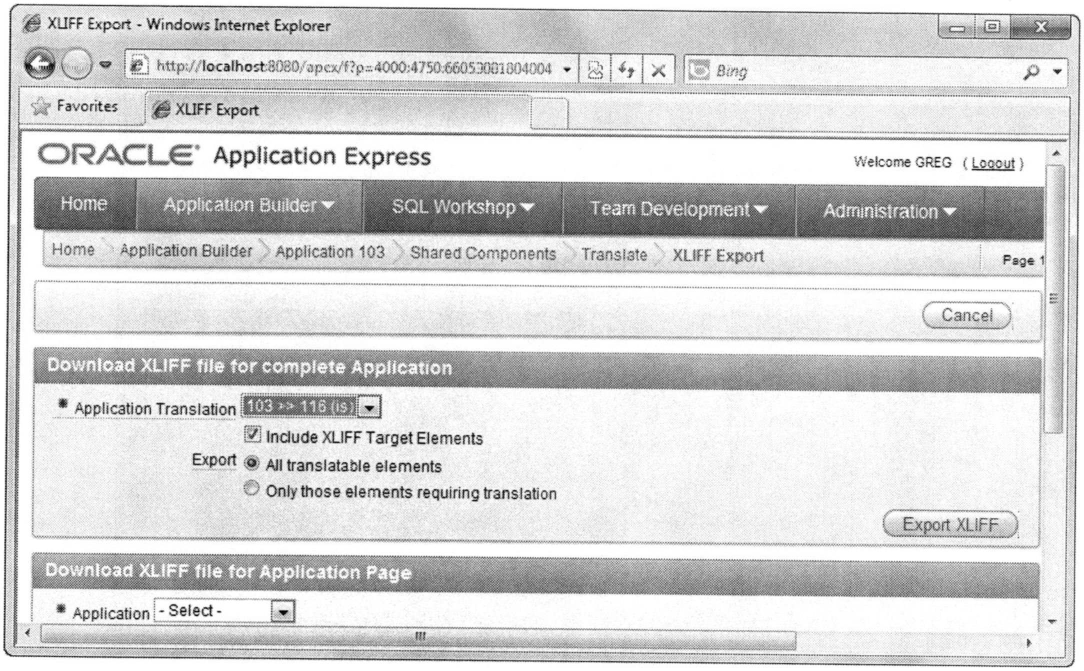

Figure 6-18. Choosing the translation mapping

5. Click the Export XLIFF button. You may need to wait several seconds before you see the next prompt. When the prompt appears, you will be given the option to download the generated XLIFF file, as shown in Figure 6-19.

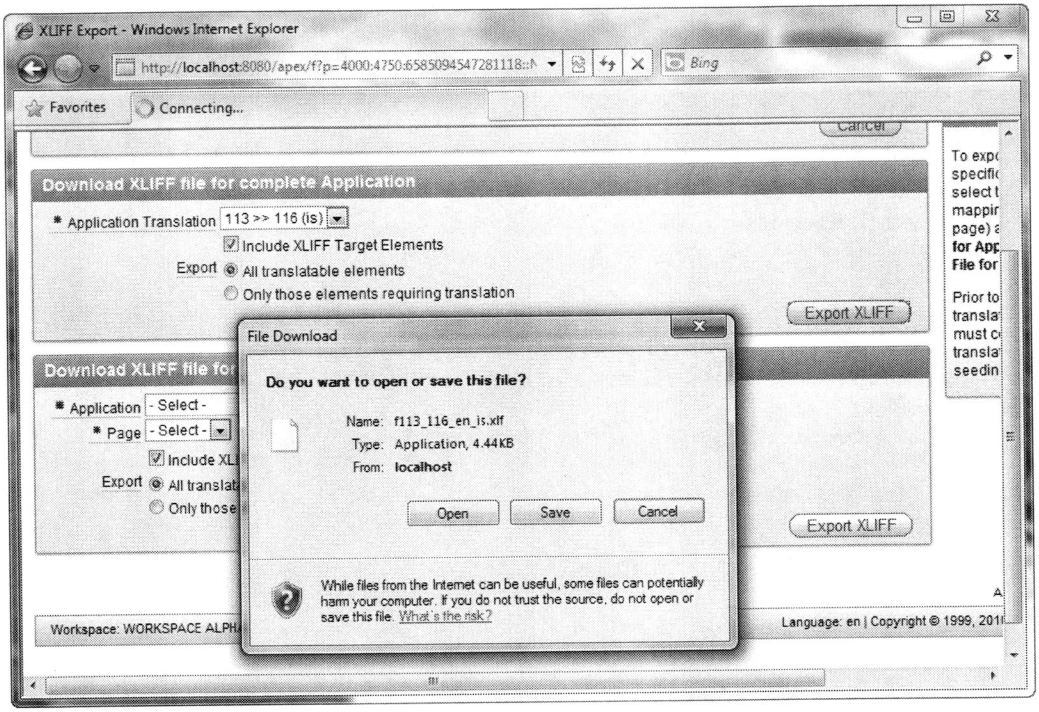

Figure 6-19. Exporting the XLIFF file

6. Save the XLIFF file to any location on your PC.

Step 4: Translate the XLIFF file

To translate the XLIFF file, follow these steps:

1. The XLIFF file is a convenient little file that contains all the text, messages, labels, and name resources used by your application.

2. You can usually send XLIFF files to real-world translators to translate its content. The XLIFF format is an open standard, and you can find many XLIFF editor tools that allow you to peek into the contents of the file and edit them by hand.

3. Open the downloaded XLIFF file using a text editor tool such as WordPad.

4. You should be able to see the generated XML with multiple translation entries, as shown in Figure 6-20.

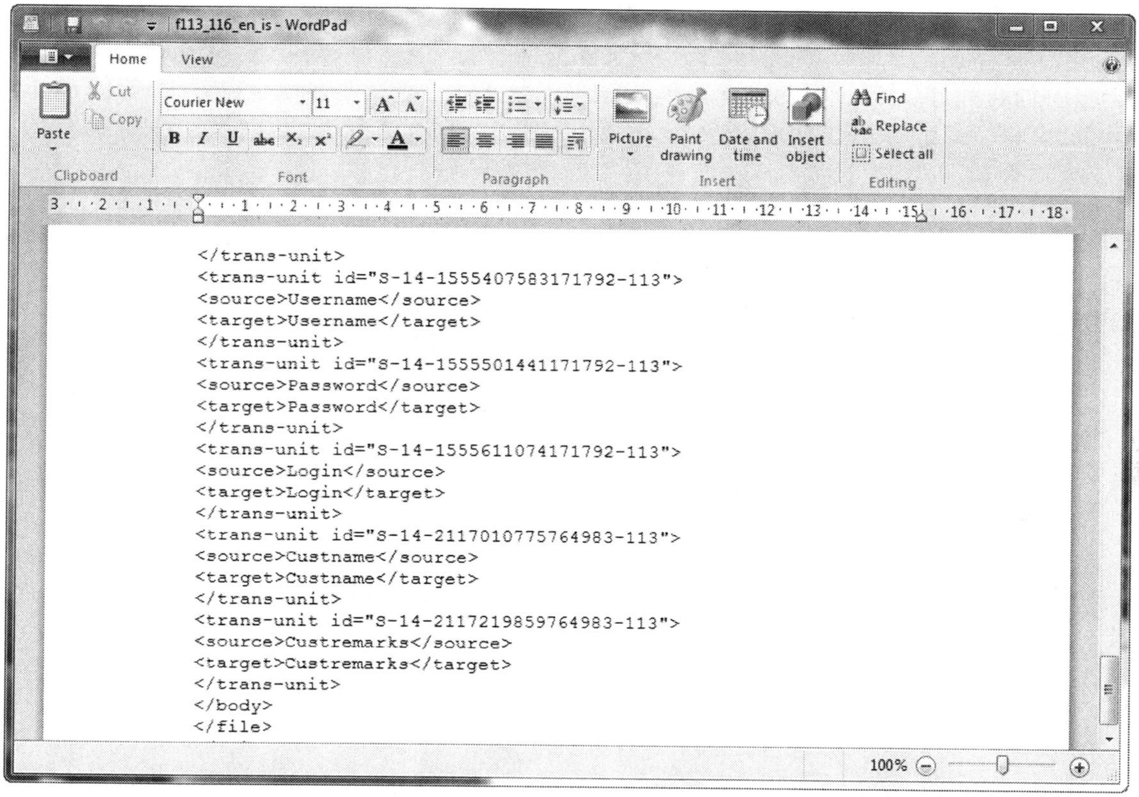

```
</trans-unit>
<trans-unit id="S-14-1555407583171792-113">
<source>Username</source>
<target>Username</target>
</trans-unit>
<trans-unit id="S-14-1555501441171792-113">
<source>Password</source>
<target>Password</target>
</trans-unit>
<trans-unit id="S-14-1555611074171792-113">
<source>Login</source>
<target>Login</target>
</trans-unit>
<trans-unit id="S-14-2117010775764983-113">
<source>Custname</source>
<target>Custname</target>
</trans-unit>
<trans-unit id="S-14-2117219859764983-113">
<source>Custremarks</source>
<target>Custremarks</target>
</trans-unit>
</body>
</file>
```

***Figure 6-20.** Taking a peek in the XLIFF file*

5. Each translation entry has the format shown in Listing 6-2. The source field represents the original untranslated text and the target field the translated text.

***Listing 6-2.** Translation Entry Format*

```
<trans-unit id="XXXXX">
 <source>Custname</source>
 <target>Custname</target>
</trans-unit>
```

6. Look for the Custname entry and change its <target> entry to its Icelandic equivalent: viðskiptavinur nafn. Change the <target> entry for Custremarks to viðskiptavinur athugasemd, as highlighted in Figure 6-21.

■ **Note** There may be several entries for Custname and Custremarks, especially if you've used these same names for different objects in your application. If you are unsure which one you should edit, always look out for the object IDs (indicated by the ID attribute of the <trans-unit> tag). These identifiers map to the actual object ids in your application.

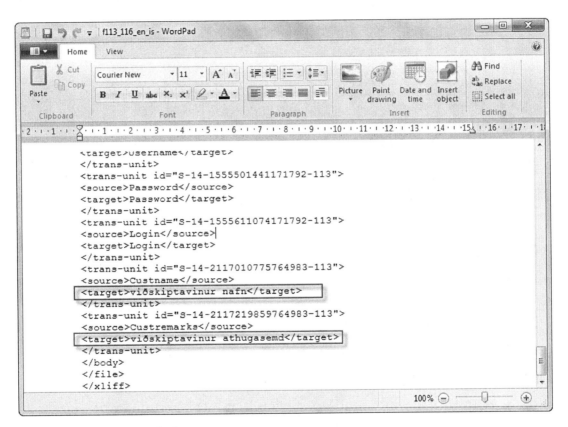

Figure 6-21.Manual translation

7.Save the changes you have made.

Step 5: Import the Translated XLIFF File

To re-import the translated XLIFF file into APEX, follow these steps:

1. Return to the main Translate page. Click the fifth link shown in Figure 6-22, "Apply XLIFF translation file to translation repository."

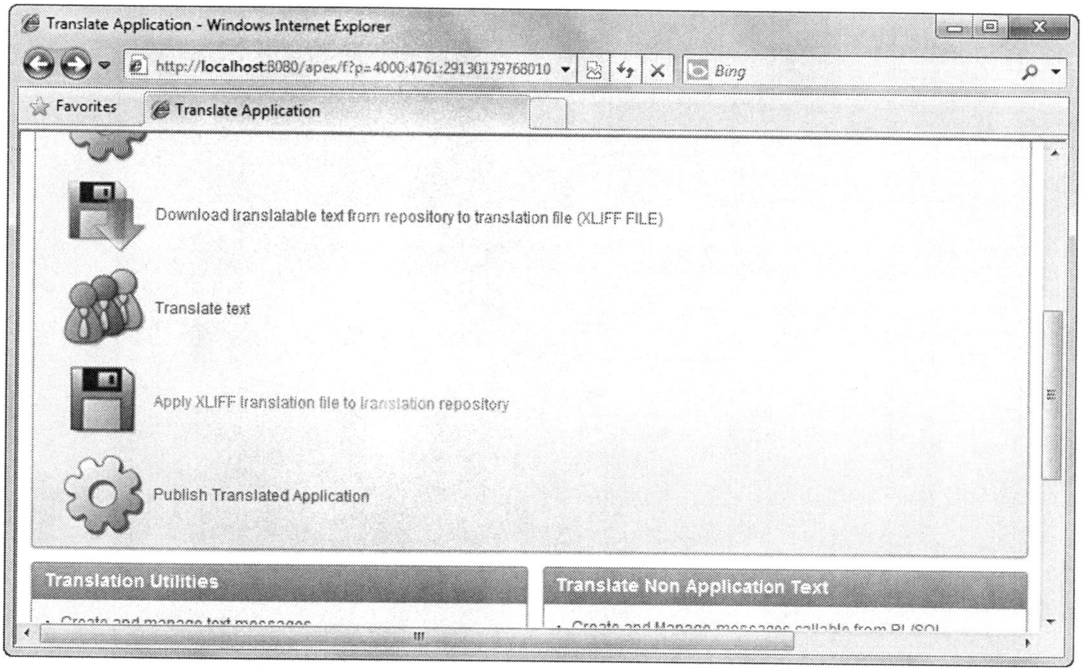

Figure 6-22. Importing the translated XLIFF file

2.   In the ensuing window, click the Upload XLIFF button. A wizard will pop up, allowing you to upload the translated XLIFF file. Specify any title you wish, and browse for the translated XLIFF file on your PC. Click the Upload XLIFF file button when you are done, as shown in Figure 6-23.

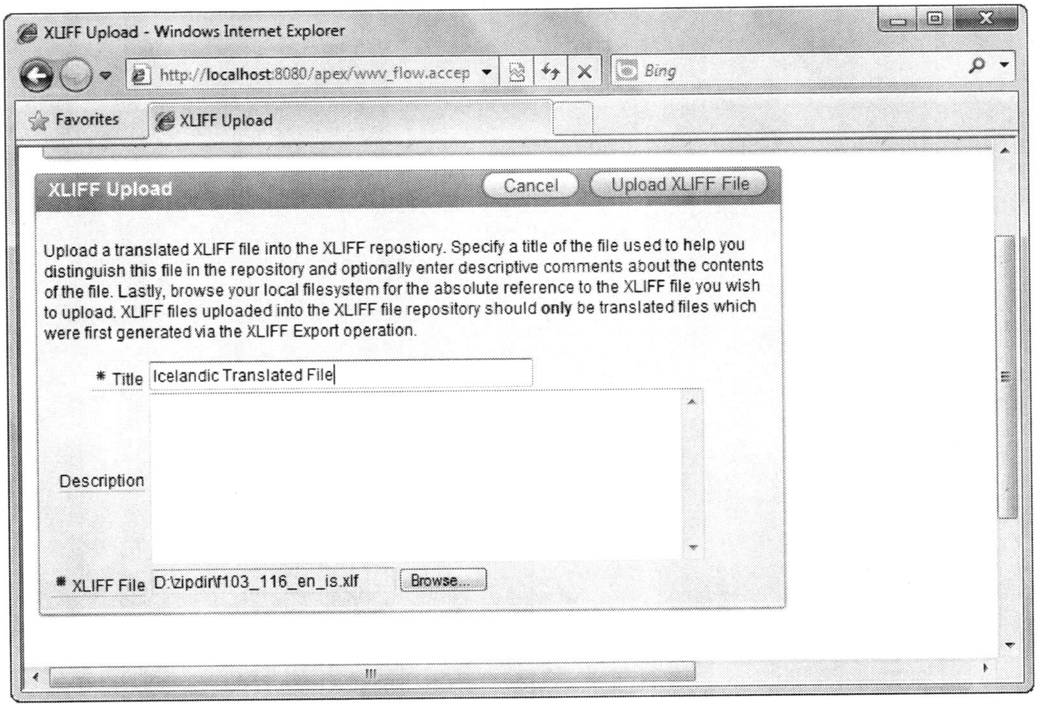

Figure 6-23. Importing the XLIFF file

3. You should see your uploaded XLIFF file in the next window (see Figure 6-24).

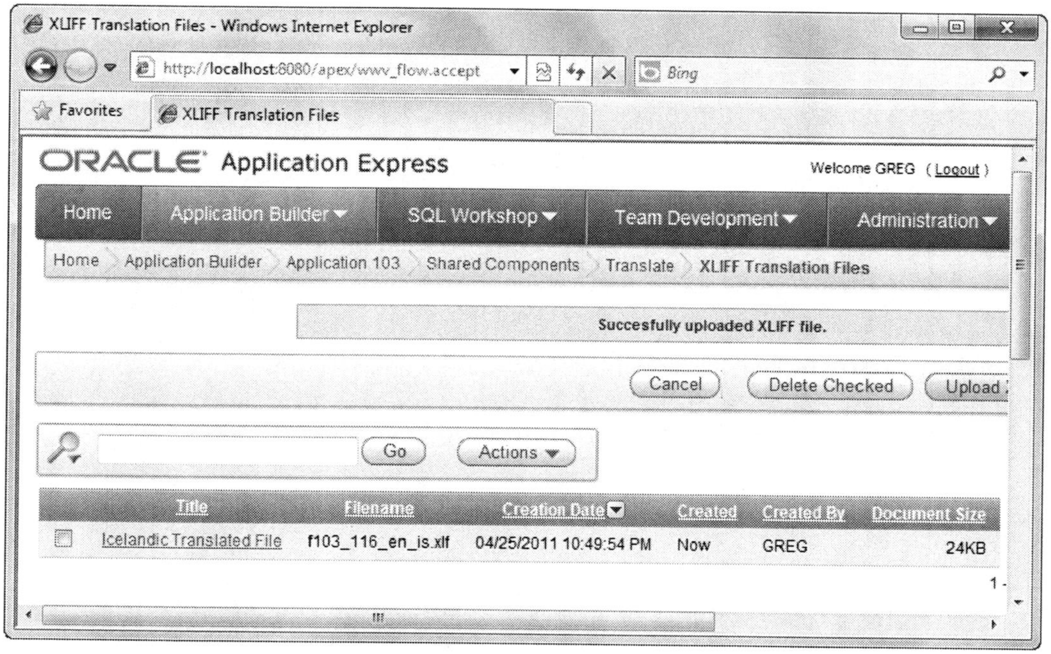

Figure 6-24. The uploaded XLIFF file

Step 6: Publish the Translated Application

To publish the translated application, follow these steps:

1. Return to the main Translate page. Click the last link shown in Figure 6-25, "Publish Translated Application."

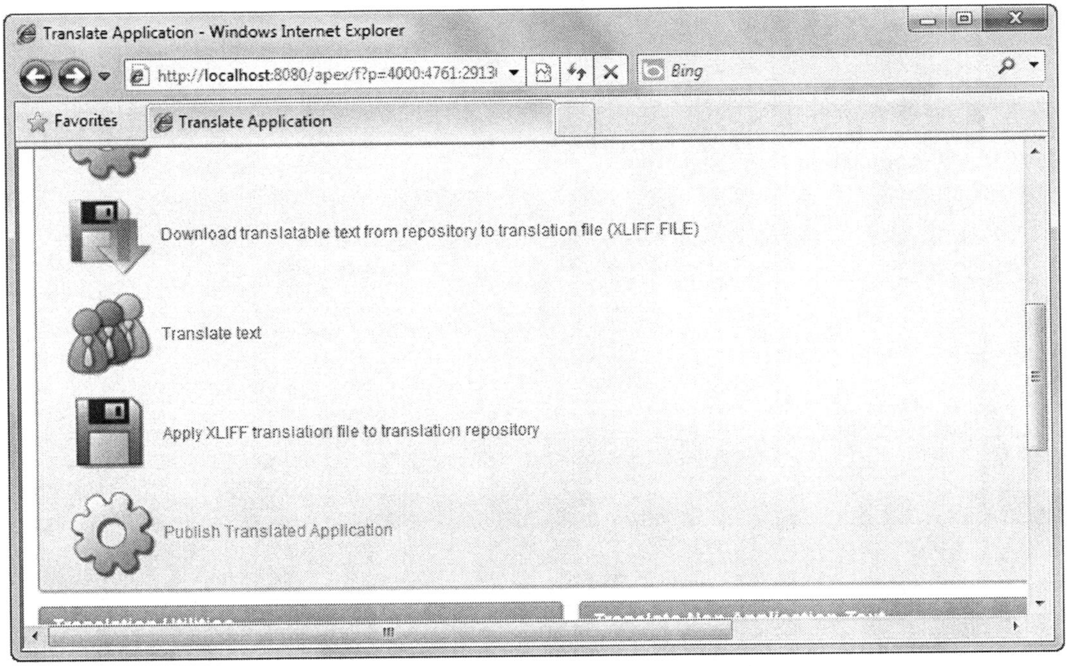

Figure 6-25. Publishing the translated application

2. In the ensuing page, set the Publish Application Translation field to the Icelandic mapping, and click the Publish Application button shown in Figure 6-26.

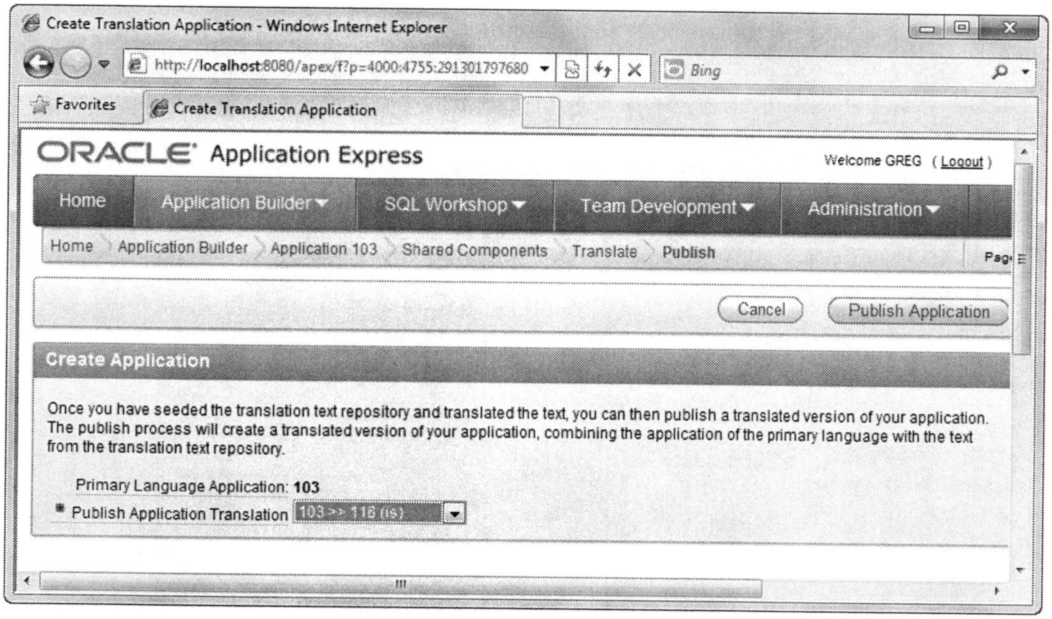

Figure 6-26. Publishing an application translation

3. You've now successfully created a (more or less) Icelandic version of your application.

Step 7: Test the Translated Application

To try out your translated application, follow these steps:

1. If you recall, you set the globalization attributes to use the language specified in the browser preference settings. To try out your translated application, you will now need to set your browser preference settings to render pages in Icelandic.

■ **Note** The example shown here applies to the Microsoft Internet Explorer browser. The screenshots and steps may differ for other browsers, so refer to your browser's documentation on the topic of language preference settings.

---

2. Open Internet Explorer and navigate to the Internet Options window. In the General tab, click the Languages button at the bottom. Add a new language to the list: Icelandic [is]. Move its preference order so that Icelandic is the top most entry, as shown in Figure 6-27.

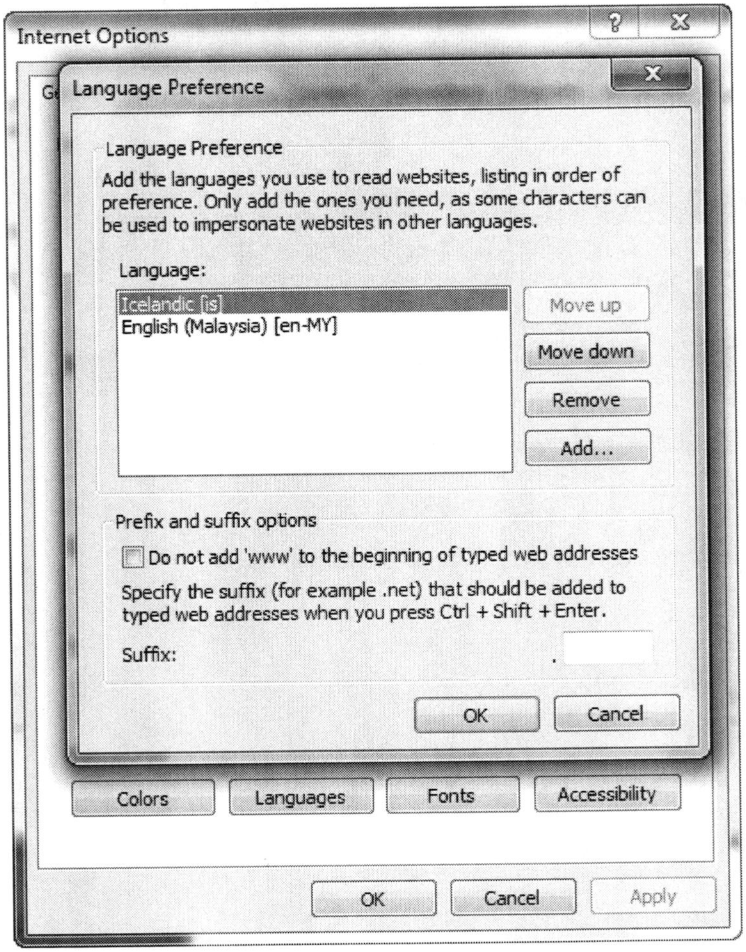

Figure 6-27. *Changing the browser language preference*

3. Save and apply all changes. Now run your application again. You should see the form rendered using the Icelandic field captions you've specified, as shown in Figure 6-28.

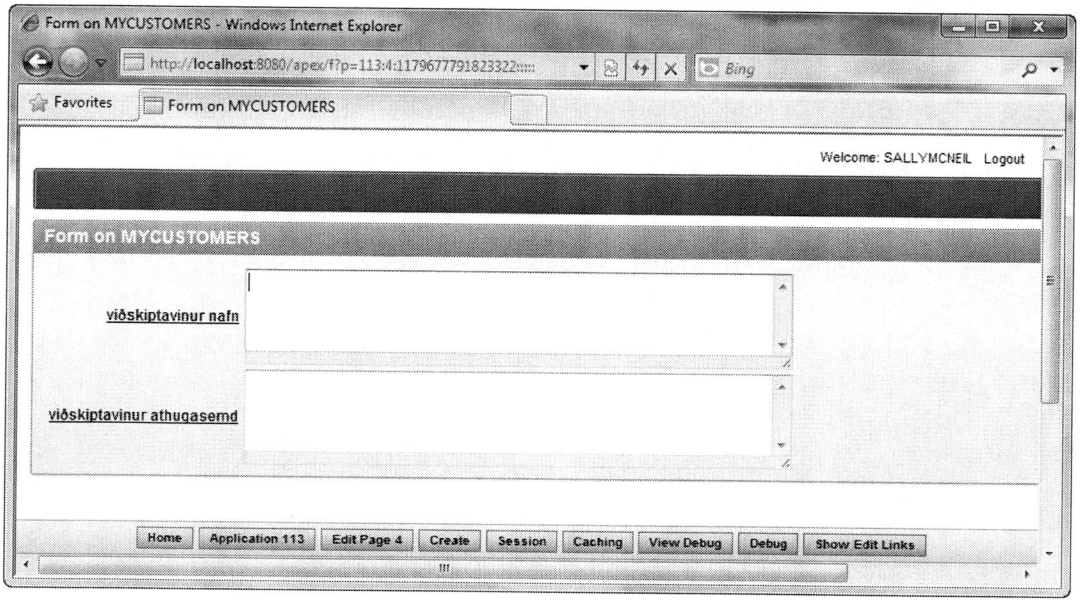

Figure 6-28. The customers page in Icelandic

How It Works

To translate an application to another language, you must first extract all the resources used in your application— which means, the error messages, labels, field captions and so on—into an XML file. This file is called an XLIFF file. The XLIFF file can be sent to real-world translators, where each entry is translated. The resulting XLIFF file is then reimported into APEX, where APEX will generate a new application using the translated text in the XLIFF file.

The example in this recipe translates only two entries from the XLIFF file. If you wish to have the entire application in 100% Icelandic, you will need to translate every entry in the file, including the form and report names, error messages, and so on.

6-4. Storing and Displaying Dates with Time Zone Information

Problem

You have a requirement to generate a report listing events that occur in different locations around the world in various time zones. Additionally, the report will be viewed by users from different countries and time zones. You need to display dates and times that correspond to the local time zone of the accessing user.

Solution

You will first need to create a table and some data for this recipe. Run the SQL in Listing 6-3 to create an EVENTS table and add a couple of events for testing purposes.

Listing 6-3. SQL to Create an EVENTS Table and Some Events

```
CREATE TABLE  "EVENTS"
    (    "EVENTLAUNCHDATE" TIMESTAMP (6) WITH LOCAL TIME ZONE,
        "EVENTNAME" NVARCHAR2(255),
        "EVENTID" NVARCHAR2(50),
         CONSTRAINT "EVENTS_PK" PRIMARY KEY ("EVENTID") ENABLE
    )
/
INSERT INTO EVENTS(EVENTID,EVENTLAUNCHDATE,EVENTNAME) VALUES(1,'22-APR-11 08:00:00 AM','GLOBAL
SALES EVENT')
/
INSERT INTO EVENTS(EVENTID,EVENTLAUNCHDATE,EVENTNAME) VALUES(2,'23-APR-11 04:00:00
PM','PROJECT KICKOFF MEETING')
/
```

Next, you will need to create the report to display the event information. Here are the steps to follow:

1. Open an existing application.

2. Click the Shared Components icon in the application page.

3. Click on the Globalization Attributes link under the Globalization section, as shown in Figure 6-29.

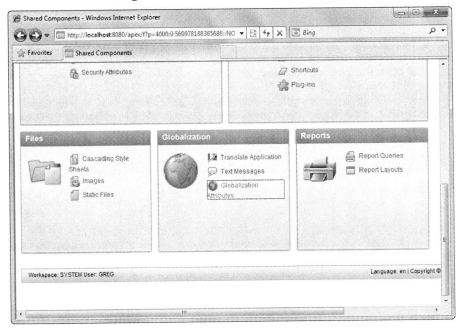

Figure 6-29. Modifying Globalization Attributes

4. In the ensuing page, change the Automatic Time Zone field from No to Yes, as shown in Figure 6-30.

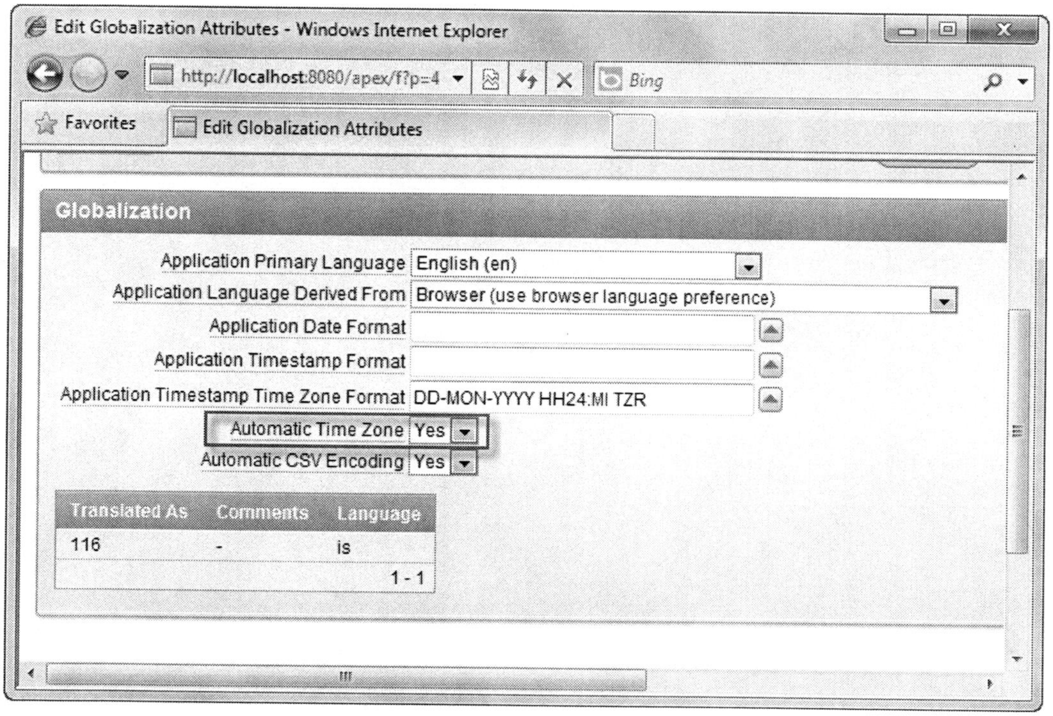

Figure 6-30. Enabling the automatic time zone feature

5. Save your changes. Now create a new report in the application. For the SQL Query for the report, specify the following SQL:

```
SELECT * FROM Events
```

6. Complete the wizard to create the report. After doing so, edit the report definition, and choose to edit the EVENTLAUNCHDATE column of the report, as shown in Figure 6-31.

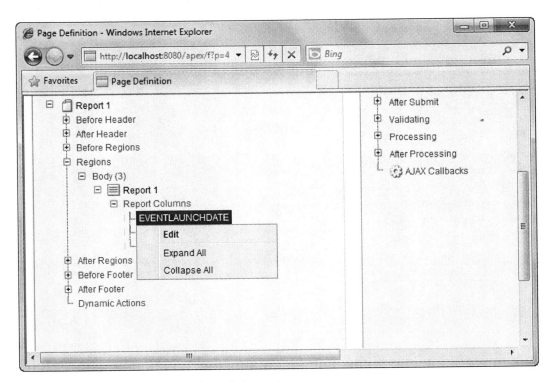

Figure 6-31. Modifying the Event launch date column

7. Change the date/time format field to the following: `DD-MON-YYYY HH24:MI TZR`
    (as shown in Figure 6-32).

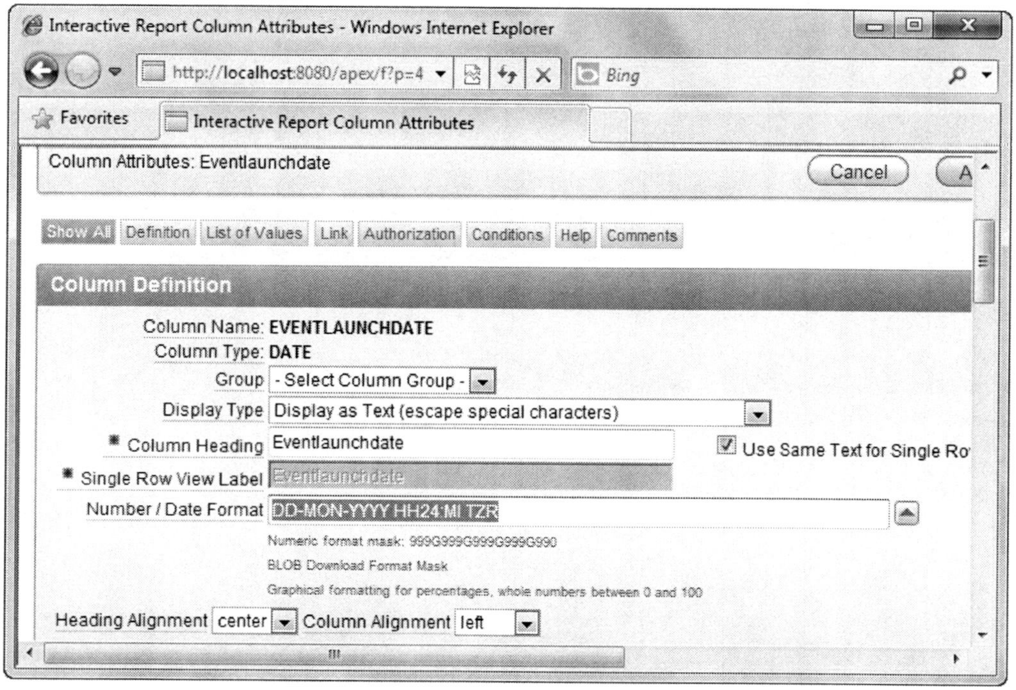

Figure 6-32. Changing the number/date format

8. Save your changes and run the report. You will instantly notice that your date and time data in the report shows your local time zone next to it (see Figure 6-33).

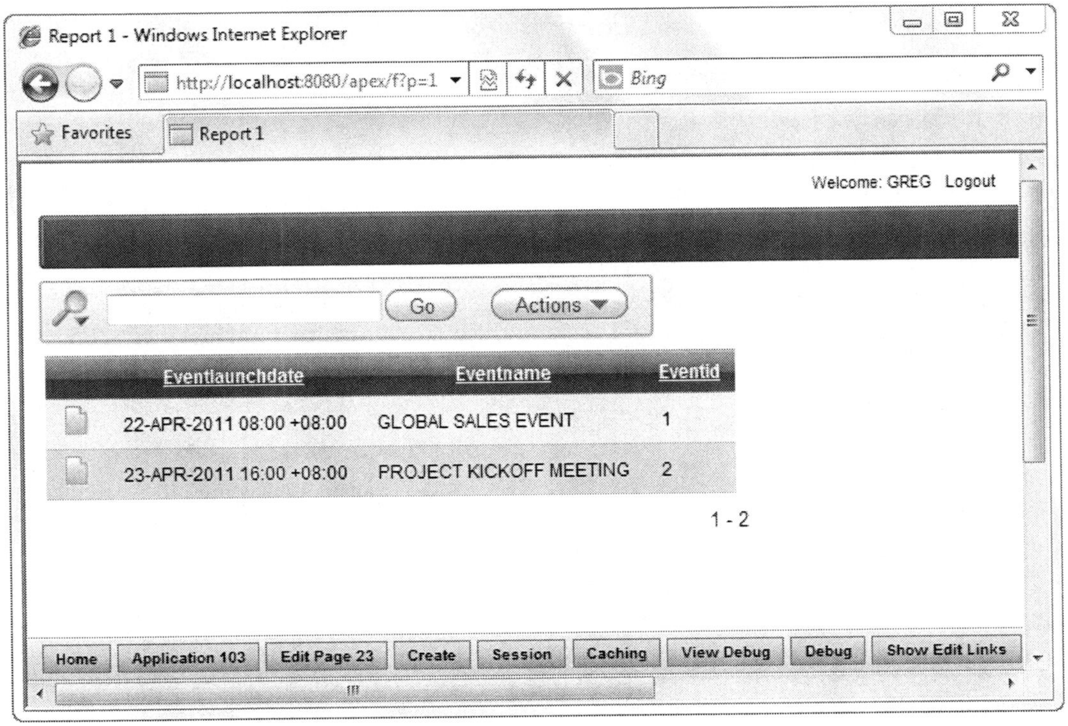

Figure 6-33. *The dates and times in Malaysian (Kuala Lumpur) time zone*

9. Log out from the application. Go to your Windows operating system date/time settings and change your local time zone to a different one. Let's pretend you now live in Tashkent, which has the time zone UTC+05:00.

10. Log in to your APEX application one more time. You will notice that the date and time data has been automatically adjusted to reflect the local time zone in Tashkent, as shown in Figure 6-34.

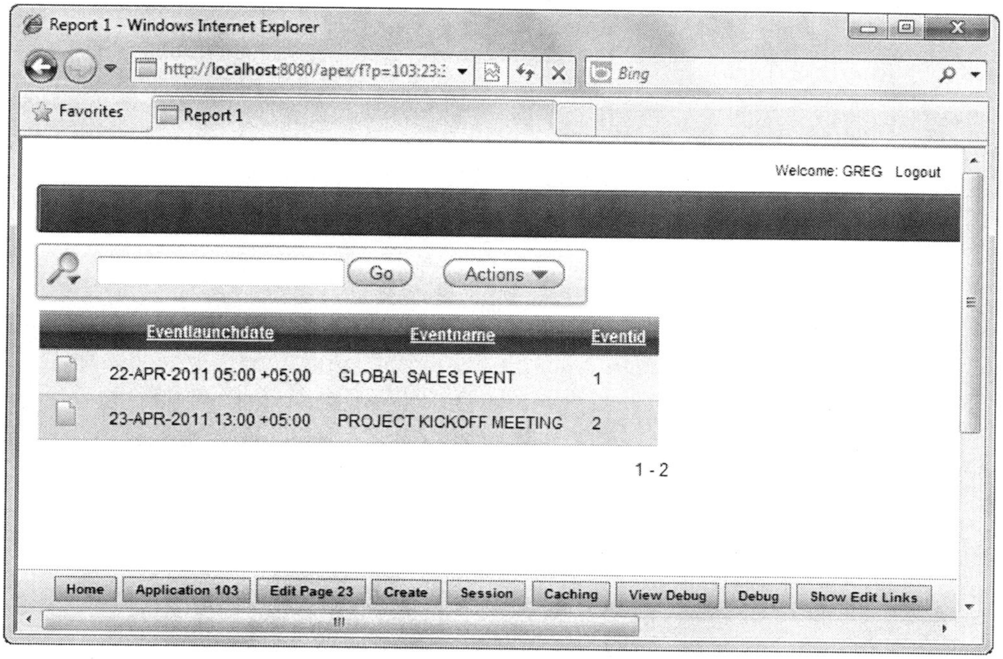

Figure 6-34. The dates and times in Tashkent time zone

How It Works

Enabling time-zone support is as easy as just using the TIMESTAMP WITH LOCAL TIME ZONE data type in your tables and setting the Automatic Time Zone support in the application settings to Yes. When you do so, APEX captures your local time zone information in a session and transmits it with every request so that the necessary adjustment can be made before saving the date/time value in the database.

CHAPTER 7

Improving Application Performance

Performance has always been a big issue when it comes to Rapid Application Development (RAD). Most developers generally share the same opinion: if it's that fast and easy to create an application, the developer will have to "pay the price" elsewhere in terms of tool flexibility or application performance.

While this may hold true for other less integrated RAD tools (and to a much lesser degree for APEX), there has been no other RAD tool quite like APEX. The entire business logic layer in APEX is written in PL/SQL and hence executes within the context of the database—leading to far better performance than with other tools. In fact, APEX is commonly used to host mission critical applications. The APEX platform has been used to handle thousands of online transactions daily for an online e-commerce site based in Singapore, to create an application to handle millions of voters in Ukraine, and to handle the thousands of leads and opportunities captured hourly during nationwide roadshows held in Malaysia. The bottom line: APEX performance is good enough to handle usage-heavy scenarios.

APEX performance can, however, be further improved through a mixture of caching, SQL query design, and best practices. The recipes in this chapter will give you an idea how to achieve this improved performance.

7-1. Measuring Page Access Frequency

Problem

Not every page in your application will be performance critical. Before you begin on any performance tuning task, you need to know which pages are in need of performance tuning—the ones that are accessed most frequently by your end users.

Solution

To measure page access frequency using the Monitor Activity tool, follow these instructions:

1. Login to APEX and click the large Administration icon.

2. You should see four icons, two of which are labeled Monitor Activity and Dashboards (as shown in Figure 7-1).

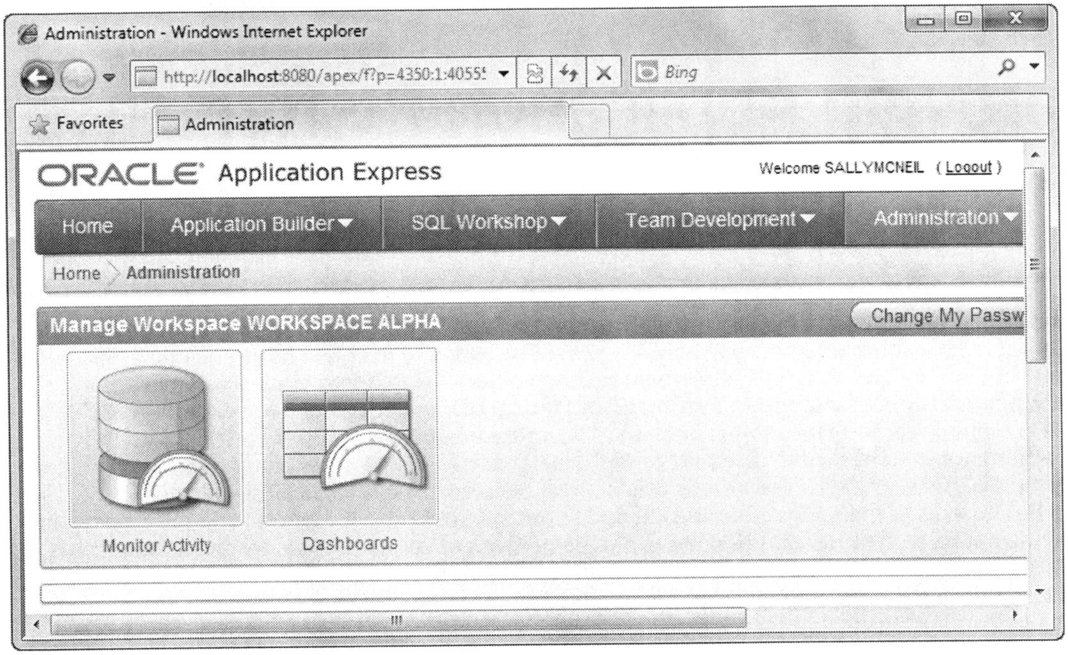

Figure 7-1. The Monitor Activity icon

3. Click the Monitor Activity icon. Scroll down to the Page View Analysis section, and click the Most Viewed Pages over All Applications link.

4. You should see a view containing every single page and application in the workspace plus the frequency of access in the Count column (as shown in Figure 7-2). You can see that the MYCUSTOMERS page in the PATIENTDBAPP application is the most frequently accessed page, with eight views.

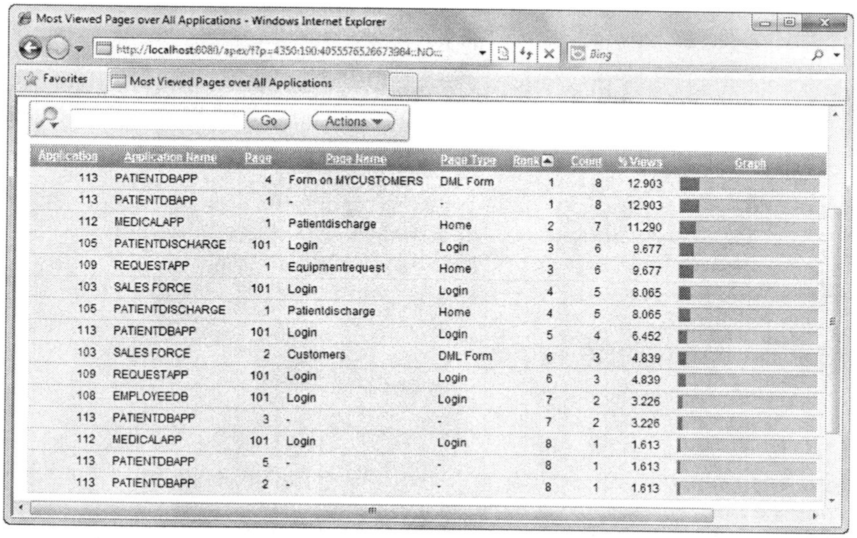

Application	Application Name	Page	Page Name	Page Type	Rank	Count	% Views	Graph
113	PATIENTDBAPP	4	Form on MYCUSTOMERS	DML Form	1	8	12.903	
113	PATIENTDBAPP	1	-	-	1	8	12.903	
112	MEDICALAPP	1	Patientdischarge	Home	2	7	11.290	
105	PATIENTDISCHARGE	101	Login	Login	3	6	9.677	
109	REQUESTAPP	1	Equipmentrequest	Home	3	6	9.677	
103	SALES FORCE	101	Login	Login	4	5	8.065	
105	PATIENTDISCHARGE	1	Patientdischarge	Home	4	5	8.065	
113	PATIENTDBAPP	101	Login	Login	5	4	6.452	
103	SALES FORCE	2	Customers	DML Form	6	3	4.839	
109	REQUESTAPP	101	Login	Login	6	3	4.839	
108	EMPLOYEEDB	101	Login	Login	7	2	3.226	
113	PATIENTDBAPP	3	-	-	7	2	3.226	
112	MEDICALAPP	101	Login	Login	8	1	1.613	
113	PATIENTDBAPP	5	-	-	8	1	1.613	
113	PATIENTDBAPP	2	-	-	8	1	1.613	

Figure 7-2. Frequency of access of each page in your applications

---

■ **Tip** You will likely get a different page access count on your system, as it depends on how many times you actually viewed each corresponding page.

How It Works

The Monitor Activity tool provides a wealth of diagnostic information pertaining to the execution of your APEX applications. The Page View Analysis section provides an eagle-eye view of application usage statistics. Table 7-1 describes some of these charts and their use. Your solution chose the Most Viewed Pages over All Applications chart, giving you a list of the most-used pages in your application.

Table 7-1. Usage Statistic Charts in the Page View Analysis Section

Chart	Description
`Most Viewed Pages over All Applications`	Displays the full list of all pages/applications and their access frequency. This is useful to find out the most frequently accessed pages in your application.
`Monthly Calendar of Page Views by Day`	Displays access frequency (and number of users) by date (populated on a visual calendar). This view is useful to determine usage peaks over a single month and the number of users accessing your applications in any single day.

Chart	Description
Line Chart of Usage by day	This chart displays total page access frequencies as a line chart on a daily or hourly timescale. This view is useful for fine-grain monitoring of usage peaks.
By Weighted Page Performance	This chart displays the average page rendering time for each page across all applications. This view is useful to gauge how each individual page performs in your application.

7-2. Measuring Page Performance in APEX

Problem

You now know which pages are important in your application. Now you want to measure the performance (in terms of rendering time) for each of those pages. You want to spend your time on pages that take the longest to render and thus maximize the return from your optimization efforts.

Solution

To measure page performance, please follow these steps:

1. Login to APEX and click the large Administration icon. Click the Monitor Activity icon and navigate to the Page View Analysis section.

2. Scroll down to the Page View Analysis section, and click the By Weighted Page Performance link.

3. Set the desired time range to collect statistical information in the Since drop-down list. If you have accessed any of the pages in your applications recently, you should see the screenshot shown in Figure 7-3. You can see the average time taken to render each particular page under the Average Elapsed column.

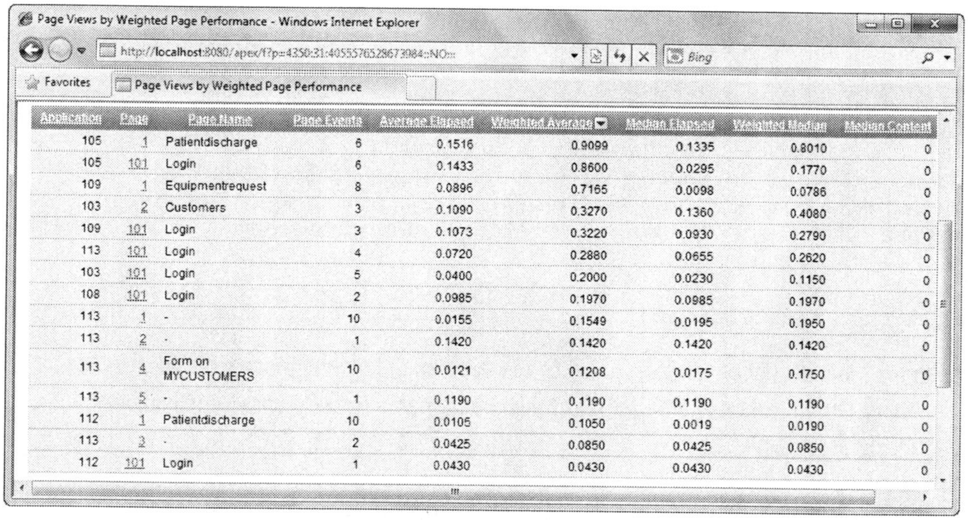

Page Views by Weighted Page Performance - Windows Internet Explorer

Application	Page	Page Name	Page Events	Average Elapsed	Weighted Average	Median Elapsed	Weighted Median	Median Content
105	1	Patientdischarge	6	0.1516	0.9099	0.1335	0.8010	0
105	101	Login	6	0.1433	0.8600	0.0295	0.1770	0
109	1	Equipmentrequest	8	0.0896	0.7165	0.0098	0.0786	0
103	2	Customers	3	0.1090	0.3270	0.1360	0.4080	0
109	101	Login	3	0.1073	0.3220	0.0930	0.2790	0
113	101	Login	4	0.0720	0.2880	0.0655	0.2620	0
103	101	Login	5	0.0400	0.2000	0.0230	0.1150	0
108	101	Login	2	0.0985	0.1970	0.0985	0.1970	0
113	1	-	10	0.0155	0.1549	0.0195	0.1950	0
113	2	-	1	0.1420	0.1420	0.1420	0.1420	0
113	4	Form on MYCUSTOMERS	10	0.0121	0.1208	0.0175	0.1750	0
113	5	-	1	0.1190	0.1190	0.1190	0.1190	0
112	1	Patientdischarge	10	0.0105	0.1050	0.0019	0.0190	0
113	3	-	2	0.0425	0.0850	0.0425	0.0850	0
112	101	Login	1	0.0430	0.0430	0.0430	0.0430	0

Figure 7-3. Measuring page performance

How It Works

The Page Views by Weighted Page Performance page shows execution statistics for each individual page in your application on an averaged basis. This report shows a few different pieces of information, which are described in Table 7-2.

Table 7-2. Page Execution Statistics

Column Name	Description
`Average Elapsed`	Displays the average time taken (in seconds) for the execution of the page.
`Weighted Average`	Each page consists of page rendering and processing events that may affect the amount of time required to render the page. The weighted average multiplies the average rendering time by the number of events on the page.
`Median Elapsed`	This column displays the median of the average rendering time of each page. This gives a more accurate reading closer to the actual elapsed rendering time of the page.
`Weighted Median`	The weighted median (for each page) is the median elapsed multiplied by the number of events in each page.

These figures are particularly useful in that they allow you to zoom in on the pages that need performance optimization. For instance, the following is a series of steps you can adopt as a strategy for optimization:

5. Sort all pages by Median Elapsed time, and take note of all the pages that exceed a certain threshold. Consider deriving that threshold from your enterprise objectives. For instance, your Quality of Service statement might include delivering every page to your end user in less than three seconds. Such an objective will let you narrow down to a smaller and more manageable subset of pages for optimization.

▦ **Tip**   It's interesting to note that public tenders issued by the Government of Singapore for IT projects typically outline the three-second maximum response time as one of the requirements for web-based applications.

---

6. Review the Page Events values. The Median Elapsed time alone is not a good indicator for the performance of the page. Looking at the Page Events column will let you make a better assessment, since the number of page events roughly correlates with the complexity of the page. For instance, a page that takes three seconds to load might actually be more performance-effective than a page that takes one second to load if that first page has 20 events and the second page has 1 event.

7-3. Measuring Region Performance in APEX

Problem

You now know the average elapsed time taken for each page. You want to drill down further into the performance of each individual region in a particular page. As in the previous recipe, your goal is to focus your optimization efforts on those pages and regions consuming the most time.

Solution

To measure region performance, please follow these steps:

1. Log in to APEX and open any application that contains a report. (To create a report page, please see Recipe 2-2). Navigate to the Page Rendering view of the report page.

2. Expand the Regions node, and right-click on any region under this node. Click the Edit menu item in the pop-up menu (as shown in Figure 7-4).

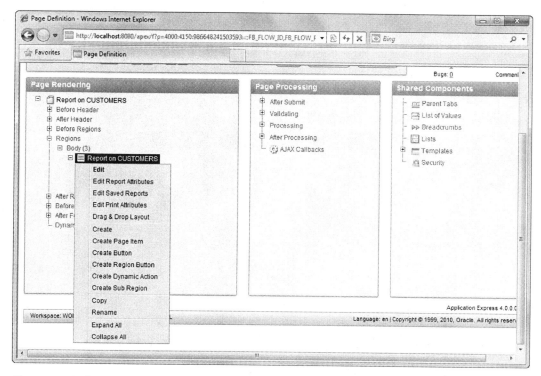

Figure 7-4. *Editing the report region*

3. In the Edit Region page, click the Header and Footer tab. In the Region Footer section, enter the following line:

```
#ROWS_FETCHED# rows fetched (from a total of #TOTAL_ROWS# rows) in #TIMING# seconds
```

4. You should now see the screenshot shown in Figure 7-5.

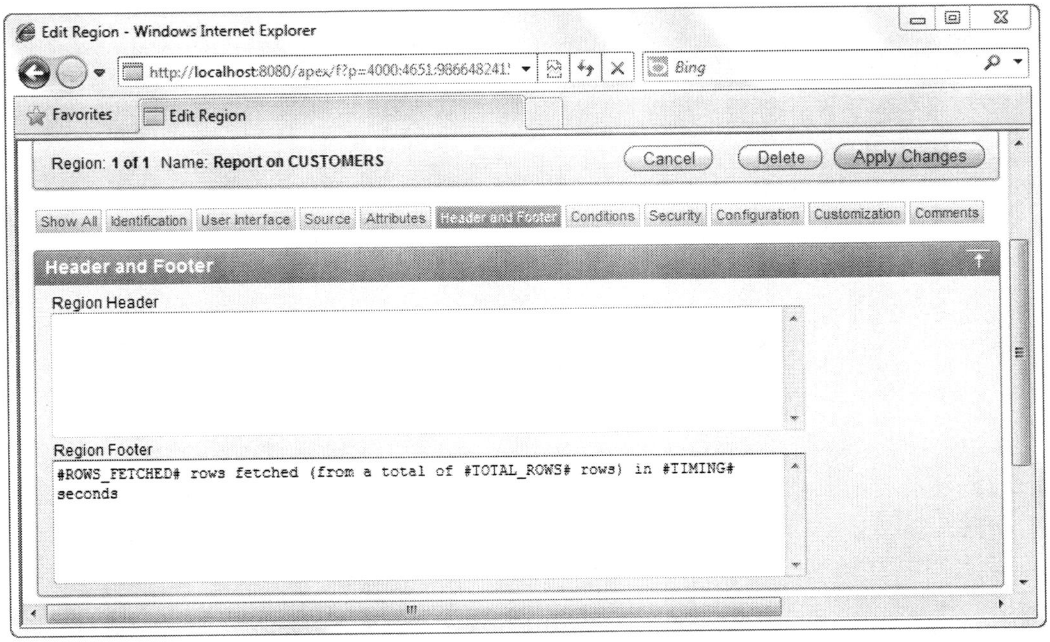

Figure 7-5. Specifying substitution strings in the region footer to collect performance statistics

5. Apply your changes and run the report. You should notice a new line at the bottom of the Report region which provides you the total time taken to run the query and render the region (and its contained items), as shown in Figure 7-6.

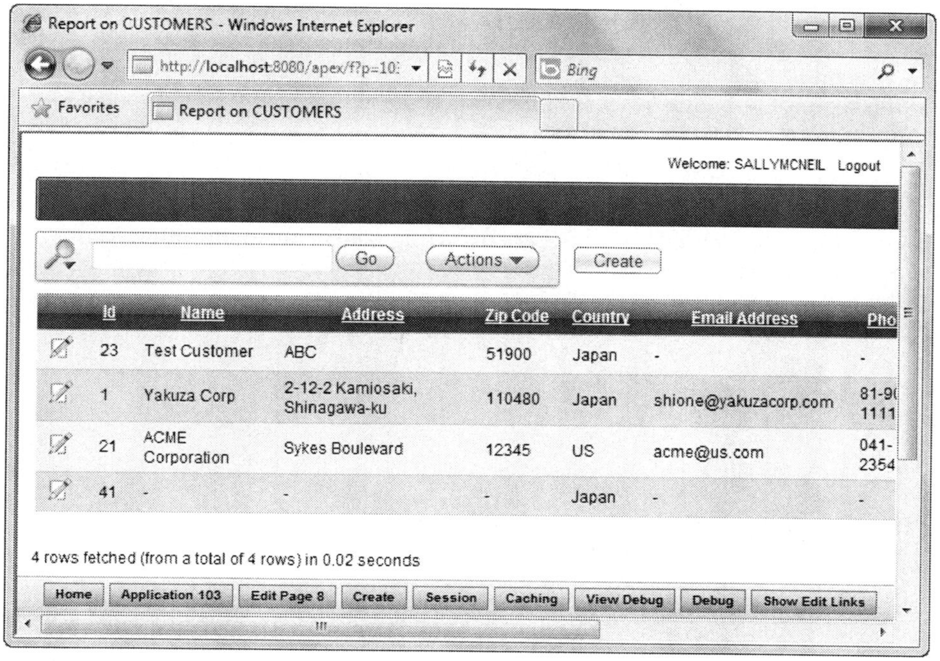

Figure 7-6. Performance statistics displayed in the footer of the region

How It Works

A page may consist of several regions; some may already be performance-optimized but others are not. When focusing on per-page optimization, it's useful to break it down further by running a quick assessment on the individual components (regions) in that page.

The best way to do this is to capture and print performance statistics for each region. This simple step will give you actual run-time statistics for all the regions in a page—and instantly reveal the particular region that's giving you performance troubles. Oracle APEX provides the substitution strings described in Table 7-3 to provide real-time information on performance statistics.

Table 7-3. Useful Substitution Strings for Performance Statistics Gathering

Substitution String	Description
#TIMING#	Shows the elapsed time (in seconds) used in rendering a particular region.
#TOTAL_ROWS#	Displays the total number of rows retrieved by the particular SQL query in a region.
#ROWS_FETCHED#	Shows the total number of rows fetched by APEX from the query for display.

215

You can place these substitution strings in more than one region on a page to find out how long each region takes to render. This will allow you to find the performance-poor region and to focus your performance tuning efforts there.

As you've seen in this recipe, these three pieces of information are indispensable in the goal of profiling your pages (and regions). It is important to look at all three parameters and not just the #TIMING# info.

For instance, consider this scenario: Region A might take three seconds in total to render, but this may be due to the fact that there are 500 rows to fetch for display, as opposed to Region B that takes one second to render but fetches only 100 rows. In this case, Region A might be better-performing than Region B despite Region B having a shorter rendering time. Thus, you should always consider all three parameters before deciding if a region needs performance optimization.

7-4. Enabling Region Caching

Problem

You have a region that retrieves a list of fixed/static data from the database for display. You want to improve the performance of this region by caching it.

Solution

To enable region caching, please follow these steps:

1. Log in to APEX and open any application that contains a form. (To create a form page, please see Recipe 2-1). Navigate to the Page Rendering view of the form page.

2. Expand the Regions node, and right click on any region under this node. Click the Edit menu item in the pop-up menu. This will bring you to the Region Definition page.

3. Click the Caching tab. Change the Caching drop-down list from Not Cached to Cached.

4. You should see several fields. Set the timeout value for the cache (the amount of time the region should stay cached) to 1 hour and the Cache condition type to Always, as shown in Figure 7-7.

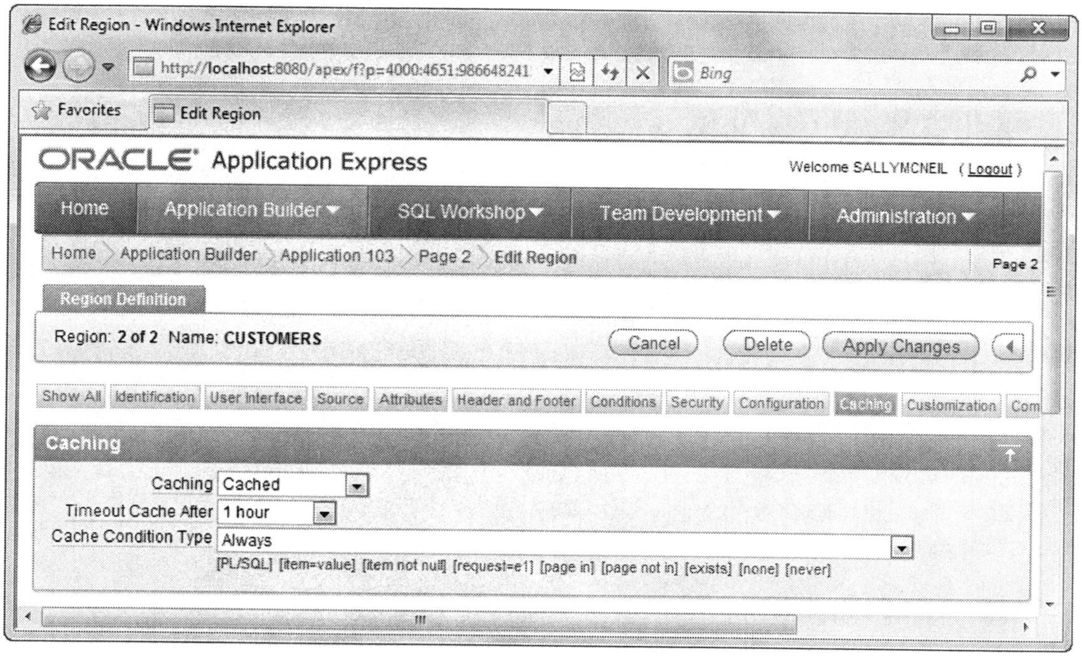

Figure 7-7. Enabling caching in a page region

5. Run your form now. If you include #TIMING# statistics in the region footer, you should observe that the amount of time elapsed in rendering the region is smaller on consecutive runs.

How It Works

It's almost inevitable that pages in your application will have to handle dynamic queries, web service calls, and so on. If, for instance, you had to call a remote web service to retrieve the list of fruits for display in a region, that would equate to a lot of calls! Imagine a user base of 2000 loading this page—this would generate 2000 web service calls.

Now if the web service retrieves exactly the same thing or something that rarely changes (for example, branch outlet phone numbers), it would be ideal to have this information cached so that the web service need only be called once. The data retrieved is then stored locally. When the next user requests the same data, it would fetch it from the local store instead of invoking another web service call.

When you cache a region, you are doing exactly this. The static HTML (generated content) of an entire region can be cached by APEX, so that when the next user renders the region, it will just grab the static HTML from the local cache store. This saves a huge amount of processing cycles and can even significantly reduce network traffic (by reducing the number of dynamic calls to physically remote systems). You can choose to cache a particular region of a form by setting the Caching property to true. If you wanted caching to be always applied, choose the Always condition type.

You can specifically state the conditions in which data should be retrieved from the cache instead of being dynamically rendered. The Cache Condition Type drop-down lists allows you to specify this condition. For instance, if you are creating an online gift ordering application, you may want to create a condition that does a check on the system date so that caching will only be applied during the month of December, when you can expect a larger number of hits from holiday shoppers.

7-5. Enabling Page Caching

Problem

You have a page that consists mostly of static data. You want to improve the rendering performance of this page.

Solution

Page caching, as opposed to region caching, caches the static HTML of an entire page. To enable page caching, please follow these steps:

1. Log in to APEX and open any application that contains a form. (To create a form page, please see Recipe 2-1). Navigate to the Page Rendering view of the form page.

2. Right-click on the root node, and choose the Edit menu item in the pop-up menu. This will bring you to the Page Definition page.

3. Click the Cache tab. Change the Cache drop-down list from No to Yes.

4. You should now be able to set the timeout value for the cache (the amount of time the region should stay cached) to 1 hour and the Cache condition type to Always, as shown in Figure 7-8.

Figure 7-8. Enabling caching in a page

5. Run your form now. If you use the Monitor Activity tool to check the weighted performance for the page, you should observe that the amount of time elapsed in rendering the page is smaller on consecutive runs.

How It Works

Caching works not only at the region level but also at the page level. Page caching is different from region caching in that it caches the static HTML of the entire page. If your objective for the page is to simply display some static information that rarely changes, it is a good candidate for page caching.

The Cache By User setting allows the page to be cached by user, as opposed to caching by session. The difference is that if you cache a page by session, all other users will use the same copy from the cache, whereas if you cached a page by user, the data is only retrieved from the cache if it was accessed by the same user that first accessed the page.

■ **Tip**   One problem with page caching is that sometimes the data for a cached page might have changed, and APEX is still retrieving the cached copy. In such cases, it might be fruitful to invalidate the cache based on a certain event. You can use the APEX_UTIL.CLEAR_PAGE_CACHE(page_number); function to invalidate the cache when the user logs out of the application or after a period of inactivity, for example.

CHAPTER 8

Securing an Application

Applications that you build on top of APEX are not, by default, magically hacker-proof. Even tight platforms such as APEX have several security concerns. In APEX, these concerns usually center around three main areas: authentication, authorization, and vulnerability exploits.

Authentication refers to the process of checking if the user has rights to access (log in to) the application. This is usually done through a username-password challenge. Authorization is the process of specifying access rights for each user to a particular resource in the application. For instance, an authorization scheme may permit a user to view a report but not to delete it. Finally, security vulnerability exploits—events like SQL injection attacks and cross-site scripting attacks—work on the premise of cleverly manipulating input data so that it ends up being executed by your application.

The good news is that APEX provides ample features and allocation to elegantly handle all three concerns. In this chapter, you will learn how to beef up security in your application.

8-1. Creating Your Own Authentication Scheme

Problem

You have an existing database table containing the list of all users in the organization, together with their passwords. This database table is a custom table proprietary to your organization. You try to convince your bosses to migrate the list of user accounts from the custom table into APEX, but they insist that your application authenticate against this table instead in real time.

And so you embark on this task. You want to create a custom authentication scheme to authenticate your APEX application against this external database table.

Solution

Your first task is to create the database objects used in this recipe. To create the CustomLogins table (and sample records), run the following SQL:

```
CREATE TABLE  "CUSTOMLOGINS"
    (    "USERID" VARCHAR2(50),
         "USERNAME" VARCHAR2(255),
         "PASSWORD" VARCHAR2(255),
          CONSTRAINT "CUSTOMLOGINS_PK" PRIMARY KEY ("USERID") ENABLE
    )
```

```
INSERT INTO CUSTOMLOGINS(USERID,USERNAME,PASSWORD) VALUES('01','greg','1234')
/
INSERT INTO CUSTOMLOGINS(USERID,USERNAME,PASSWORD) VALUES('02','zehoo','7890')
/
```

Your next task is to define the actual authentication function itself. You will create a very simple authentication function that simply checks if the specified username and password exists in the table. If they do, access is granted. To create this function, open the SQL workshop, and run the PL/SQL shown in Listing 8-1.

Listing 8-1. Defining the Authentication Function

```
CREATE OR REPLACE FUNCTION MyCustomAuthenticator (
  p_username IN VARCHAR2,
  p_password IN VARCHAR2
)
  RETURN BOOLEAN
IS
  l_count NUMBER;
BEGIN
  SELECT COUNT(*) into l_count from CUSTOMLOGINS WHERE Username=p_username AND
 Password=p_password;
  IF l_count > 0 THEN
    RETURN TRUE;
  ELSE
    RETURN FALSE;
  END IF;
END;
```

Your next task will be to define a new authentication scheme. To do so, follow these steps:

1. Open an existing application and click the Shared Components icon.

2. Under the Security section, click on the Authentication Schemes link, as highlighted in Figure 8-1.

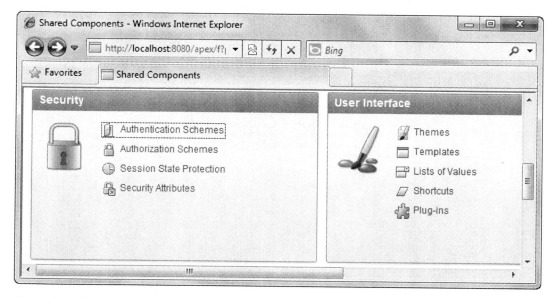

Figure 8-1. The Authentication Schemes link

3. In the ensuing page, click the Create button to create a new authentication scheme.

4. In the first step of the wizard, choose to create the scheme from scratch.

5. In the next step, name your authentication scheme MYCUSTOMAUTH_SCHEME.

6. Click the Next button until you arrive at the Authentication Function step.

7. In this screen, choose the Use my custom function to authenticate option. This will cause an Authentication Function textbox to appear at the bottom of the option.

8. Type the following text into the textbox: return MyCustomAuthenticator. This is shown in Figure 8-2.

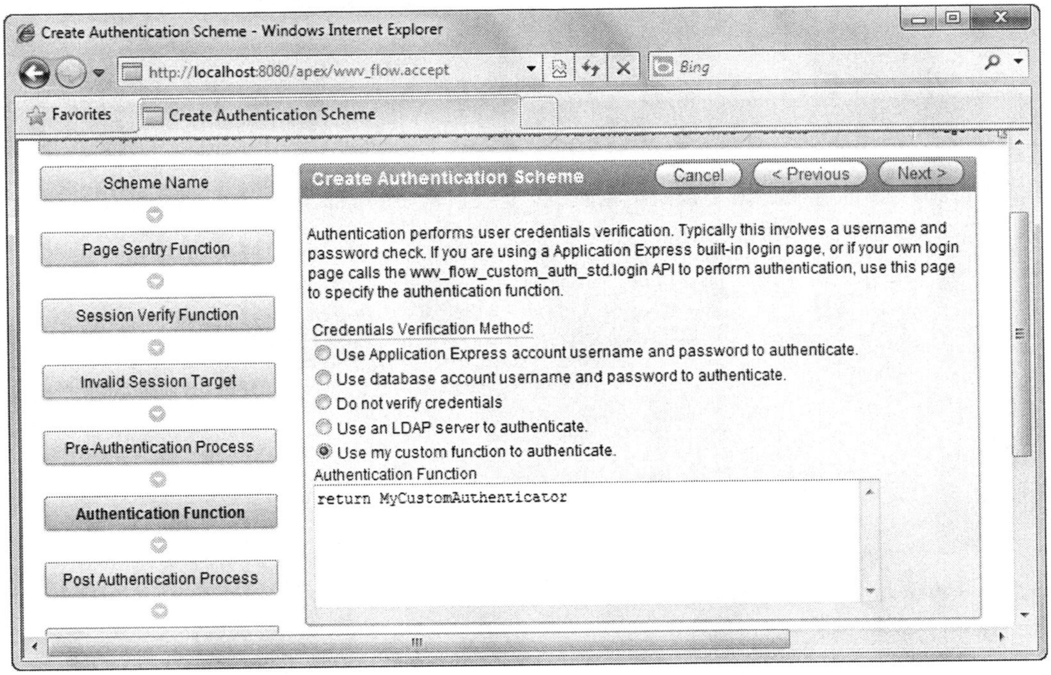

Figure 8-2. Defining the Authentication Function call

9. Complete the rest of the wizard using the default settings provided.

10. Back in the Authentication Schemes page, you should see your newly created authentication scheme. Now you will need to set it as the active authentication scheme for your application.

11. In the authentication schemes page, click the Change Current tab. Choose the MYCUSTOMAUTH_SCHEME scheme from the drop-down list, as shown in Figure 8-3.

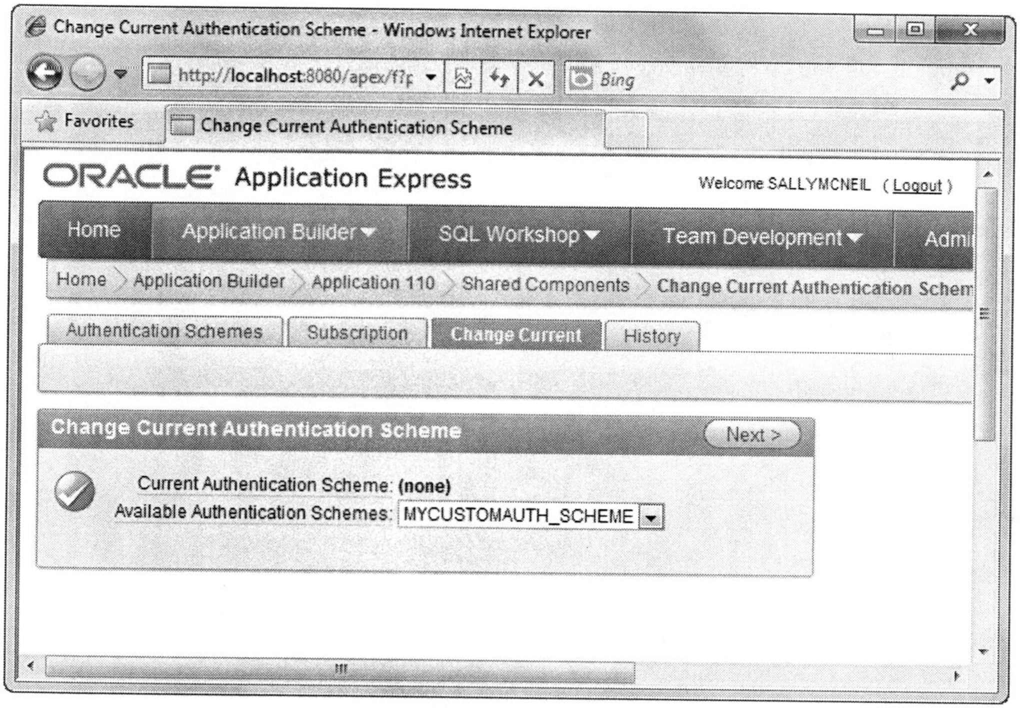

Figure 8-3. Setting the current authentication scheme

12. Click the Make Current button to complete the wizard and make the change.

13. Now run the Login form in your application. Try to key in a random username and password. You will find that you can't login to the application, as shown in Figure 8-4.

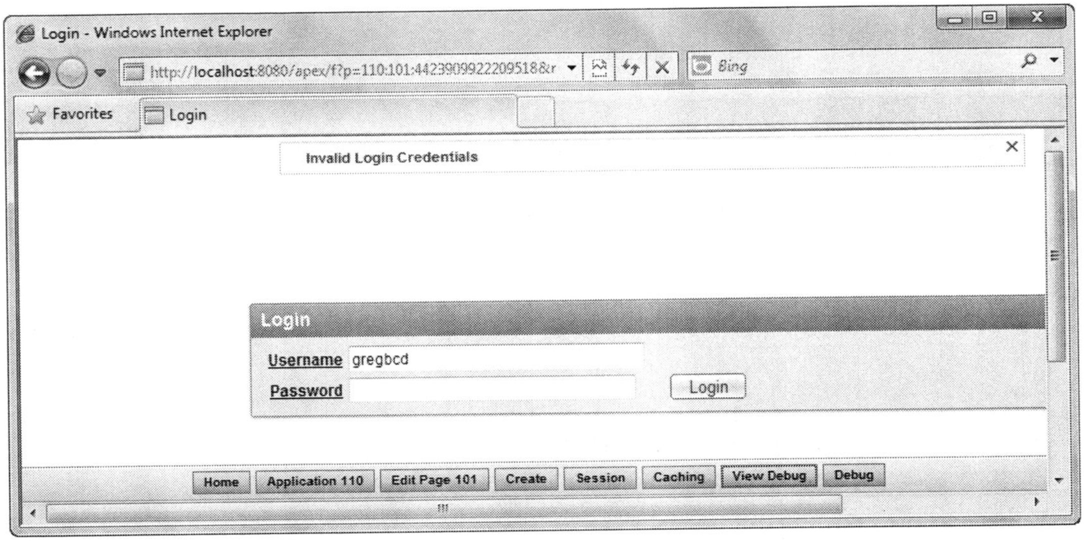

Figure 8-4. Access denied

14. However, if you specify the credentials greg with the password 1234, you will find that you can successfully login to the application. This proves that the login page is now using your custom authentication scheme.

How It Works

APEX is flexible enough to allow you to modify even the underlying authentication mechanisms for your applications. The method shown in this recipe uses a very simple authentication function (that hardcodes the username and password in PL/SQL); the objective of this recipe, however, is to give you an idea of how to go about switching the authentication mechanism from APEX's default to a custom one.

▪ **Note** Using APEX's flexible authentication framework, you can create schemes to authenticate against LDAP stores or to specify not to have authentication at all in your application. You can change these settings in the properties area of the authentication scheme.

Let's take a further look at how the PL/SQL authentication function works. The skeleton for this function is described in Listing 8-2.

Listing 8-2. Skeleton of the Authentication Function

```
CREATE OR REPLACE FUNCTION AuthenticationFunction (
```

```
  p_username IN VARCHAR2,
  p_password IN VARCHAR2
)
  RETURN BOOLEAN
AS
BEGIN
    /* Do your thing here and return TRUE if access should be granted and
       FALSE if access should be denied. */
END;
```

You can modify this authentication function to do whatever you need. For instance, you could have the function run an SELECT query against an external table, and if the user account exists, return TRUE from the function.

In fact, there is nothing stopping you from authenticating in real-time against usernames or passwords stored in text files (although it would be a rather bad idea to do so). This, however, gives you an idea of the extremes that you can go to with APEX's flexible authentication schemes framework.

8-2. Defining User Access Rights

Problem

You have an interactive report showing a list of job vacancy records. You want to allow John to create new job vacancy record, but you don't want to give Barry this same privilege. In other words, you need to configure access rights for this report.

Solution

First you need to create the sample objects used in this recipe. To do so, please follow these steps:

1. Create the sample Jobs table as shown in Listing 8-3.

Listing 8-3. *The Sample Jobs Table*

```
CREATE TABLE  "JOBS"
   (    "JOB_ID" VARCHAR2(10),
        "JOB_TITLE" VARCHAR2(35) CONSTRAINT "JOB_TITLE_NN" NOT NULL ENABLE,
        "MIN_SALARY" NUMBER(6,0),
        "MAX_SALARY" NUMBER(6,0),
         CONSTRAINT "JOB_ID_PK" PRIMARY KEY ("JOB_ID") ENABLE
   )
```

2. Enter some sample data in this table using the code in Listing 8-4.

Listing 8-4. *Sample Data in the Jobs Table*

```
INSERT INTO JOBS(JOB_ID,JOB_TITLE,MIN_SALARY,MAX_SALARY)
VALUES('AD_PRES','President',20000,40000)
INSERT INTO JOBS(JOB_ID,JOB_TITLE,MIN_SALARY,MAX_SALARY) VALUES('AD_VP','Administration Vice
President',15000,30000)
```

3. Now, create a new application. In the application, create a new form, and choose the Form on a Table with Report template.

■ **Note** You can refer to Recipe 2-1 on how to create a new application and form

---

4. When you are prompted to specify the base table for your form and report, choose the Jobs table, as shown in Figure 8-5.

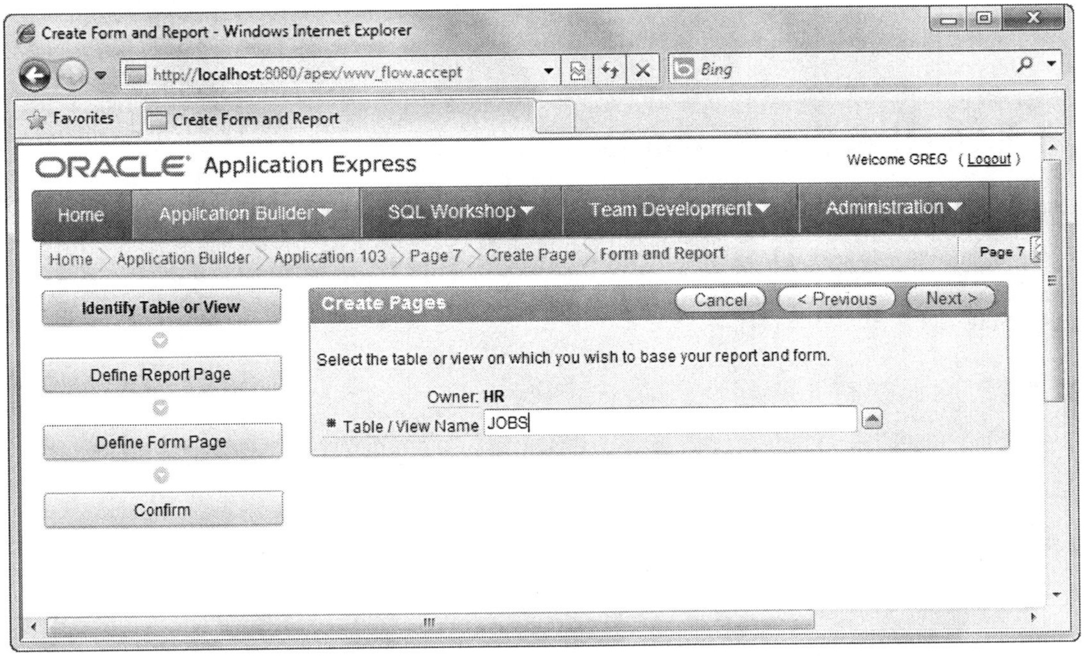

Figure 8-5. Choosing the base table for your form and report

5. Step through the rest of the wizard using the default settings provided and complete the wizard.

6. Log out from the workspace, and log in to the INTERNAL workspace using the ADMIN account. Navigate to Manage Workspaces ➤ Existing workspaces. Click on the workspace you were working on earlier, and click the Manage Users button.

7. Create a new user with the username of greg. Set any password you desire for this account.

Now that you've successfully created the sample objects successfully, let's move on to creating an authorization scheme. Please follow these instructions to do so:

1. Open your application and click the Shared Components icon.

2. In the Security area of the page, click the Authorization Schemes link (highlighted in Figure 8-6).

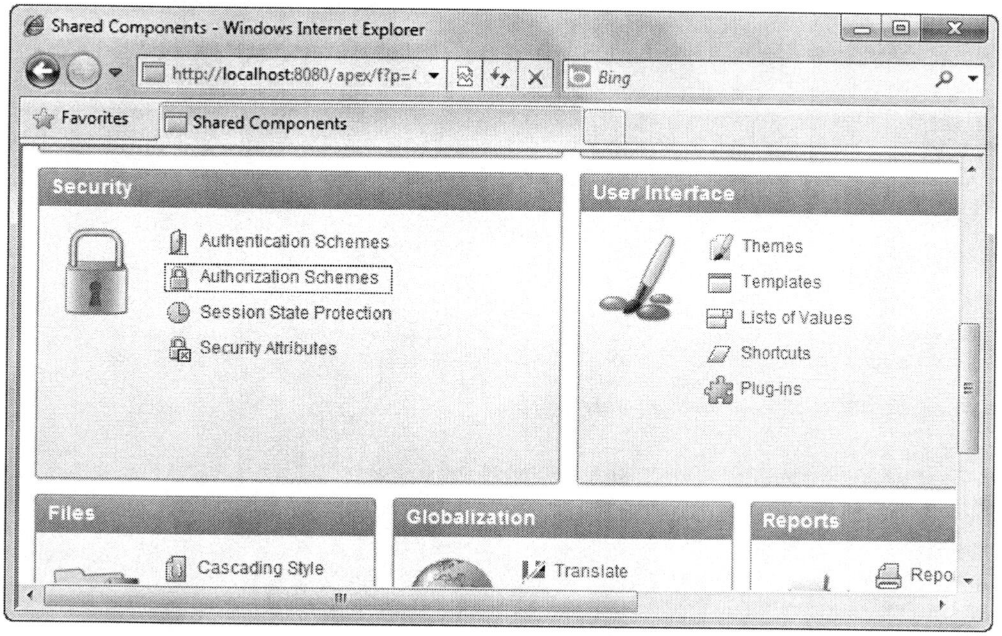

Figure 8-6. Authorization Schemes link

3. On the next page, click the Create button to create a new authorization scheme.

4. Choose to create the scheme from scratch when prompted, as shown in Figure 8-7.

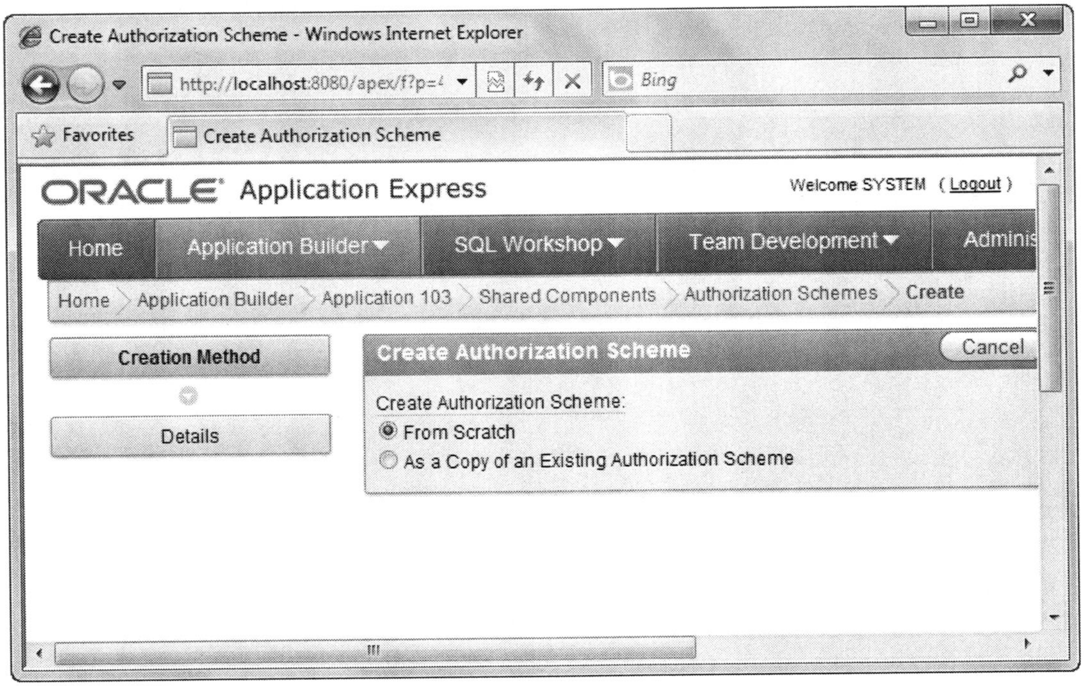

Figure 8-7. Creating an authorization scheme from scratch

5. On the next page, give your authorization scheme the name of CHECKFORGREG.

6. Choose Exists SQL Query as the Scheme Type, and in the Expression 1 field, enter the following PL/SQL:

```
select 1 from jobs where LOWER(v('APP_USER')) = 'greg'
```

7. Specify "Scheme Violated" as the scheme violated error message. You should now have the screen shown in Figure 8-8.

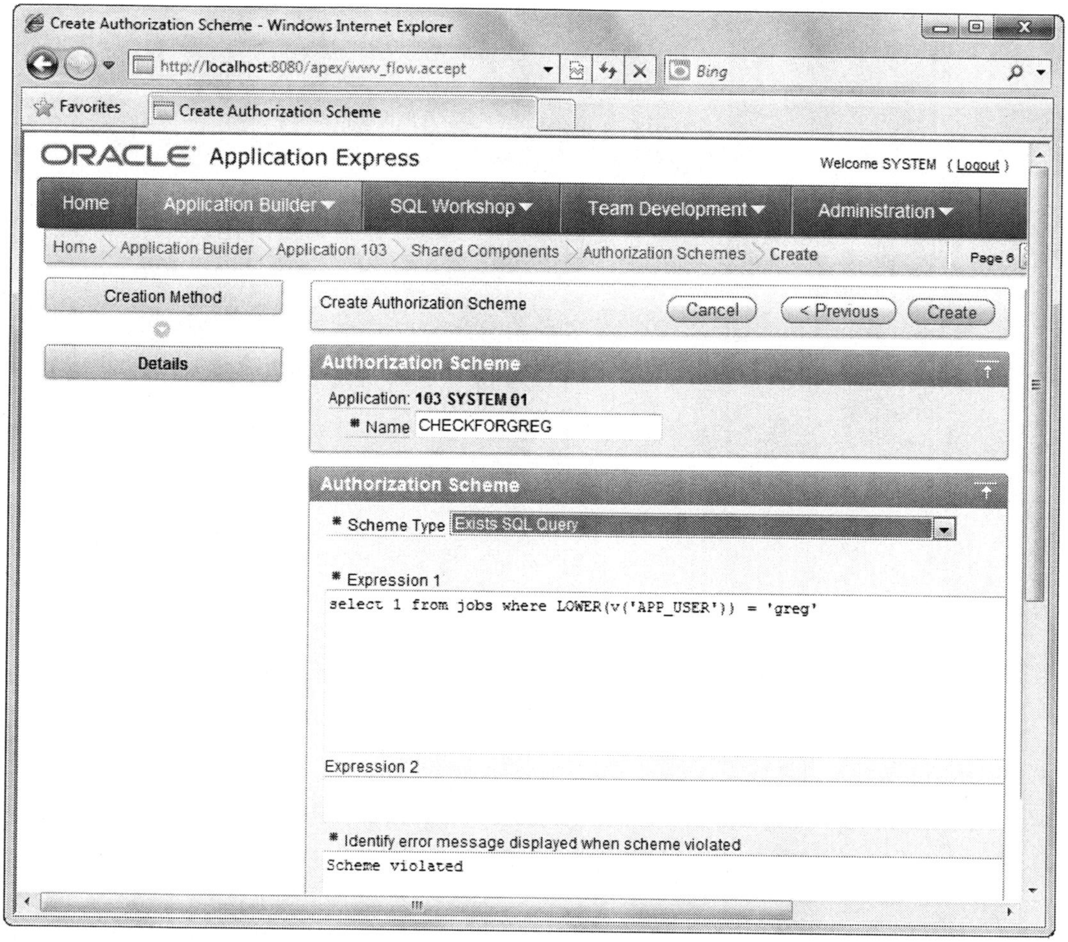

Figure 8-8. Defining the authorization scheme

8. Click the Create button to create the authorization scheme.

Now you will need to apply the authorization scheme to the report.

1. Open the Jobs report you created earlier in this recipe.

2. In the Page Rendering area of the report, right-click on the Create button, and choose to edit it, as shown in Figure 8-9.

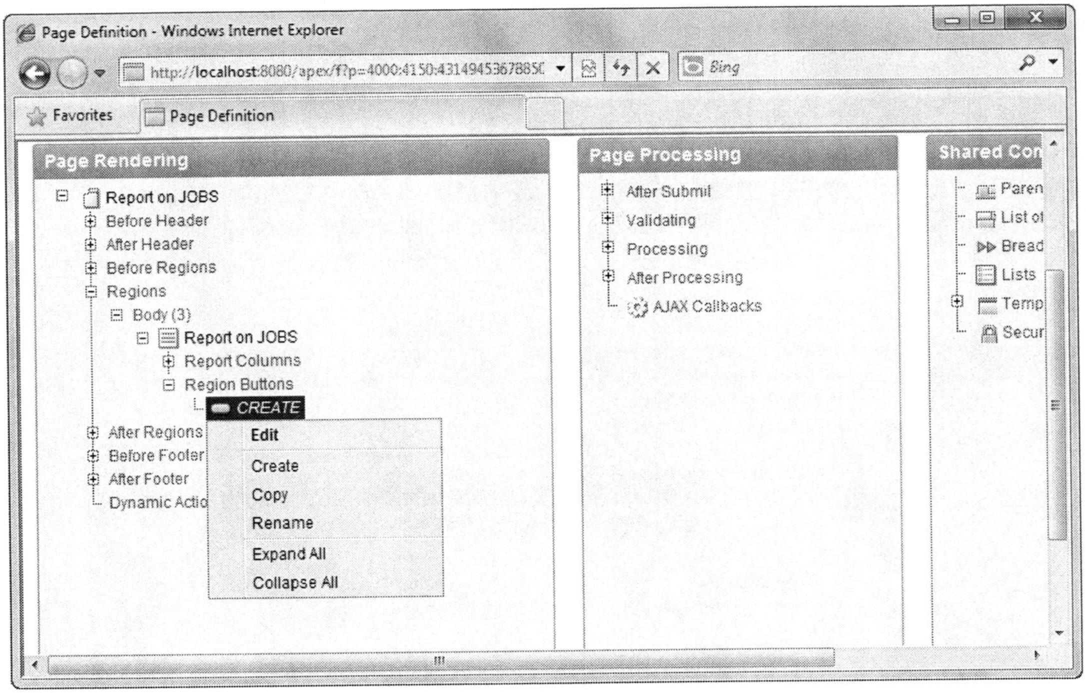

Figure 8-9. Modifying settings for the Create button

3. On the next page, scroll down to the Security section and select CHECKFORGREG as the authorization scheme for this button item. This is shown in Figure 8-10.

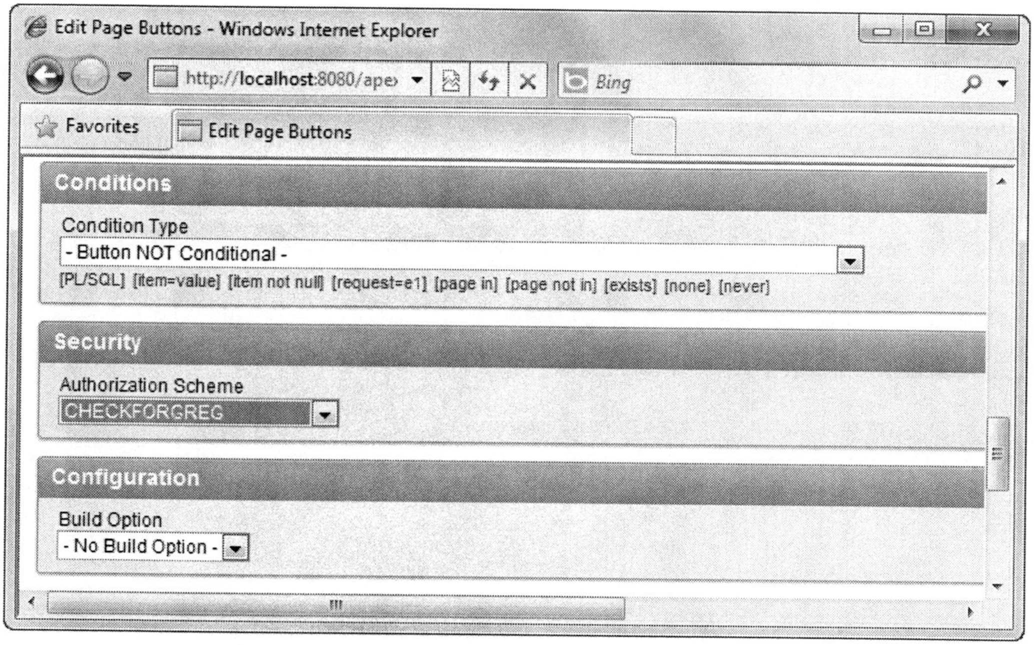

Figure 8-10. Settings the authorization scheme for the Create button

4. Save your changes and run the report. If you log in to the application as greg, you will see the Create button at the top right corner of the report, as shown in Figure 8-11.

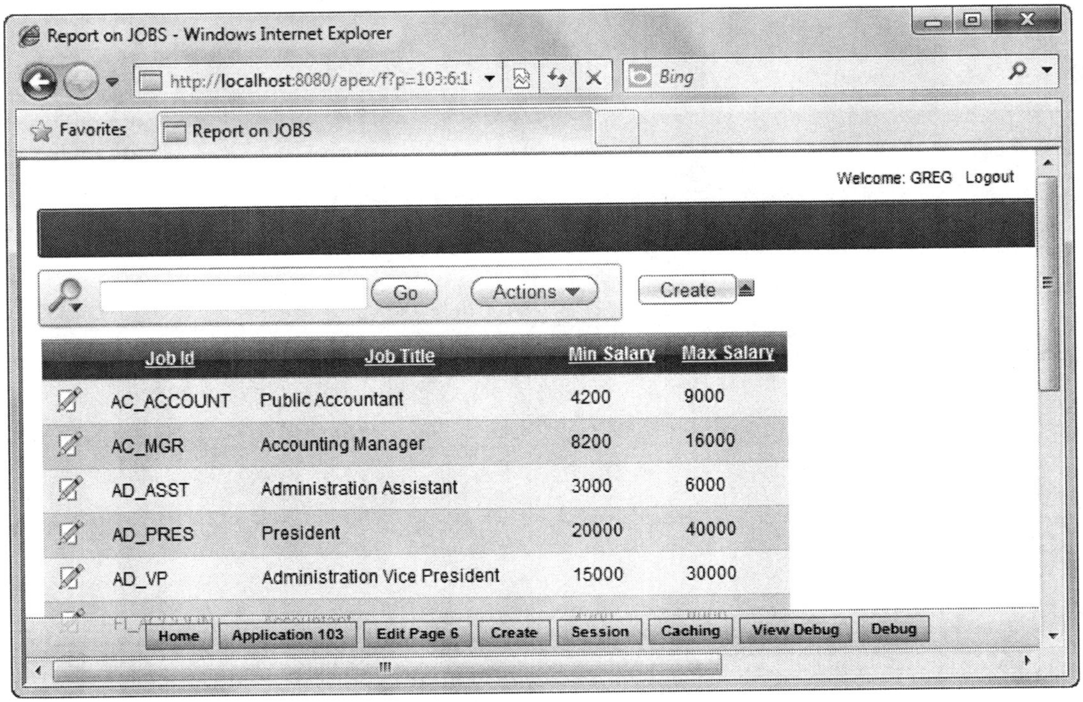

Figure 8-11. Create button visible for user named greg

5. Now, log out from the application and log in as any other user. You will notice that the Create button does not show for this user, as illustrated in Figure 8-12.

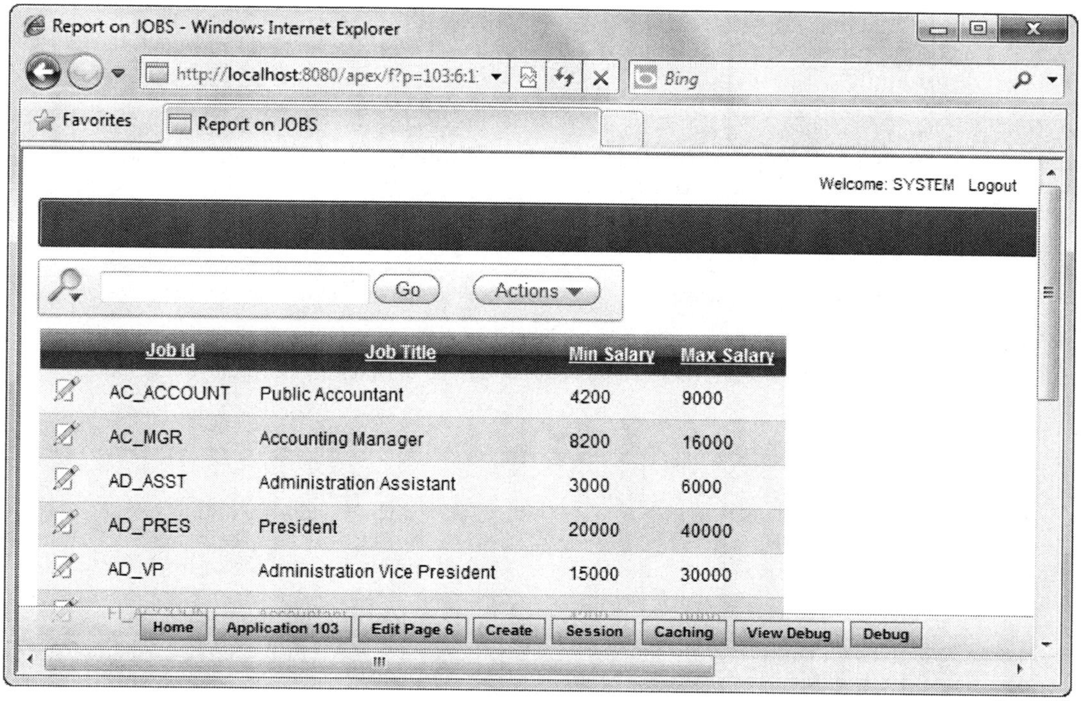

Figure 8-12. Create button missing for user named system

How It Works

An authorization scheme lets you define a condition (logic) that evaluates to either a true or false. The authorization scheme can then be applied to any element in your application, be it a report column, a button on a report, or even an entire form itself. When the scheme (your logic) returns true, the current user is granted access to the element. If it returns false, the current user is denied access.

Let's take a closer look at the configuration of the authorization scheme that you created earlier. Note that you chose the Exists SQL Query scheme type; it means that if the PL/SQL you wrote returned a record, then the scheme evaluates to true (access granted). If an empty result set was returned, the scheme would evaluate to false (access denied).

Now, let's take a look at the PL/SQL from earlier in this recipe:

```
select 1 from jobs where LOWER(v('APP_USER')) = 'greg'
```

> ■ **Tip** v('APP_USER') is a dynamic field (called a built-in substitution string) that returns the username of the currently logged on user. There are other built-in substitution strings defined in APEX; a comprehensive list of all the substitution strings available in APEX is here:
>
> http://download.oracle.com/docs/cd/B32472_01/doc/appdev.300/b32471/concept.htm#BEIIBAJD

You've practically defined that if the current user had the username greg, then it would return something (here you simply return 1 but it could also be abc if you desire, as long as a single record was returned). Hence the authorization scheme you created in this recipe can be interpreted as: if the current user has the username greg, he should be granted access to the element.

Based on this simple concept, you can apply very complex access rights control to your application. For instance, you can create an Employee report that shows all columns to a manager, but hides the Current Salary column when a normal clerk views it.

■ **Tip** The hardcoding of data (such as username greg) in the authorization scheme is for purpose of demonstration and is certainly not encouraged. You would usually do something more meaningful in the authorization scheme, such as checking if a user is a manager or a Head of Department (against another database table and so on).

As a side note, the concept of authorization schemes also promotes reusability and ease of maintenance. It is reusable because you can reuse the same logic for multiple elements in your application without rewriting the same logic many times. More importantly, this makes it easier for you to maintain your application. For instance, if the logic changes one day, such that you need to include an additional check in your PL/SQL, you can just change it at one location, and it will instantly be applied to all elements that use the said authorization scheme.

8-3. Preventing SQL Injection Attacks

Problem

You have a dynamic report showing the list of customers in the system. By default, your application requires the end user to specify the customer name before it retrieves the matching customer from the database. An APEX hacker has managed to retrieve the full list of all customers in the database via an SQL injection attack. You want to protect your application against similar attacks in the future.

Solution

First, you need to set up the sample tables and forms needed to duplicate the scenario for the attack. To do this, please follow these steps:

1. Create the table shown in Listing 8-5 if it doesn't yet exist in your database.

Listing 8-5. Sample Customers Table

```
CREATE TABLE  "CUSTOMERS"
   (    "ID" NVARCHAR2(255) NOT NULL ENABLE,
        "NAME" NVARCHAR2(255),
        "ADDRESS" NVARCHAR2(2000),
        "ZIP_CODE" NVARCHAR2(6),
        "COUNTRY" NVARCHAR2(255),
```

```
    "EMAIL_ADDRESS" NVARCHAR2(255),
    "PHONENUMBER" NVARCHAR2(255),
    "EMPLOYEEHEADCOUNT" NUMBER(9,0),
     CONSTRAINT "CUSTOMERS_PK" PRIMARY KEY ("ID") ENABLE
)
```

2. Create the following sample data shown in Listing 8-6.

Listing 8-6. Sample Data for the Customers Table

```
INSERT INTO CUSTOMERS (ID, NAME, ADDRESS, ZIP_CODE, COUNTRY, EMAIL_ADDRESS, PHONENUMBER,
EMPLOYEEHEADCOUNT) VALUES ('1','Yakuza
Corp','Akihabara,Tokyo','551119','Japan','yakuzacorp@test.com','+8112345678',30)

INSERT INTO CUSTOMERS (ID, NAME, ADDRESS, ZIP_CODE, COUNTRY, EMAIL_ADDRESS, PHONENUMBER,
EMPLOYEEHEADCOUNT) VALUES ('2','ACME Corp','ACME City, Texas','12345','United
States','acmecity@test.com','987654321',10)

INSERT INTO CUSTOMERS (ID, NAME, ADDRESS, ZIP_CODE, COUNTRY, EMAIL_ADDRESS, PHONENUMBER,
EMPLOYEEHEADCOUNT) VALUES ('3','Shin Corp','Bangrak,
Bangkok','123456','Thailand','shincorp@test.com','12468086',15)
```

3. Now, create a new application, and create a report page in the application.

4. In the Report Page Creation wizard, choose to create the Classic Report type. Use the default settings for all the steps in the wizard, and click the Next button until you reach the step that lets you specify the SQL statement for the report.

5. Just specify SELECT * FROM CUSTOMERS in this area for the time being.

6. When the report has been created successfully, choose to edit the report.

7. In the Page Rendering area of the report, you should see the report node under the Regions ➤ Body node. Right click on the report item (Report 1), and choose to Create a new page item, as shown in Figure 8-13.

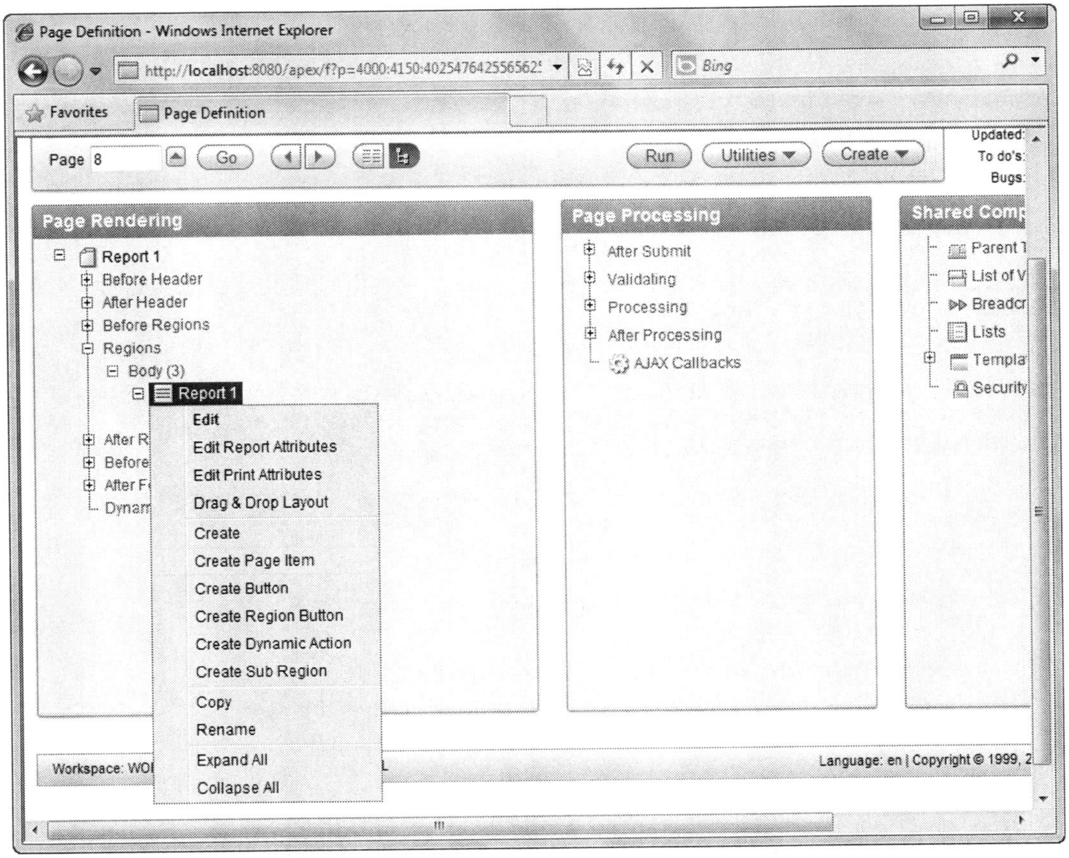

Figure 8-13. Creating a new page item in the report

8. In the wizard, choose to create a Text field. In the next step of the wizard, name the text field PSEARCH_BYNAME, and set its label to Search by Name. Click Next all the way to the end of the wizard and use the default settings provided by APEX.

9. After you've created the field, right-click on the PSEARCH_BYNAME item in the Page Rendering area, and choose the Create Button item in the pop-up menu. Name the button PSEARCH_GO and create the button. You should now have the screen shown in Figure 8-14 in the Page Rendering area of your report.

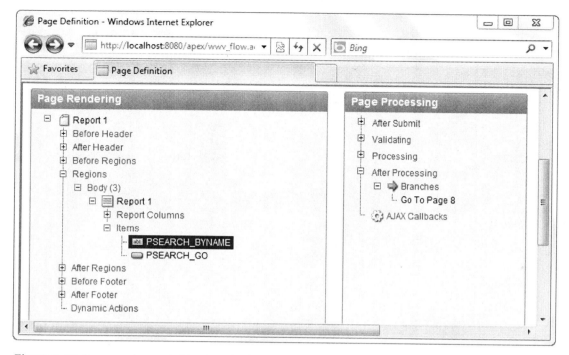

Figure 8-14. *Your newly created buttons in the report*

10. Right-click on the Report 1 item, and choose to edit the report. Scroll down to the Source section, and in the Region source field, enter the SQL statement shown in Listing 8-7.

Listing 8-7. *Specifying the Customer Search SQL*

```
SELECT * FROM CUSTOMERS WHERE NAME = '&PSEARCH_BYNAME.'
```

■ **Note** There is a full stop right after PSEARCH_BYNAME; don't forget to leave that out!

---

11. You should now have the screen shown in Figure 8-15. Click on the Apply Changes button to save your changes.

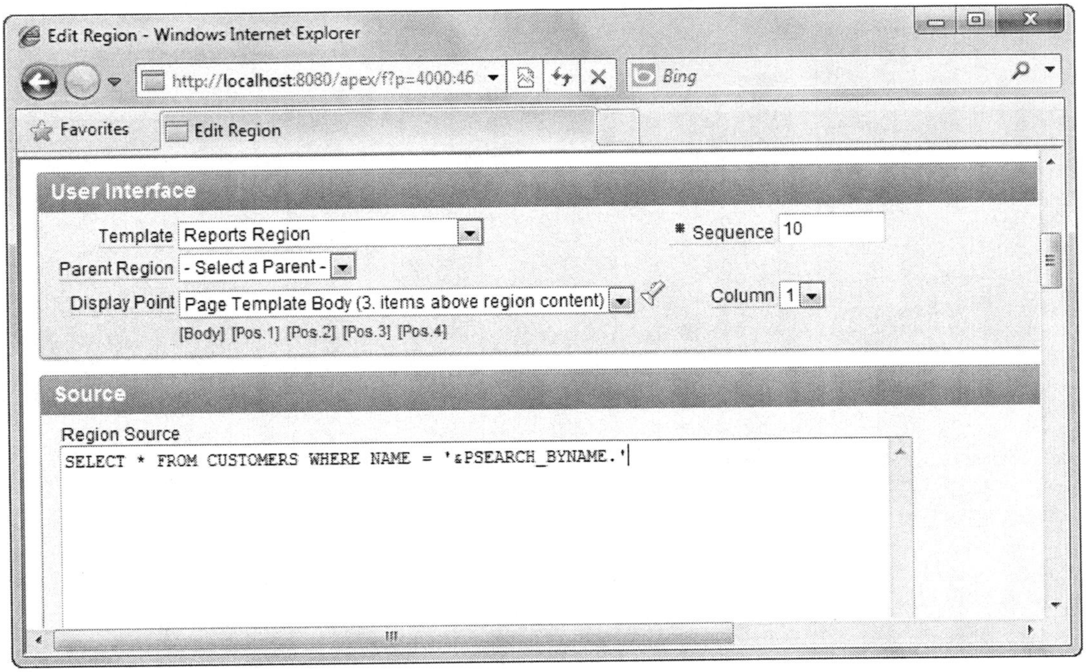

Figure 8-15. *Defining the SQL for the report*

12. Now run the report. You should see a blank report (without any data). However, upon entering Yakuza Corp in the search textbox and clicking the Go button, the report refreshes itself, showing the matching customer, as shown in Figure 8-16.

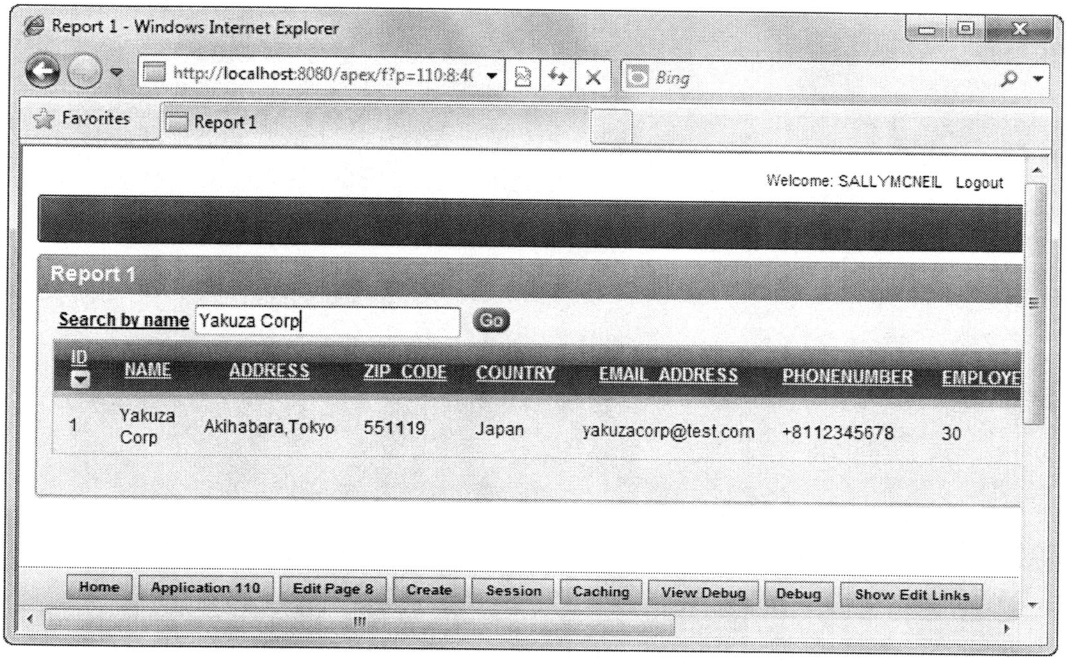

Figure 8-16. Running your report

To perform the SQL injection attack, follow these steps:

   1.   Specify the text shown in Listing 8-8 in the search field, and click the Go
        button.

Listing 8-8. Conducting the SQL Injection Attack

```
' OR 1=1--
```

   2.   You should now see every single customer retrieved from the table, as shown
        in Figure 8-17.

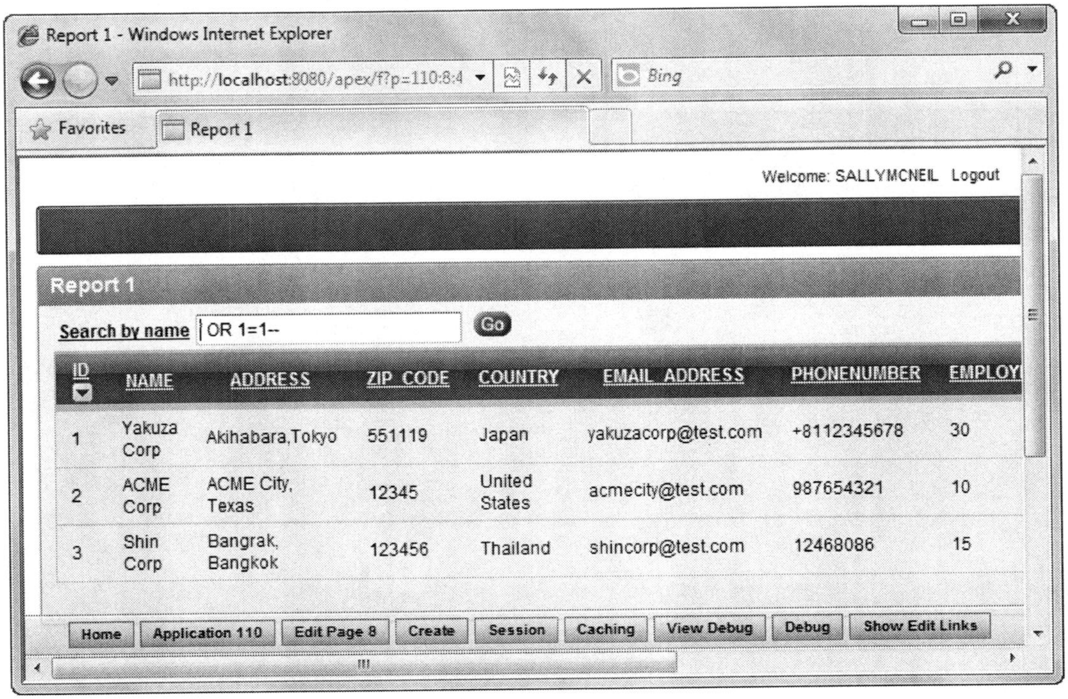

Figure 8-17. Conducting the SQL injection attack

3. Congratulations! You've successfully hacked your own application.

To prevent a SQL injection attack from being used against your application, follow these steps:

1. Navigate to the Page Rendering area of your report again. Right click on the Report 1 node, and choose to edit the report.

2. In the Region source field, change the SQL query to the one shown in Listing 8-9.

Listing 8-9. Using Bind Variables

```
SELECT * FROM CUSTOMERS WHERE NAME = :PSEARCH_BYNAME
```

3. You should now have the screen shown in Figure 8-18.

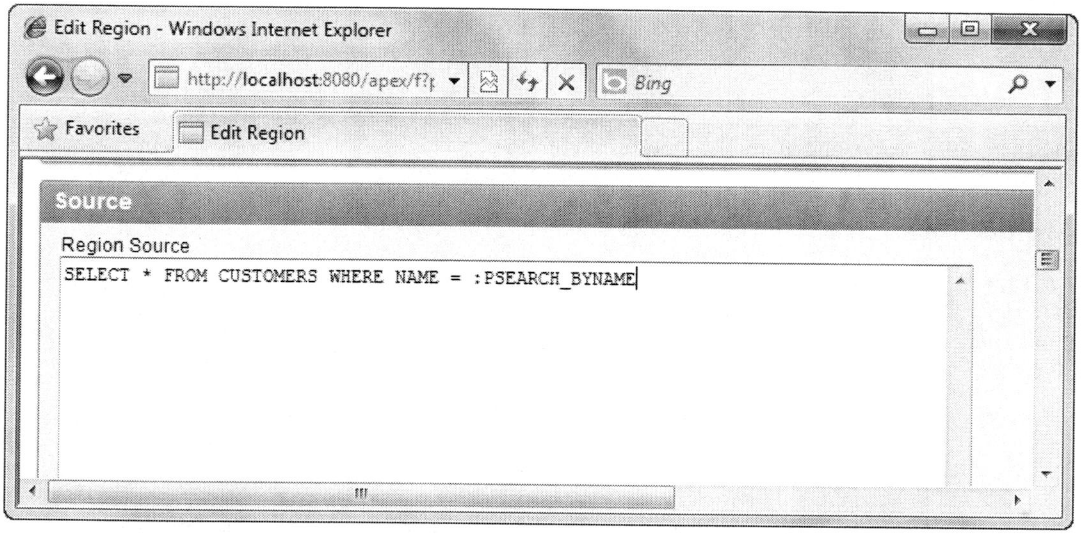

Figure 8-18. Using bind variables to protect against SQL injection attack

4. Apply your changes and run your report one more time. You will find that your report works as usual, and you can search for a customer by name. This time, however, if you specify ' OR 1=1-- in the search field and click the Go button, instead of retrieving the full list of customers from the table, it returns an empty result set. This is shown in Figure 8-19.

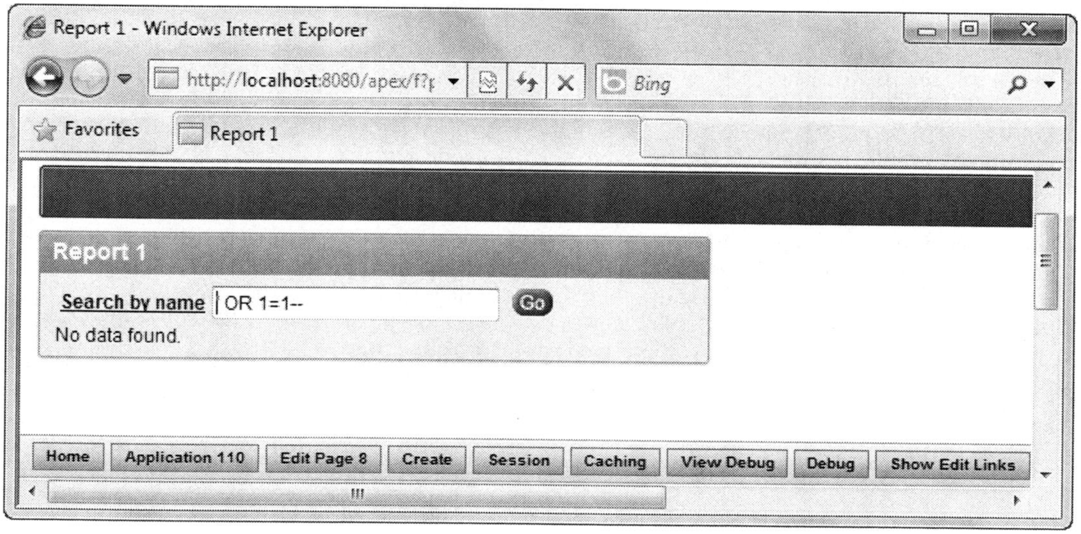

Figure 8-19. Trying the SQL injection attack again, this time on a protected form.

5.   You've successfully protected your report against the SQL injection attack.

How It Works

The SQL injection attack is one of the most common forms of attack against web applications. It usually involves a malicious user gaining unauthorized access to data by manipulating dynamic SQL statements generated by your application. This is done so by massaging input data so that becomes part of the SQL statement itself. For instance, take a look at your original SQL statement.

```
SELECT * FROM CUSTOMERS WHERE NAME = '<INPUT DATA FROM SEARCH FIELD>'
```

If the malicious user keys in ' OR 1=1-- in the search field, this is concatenated with your SQL code, and it becomes

```
SELECT * FROM CUSTOMERS WHERE NAME = '' OR 1=1--'
```

■ **Tip**   The -- symbol is the comment indicator symbol in PL/SQL, and it comments out the last single quote character, effectively turning your active SQL statement into

```
SELECT * FROM CUSTOMERS WHERE NAME='' OR 1=1
```

This allows the end user to retrieve the entire list of customers from your database! A SQL injection attack can be used in many different ways. For instance, it can be used against an unprotected login page where an end user can gain unauthorized access to your application simply by manipulating the data entered in the username or password field.

Earlier in this recipe, you saw that the following notation was used: &PSEARCH_BYNAME. The ampersand indicates that this is a substitution variable; substitution variables are used to retrieve data from form fields on a page. This data is then (as its name implies) substituted as-is into the target string. Substitution variables are the root causes of most SQL injection attacks. Since data is simply substituted into the SQL statement, this allows apostrophes keyed in by the end user to end up in the final SQL string, causing the previously mentioned scenario.

Traditionally, in most web applications, SQL injection attacks are prevented by escaping single quote characters in the input data. "Escaping" the single quote characters simply meant placing an escape character at the front of each single quote in the input data to render them harmless.

Duplicating the single quote character is a way to escape the single quote in PL/SQL. For instance, the final SQL generated if the input data was escaped would look like this:

```
SELECT * FROM CUSTOMERS WHERE NAME=''' OR 1=1--'
```

■ **Note**   The ' OR 1=1-- input phrase in the previous SQL (after escaping its single quotes) is correctly treated as a string instead of as PL/SQL code.

In Oracle APEX, there is a better way to prevent SQL injection attacks: through the use of bind variables. Bind variables work in much the same way as passing data to a stored procedure. Bind variables automatically treat all input data as "flat" data and never mistake it for SQL code.

The syntax to declare a field item as a bind variable is through the use of the colon character (:). Simply prefix the colon to your field item name, like this:

```
:PSEARCH_BYNAME
```

▓ **Note** You don't have to explicitly specify any enclosing single quote characters. APEX is already aware of the data type of your variable.

The use of bind variables is often encouraged in APEX. Besides the prevention of SQL injection attacks, there are other performance-related benefits to its use (please see Chapter 7 for more information).

8-4. Preventing Cross-Site Scripting (XSS) Attacks

Problem

Your boss opens an APEX report, but instead of seeing the daily financial data, he is automatically redirected to an adult web site containing inappropriate photos. Your boss is obviously not amused. Upon closer inspection of the report, you find that someone has entered malicious JavaScript in one of the fields in the database. Upon displaying the report, the output data (containing the JavaScript) executed, causing the malicious script to run. You recognize this as the cross-site scripting attack. You want to prevent future attacks by rendering any JavaScript code found in report data harmless when it is retrieved for display.

Solution

First, try to set up the same environment that made the cross site scripting attack possible. Please follow these steps:

1. Create a new report in the same application you created in Recipe 8-3.

2. In the Report wizard, choose the Interactive Report Type.

3. In the SQL query step of the wizard, enter the following SQL query:

```
SELECT * FROM CUSTOMERS
```

4. Complete the wizard for the report.

5. In the Page Rendering area of the report, right-click on the NAME report column, and choose to edit it, as shown in Figure 8-20.

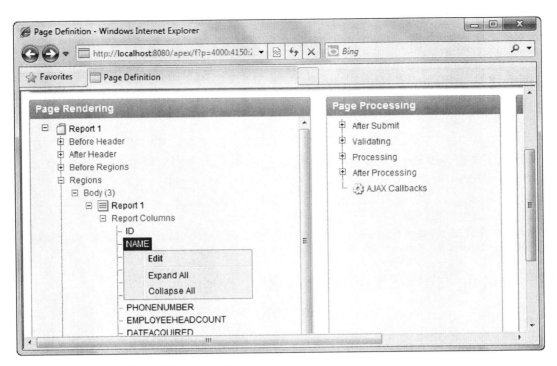

Figure 8-20. *Editing the NAME column in the report*

6. Set the value of the Display Type field to Standard Report Column, as shown in Figure 8-21.

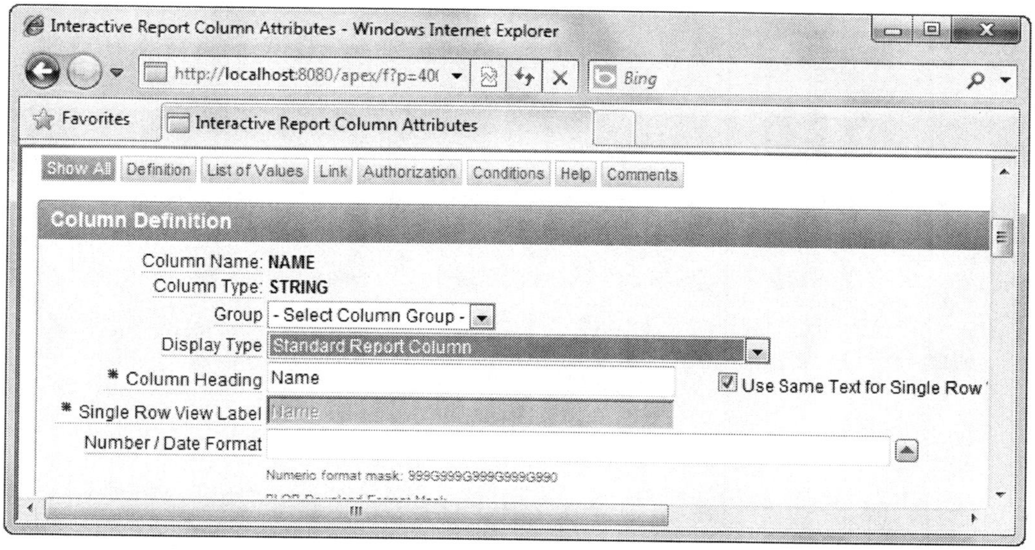

Figure 8-21. Changing the display type of the column to Standard Report Column

7. Apply your changes. Now create a new form in the same application. Choose the Form on a Table or View form type.

8. Choose the Customers table or view in the next step of the wizard.

9. Complete the rest of the wizard using the default settings.

You are now ready to initiate the attack. Let's irritate your end users by having the Customers report automatically redirect to the Google site every time they try to view the report.

1. Run the form you've just created.

2. In one of the text fields on the form, specify the JavaScript shown in Listing 8-10.

Listing 8-10. The Malicious Script

```
<script>window.location='http://www.google.com';</script>
```

3. You should now see the screen shown in Figure 8-22. Click the Create button to save your data.

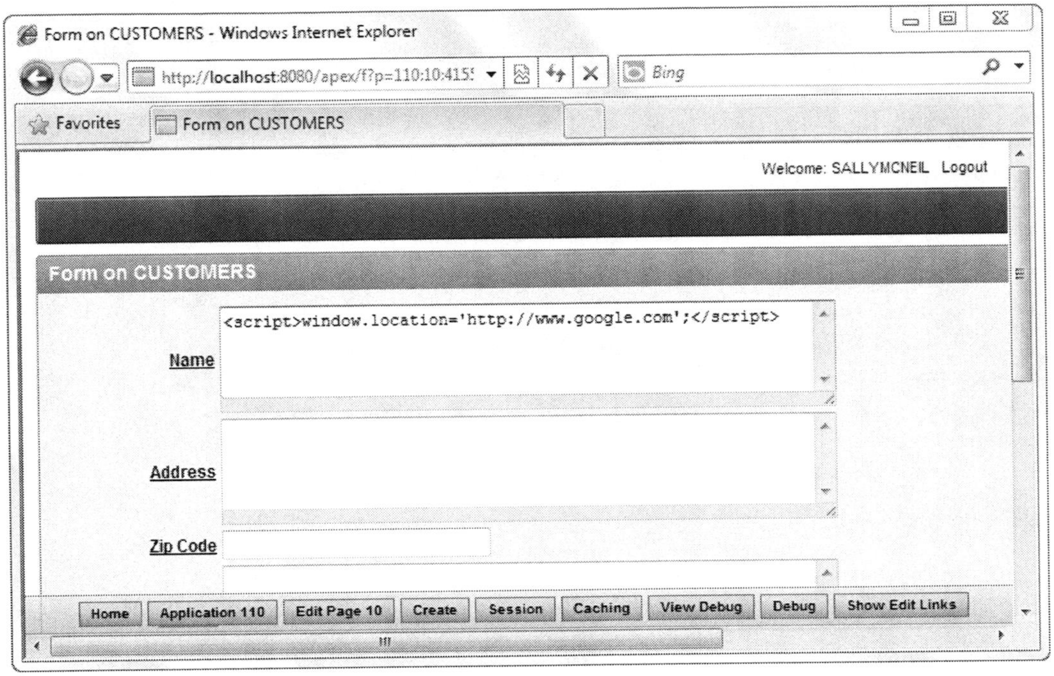

Figure 8-22. Conducting the cross-site scripting attack

4. Now run the report you created earlier. You will find that it is impossible to view the report, as you will keep getting redirected to the Google web site. You have just successfully conducted the cross-site scripting attack.

To prevent the cross-site scripting attack, you have to do the following:

1. Edit the report you created earlier.

2. In the Page Rendering area, right-click on the NAME field and choose to edit it.

3. Set the Display Type field to Display As Text (escape special characters).

4. Save your changes and run the report one more time.

5. You will find that your report now shows; also, the JavaScript that you entered earlier has been escaped appropriately and is now treated as report data rather than code, as highlighted in the red box in Figure 8-23.

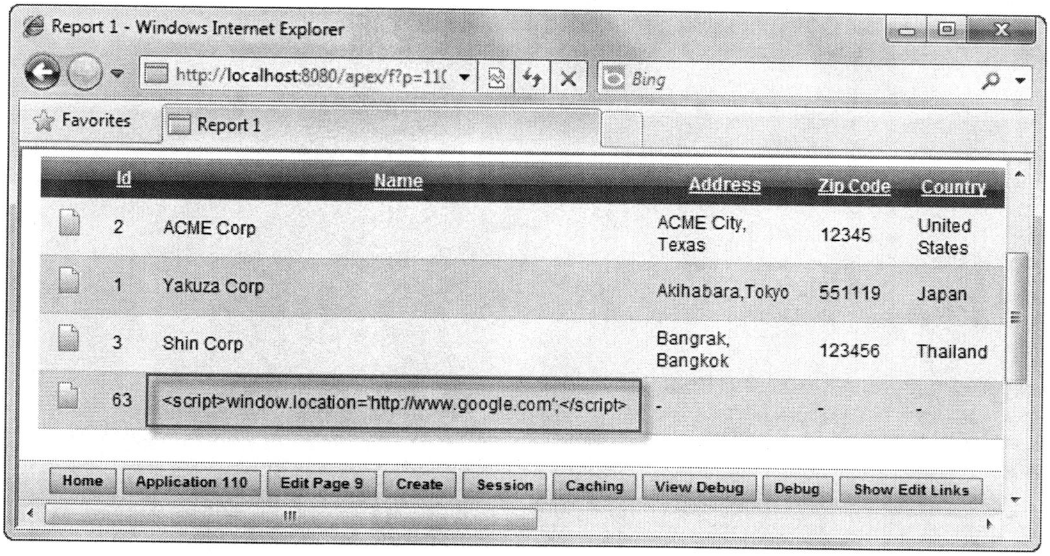

Figure 8-23. The malicious script, now rendered harmless

6. You can repeat steps 1 to 3 above for all other report columns you wish to protect.

How It Works

The cross site scripting (XSS) attack attempts to get client-side JavaScript code to run by injecting it into data entry fields. Such attacks may simply harbor mischievous intent (as outlined in this recipe's example scenario) or can be downright dangerous; imagine an attack that redirects you to a replica of the original site requesting you to enter your password or personal details.

The XSS attack is a rather simple type of attack that works due to the following weaknesses:

•   No validation of input data at the data entry-end.

•   No escaping of special characters during data display.

To explain how the attack works, consider a form that lets you enter the name of a customer via a textbox. Ideally, the form would take in the data and save it in the database. When it needs to be displayed, the data is retrieved as-is and displayed via HTML (for instance, placed inside a table row of a table). The output result might look like Listing 8-11.

Listing 8-11. Usual Output

```
<table>
 <tr>
  <td                 width='100%'>ACME CORP</td>
 </tr>
</table>
```

If you didn't place any checks in your application and if a malicious user keyed in some JavaScript instead of ACME CORP, you would get the following (shown in Listing 8-12) as the output result:

Listing 8-12. Output with Malicious Script

```
<table>
 <tr>
  <td              width='100%'>
  <script>window.location='http://www.google.com';</script>
  </td>
 </tr>
</table>
```

The browser misinterprets the data as client-script code and executes the JavaScript.

One way to prevent this from happening is by validating input data during data entry (for instance, rejecting data with tags such as <script> in its content). One downside of this approach is that if you really needed to key in some data containing such a tag, it would not be possible.

■ **Tip**   One application that might need to take in data containing HTML tags is an online developer forum. Users usually share their code for other developers to view, and it wouldn't be uncommon for them to paste examples of their code into these data fields. It would not make much sense in this case for the application to reject data with HTML tags.

The preferred way is to escape special characters, not during data entry but during data display. APEX provides an easy way to do this, which is to change the Display Type property of the report column, as you saw earlier in this recipe.

■ **Note**   Happily, with the latest release of APEX, all report columns are set to escape special characters by default, so if you create a report, it will be protected from cross-site scripting attacks automatically. By further coupling this with frequent usage of bind variables instead of substitution strings, you can keep common web and database attacks at bay.

CHAPTER 9

Deploying the Application

The last mile in getting your application into the hands of your intended audience is the deployment process. In traditional programming, a programmer would typically compile an application into an executable file and then package it into an automated installer for distribution.

In the world of APEX, your entire application sits inside the database. Deployment is therefore just a matter of copying all the database objects and dependencies from one database instance to another. Having said that, it is still important to make sure you copy the right objects, lest you accidentally leave out a table or resource that is crucial to the correct functioning of your application. The last thing your users want is to painstakingly track down missing files after deploying an application that doesn't work.

Obviously, a complete packaged application should contain all the resources necessary to run an application. A solid deployment strategy will help reduce the common "Oops, I left that out in the patch" problem inherent in rushed deliverables. As you will see in this chapter, APEX provides a few ways to package an application (or a part of it). You will learn the basics of application deployment and the pitfalls to avoid along the way.

9-1. Deciding on a Deployment Approach

Problem

You've spent a lot of time creating the perfect application in your workspace. Now you need to deploy it, but you need to know which objects from your application or workspace to include in the deployment package.

Solution

For smaller organizations where convenience and speed of deployment is favored over security (and if you want the quickest and simplest deployment method possible), adopt the following deployment approach:

1. Create the necessary end users for the application.

2. Simply expose the application URL to the end users.

3. The end users run the application from the same instance in which you developed it.

If these applications frequently change (but with relatively little changes to the database objects), adopt the following deployment approach:

1. Export the application.

2. Import the application into the same workspace/schema using a new application ID.

For larger organizations, a development server (for development and testing or your applications) that is separate from the production server should be adopted. In this case, the following deployment approach may be more suitable:

1. Export the application.

2. Import the application into a different workspace (and/or schema).

If you need to deploy to an entirely separate server (for example, deploying at your customer's office), adopt the following deployment approach:

1. Export the application.

2. Import the application into the target Oracle APEX instance (install it using a different schema/database).

How It Works

Many large organizations develop on a development server, move their applications over to a staging or User Acceptance Testing (UAT) server, and after the system has been approved by the users, to the production server. This type of deployment is quite common, and there are numerous ways to segregate or share your APEX instances, workspaces, and schema. A common setup is shown in Figure 9-1.

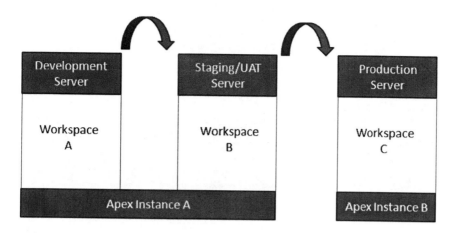

Figure 9-1. A typical deployment strategy

For very small deployments (and non-critical systems), it is sometimes acceptable to deploy the development and production version of your application in the same instance and workspace. The benefits of this approach include not having to manage many different workspaces and saving time by eliminating any deployment needed to get the application to its users.

For everything else, however, a good rule of thumb is that the development instances and production instances should be on different APEX instances entirely. Since development instances are usually used as testbeds, it is never a good idea to put a live production system in the same APEX instance. At the very least, you should separate the development instance and production instance using different workspaces so that it's not possible for developers to modify a live and running application.

9-2. Generating a List of Application Dependencies

Problem

You are prepared to export your application, but your application uses a wide array of database objects across multiple schemas, and you are unsure if you have covered the full list of underlying database objects used by your application in the export.

Solution

To use the Database Object Dependencies report to view all the dependencies of your application, follow these steps.

1. Log in to the application builder.

2. Open the application you wish to export.

3.   Click on the Utilities icon at the top of the page, as shown in Figure 9-2.

Figure 9-2. *The Utilities icon*

4.   Click on the Database Object Dependencies icon in the following page, as shown in Figure 9-3.

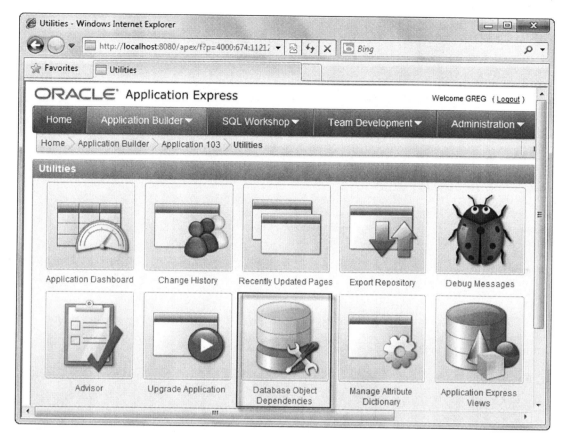

Figure 9-3. The Database Object Dependencies icon

5. On the following page, click the Compute Dependencies link in the top right corner.

6. You should now see a table in the main area of the page describing all the objects currently used by the application, as shown in Figure 9-4.

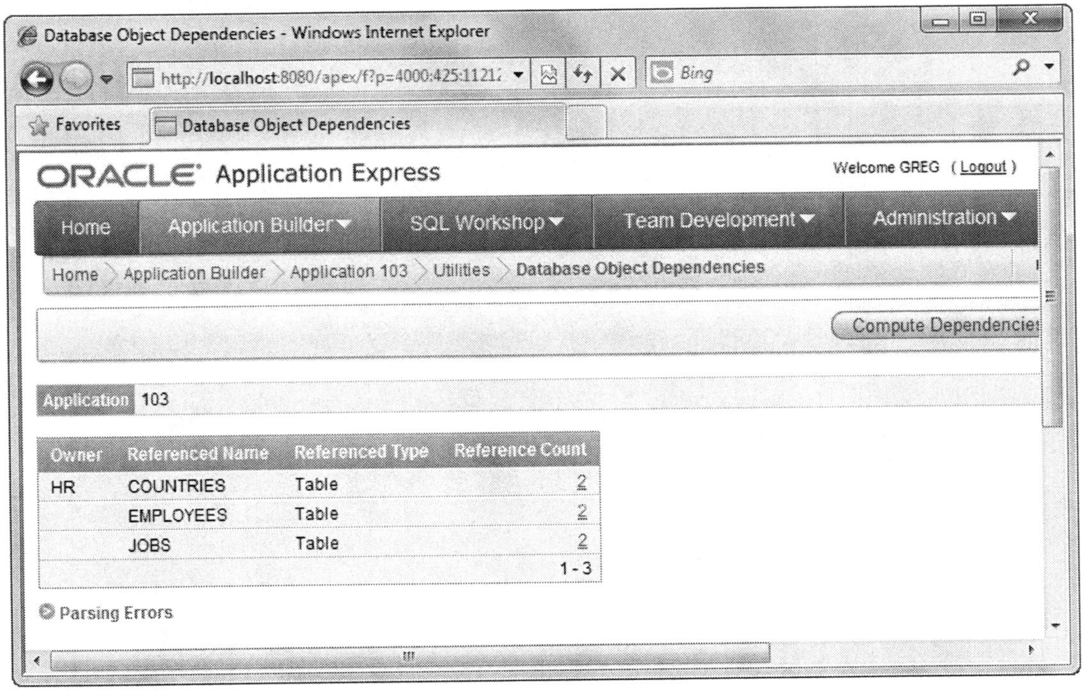

Figure 9-4. The Database Object Dependencies report

How It Works

The Database Object Dependency viewer provides a one-page summary of all the database objects that are used by your application. This will be useful when deciding which objects to export from your application.

9-3. Exporting an Application

Problem

You want to export an application from one schema or instance in preparation for deploying that application to a production environment.

Solution

To export an application, follow these steps:

1. Log in to the application builder

2. Open the application you wish to export.

3. Click the Import/Export icon at the top of the page, as highlighted in Figure 9-5.

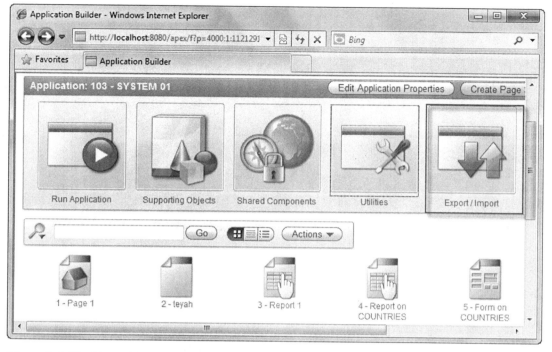

Figure 9-5. The Export/Import icon

4. On the next page, choose Export and click the Next button.

5. On the next page, confirm the application that you wish to export, and choose the DOS file format, as shown in Figure 9-6.

■ **Tip**   For users of UNIX operating systems, choose the UNIX file format instead. The main difference in the different exported file formats is how lines end: UNIX-based file formats end with an LF character and Windows-based file formats end with a CR/LF character.

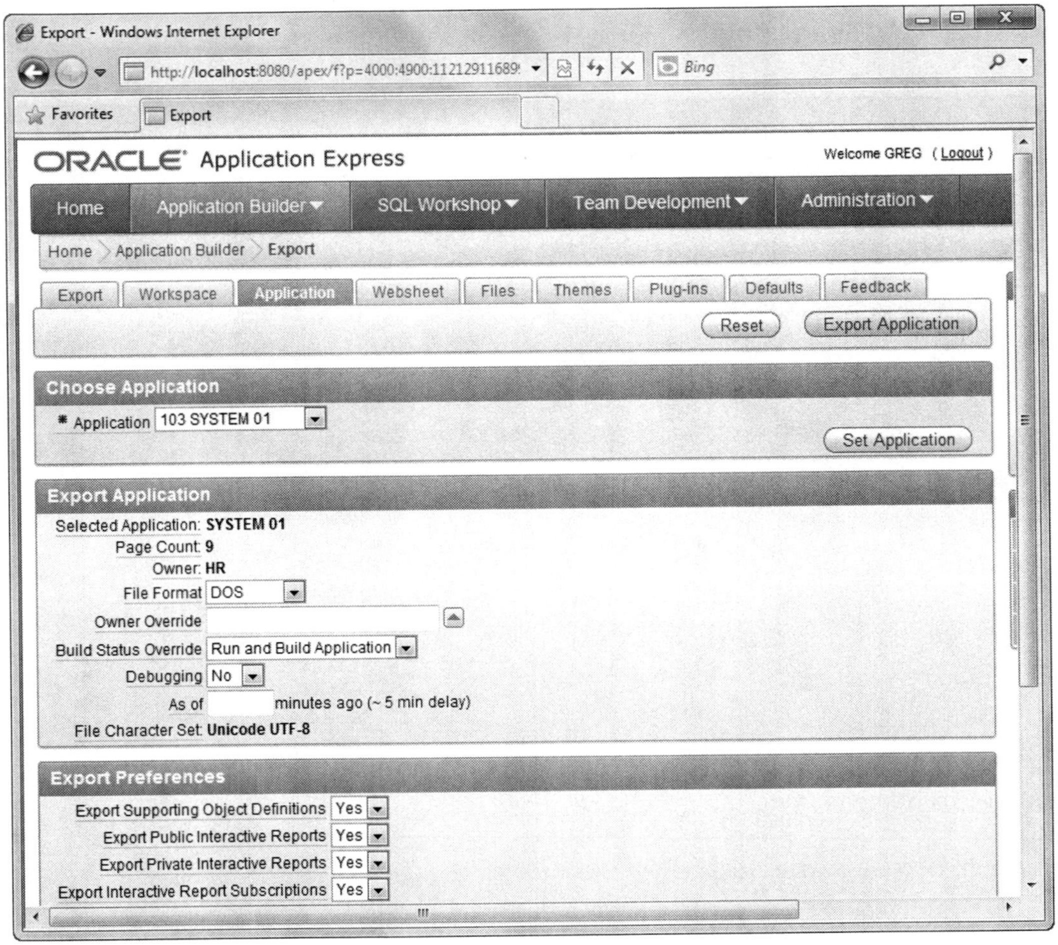

Figure 9-6. Exporting the application

6. Click the Export application button. This will prompt the export. At the end of the process (which should take a few seconds), you will be prompted to download the generated file (an .sql file), as shown in Figure 9-7.

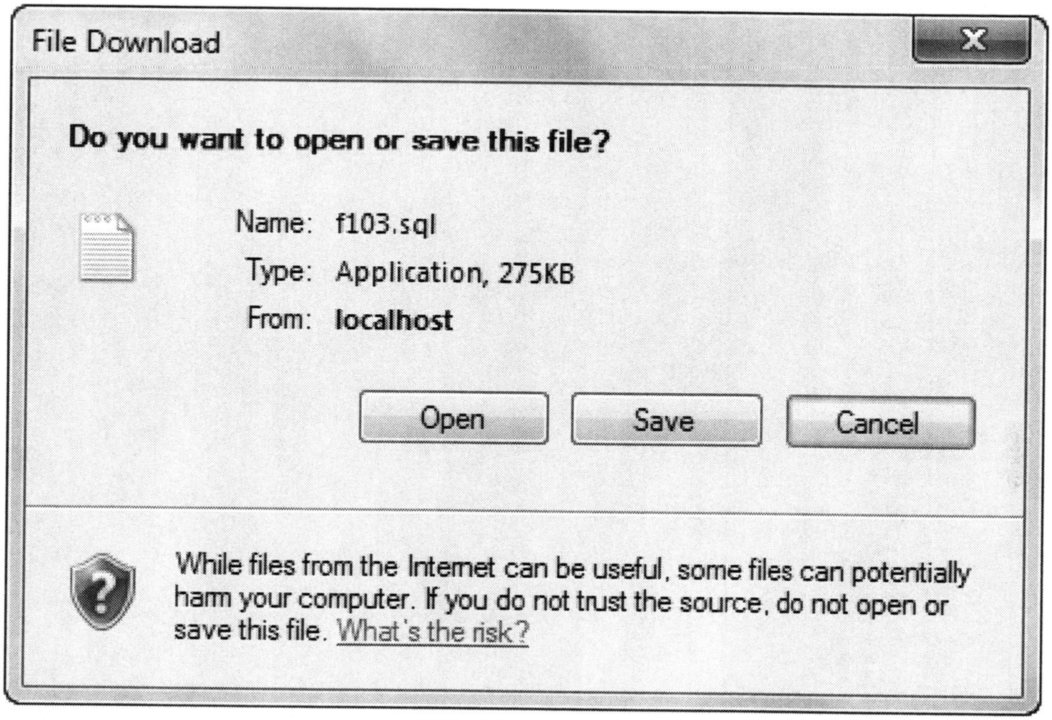

Figure 9-7. Saving the exported SQL file

How It Works

An application in APEX consists of metadata, data, and business logic, and all of it sits nicely in the Oracle database. When you export an application, it exports all the metadata into an SQL file. By running this SQL file, it will rebuild the entire application from scratch on the target machine.

If you open the exported file in a text editor (such as Notepad), you will see that the content of the file are mostly PL/SQL function calls and DML that specifies the schema of your database and application objects. This is shown in Figure 9-8.

```
f103 - Notepad

File   Edit   Format   View   Help

begin

null;

end;
/

--application/comments
prompt  ...comments: requires application express 2.2 or higher
--

--application/pages/page_00001
prompt  ...PAGE 1: Page 1
--

begin
wwv_flow_api.create_page (
 p_flow_id => wwv_flow.g_flow_id
,p_id => 1
,p_tab_set => 'TS1'
,p_name => 'Page 1'
,p_step_title => 'Page 1'
,p_step_sub_title => 'Page 1'
,p_step_sub_title_type => 'TEXT_WITH_SUBSTITUTIONS'
,p_include_apex_css_js_yn => 'Y'
,p_cache_page_yn => 'N'
,p_help_text =>
'No help is available for this page.'
,p_last_upd_yyyymmddhh24miss => '20110321203343'
 );
null;

end;
/

declare
```

Figure 9-8. Exploring the contents of the exported SQL file

■ **Tip** It is thus possible to open the SQL file in a text editor, hand-edit the values and import the updated SQL into another APEX instance. (This is only recommended if you know what you are doing!)

9-4. Importing an Application

Problem

You need to import an application that you have just exported from another instance of APEX.

▨ **Note** This recipe demonstrates a manual import method. Recipe 9-5 shows how to use SQL*Plus to script an import to run automatically.

Solution

Use the Application Builder to walk through the import process using a convenient, GUI interface. Follow these steps:

1. Log in to the application builder.

2. Open the application you wish to import.

3. Click the Import/Export icon at the top of the page.

4. In the next page, choose Import and click the Next button.

5. In the next page, browse for the .sql file in the Import File field.

6. In the File Type field, choose the Database Application, Page, or Component Export option, as shown in Figure 9-9.

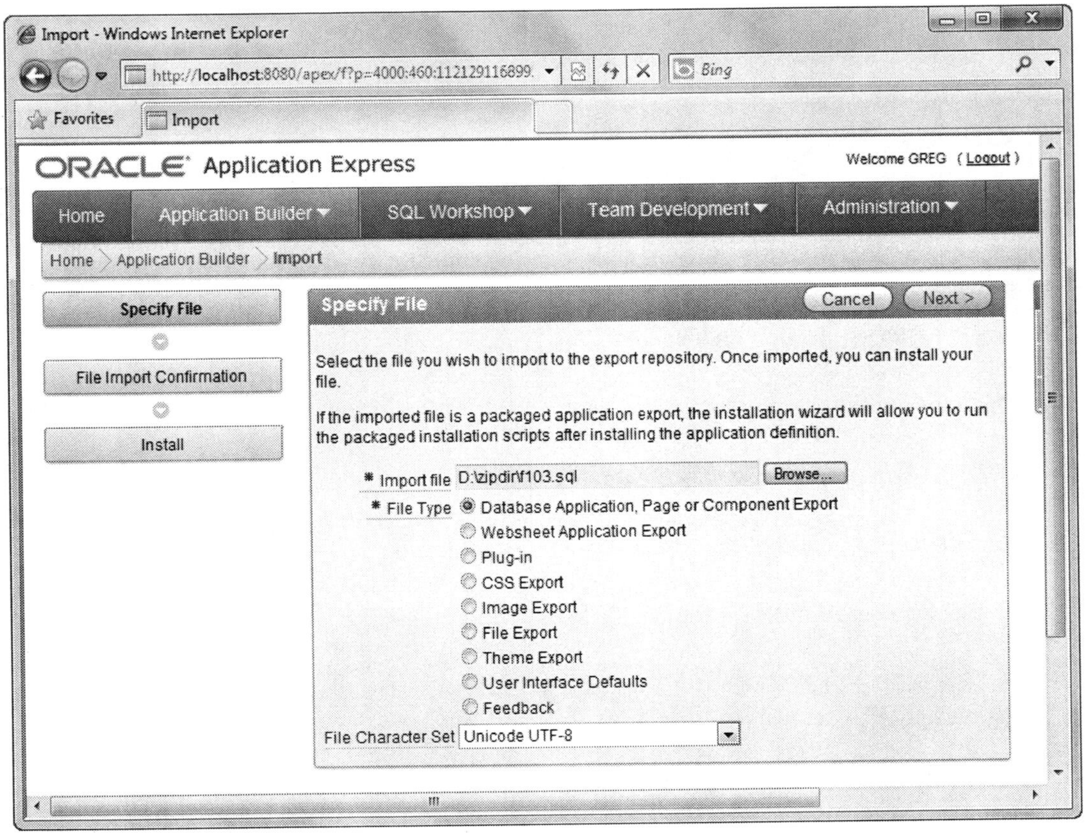

Figure 9-9. Importing an SQL file

7. Once you click the Next button, a little progress bar will appear at the top of the page indicating the progress of the import.

8. Once the import has successfully completed, you are given the option to install the application, as shown in Figure 9-10.

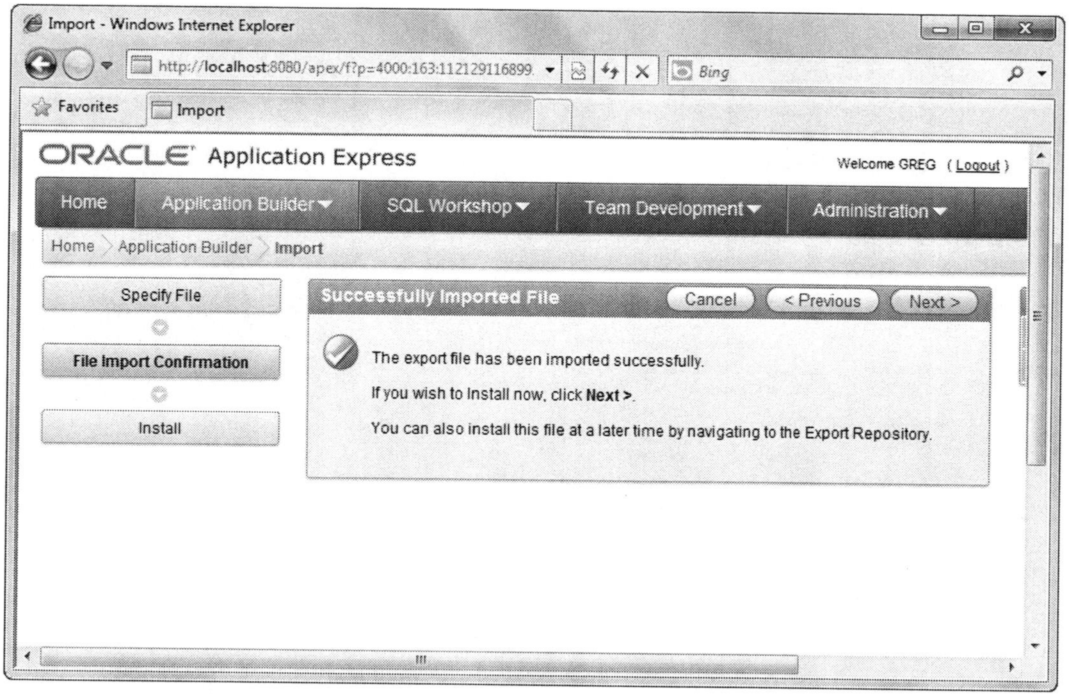

Figure 9-10. Successfully imported message

9.   Click the Next button to install the application.

▓ **Tip**   After you import a file, it ends up in an internal repository called the APEX export repository. You can't use an imported file in any way until you install it.

---

10. You are now greeted with a page that allows you to specify the schema and the application ID to use for the new application.

11. Choose the Auto Assign New Application ID item, as shown in Figure 9-11 below, and click the Install button to proceed.

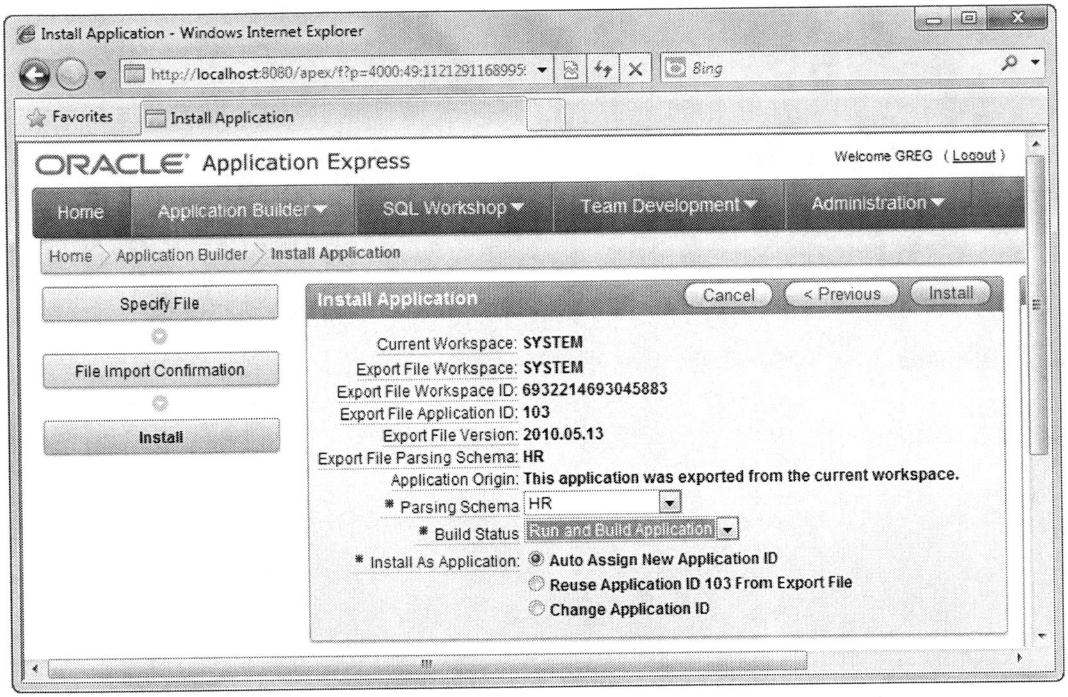

Figure 9-11. Installing the application

12. You should see a progress bar indicating the progress of the import.

13. Once the import has completed, you should see a screen that lets you choose to create the supporting objects for the application. In this page, choose the Yes option for the Install Supporting Objects field, as shown in Figure 9-12.

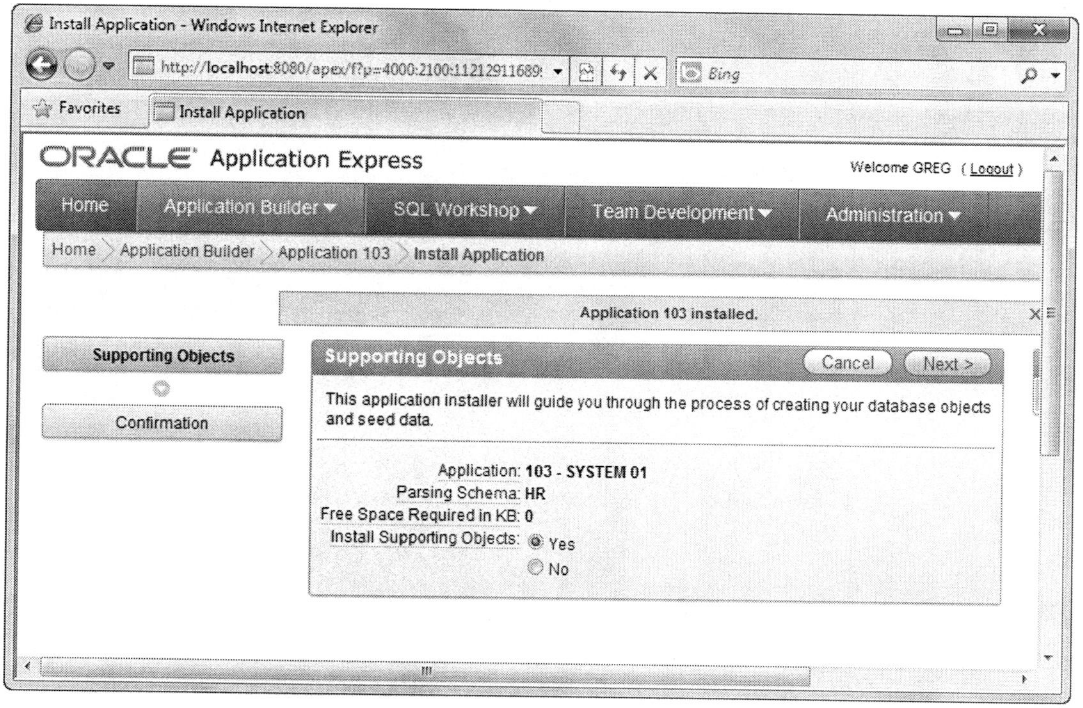

Figure 9-12. Creating the database supporting objects

14. Click the Next button to proceed.

15. You will be presented with a confirmation screen. Click the Install button to continue with the installation.

16. After the installation completes, you will be presented with the screen shown in Figure 9-13.

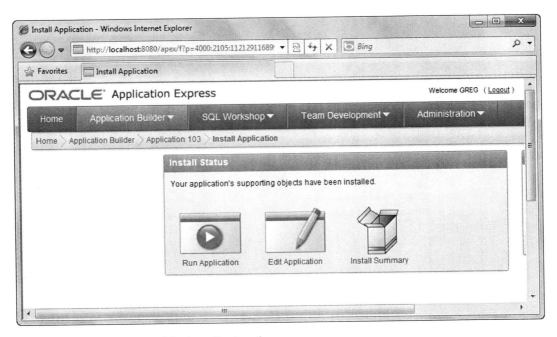

Figure 9-13. The last step of the install wizard

17. Now go back to your main workspace area. You should see your new
    application. If you open the application, you can see that the set of forms in
    the exported application has been created in your APEX instance, as shown in
    Figure 9-14.

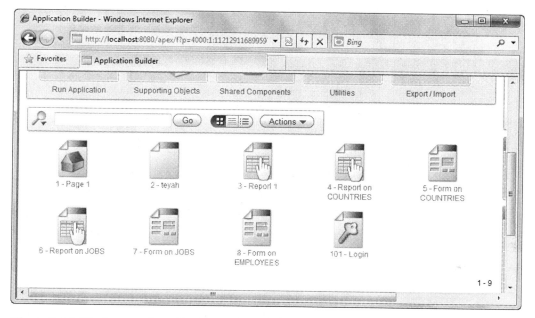

Figure 9-14. The imported application and its contents

How It Works

There are two ways to import an application.

- Import an application visually through the APEX Application Builder window.

- Import an application through SQL*Plus.

Recipe 9-5 describes how you can import an application through SQL*Plus.

9-5. Scripting an Application Import

Problem

You need to automate the import of an application via batch script, and therefore you can't import the application through the Application Builder interface.

Solution

Import that application using SQL*Plus. By using SQL*Plus, you trade the GUI interface of Application Builder for the ability to script and automate your import. Here are the steps to follow:

1. Run SQL*Plus.
2. Log in as the System Administrator to SQL*Plus.

3. Change your current active folder to the location of your exported .sql file. For instance, if your current active folder is **d:\zipdir**, you must first change the active folder to this location. You can do so using this code:

define dir=D:\zipdir

4. In the next line, type in **&dir** (prefixed with the alias symbol (@)), followed by the name of the exported file. For example, if you exported your file earlier as f103.sql, type **@&dir\f103** in the SQL*Plus command prompt (as shown in Figure 9-15).

■ **Tip** You can also declare the full path directly in this fashion: **@d:\zipdir\f103.sql**

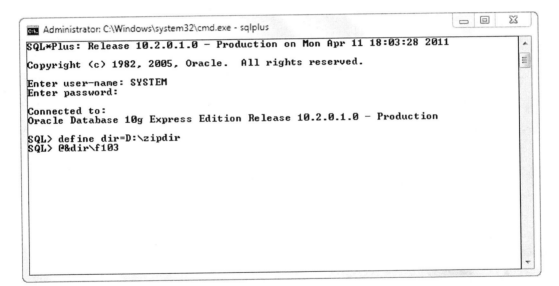

*Figure 9-15. Setting the active directory in SQL*Plus*

5. When you run the script, you should see a bunch of log messages scroll by. At the end of a successful installation, you should see the screen shown in Figure 9-16.

```
...calendar templates
......template 2828106592158458
......template 2828312213158458
......template 2828500789158460
...application themes
......theme 2828804719158461
...build options used by application 103
...messages used by application: 103
...dynamic translations used by application: 103
...Language Maps for Application 103
...Shortcuts
...web services (9iR2 or better)
...shared queries
...report layouts
...authentication schemes
......scheme 2828909457158472
......scheme 2829020317158472
......scheme 2829106439158472
...plugins
...application deployment
...application install scripts
...application deployment checks
...application deployment build options
...done
SQL>
```

Figure 9-16. Executing the exported SQL file

6. The lack of error messages in Figure 9-16 indicates that the application has been successfully imported.

7. Now try logging on to the Application Builder. You should see your newly imported application.

How It Works

The ability to import a file through SQL*Plus makes it possible for you to automate the importing process using batch scripts and so on. You might, for example, decide to create a batch script to automate the weekly import of new and updated pages from an application sitting in the development server to one sitting on the production server.

9-6. Exporting a Single Page

Problem

You've already deployed your application on a production server at your customer's office. Your team has updated a page in the application back at your office, and you want to bring this updated page to the customer's place to deploy it on their servers.

Solution

To export a single page, please follow these steps:

1. Open an existing application.

2. Open the page you wish to export in your application.

3. In the Page Definition area, choose the Utilities ➤ Export menu item, as shown in Figure 9-17.

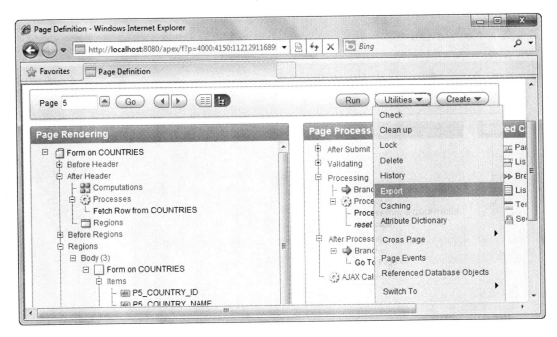

Figure 9-17. Exporting a single page

4. In the next page, you are given the option to choose the file format for the export. Choose the DOS file format, as shown in Figure 9-18.

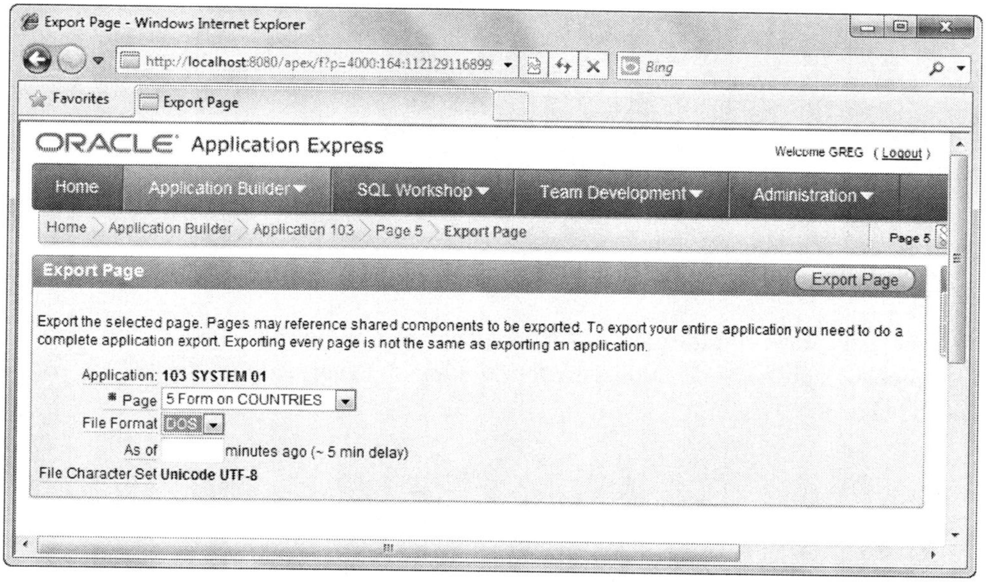

Figure 9-18. *Export page wizard*

> 5. You should now be prompted to download the exported page (a .sql file).

How It Works

Exporting a single page is useful when you don't wish to export every other part of the application. Other advantages of exporting a single page include:

- Reducing of the size of the exported application (to keep sizes of .sql files manageable for transmission over the Internet).

- Reducing the impact to a production server by localizing the import to only one or two page files.

- A convenient way to upload bug fixes or updates to a production or UAT server.

- As a means of exporting individual pages from a development server to a production server.

Thus, if you've only changed one or a few pages, you can minimize the impact on the production environment by moving only the pages that you have changed.

9-7. Importing a Single Page

Problem

You have already exported a page following the instructions in Recipe 9-6. You now need to import the page into the target application.

Solution

To import a single page into your application, please follow these steps:

1. Open the target application you wish to import the page to.

2. Click the Export/Import icon at the top of the page.

3. Choose the Import option when prompted.

4. In the next page, browse for the page you exported earlier. For the File Type option, choose Database Application, Page, or Component Export option, as shown in Figure 9-19.

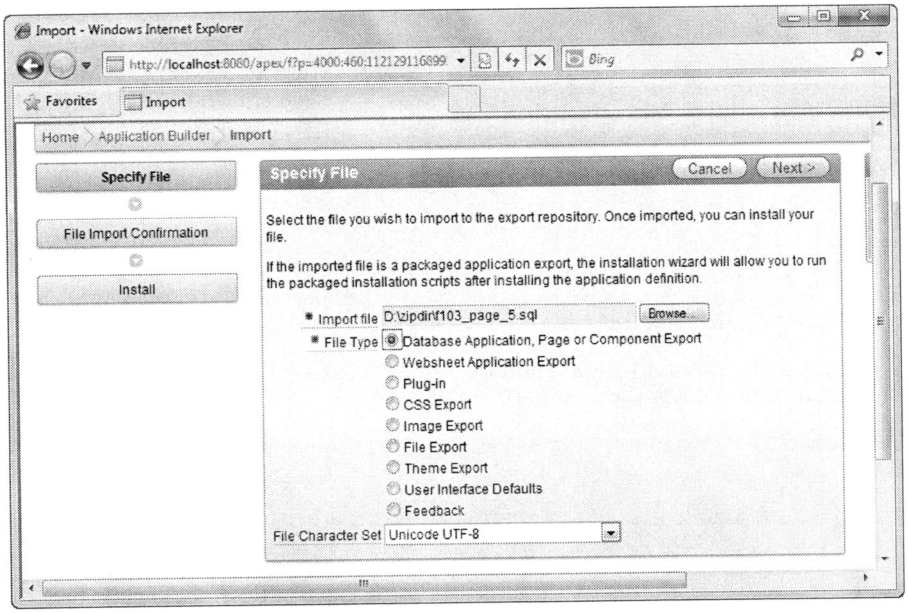

Figure 9-19. Importing a page

5. Click the Next button to continue. You will see the page installation confirmation step shown in Figure 9-20. Click the Install Page button to continue.

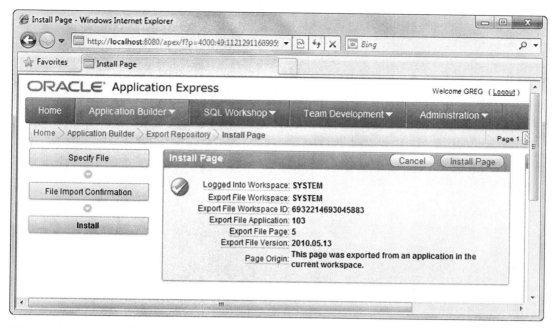

Figure 9-20. Install page confirmation step

6. Because you are deploying an updated version of an existing page, the wizard will prompt you to overwrite the page, as shown in Figure 9-21.

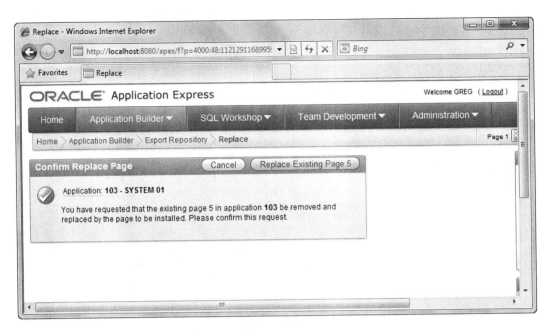

Figure 9-21. Replace page confirmation

7. After the page has been replaced successfully, you should see the screen shown in Figure 9-22. Your page has been successfully deployed.

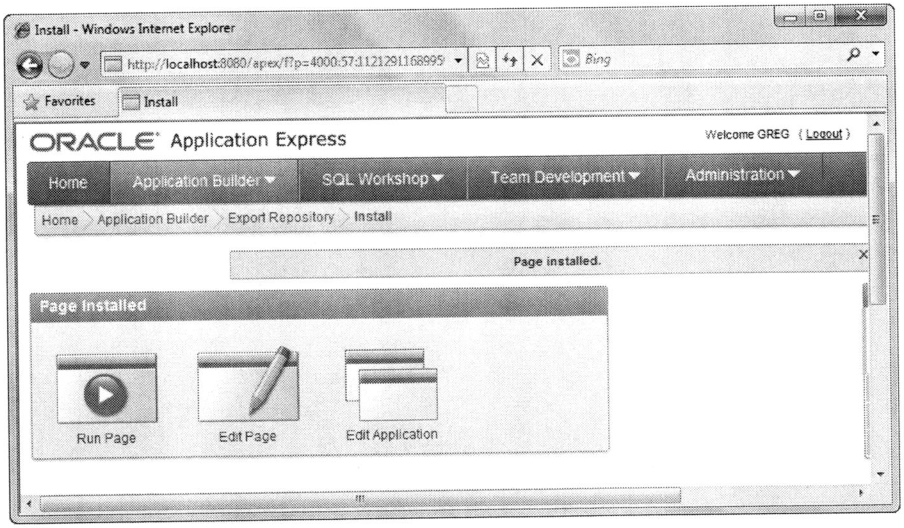

Figure 9-22. Page installed message

How It Works

You can also easily import a page file into the same application or another application on another APEX instance using the methods described in this recipe. In fact, most of the other application resources (such as theme files, image files, shared objects, and so on) can be exported and imported in the same manner.

9-8. Publishing the Application URL

Problem

After you have deployed your application, you need to publish your application URL so that your end users can access the application, but you don't know it. You need to locate the application URL.

Solution

To discover the application URL, follow these instructions:

1. Open an existing application.

2. Mouseover the Run Application icon, right-click on it, and choose to view the shortcut/link for the icon, as shown in Figure 9-23.

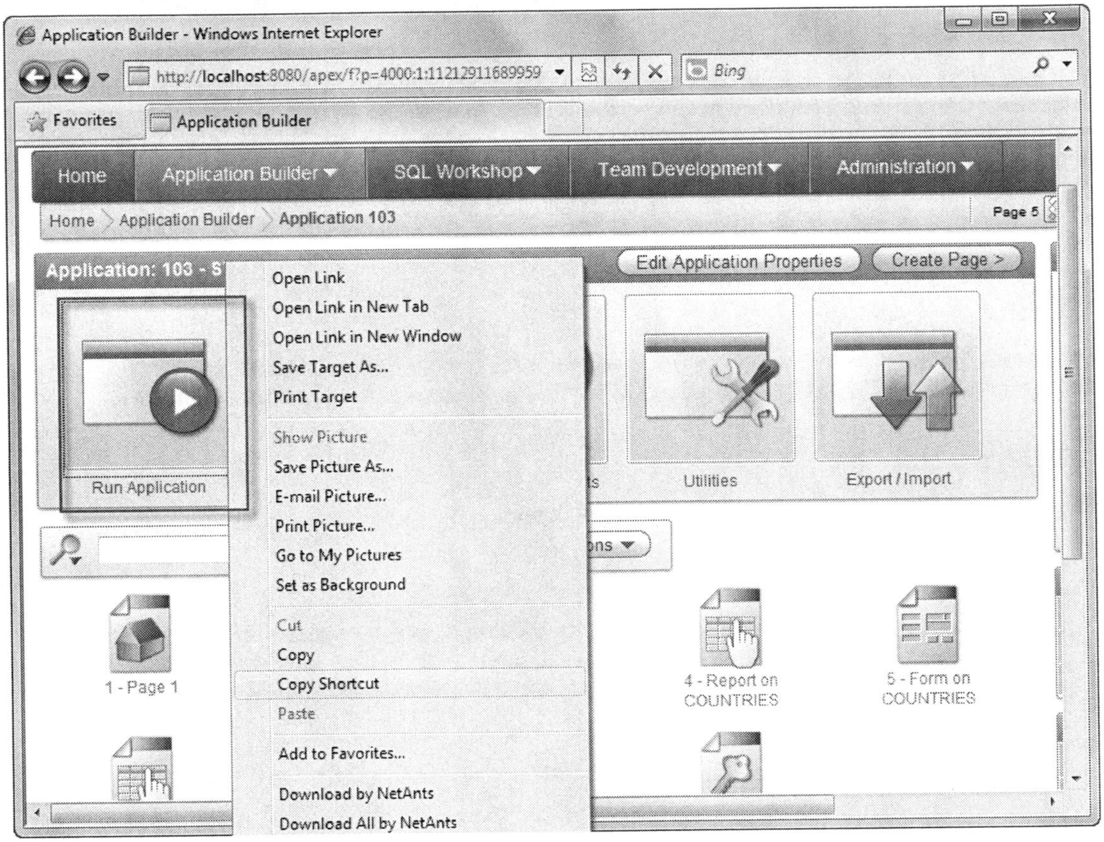

Figure 9-23. Accessing the URL for the application

■ **Tip**   In Microsoft Internet Explorer, right-click on the icon and choose the `Copy Shortcut` menu item. For other browsers, look for the equivalent menu item that lets you inspect the full URL for the link.

---

3.   If you paste the link of your application somewhere (for instance, in a text file), you will see that the full link to your application looks something like this:

```
http://localhost:8080/apex/f?p=103:1:1121291168995976:::::
```

4.   You can paste this link in any browser to directly access the login page of your application.

How It Works

The following URL is actually made up of a few parts. Let's dissect each part in detail to understand what they mean. Table 9-1 describes the URL in detail.

```
http://localhost:8080/apex/f?p=103:1:1121291168995976:::::
```

Table 9-1. An APEX Application URL in Detail

Component	Description
`http://localhost:8080`	**localhost** refers to the name of the server hosting the APEX instance, and **8080** is the port number that the APEX service is listening on.
Apex	This is the name of the database access descriptor (DAD). This portion describes how the Oracle HTTP server connects to the database server to fulfill an HTTP request.
`f?p=`	This is a special prefix used by APEX to indicate the data that follows.
103	This is the ID of the application being accessed.
1	This is the page number in the application being accessed.
1121291168995976	This is an ID identifying the current session. It is useful to note that this value doesn't need to be part of the URL that is exposed to the end users since it is generated by APEX for every session. Hence, it is sufficient to publish the following URL to the end users: `http://localhost:8080/apex/f?p=103:1:::::`

CHAPTER 10

A Mini Book Catalog Site

In this last chapter you will explore a real-life scenario of an online book catalog and how to apply APEX to create it in a matter of hours. Think of this catalog as the bare beginnings of a bookstore—you aren't even going to implement anything like shopping-cart functionality but you will use the various APEX techniques and features you learned throughout the earlier chapters in the book.

Before you create the online book catalog, let's define the scope of what you want to build. The application will be divided into two main areas—the Administration part of the web site (where the user can manage the list of available books) and the front end (which is the actual book catalog visible to the public).

In addition, you'll create a chart report to let the storekeeper view the current stockcount of all books in the store. Last of all, you'll pull all these separate pages together by providing a proper navigation scheme for your application using navigation lists and tabs.

10-1. Setting Up the Main Objects for Your Book Catalog

Problem

You need to set up the underlying database tables and sample records (books) required for the book catalog.

Solution

To set up the book catalog tables, follow these steps. (Note that you can find the code in the in the example download for this book—you don't need to type it in manually.)

1. Create the main Books table as follows, together with the sample data:

```
CREATE TABLE "BOOKS"
    (    "BOOKID" NVARCHAR2(255),
         "BOOKTITLE" NVARCHAR2(255),
         "BOOKISBN" NVARCHAR2(255),
         "BOOKPUBLISHER" NVARCHAR2(255),
         "BOOKEDITION" NVARCHAR2(255),
         "BOOKCATEGORY" NVARCHAR2(255),
         "BOOKDESCRIPTION" NVARCHAR2(255),
         "BOOKPRICE" FLOAT(9),
         "AUTHOR" NVARCHAR2(255),
         "BOOKIMAGE" BLOB,
```

```
        CONSTRAINT "BOOKS_PK" PRIMARY KEY ("BOOKID") ENABLE
  )
/

INSERT INTO BOOKS(BOOKID, BOOKTITLE, BOOKISBN, BOOKPUBLISHER, BOOKEDITION, BOOKCATEGORY,
BOOKDESCRIPTION, BOOKPRICE, AUTHOR) VALUES('B1','PRO ODP.NET
PROGRAMMING','9781430228202','APRESS PUBLISHING','2010','C3','This book is a comprehensive and
easy-to-understand guide for using the Oracle Data Provider (ODP) version 11g on the .NET
Framework',59.99,'ED ZEHOO')
/

INSERT INTO BOOKS(BOOKID, BOOKTITLE, BOOKISBN, BOOKPUBLISHER, BOOKEDITION, BOOKCATEGORY,
BOOKDESCRIPTION, BOOKPRICE, AUTHOR) VALUES('B2','IPHONE PROGRAMMING','9781430228400','WROX
PUBLISHING','2011','C3','This book describes the basics of iPhone and iPad development using
Objective C',49.99,'GREG YAP')
/

INSERT INTO BOOKS(BOOKID, BOOKTITLE, BOOKISBN, BOOKPUBLISHER, BOOKEDITION, BOOKCATEGORY,
BOOKDESCRIPTION, BOOKPRICE, AUTHOR) VALUES('B3','HOW MASTER CHIEF BECAME MASTER
CHIEF','1123433328400','TOR BOOKS','2010','C2','Master Chief goes on a vacation in China. Read
about his exploits in this book!',39.99,'JAMES BURKE')
/

INSERT INTO BOOKS(BOOKID, BOOKTITLE, BOOKISBN, BOOKPUBLISHER, BOOKEDITION, BOOKCATEGORY,
BOOKDESCRIPTION, BOOKPRICE, AUTHOR) VALUES('B4','THE CURSE OF AMMATTAR','9781430228400','TOR
BOOKS','2011','C4','Classic horror story set in medieval Thailand',29.99,'SARAH HAWKINS')
/

INSERT INTO BOOKS(BOOKID, BOOKTITLE, BOOKISBN, BOOKPUBLISHER, BOOKEDITION, BOOKCATEGORY,
BOOKDESCRIPTION, BOOKPRICE, AUTHOR) VALUES('B5','CHING CHONG: THE RISE AND FALL OF
JACKSON','343322221400','NIECA BOOKS','2011','C1','A story about the misfortunes of Jackson
Junior as he travels across Asia',12.99,'TARA WILLIAMS')
/

INSERT INTO BOOKS(BOOKID, BOOKTITLE, BOOKISBN, BOOKPUBLISHER, BOOKEDITION, BOOKCATEGORY,
BOOKDESCRIPTION, BOOKPRICE, AUTHOR) VALUES('B6','UNFORTUNATE
CIRCUMSTANCES','115062221400','PARAMOUNT BOOKS','2011','C1','Read about the unfortunate
circumstances of Ali, someone you will absolutely not care about',19.99,'DANA T. ROLLS')
/

INSERT INTO BOOKS(BOOKID, BOOKTITLE, BOOKISBN, BOOKPUBLISHER, BOOKEDITION, BOOKCATEGORY,
BOOKDESCRIPTION, BOOKPRICE, AUTHOR) VALUES('B7','SCARY LIONS','11553221400','PARAMOUNT
BOOKS','2011','C1','A book about the greasy politicians in Mootawambaland and how Alex becomes
one of them',15.99,'TERRY BARRACK')
/

INSERT INTO BOOKS(BOOKID, BOOKTITLE, BOOKISBN, BOOKPUBLISHER, BOOKEDITION, BOOKCATEGORY,
BOOKDESCRIPTION, BOOKPRICE, AUTHOR) VALUES('B8','THE LIME TREE','22113221400','ZACK
PUBLISHING','2011','C1','A book about how Sally became a top salesperson when she decides to
sell lime as lemon',16.99,'JAMES LEE')
/
```

2.   Create the Inventory table as follows:

```
CREATE TABLE  "INVENTORY"
   (    "ID" NVARCHAR2(255),
        "BOOKID" NVARCHAR2(255),
        "COPIESINSTOCK" NUMBER(9,3),
         CONSTRAINT "INVENTORY_PK" PRIMARY KEY ("ID") ENABLE
   )
/

INSERT INTO INVENTORY(ID,BOOKID,COPIESINSTOCK) VALUES('1','B1',10)
/

INSERT INTO INVENTORY(ID,BOOKID,COPIESINSTOCK) VALUES('2','B2',15)
/

INSERT INTO INVENTORY(ID,BOOKID,COPIESINSTOCK) VALUES('3','B3',1)
/

INSERT INTO INVENTORY(ID,BOOKID,COPIESINSTOCK) VALUES('4','B4',6)
/

INSERT INTO INVENTORY(ID,BOOKID,COPIESINSTOCK) VALUES('5','B5',17)
/

INSERT INTO INVENTORY(ID,BOOKID,COPIESINSTOCK) VALUES('6','B6',9)
/

INSERT INTO INVENTORY(ID,BOOKID,COPIESINSTOCK) VALUES('7','B7',14)
/

INSERT INTO INVENTORY(ID,BOOKID,COPIESINSTOCK) VALUES('8','B8',9)
/
```

3.   Create the Category table as follows:

```
CREATE TABLE  "CATEGORY"
   (    "CATEGORYID" NVARCHAR2(255),
        "CATEGORYNAME" NVARCHAR2(255),
        "DESCRIPTION" NVARCHAR2(255),
         CONSTRAINT "CATEGORY_PK" PRIMARY KEY ("CATEGORYID") ENABLE
   )
/

INSERT INTO CATEGORY(CATEGORYID, CATEGORYNAME, DESCRIPTION) VALUES('C1','FICTION','Fiction
selection')
/

INSERT INTO CATEGORY(CATEGORYID, CATEGORYNAME, DESCRIPTION)
VALUES('C2','SCIENCEFICTION','Science Fiction Selection')
/
```

```
INSERT INTO CATEGORY(CATEGORYID, CATEGORYNAME, DESCRIPTION) VALUES('C3','COMPUTERS','Computer
Books Selection')
/

INSERT INTO CATEGORY(CATEGORYID, CATEGORYNAME, DESCRIPTION) VALUES('C4','HORROR','Best Horror
Selections')
/
```

How It Works

The Books table is the main table that stores the list of books in the book catalog; the Inventory table stores the stockcount of each available book; and the Category table stores the full list of book categories (genres) available in the catalog. Table 10-1 describes the mapping between the various keys in each respective table.

Table 10-1. Foreign Key Mapping Between Different Tables in the Book Catalog Application

Foreign key mapping	Description
Books.BookID = Inventory.BookID	Each book has a corresponding entry in the Inventory table that stores the stockcount details for the book.
Books.BookCategory = Category.CategoryID	Each book belongs to a genre/category, the details of which are stored in the Category table. The ID stored in the Books.BookCategory column looks up the corresponding entry in the Category table.

10-2. Creating the Pages to Manage the List of Books

Problem

The storekeeper needs a way to manage the list of books in his book catalog.

Solution

You must first create the forms that allow the storekeeper to add, edit, and delete book titles in the book catalog.

To create the page that allows the storekeeper to add/edit/delete books, please follow these instructions:

1.   Create a new Database application named Book catalog.

2. During the Pages step of the Create Application wizard, choose the Report and Form page type linked to the Books table, as shown in Figure 10-1.

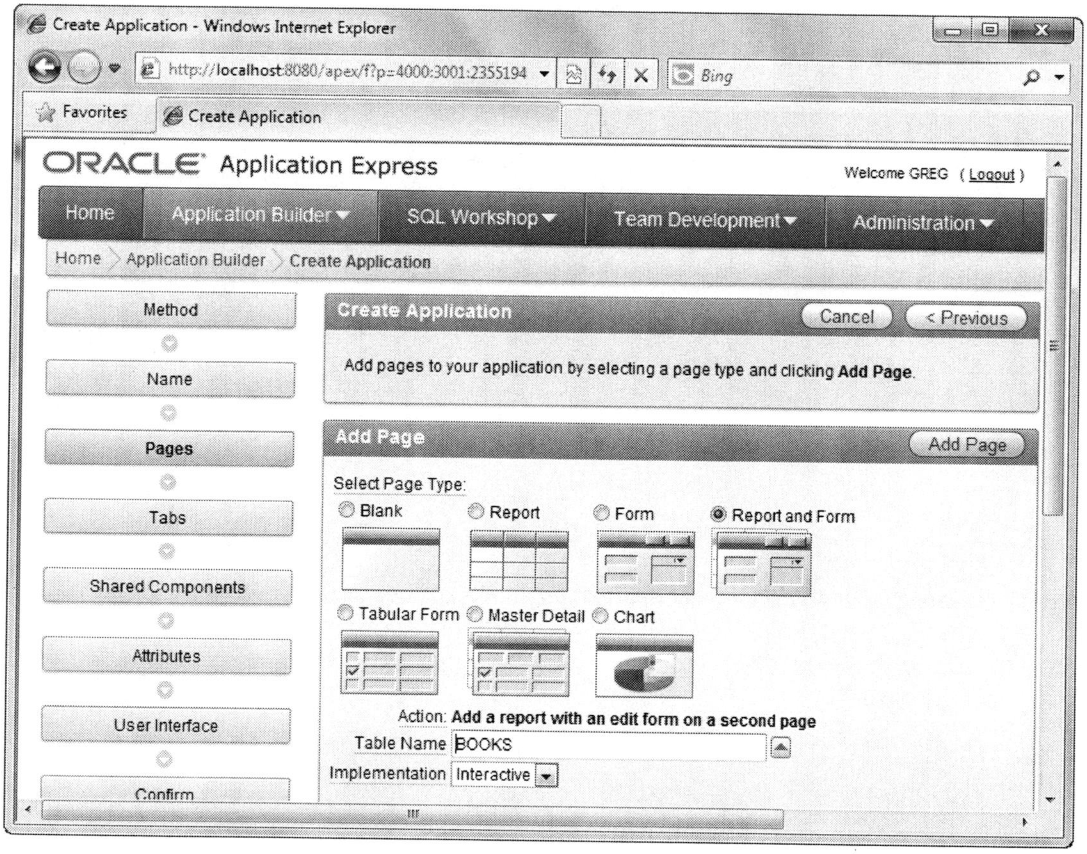

Figure 10-1. Adding a Report and Form

3. Click the Add Page button to add the form and report. After doing so, finish the wizard to create the application.

4. You should now have the screen shown in Figure 10-2.

Figure 10-2. The current list of pages in your application

5. If you launch the main Books form, you should see the screen shown in Figure 10-3.

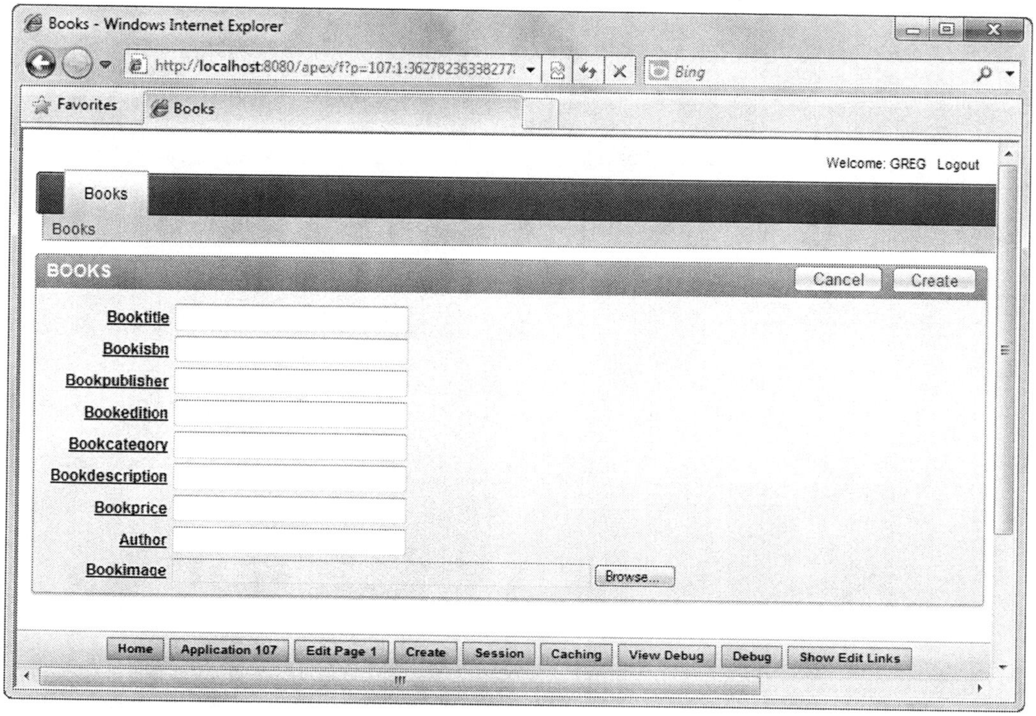

Figure 10-3. The book details entry form

6. The book details entry form from Figure 10-3 lets the storekeeper add a new book to the book catalog, but the form is not complete yet. The BookCategory field should show a drop-down list of categories so that the storekeeper can pick from a list of categories instead of manually typing in the category code.

7. Edit the form. In the Page Rendering section, right-click the P1_BOOKCATEGORY field, and choose to edit the field (as shown in Figure 10-4).

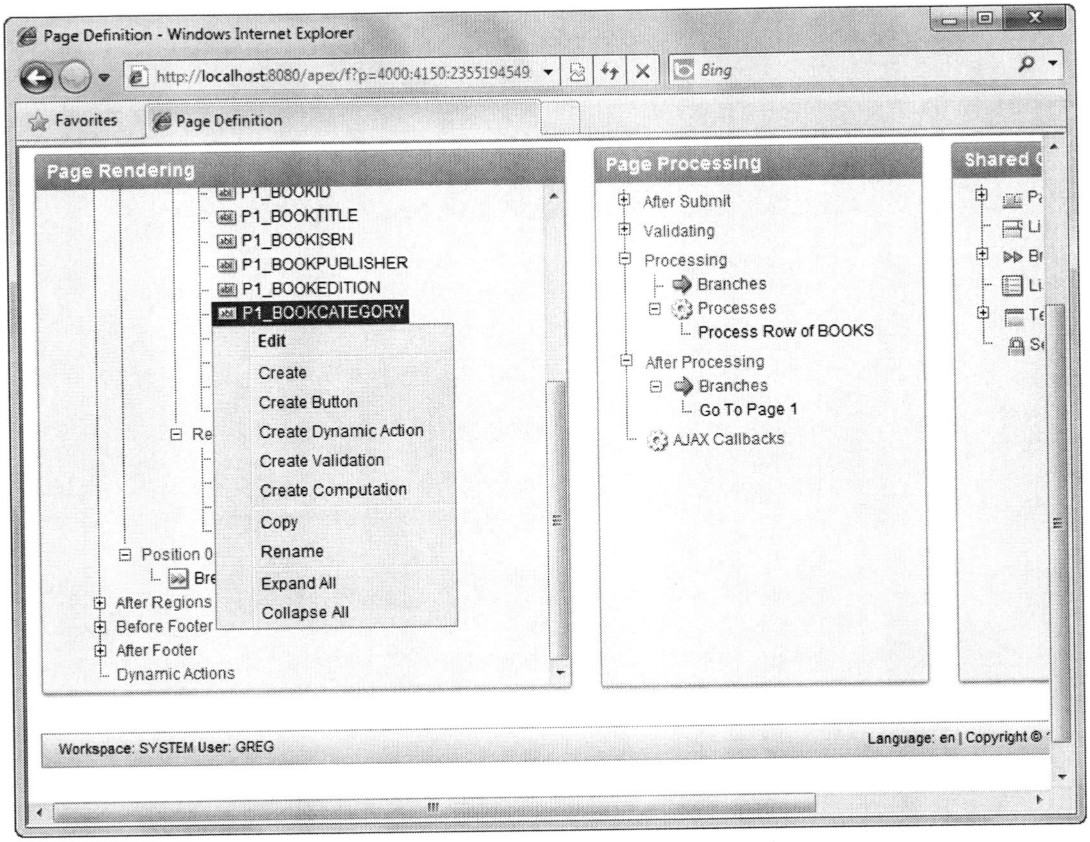

Figure 10-4. Editing the Book Category field

8.   In the Field Properties page, change the Display As field from Text Field to Select List, as shown in Figure 10-5.

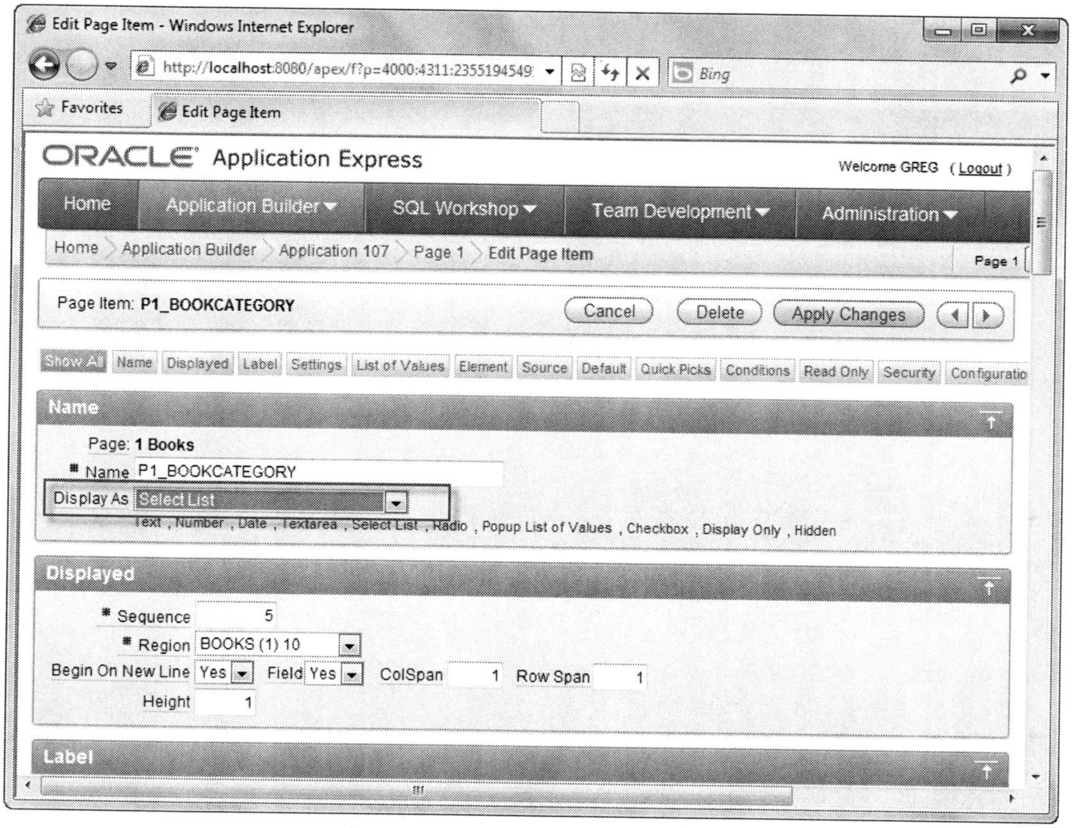

Figure 10-5. Changing the Display As field

9. Scroll down to the List Of Values area, and specify the following SQL:

```
SELECT Description, CategoryID FROM Category
```

10. You should now have the screen shown in Figure 10-6.

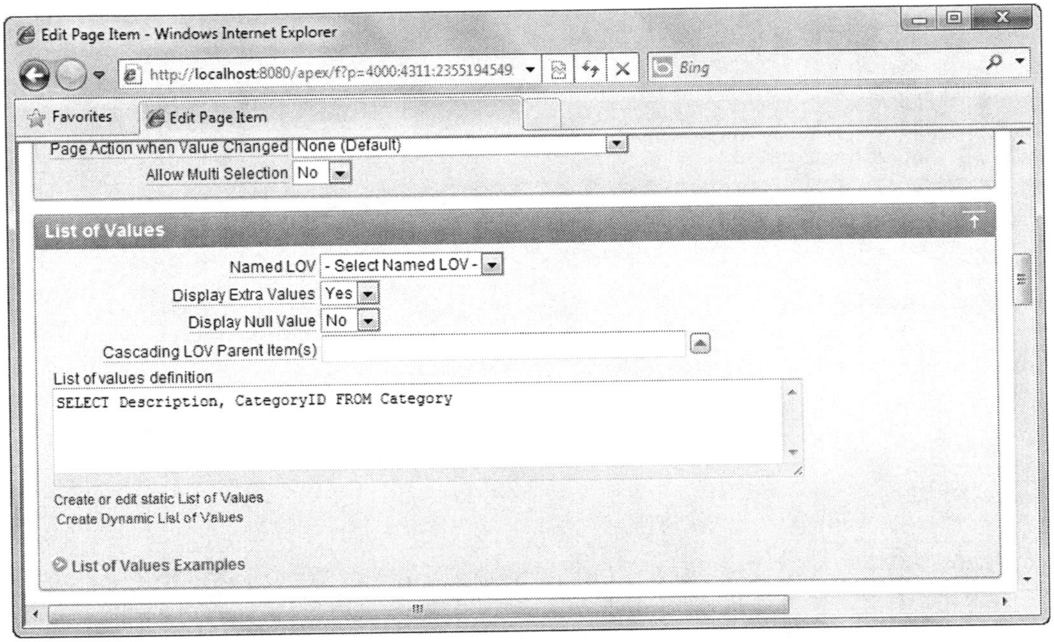

Figure 10-6. Specifying the SQL for the list of values area

11. Save your changes and run the form. You should be able to select the book category from a list of values, as shown in Figure 10-7.

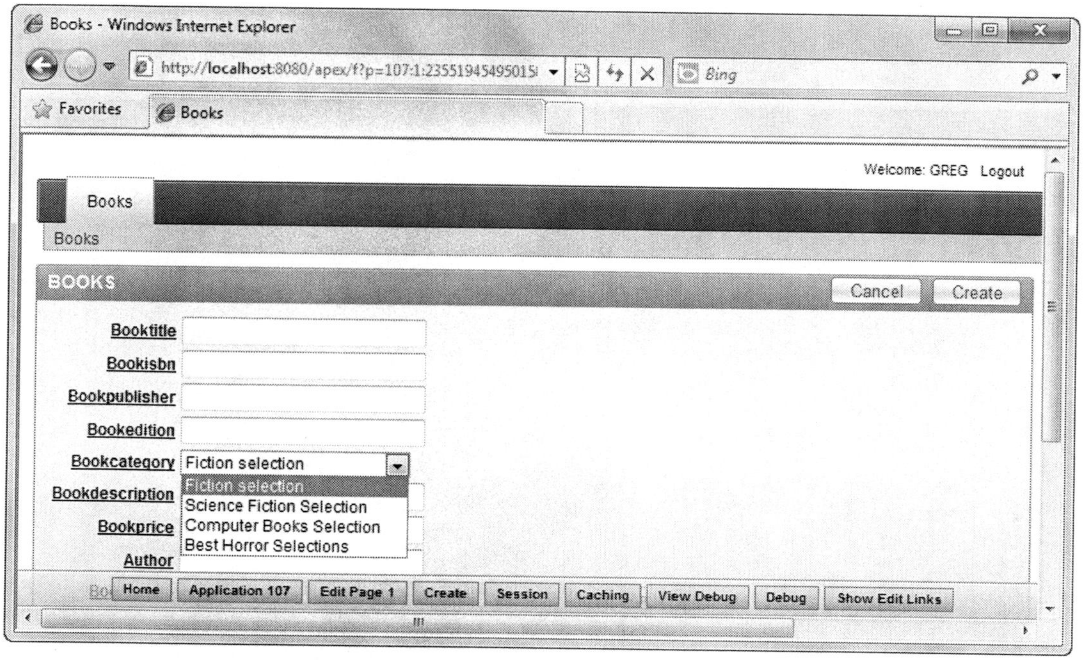

Figure 10-7. The book category selection list in action

12. Let's turn to the report that was generated earlier. When you run the report in the application, you should see the list of books shown in Figure 10-8.

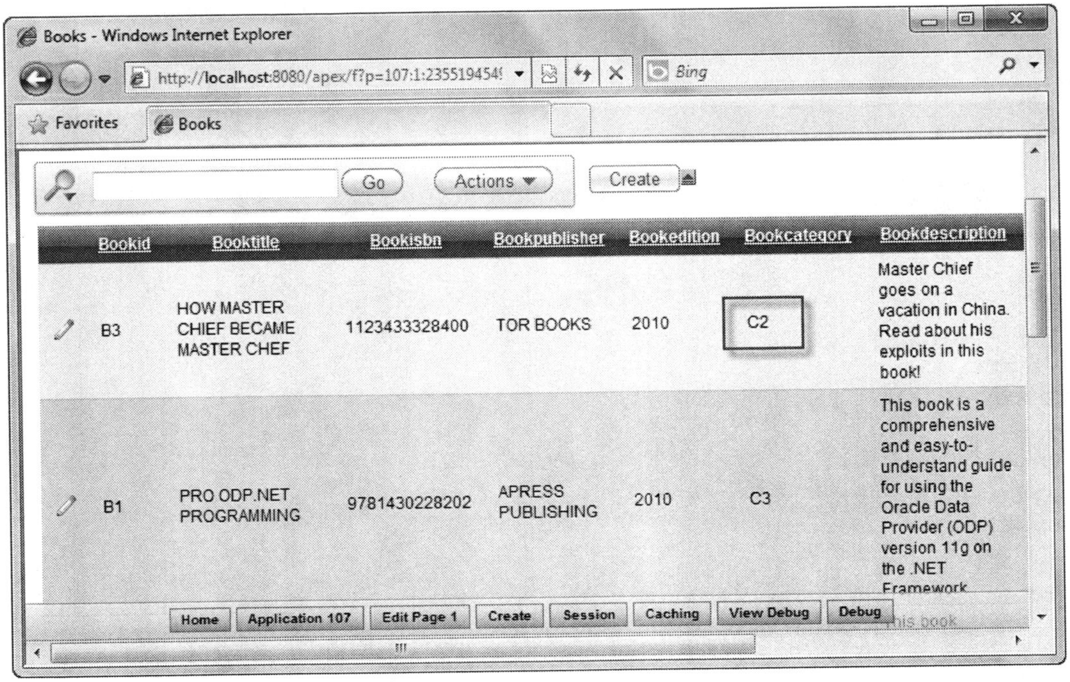

Figure 10-8. List of books

13. There's still one last thing to do at this point, which is to change the BookCategory column so that it displays the full category description instead of the category code. To do so, edit the report.

■ **Tip**   You might also want to change the heading of the report columns to display a more user friendly/readable title. You can do so by editing the report column and changing the Column Heading field.

---

14. In the Page Rendering area of the report, right click on the Books node, and choose the Edit link (as shown in Figure 10-9).

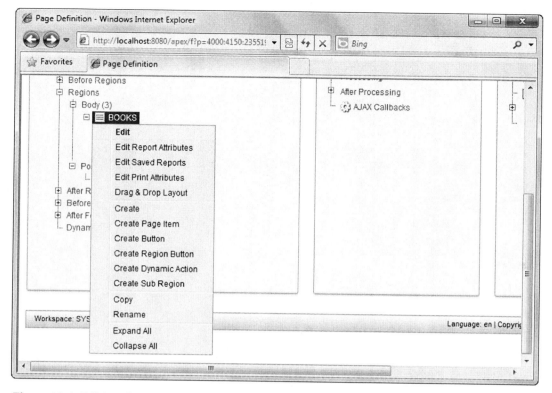

Figure 10-9. *Editing the Books region*

15. Scroll down to the source of the report, and change the existing SQL to the following:

```
select
"BOOKID",
"BOOKTITLE",
"CATEGORY"."DESCRIPTION" "BOOKCATEGORY",
"BOOKISBN",
"BOOKPUBLISHER",
"BOOKEDITION",
"BOOKDESCRIPTION",
"BOOKPRICE",
"AUTHOR",
dbms_lob.getlength("BOOKIMAGE") "BOOKIMAGE"
 from   "BOOKS" LEFT JOIN "CATEGORY" ON "BOOKS"."BOOKCATEGORY" = "CATEGORY"."CATEGORYID"
```

16. You should now have the screen shown in Figure 10-10.

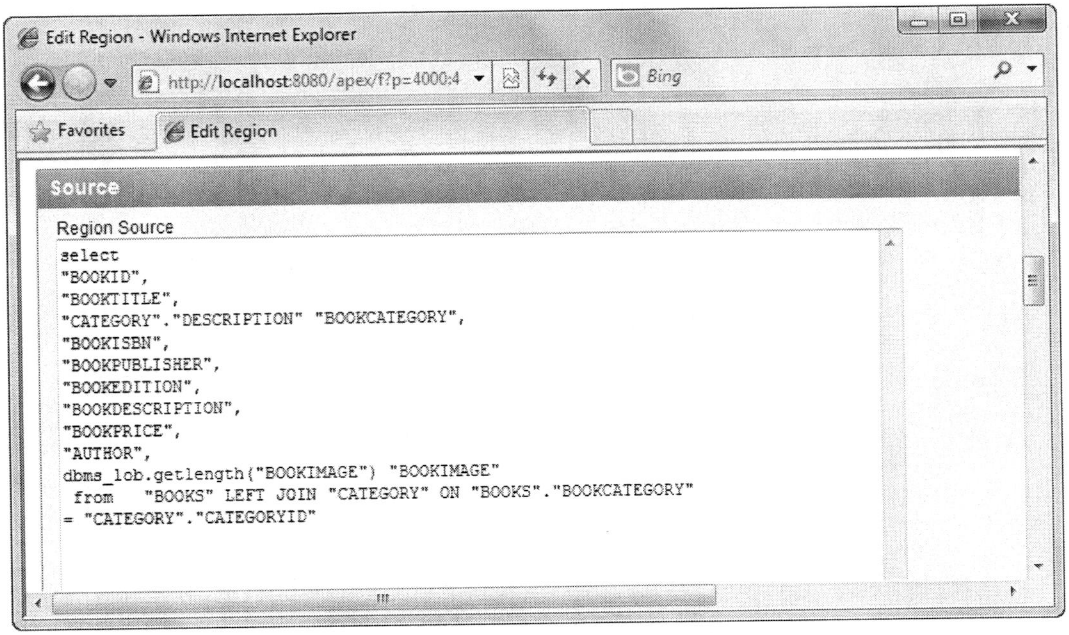

Figure 10-10. Changing the SQL for the region source

17. Apply the changes and run the report again. Note that the report displays the full category name instead of the category code, as shown in Figure 10-11.

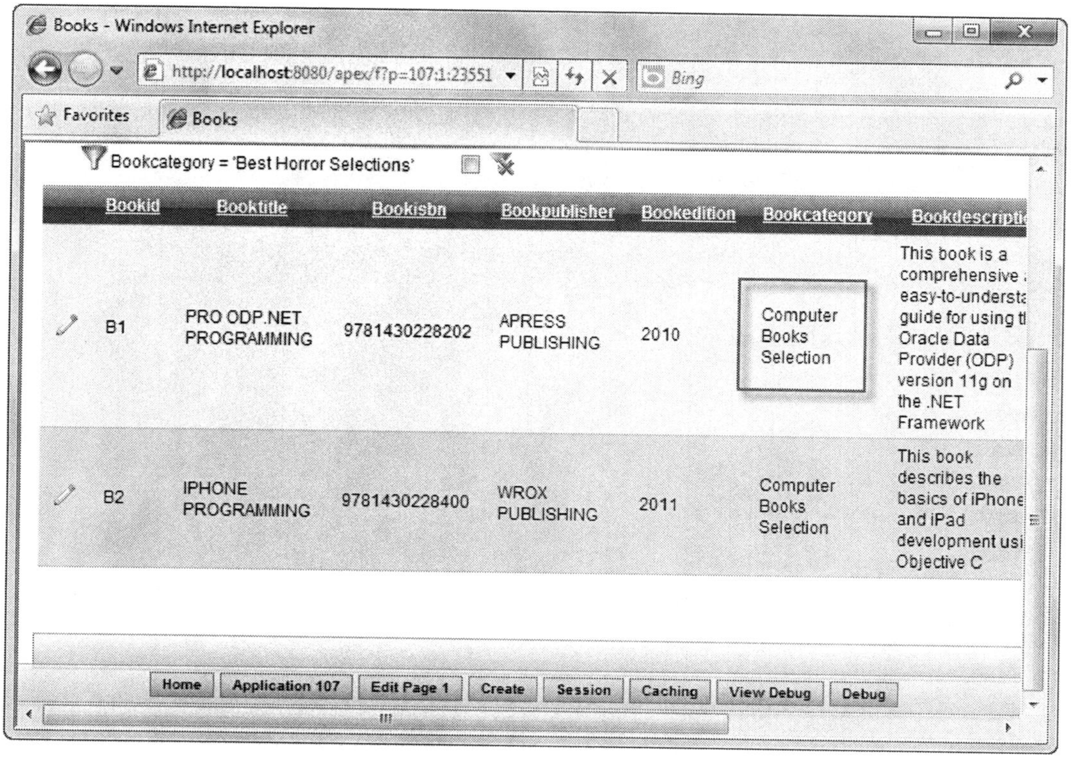

Figure 10-11. The full category name of the book displayed in the report

18. Try uploading book photos through your newly created form/report. In the report, edit a book by clicking the edit icon at the far left of each row.

19. Browse for an image of the book and upload it through the form, as shown in Figure 10-12. Save all changes to the record.

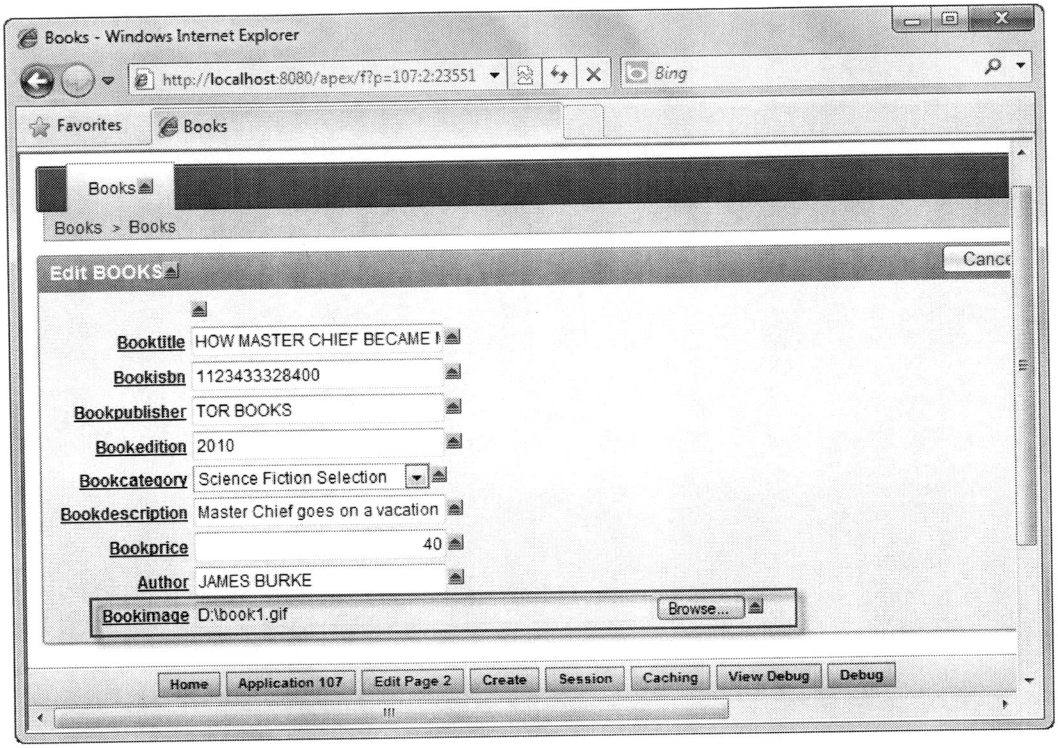

Figure 10-12. Uploading a book image

20. To confirm that the image was successfully uploaded, edit the record again; this time you see a Download link next to the control. Clicking the download link will bring you to the uploaded image file shown in Figure 10-13.

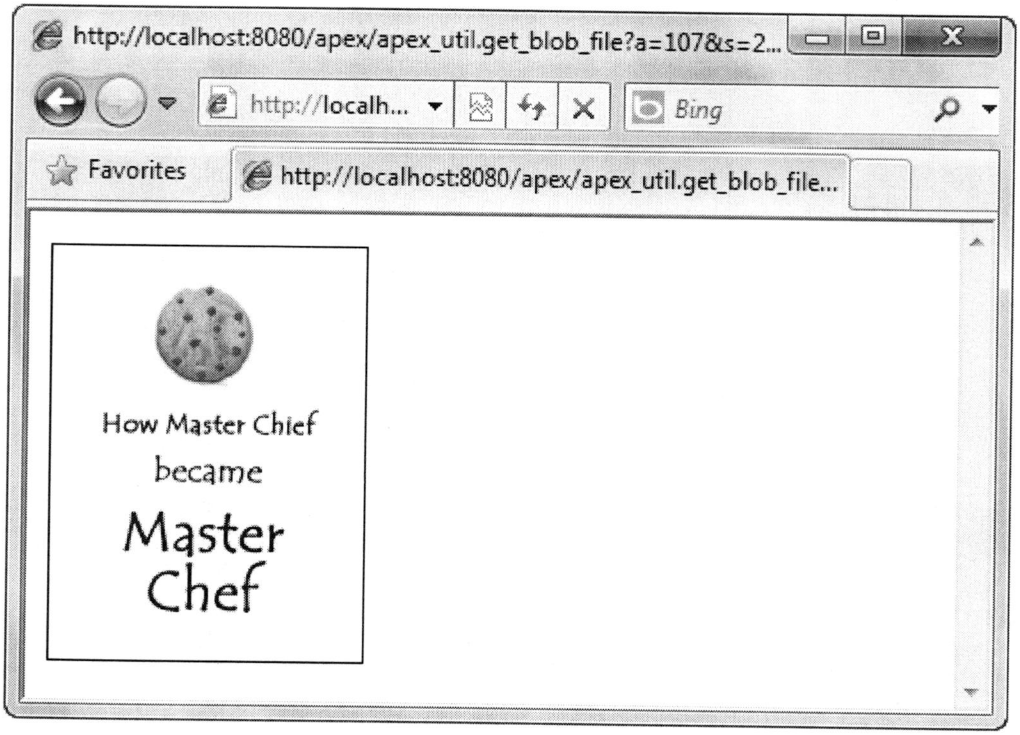

Figure 10-13. Sample book image

21. Upload your own photos for all the other books in the Books table.

How It Works

As demonstrated in the earlier chapters of this book, APEX lets you easily create a form and report combination from a database table. This, in turn, allows you to easily and quickly setup CRUD (Create, Read, Update and Delete) functionality in your application.

Also covered in the previous chapters of this book was the use of List of Values (LOVs) dynamically generated from a specified SQL statement. LOVs can be used as the data source for Select Lists (drop-downs), as seen in this recipe.

**Exercise 10-1: Create Pages to Manage the List
of Categories and Book Inventory**

As an exercise, I leave it to you to create the form and report pages to manage the list of different categories as well as book inventory in the book catalog application. The approach is similar to the steps outlined in this recipe. Use the Category and Inventory tables as the base for these pages.

To verify if what you've done is correct, you should have the List of Categories report shown next. This will provide the storekeeper an interface to manage the list of available book categories in the book catalog.

For the inventory report, you should eventually have the report shown next. To display the book title in place of the Book ID in the report, you can use the following SQL:

```
select "ID",
"BOOKS"."BOOKTITLE" "BOOKID",
"COPIESINSTOCK"
from "#OWNER#"."INVENTORY" LEFT JOIN "BOOKS" ON "INVENTORY"."BOOKID"= "BOOKS"."BOOKID"
```

The Inventory report and form will allow the storekeeper to manage (and view) the number of copies of each book in stock in the book catalog.

10-3. Setting Up the Book Catalog Front End

Problem

You completed the bulk of the catalog back end in Recipe 10-2. Now you need the accompanying front-end portal that displays the list of books available in the catalog to the public, in a typical online book catalog format.

Solution

To create the catalog front end, follow these steps:

1. In the same Book catalog application, create a new Report.

2. In the wizard, choose to create a Classic Report.

3. Name this report "My Mini Book catalog" and the region title as "Browse our books".

4. In the SQL Query section of the report, write the following SQL:

```
SELECT "BOOKID",
"BOOKTITLE","BOOKISBN","BOOKPUBLISHER","BOOKEDITION","BOOKCATEGORY","BOOKDESCRIPTION","BOOKPRI
CE","AUTHOR", dbms_lob.getlength("BOOKIMAGE") "BOOKIMAGE" FROM Books
```

5. Complete the wizard to create the report. After you have done so, edit the report again. You should have the screen shown in Figure 10-14.

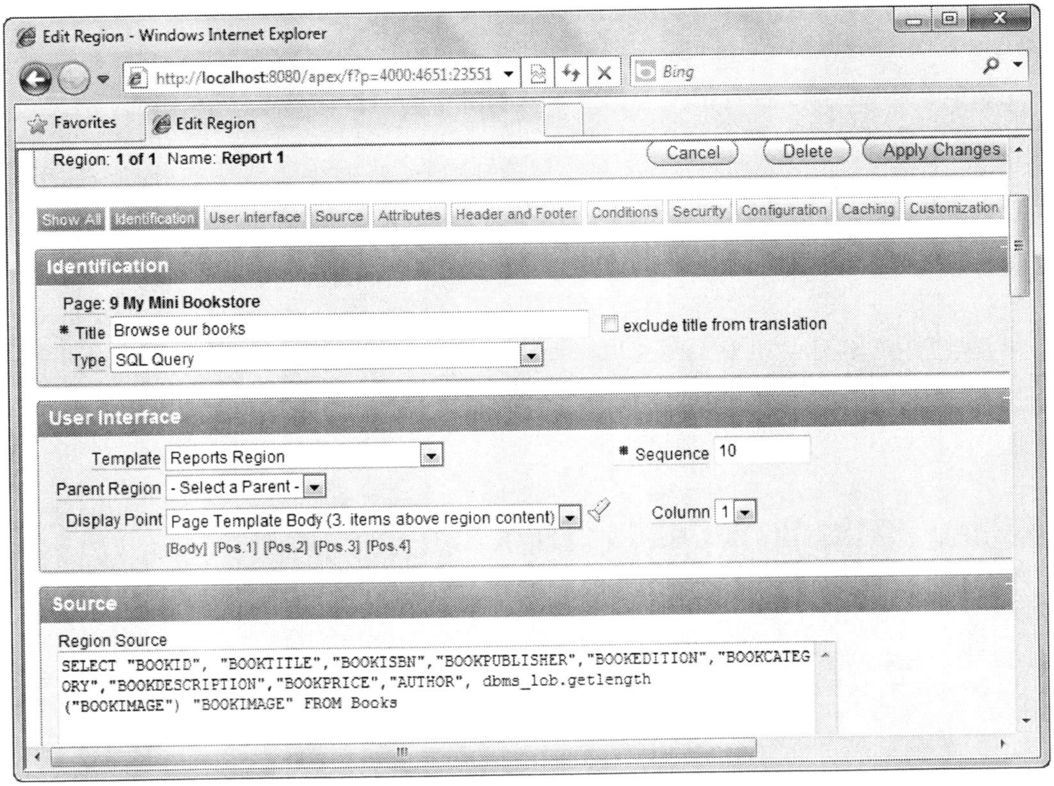

Figure 10-14. Changing the SQL for the region source

6. Complete the rest of the wizard using the default settings.

7. If you run your report, you should see the standard layout shown in Figure 10-15.

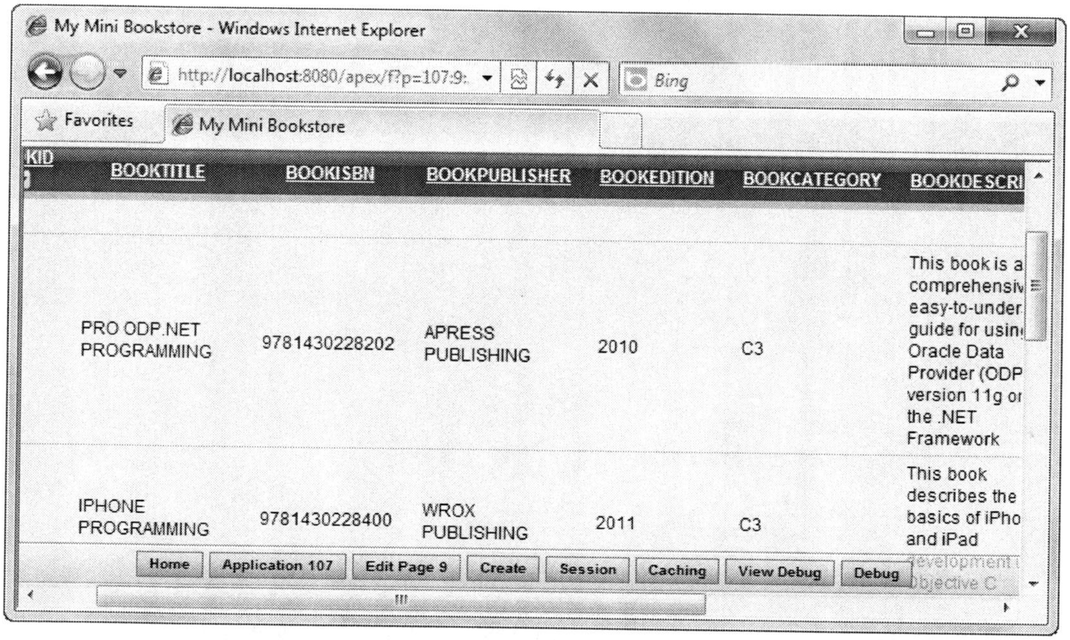

Figure 10-15. The standard report layout

8. This layout works, of course, but it's not a very user-friendly book catalog. It would be nicer to list each item in the format shown in Figure 10-16.

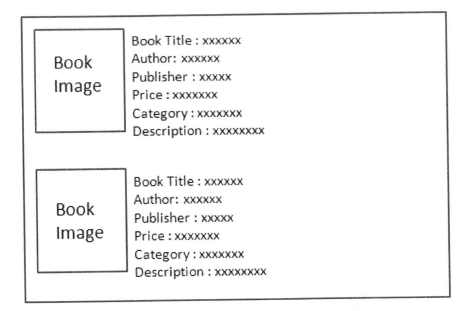

Figure 10-16. The desired layout for the book listing in the front end catalog

9. First, you will need to change the report slightly so that the actual book images will appear in each row. To do this, edit the report. In the Page Rendering area of the report, right click on the BookImage column and choose to edit it.

10. In the Number/Date Format field, type in the following text:

```
IMAGE:BOOKS:BOOKIMAGE:BOOKID
```

11. You should now have the screenshot shown in Figure 10-17.

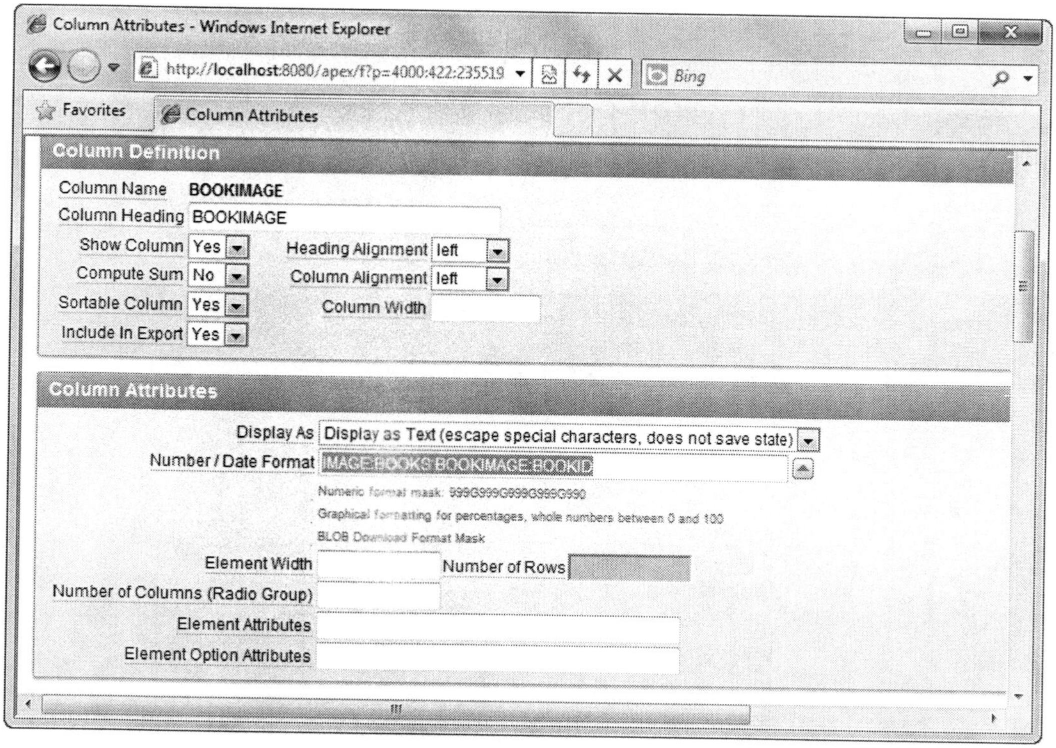

Figure 10-17. Setting the Number/Date format to display images in a report

12. Save your changes and return to the main page definition area of the report.

13. Click on the Report Attributes tab. Change the sorting of the columns so that the BookImage column appears first, as shown in Figure 10-18.

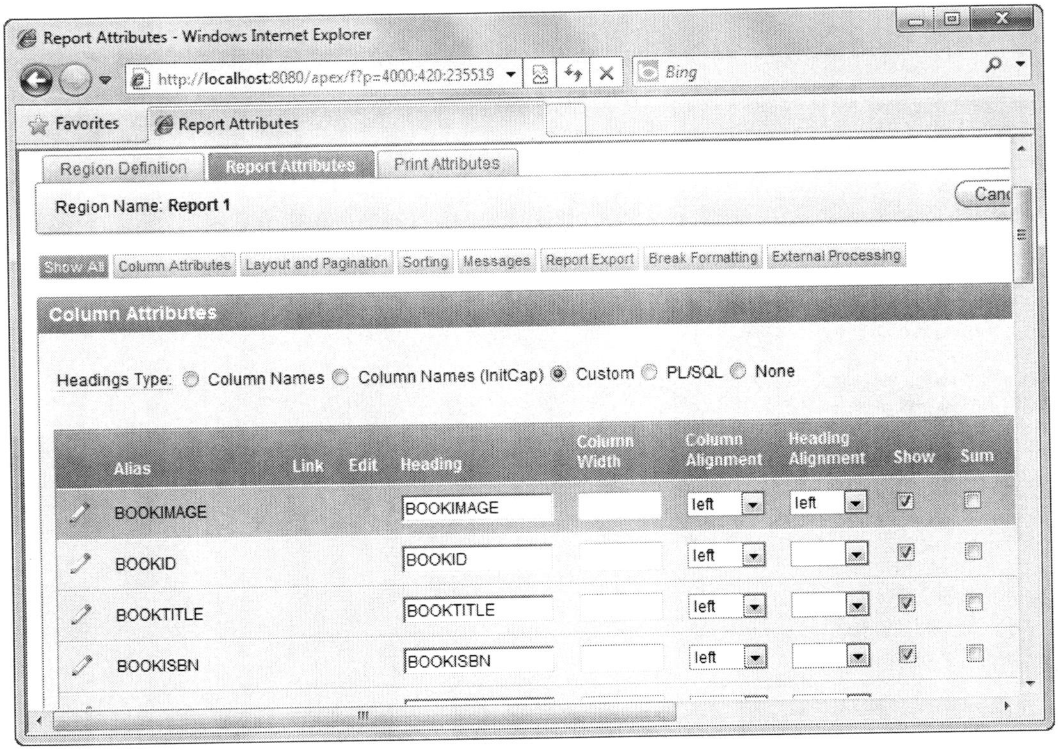

Figure 10-18. Shifting the viewing order of the BOOKIMAGE column

14. Save your changes and run the report. You should now have something that looks like Figure 10-19.

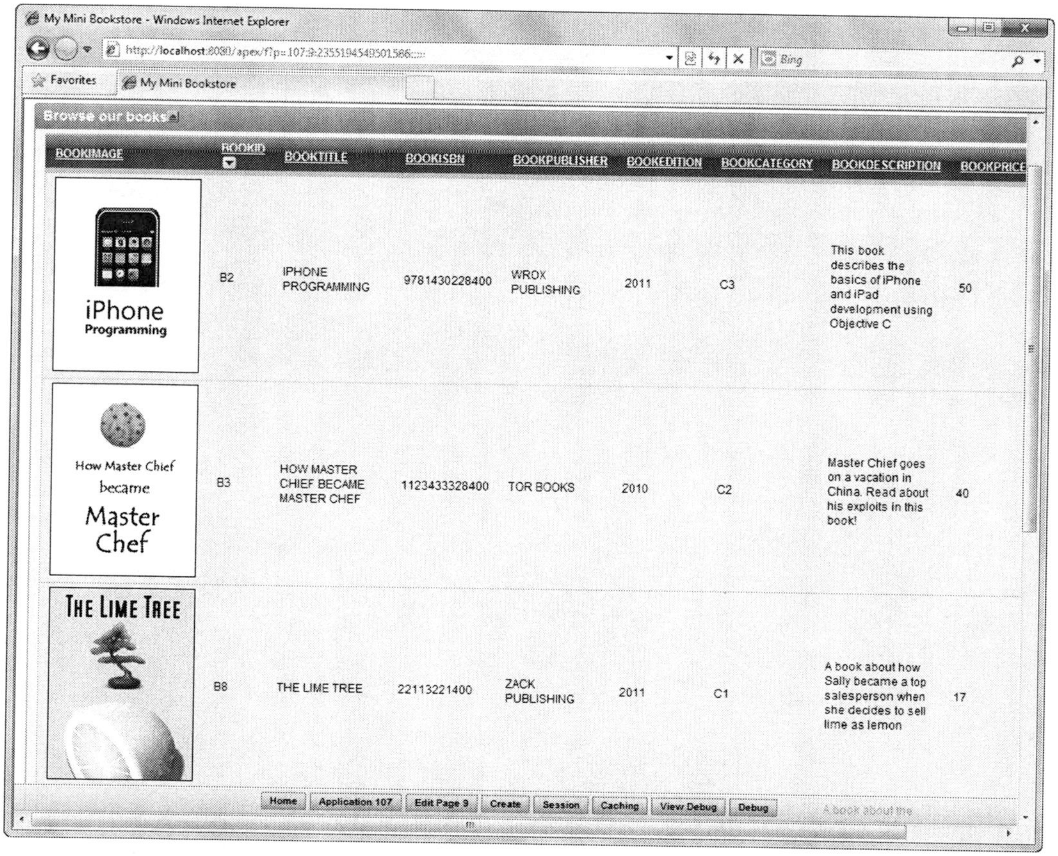

Figure 10-19. The book images displayed in the report

15. Edit the report again. In the Page Rendering area of the report, right-click on the "Browse our books" region and choose to edit it. Click on the Reports Attribute tab.

16. In the list of columns, hide all columns (untick the checkbox in the Show column) except for the BOOKIMAGE and BOOKTITLE columns, as shown in Figure 10-20.

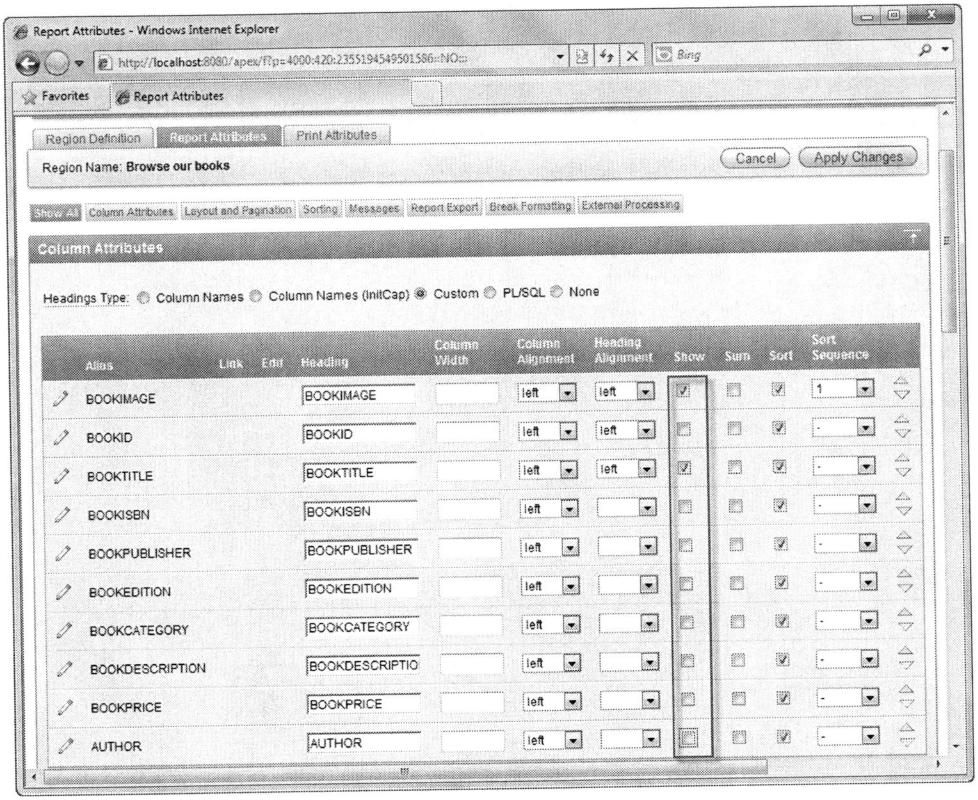

Figure 10-20. Hiding all the other columns

17. Save your changes, and edit the report again.

18. In the Page Rendering area, right click on the BOOKTITLE field and edit it.

19. Scroll down to the Column Formatting area, and in the HTML Expression field, type the following HTML:

```
<b>Title :</b> #BOOKTITLE#<br>
<b>Author :</b> #AUTHOR#<br>
<b>Publisher :</b> #BOOKPUBLISHER#<br>
<b>Price :</b> USD #BOOKPRICE#<br>
<b>Description :</b> #BOOKDESCRIPTION#<br>
```

20. You should now have the screen shown in Figure 10-21.

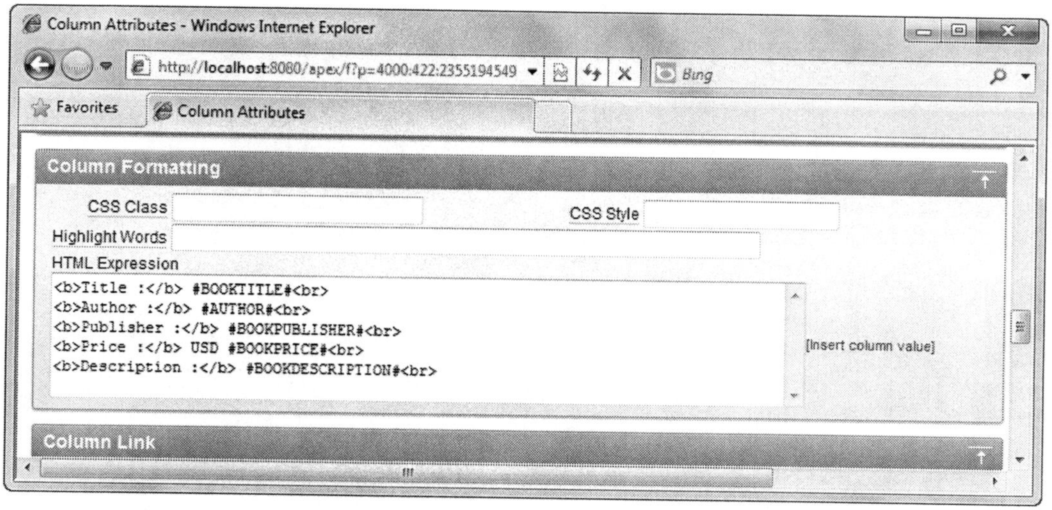

Figure 10-21. Defining a display template for the row via the HTML Expression field

21. Save and apply your changes. Now try running the report again. You should now see the books laid out in a more user-friendly and readable fashion, as shown in Figure 10-22.

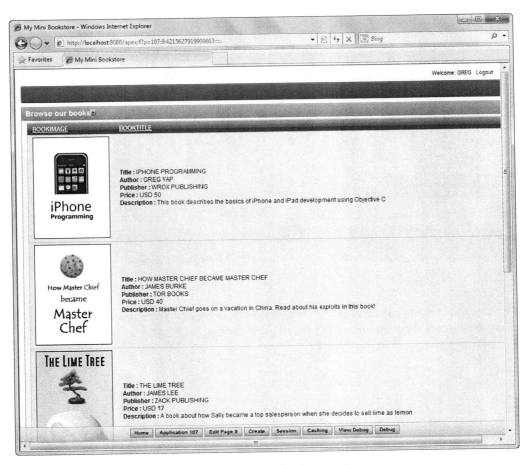

Figure 10-22. The revised layout for the book catalog front end

How It Works

The HTML Expression field allows you to define your own template to display columnar data in a report for each row. Using the #FIELDNAME# notation, you can display data from any report column inside your HTML block.

■ **Tip**   Again, you might want to tidy up your interface by providing column captions that are more intuitive.

10-4. Changing the Home Page of the Application

Problem

The current home page of the Book catalog application is the administration back end Books report. You would like to change it to be the catalog front end page.

Solution

To change the home page of an application, follow these instructions:

1. In the same Book catalog application, click on the Shared Components icon.

2. Under the Security area, click on the Security Attributes link, as shown in Figure 10-23.

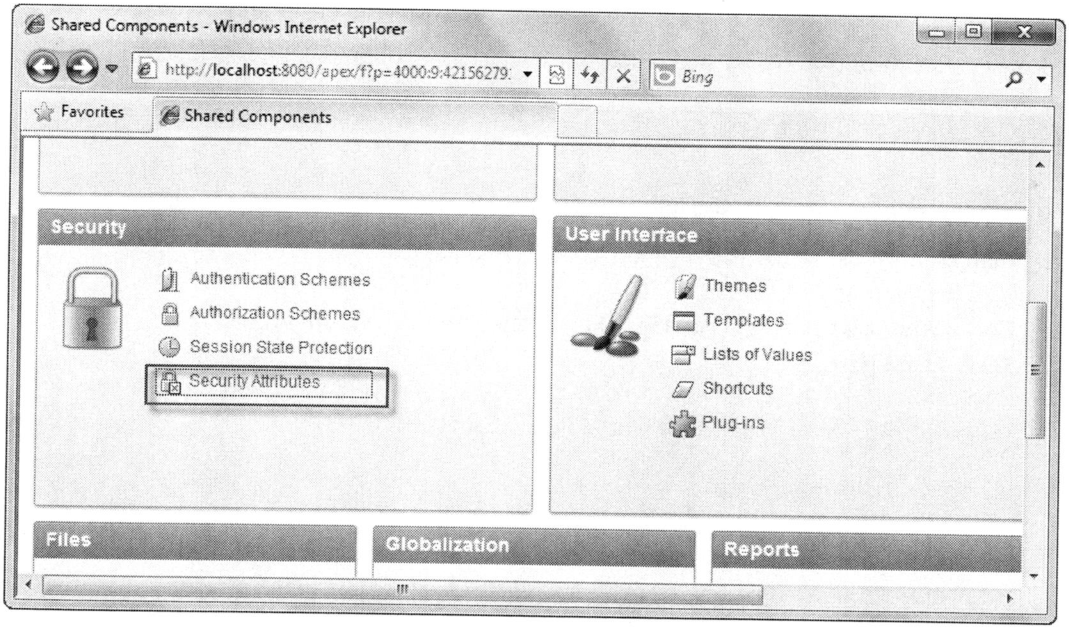

Figure 10-23. The Security Attributes link

3. In the ensuing page, change the page number in the Home link property from 1 to the page number of the front end catalog page. For example, if the page number of your front end catalog page is 9, your Home link property should be set to the following:

```
f?p=&APP_ID.:9:&SESSION.
```

4. Save and apply your changes. Now run your application by clicking the Run Application icon. The application will now redirect you to the front end catalog page.

How It Works

As mentioned in Chapter 9, a typical link to a page in APEX has the following format:

```
f?p=(ApplicationID):(PageNumber):(SessionID):::::
```

This recipe shows you the &APP_ID. and &SESSION. substitution tags to dynamically place the application ID and session identifier respectively in the final generated link. In this recipe, the page number (id: 9) is hardcoded in the link.

10-5. Creating the Stockcount Report for the Storekeeper

Problem

The storekeeper's boss wants to see a visual report (pie chart) of the number of books (stockcount) by genre.

Solution

To create the stockcount pie chart, please follow these instructions:

1. In the same Book catalog application, create a new page.

2. Choose the Chart page type, and in the next step of the wizard, opt for the Flash Chart type.

3. Choose the Pie & Doughnut chart type, as shown in Figure 10-24.

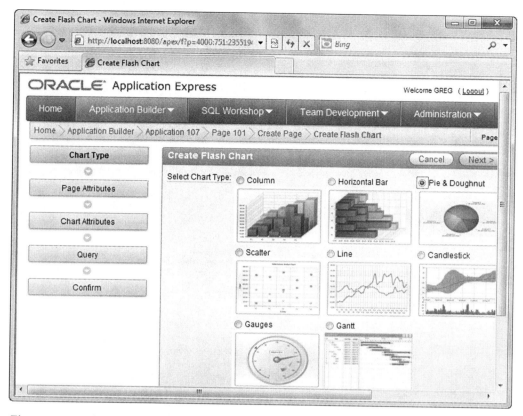

Figure 10-24. The Pie & Doughnut chart type

4. Choose the 3D Pie chart type in the next step of the wizard, and for the page
    name and chart title, enter "Stockcount by Genre".

5. When you are prompted to enter the SQL data source for the chart, enter the
    following SQL:

```
SELECT NULL LINK,
  Category.CategoryName        LABEL,
      SUM(Inventory.CopiesInStock) VALUE
FROM Category,Books,Inventory WHERE Category.CategoryID= Books.BookCategory AND
Books.BookID=Inventory.BookID GROUP BY Category.CategoryName
```

6. You should now have the screen shown in Figure 10-25.

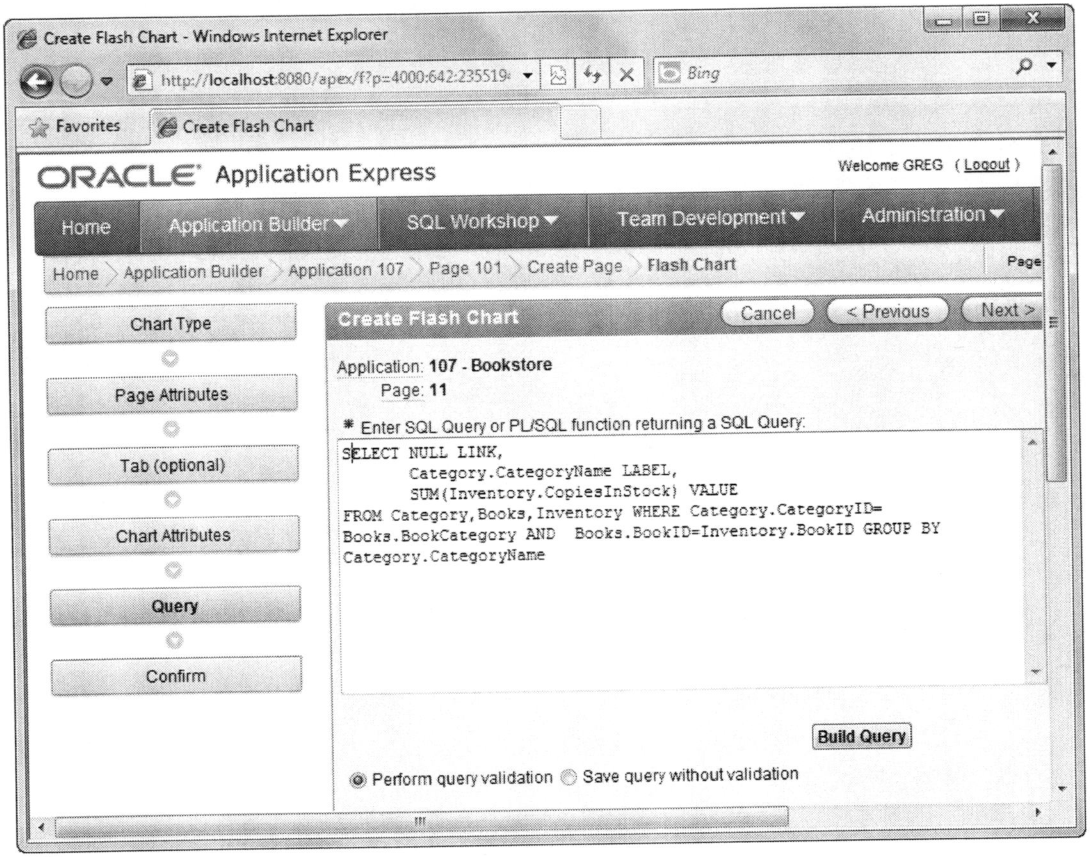

Figure 10-25. Defining the SQL datasource for the chart

7. Complete the wizard and run the page. You should see the total number of books instantly computed by genre, as shown in Figure 10-26.

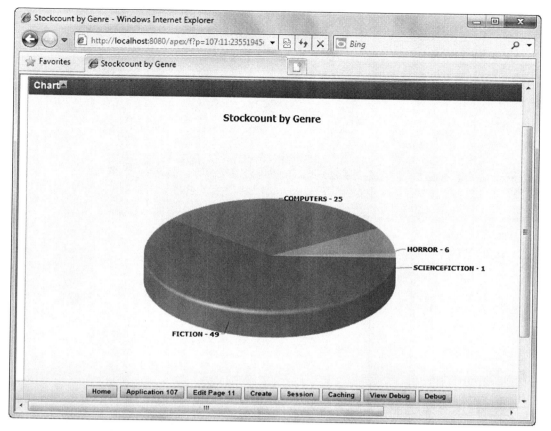

Figure 10-26. The stockcount chart in action

How It Works

As you saw earlier in this book, you can easily generate a variety of visual charts from an SQL statement. In this recipe's example, you combine information from three different tables to retrieve the sum of the stockcount for each different book category.

10-6. Setting Up the Central Administration Page

Problem

You now have various pages, but they're all in pieces. You need to provide a central Administration page from which the storekeeper can navigate to the various administration pages.

Solution

First, you must set up a navigation list. To do so, please follow these steps:

1. In the same Book catalog application, click the Shared Components icon.

2. In the Navigation area, click the Lists link shown in Figure 10-27.

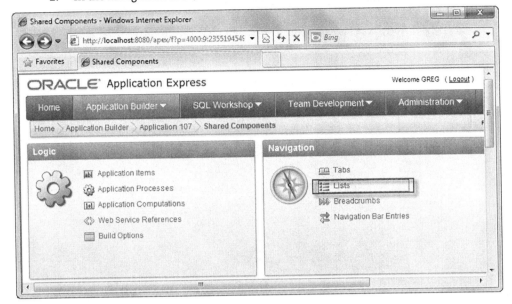

Figure 10-27. The Lists link

3. Create a new navigation list by clicking the Create button in the top right corner.

4. In the first step of the wizard, name the navigation list as "AdministrationOptions".

5. In the next step of the wizard, create the following four entries:
   - Book Categories
   - Inventory & Stockcount
   - Books Listing
   - Stockcount by Genre report

6. Tie each item to their respective report pages by clicking the little arrow icon next to each Target Page ID or Custom URL box, and choosing the correct page to link to from the pop-up window. This is illustrated in Figure 10-28.

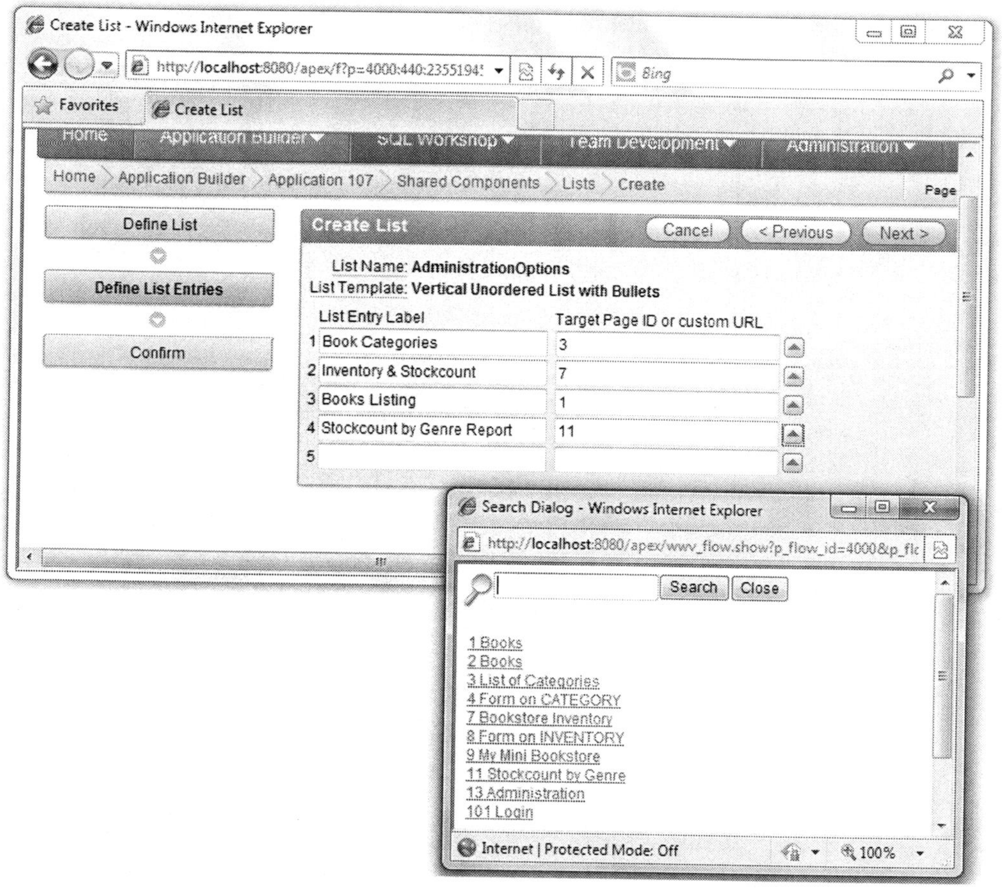

Figure 10-28. Setting up a navigation list

7. When you are done, complete the wizard to create the list.

Now that you've created the navigation list, you need to host it inside a page—the Central Administration page. To set up this page, please follow these steps:

1. In the same Book catalog application, create a new blank page.

2. Specify "Administration" as the page name.

3. Complete the rest of the steps of the wizard using the default settings to create a blank page.

4. Choose to Edit the page.

5. In the Page Rendering area, right click on the Regions node, and choose to Create a new region.

6. Choose the List region type, as shown in Figure 10-29.

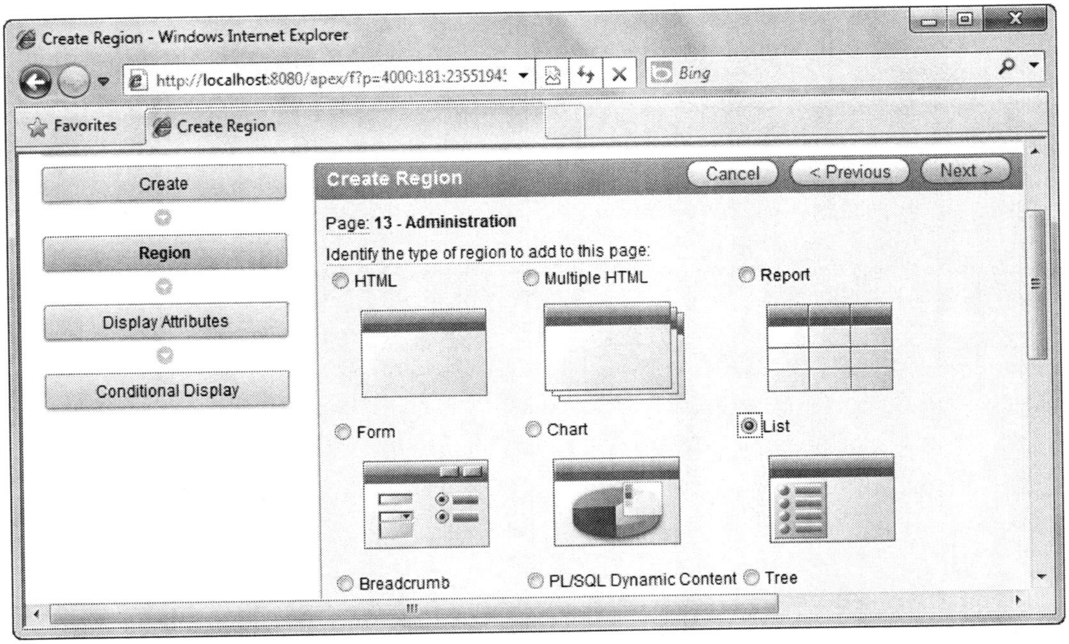

Figure 10-29. Creating a List region

7. Set "Please pick an option below" as the title of the region.

8. In the Source step of the wizard, choose the AdministrationOptions list you created earlier, as shown in Figure 10-30.

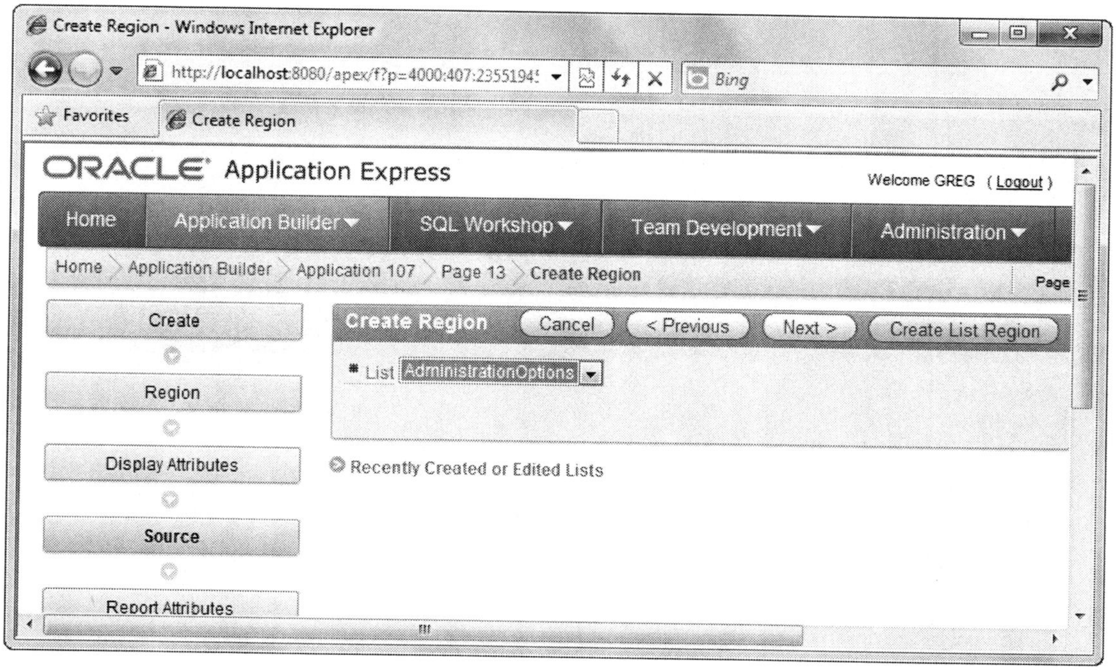

Figure 10-30. Choosing the AdministrationOptions list for the region

9. Click the Create List Region button to complete the wizard.

10. Now run the page. You should see the various links to the various administration pages, as shown in Figure 10-31. Try clicking each link to ensure you land at the correct page.

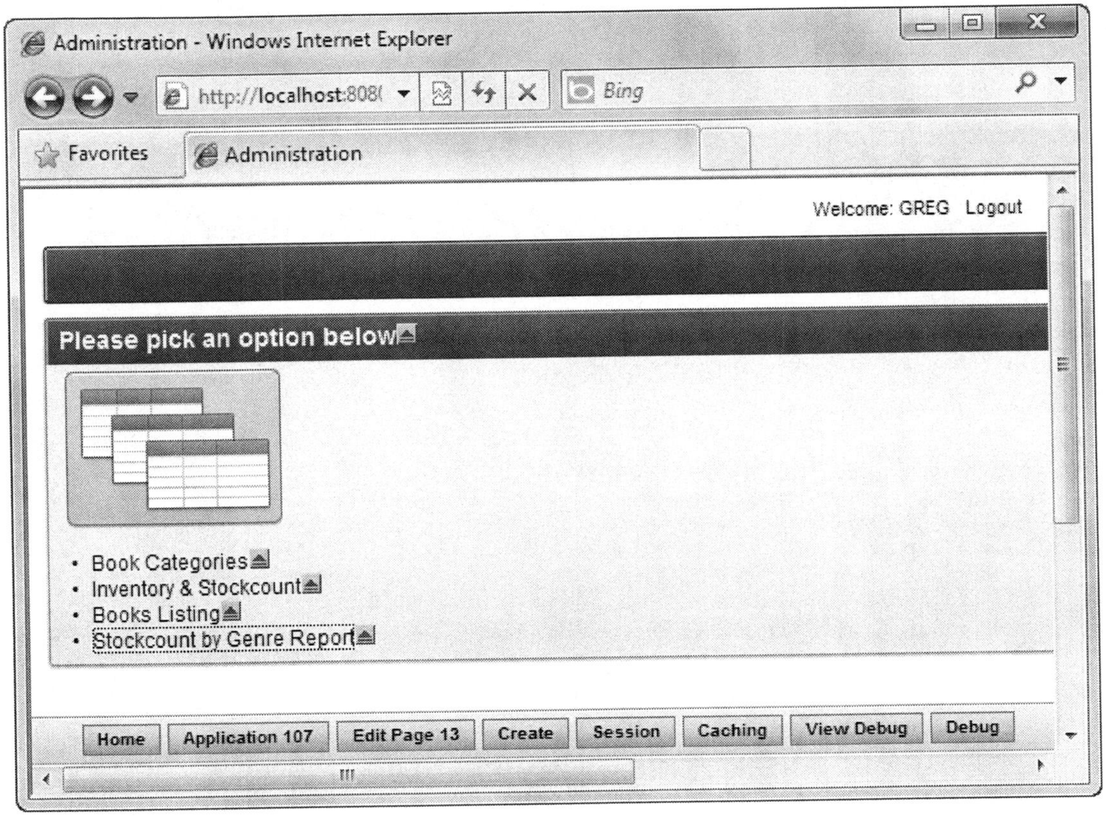

Figure 10-31. The Central Administration page in action

How It Works

Navigation Lists provide an easy way to setup a bunch of links that can be displayed as is (as shown in this recipe), or even hosted within a drop-down menu.

There is actually a side-benefit to setting up navigation lists. Once it is set up, it can be reused many times in an application. This can lead to easier maintenance of your application in the future. For instance, when a link is to be dropped, you don't have to go through every place in your application looking to delete that link. You could just remove it from the navigation list, and all areas that use the navigation list will be instantly updated.

10-7. Creating Tabs in Your Application

Problem

You have a Central Administration page—that's fine. But how do you navigate there from your main catalog page (which is the front end catalog page). You realize you need tabs.

Solution

To create tabs in your application, follow these steps:

1. In the same Book catalog application, click the Shared Components icon.

2. Under the Navigation area, click the Tabs link shown in Figure 10-32.

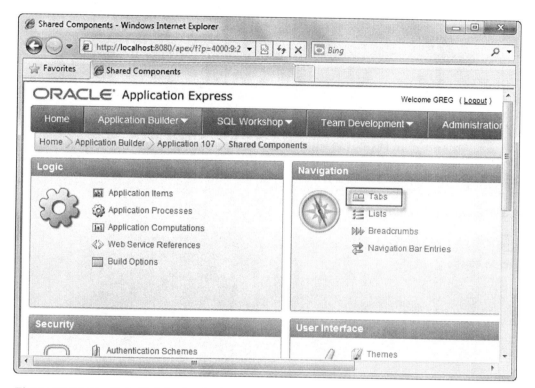

Figure 10-32. The Tabs link in the Navigation area

3. Click on the Manage Tabs button in the top right corner of the ensuing page.

4. Click the Edit Standard Tabs tab.

5. Remove any and all existing tabs from this list (if an entry exists, click the Edit icon, and then click the Delete icon on the following page).

6. You should now see the screen shown in Figure 10-33.

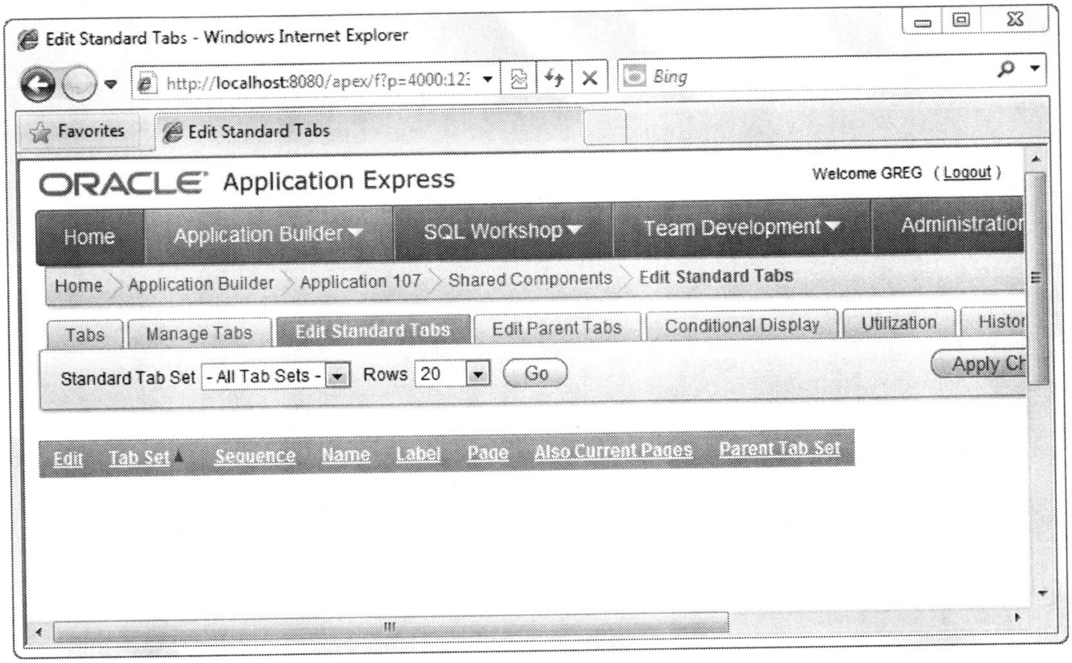

Figure 10-33. Removing all standard tabs

    7.   Now click the `Manage Tabs` tab, and click the little Add button highlighted in Figure 10-34.

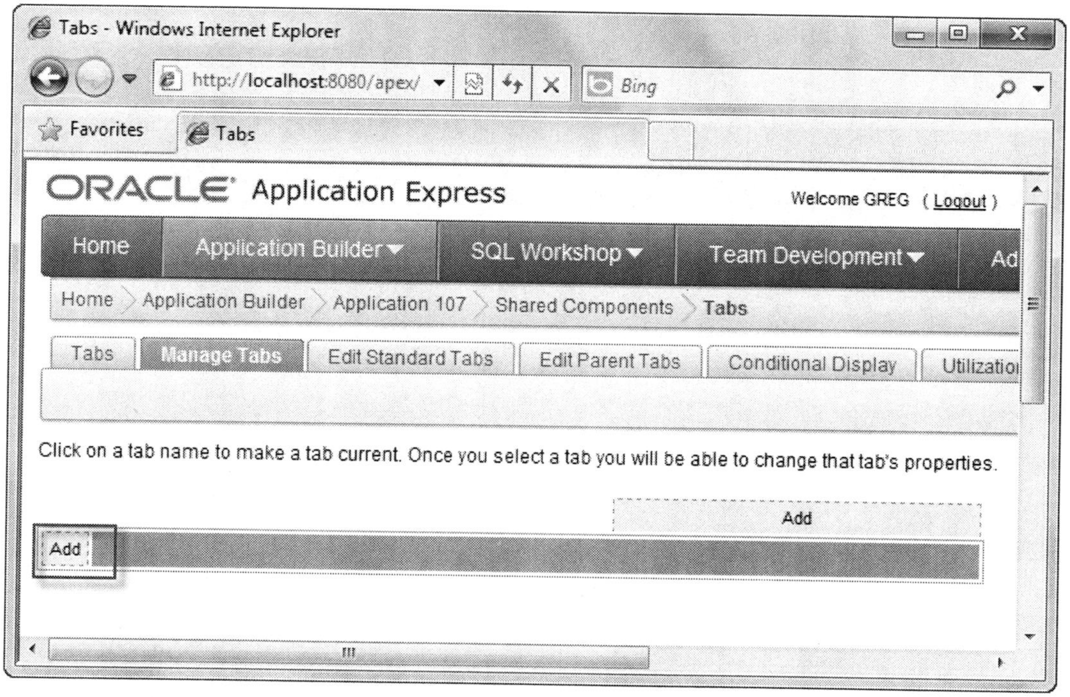

Figure 10-34. *Adding a new tab*

8.   Specify "Book catalogTabs" for the new tabset name, and skip the next few steps until you arrive at the "Tab Name" step of the wizard.

9.   Specify "Store" as the tab label, as shown in Figure 10-35.

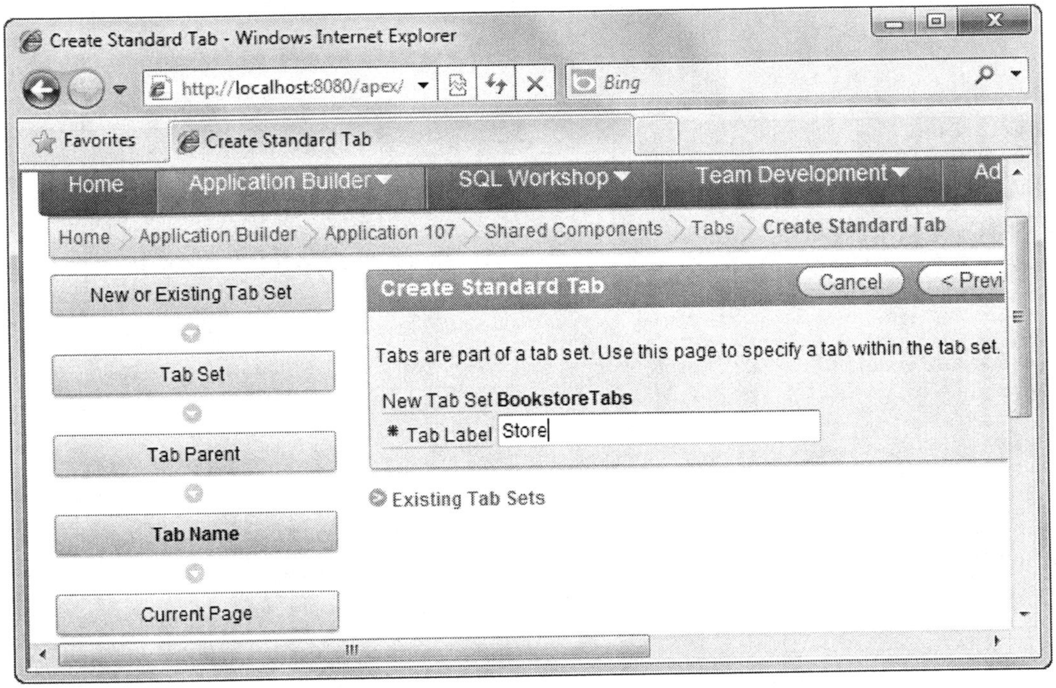

Figure 10-35. *Creating the Store tab*

10. Click the Next button. Now you'll be able to specify the page that is associated with this tab. Choose the My Mini Book catalog page by clicking the arrow highlighted in Figure 10-36.

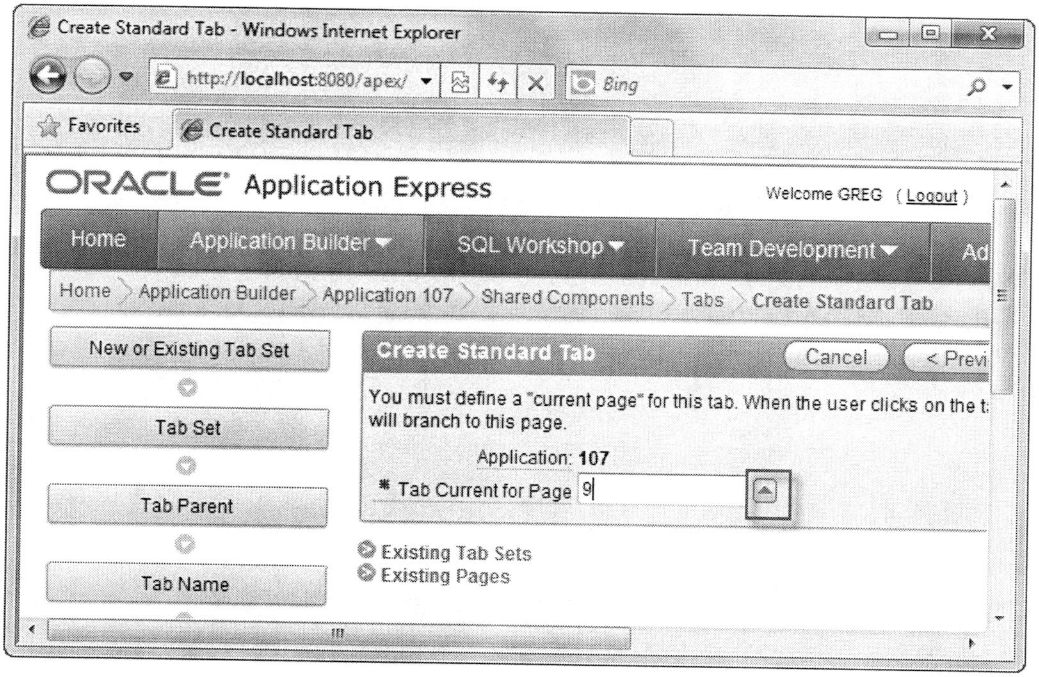

Figure 10-36. Choosing the associated page for the tab

11. Complete the rest of the wizard using the default settings provided.

12. You should see your newly created tab displayed in the screen shown in Figure 10-37.

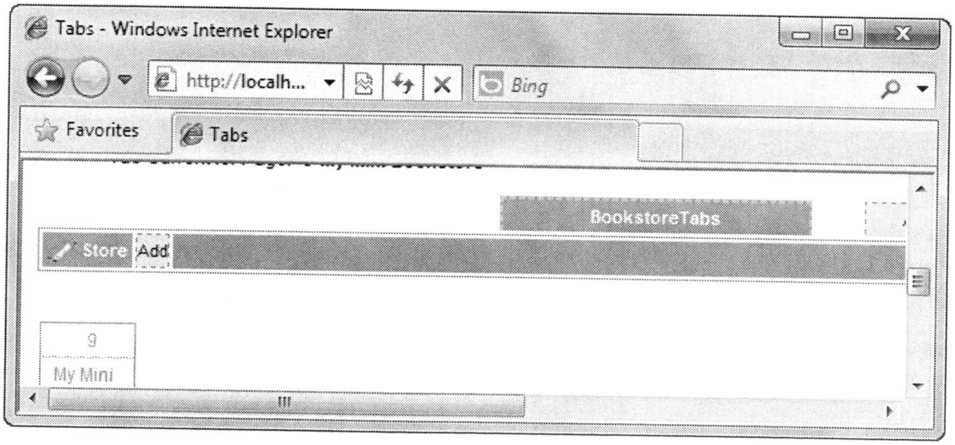

Figure 10-37. The newly created Store tab

13. Add another tab, and label it "Administration".

14. When you are prompted to provide the page associated with this tab, choose the Central Administration ("Administration") page.

15. Complete the rest of the wizard using the default settings.

16. Now run your application again. You will see two tabs at the top of your application, as shown in Figure 10-38. One will bring you to the catalog front end page and the other will bring you to the Central Administration page.

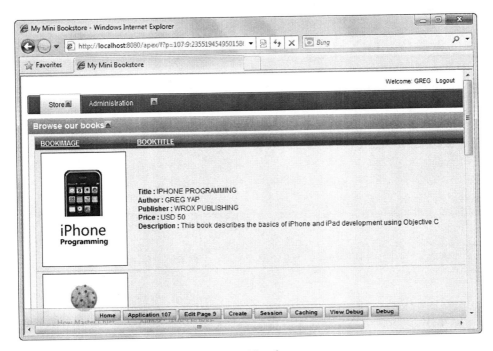

Figure 10-38. The final book catalog site with tabs

How It Works

APEX takes away most of the work of visual representation of a tab from the developer. Once you associate a tab with a particular page, APEX will automatically highlight the tab for you (when you are on the page) and unhighlight the other tabs.

Tabs, like navigation lists, are also reusable throughout the application and provide the same benefit of easier maintenance: when a new tab needs to be added, just add it to an existing tabset, and voila! The new tab will instantly appear on every page in your application.

Index

■ W

web server
  calling web service reference from form, 99–101
  using Oracle XML DB HTTP server as, 5
Web Service References section, 101
web services
  adding reference, 98–99
  enabling region caching, 217
  interacting with, 96–101
  types supported in APEX, 101
Websheet application, 13
  changing item type of column, 65–68
  creating, 61–65
  creating drop-down list for column, 66
  modifying values in bulk, 69–70
Windows 7-based operating system
  setting up for double-byte character input, 173
working directory, SQL*Plus
  installing Oracle APEX, 8

Workspace Administrator user
  setting up workspace for team-based development, 19, 20
WORKSPACE_IMAGES substitution string, 114, 120
workspaces, 13, 14
  creating Customers table, 32
  creating, 17, 18
  creating schema for, 18, 19
  database workspaces, 25
  home page, 23, 24
  logging on to, 22, 23
  mapping to database schemas, 24
  setting up for team-based development, 17–25

■ X, Y, Z

XLIFF file, 199
  exporting, 187–190
  importing translated file, 192–195
  translating, 190–192

CPSIA information can be obtained at www.ICGtesting.com
234666LV00002B/1/P